AN INTRODUCTION TO
ISLAM

AN INTRODUCTION TO ISLAM

GERHARD ENDRESS
translated by Carole Hillenbrand

NEW YORK
COLUMBIA UNIVERSITY PRESS

Printed in Great Britain

LIBRARY OF CONGRESS
Library of Congress Cataloging-in-Publication Data
Endress, Gerhard, 1939–
[Einführung in die islamische Geschichte. English]
An introduction to Islam / Gerhard Endress; translated by Carole Hillenbrand.
p. cm.
Translation of: Einführung in die islamische Geschichte.
Bibliography: p.
Includes index.
ISBN 0-231-06580-9 ISBN 0-231-06581-7 (pbk)
1. Islamic countries. 2. Islam. I. Title.
DS35.6.E5313 1988
909'.097671—dc19 87-38182
CIP

c 10 9 8 7 6 5 4 3 2 1
p 10 9 8 7 6 5 4 3 2

CONTENTS

ILLUSTRATIONS

PREFACE

This book was written to give students of Islam and the history of the Muslim peoples an introduction to the basic concepts and problems. It is not another narrative history, but a companion to the many accounts which are available: a perspective on the common denominators given to fourteen centuries of the Middle East and North Africa by Islamic rule and the Muslim creed. It is hoped that the indexed chronology will be found convenient as a reference guide to the main events, and that the bibliography will be useful as a guide to further reading for beginners and specialists alike. The publication of an English version four years after the original German edition has been a welcome opportunity to correct the text and to update the bibliography. I am grateful to Dr Carole Hillenbrand, who has doubled toil and trouble to translate the book into fair English, for making lucid even my obscurities.

Ruhr-Universität Bochum G.E.

NOTE ON THE TRANSLITERATION

The transliteration system used here and in the other Islamic Surveys follows that of the *Encyclopedia of Islam* (second edition) with the following modifications:

ḳ, d̲j̲, d̲h̲, k̲h̲, and s̲h̲ are rendered as q, j, dh, kh, and sh.

Chapter One

INTRODUCTION: THE CONCEPT AND UNITY OF ISLAMIC HISTORY

'When God sent him, in the month of Ramaḍān in which God willed concerning him what He willed of His grace, the apostle set forth to Ḥirā' as was his wont, and his family with him. When it was the night on which God honoured him with his mission and showed mercy on His servants thereby, Gabriel brought him the command of God. "He came to me," said the apostle of God, "while I was asleep, with a coverlet of brocade whereon was some writing, and said, 'Recite!'. I said, 'What shall I recite?' He pressed me with it so tightly that I thought it was death; then he let me go and said, 'Recite!'. I said, 'What shall I recite?' He pressed me with it again so that I thought it was death and said 'Recite!' I said, 'What shall I recite?'—and this I said only to deliver myself from him, lest he should do the same to me again. He said:

'Recite in the name of thy Lord who created,
Who created man from a clot.
Recite! Thy Lord is the most bounteous,
Who taught by the pen,
Taught man that which he knew not.'"'

(Ibn Hishām: *Sīrat Muḥammad Rasūl Allāh* [The Life of Muḥammad, the Messenger of God]. Ed. Muṣṭafā al-Saqqā, Ibrāhīm al-Abyārī, 'Abdalḥafīẓ Shalabī, Cairo, 1955, Volume 1, pp.236–7—cf. English translation based on *The Life of Muhammad*, tr. A. Guillaume, Oxford, 1955, pp.105–6. The text of the first revelation is Sura 96 of the Koran, verses 1–5).

Thus around the year 610 AD the history of Islam began. Muḥammad, the merchant of Mecca, became convinced of a truth which manifested itself to him as a revelation 'like the light of the morning', the 'reciting' and spreading of which became the meaning and work of his life from that day onwards. Already in his lifetime the horizon broadened with the circle of believers. The message spoke of the goodness and omnipotence of the one God; it also provided, however, the elements of a legal and government system which formed the foundations of the first community in the name of this God. The message which was given to the Arabs in their language became, in the view of the founder, the renewal and perfection of all revelation, aimed at all nations. The Arab kingdom which spread rapidly after his death beyond the borders of the Arabian peninsula became an Islamic world empire, whose ruler controlled, in the name of God and in succession to the Prophet, the temporal fate and eternal salvation of believers of all countries, and who also took the unbelievers under his protection. The unity of faith and of theocratic government within the empire collapsed; but even in collapse and in strife the unity of Islam remained inextinguishably preserved for centuries in the consciousness of Muslims.

We can, therefore, speak of Islamic history in a broader sense than Christian history. It is true that there are analogies in the picture both religions have of their own history. Christianity too has its starting point in history 'when the time was fulfilled'. In both religions, believers see this beginning as the culminating point of sacred history, as the event which gives their life sense and reality. The Christians of medieval Europe also saw themselves as the people of God, the inhabitants of God's state (the *Civitas Dei*). Moreover, both religious communities share the same historical foundation. They participated in the bankruptcy of the Roman Empire (the *Imperium Romanum*); in both cases the inheritance of antiquity lived on and preserves in east and west a common basis of mutual understanding. The continuity of the transmission of knowledge, notably in philosophy and the Hellenistic sciences, is the most well-known manifestation of this; yet in urban culture too, in the power struggle of institutions, and in many a facet of political life, there are striking parallels. In the West, however, by the high Middle Ages, developments appeared which either did not take place in the Islamic East at all or occurred only very much later. Above all, the Christian state lost its identity with the community of the faithful much earlier than did the Islamic state.

The Islamic state was never called into question in the same way as, at the beginning of the era which we call modern, the Church itself—already long-divided—was called into question by people who experienced their encounter with God afresh as individuals. The Islamic world empire has also collapsed; Islam, too, has experienced erosion through schism and disagreement; it also is acquainted with the awakening of personal piety and the revolts of intellectual scepticism against the institutions of theocracy. But division between the people of God and the inhabitants of the State never became an accepted reality; the Islamic character of the political community is today a reality even in places where the ruling institutions no longer proclaim Islam as the state religion.

Islam, which entered history as the message of the Prophet, manifested itself as a religious and political order which encompassed the society of the Near East and North Africa from the seventh to the nineteenth century and which in all the variety of geographical and historical individuality gave unity and cohesion to the Arabs, Aramaeans, Berbers, Persians, Turks and others, even when they were in conflict with each other. Even today, long after the appearance of secular states in the East, the ideal of Islamic theocracy still has political impact. It is the ideal of a state whose ruler unites spiritual and secular command of all Muslims: guardian of the true faith, leader of public communal prayer and overlord of political, religious and legal institutions; in this he follows the example of the Prophet and in direct succession to him. It is true that this ideal could no longer be realised after the death of the Prophet. The question of succession (*khilāfa*, 'succession', caliphate) already divided the community under the first caliphs, kindling civil war and religious division. The dynasty of the Umayyads, the *Realpolitiker* of Arab expansion and occupation, could not satisfy the aspirations of a community which comprised so many peoples. Their successors, the 'Abbāsids, who came from the tribe of the Prophet, appeared after a victorious revolution (750) claiming that they were truly the leaders not only of Arab believers but also of all Muslims. They created, however, in a centralised government apparatus of 'scribes' (*kuttāb*) and in the military force of an absolutist government, institutions which were alien to the community of believers. The champions of the religio-legal institutions rose up against an attempt by the caliph al-Ma'mūn (813–33) and his two successors to make a rational and logically-argued meaning of the Holy Book universally accepted. Their success freed Islam from the grasp of an autocrat, binding it once again to a codified, sanctioned tradition: the Sunna. From that time onwards—i.e., from the middle of the ninth century—dogma, law and the system of government in the Islamic world were created as a result of the effort of 'Sunni' orthodoxy to uphold the universal claim of Islam and the unity of the faith against external and internal challenges. When this aim came near to realisation, political unity was shattered and the caliphate had fallen under the tutelage of foreign—Iranian and Turkish—dynasties. But in the process of co-operation between the Islamic peoples and the multiplicity of their intellectual traditions from east and west—a Semitic, Iranian and classical Greek inheritance—there emerged the 'international' society and culture of Islam. It survived the end of the caliphate (1258) for another six centuries—the same length of time as the caliphate had lasted.

With the rise of modern nation states in the course of the nineteenth and twentieth centuries we leave our subject. The history of Islam has continued, but in place of a community which—although divided and split—recognises as its sovereign the leader of orthodox prayer (even if he be a foreign usurper) there have appeared nations of Arabs—Egyptians, Syrians, Iraqis—as well as Persians, Turks and all the other Islamic peoples and regions. Their institutions are modelled on examples of western legal and government doctrines. Most of their kings, presidents and dictators cannot, and do not want to, lay claim to a spiritual role or religious authority. Others cherish this claim, attempt to legitimise their state as an Islamic one and try to turn back the wheel of history. Powerful movements aimed at reasserting the fundamentals of Islam flourish. It is questionable whether they can solve the problems of a society in flux as once the message of the Prophet at Mecca did; it is clear that they pursue different, indeed contradictory aims although many of them use the same slogans. As always, and recently even more than ever, politicians of all persuasions invoke the community of the Islamic peoples. Whether it can bring back unity of political activity remains to be seen. But their shared past exerts a profound influence on their present.

Chapter Two

EUROPE AND ISLAM: THE HISTORY OF A SCIENCE

'There are many wonderful things in oriental history which cannot be grasped by human understanding. A poor despised person, such as Muhammed was, acquired through his piety and other virtues such power that he is revered hardly less than God Himself by a great part of the inhabited earth—is that not wonderful? The same person tamed a wild and intractable people without force and educated them by giving them moral standards. He founded a religion which swept Christianity out of the east like a broom; from the smallest beginnings he established an empire which in half a century subjugated more provinces than the Roman empire in three entire centuries and defeated two flourishing empires, the Byzantine and the Persian, severely upsetting and shaking the former, and completely destroying the latter—all this, I say, did not happen without higher decree and must inwardly instil in our spirit, filled with love and respect for our own religion, a feeling of fear and pain . . . In short, anyone who wants to learn the different articles of the faith of nations about God and divine things and the history of religions, or the customs, laws and rules of tribes and states and forms of government, anyone moreover who is captivated by the history of natural objects, of illnesses and cures, or who likes to observe the form of the earth through the passage of time, and the rise and fall of cities, will find in the study of Muhammedan history a sufficiency and an abundance to occupy and satisfy him. Anyone who values literary history will be amazed how many men in the east had wandered in all avenues of literature at a time when our Europe was as if shrouded in a dark night of ignorance and barbarism, and will recognise with pleasure what contribution every one of them has made to the development of culture. He who studies such things has one of the most thoroughly worthwhile activities of the human mind and the most agreeable quickening of the spirit.'

(Johann Jacob Reiske: *Prodidagmata ad Hagji Chalifae librum memorialem rerum a Muhammedanis gestarum exhibentia introductionem generalem in historiam sic dictam orientalem* [written in 1747]. In: J.B.Koehler: *Abulfedae tabulae Syriae.* Leipzig 1766; ^{2}1786, pp.239–40.)

With such words Johann Jacob Reiske canvassed the study of Islamic history and its Arabic sources in the year 1747. It was to Reiske that Arabic studies (according to Johann Fück [20.01], p.108) owes its 'coming of age'. It was the Enlightenment which had in broad outline prepared the ground in wider circles for an unbiased interest in the history and culture of the Islamic countries. To medieval Europe, Islam was a heresy; Muḥammad, who claimed that he was renewing and perfecting the pure religion of Abraham, was viewed as a false prophet influenced by Christian and Jewish heretics. Only a few learned scholars pressed for a more thoughtful judgement. The strife-ridden relationship between Christendom and Islam was characterised by centuries of threats and military conflict. Rapidly and insuperably the Arabs had fallen upon the provinces of Sasanian Iran and then of the Byzantine empire, had conquered Christian territories in Asia Minor, Syria and Egypt, and had broken Byzantine seapower in Sicily. After taking North Africa they had acquired Spain and, in spite of the efforts of Charles Martel (732), they threatened the heartlands of Europe for decades. These events could still fill a later observer 'with fear and pain'—Reiske's words quoted at the beginning reveal this clearly—and could prevent him from making an objective judgement; even nineteenth-century biographies of Muḥammad exude a spirit of prejudice and polemic, depicting the Prophet as a cunning and self-seeking politician and the Koran as a grotesque medley of fragments derived from Jewish and Christian traditions.

1. Early studies of Islam in the context of religious war

The Crusades made the Franks familiar with a superior culture; contacts with the Muslims in Spain and Sicily gave Christian Europe access to the Arabic transmission and continuation of the scientific heritage of the ancient world; translations from the end of the eleventh century onwards enriched scientific, medical and philosophical studies. A deeper understanding of Islam and its history did not, however, accompany these developments. It was the defeats of the Crusaders—Edessa fell in 1144, as did Jerusalem in 1187, to Saladin—that awakened in intelligent men of the Church an awareness that coming to grips with the 'Saracens' demanded spiritual armour, and especially a precise knowledge of the Koran. The abbot Peter of Cluny (Peter the Venerable) who became acquainted in Spain with the conflict between Islam and Christianity, and the spirit of the

Reconquista—the *Song of the Cid* appeared at just this time—commissioned Robert of Ketton in the year 1143 to produce the first Latin version of the Koran. (This was more a comprehensive paraphrase than a translation.) He also ordered certain Christian-Arab polemical and apologetic writings about Muḥammad and Islam, which were then accessible in Toledo, to be translated. He sent the translations to Bernard of Clairvaux and undertook in his *Liber contra sectam sive haeresim Saracenorum* to confront 'the wicked sect of the Saracens' with the power of the word and reason. Dominicans and Franciscans of the thirteenth century followed this example; the call for a thorough linguistic training of missionaries—taken up above all by the famous Raymond of Lull, whose religious zeal brought about his death in Tunis in 1316—soon bore its first-fruits. A standard work of polemic which on the other hand corrected many errors was the *Propugnaculum* of the Florentine Ricoldo da Monte Croce, who studied the language and religion of the Arabs around 1290 in Baghdad (Martin Luther translated this work into German in 1542!). But the sources of information on Islam remained sparse. Until the seventeenth century, Robert of Ketton's version of the Koran, commissioned by Peter the Venerable, provided the basis for other translations into European languages. It was replaced and improved only in 1698 by the version of the Italian Ludovico Marracci.

The Ottoman conquests in the Balkans and Asia Minor in the fifteenth century brought new danger for Europe and Christianity. Constantinople fell in 1453; but even then the information assembled by Peter and Ricoldo formed the major sources used by a re-awakening polemical literature. 'So much blood has been spilt that streams of blood flowed through the city. Thus has the noble city founded by Constantine fallen into the hands of the infidels. . . . What the fury of the Turks will bring about in the imperial city I do not know; but it is easy to guess: a nation which is hostile to our religion will not leave behind anything holy or pure'—in these terms Enea Silvio Piccolomini (the future Pope Pius II) wrote to Cardinal Nicholas of Cusa under the influence of the contemporary crisis (correspondence published by R. Wolkan, Vol. III, 1, Vienna 1918, p. 207) and he called for a unified and determined counter-attack on the part of the Christians. The reply of the great man of Cusa must demand respect: his *Cribratio Alkorani* (1461) is no strident polemic, but is written with the intention 'of viewing the book of Mahumet from the standpoint of the Gospel of Christ, and of showing that there is, in this very book too, material through which the Gospel, if it needed further attestation, would indeed be confirmed'. It is written with the certainty that all religions have a share in the absolute truth of the one religion. (*Cribratio Alkorani*, prologue, n. 10, 1–3, ed. L. Hagemann, Nicolai de Cusa Opera Omnia, Vol. VIII, Hamburgi 1985, p. 11.)

In Spain, contacts between Muslims and Christians continued after the Reconquest too. In 1492, the last Arab ruler had to leave Granada, but the Muslims long remained in the Iberian peninsula as an important minority. Both the notorious Inquisition and serious studies of the Arabic language to help missionary work were the results of this precarious coexistence. Moreover, contacts between the Church of Rome and the Christians of the Near East encouraged such studies, in attempts to achieve union with the Oriental churches and to support missionary activity there. Efforts on the part of the Curia to achieve union were likewise behind the setting up of a printing press by Cardinal Fernando dei Medici, which from 1586 to 1610 published for the first time important Arabic works in beautiful Arabic type. Amongst these were not only Christian theological writings for use by Arab clerics but also the medical encyclopedia of Avicenna, grammatical teaching manuals and an extract from the geography of al-Idrīsī—signs of scientific interest in the spirit of the Renaissance. An example was set, which was soon to be followed in France, Holland and Germany.

2. *From confrontation to co-existence*

The Islamic lands had been, since ancient times, stations for European trade on the road to India and the Far East. Nevertheless, this route—which was always precarious—had lost much of its importance from the thirteenth century, as contacts with the Mongols had opened up an alternative route through Russia and Central Asia. The discovery of America and of the sea route to India caused a complete eclipse in the commercial importance of the Islamic east. Soon, however, European governments found themselves obliged to enter into a new and completely different relationship with the Islamic world. Under Selīm I (1512–20) the Ottomans had risen as the new power of the Near East, and under his successor, Süleymān, theatened the Balkans; in 1529 the Turks stood, for the first time, before Vienna. In the same year Charles V sent a diplomatic mission to Persia in the forlorn hope that he would gain the Ṣafavid Shāh in Isfahan as an ally against the Ottomans. More successful were the negotiations of his rival François I of France with the Turks. They bore political as well as other fruits: in the year 1543 the king sent with an embassy to the Sublime Porte the scholar Guillaume Postel, who bought Arabic manuscripts in the east, produced a first grammar of the classical Arabic language and published an idealised representation of 'The Republic of the Turks'. His pupil, Joseph Scaliger (1540–1609) produced, in his major work *De emendatione temporum* (1583), a thorough chronology of history according to all the sources then available, even oriental ones; the Islamic calendar was also shown. Moreover, the manuscripts of Postel which had reached the library of the Elector of the Palatinate in Heidelberg enriched Arabic and Islamic studies in both Germany and Holland. Holland soon took the lead; the cosmopolitan atmosphere of a trading nation and the energy of important scholars contributed to this. Thomas Erpenius (van Erpe, 1584–1624) studied the geography of Abu'l-Fidā' and the Persian chronicle of Mīrkhwand; he had the Annals of al-Ṭabarī in a Turkish version, and with it access to the major source of early Islamic history; and he was the first to make available, by means of a textual edition and a Latin translation of the world chronicle of the Copt al-Makīn, an overview of Islamic history from its beginnings until the time of the Crusades, an overview which went back to authentic Islamic sources. The successor of Erpenius in the Chair of Arabic at Leiden was his pupil, Jacobus Golius (1596–1667), whose Arabic-Latin dictionary (1653) remained for nearly 200 years the standard work for Arabic studies. Moreover, he brought back to Leiden valuable manuscripts from the east. Around 1609 the pupil of Golius, Levinus Warner—who represented the States-General at the Sublime Porte in Constantinople—bequeathed to the library at Leiden a legacy of almost a thousand manuscripts, and thereafter Leiden became the Mecca of European Arabic studes. To this day its treasury of early Arabic manuscripts is unique of its kind. Of comparable importance there were only the ancient holdings of the Escurial and of the Vatican (these were described for the first time only in the course of the eighteenth century) and the already important collection of the Bibliothèque Royale (the present Bibliothèque Nationale) in Paris. Nevertheless, it was only in the course of the nineteenth century that the holdings in Paris reached their present-day level when diplomats and colonial officials, scholars and travellers, in London and in Berlin, helped to found libraries of oriental manuscripts. Only during the twentieth century did the disproportionately greater holdings in the capital cities of the East become accessible and available to scholarship.

Researchers and adventurers, who by their travel accounts made known to Europe the customs, culture and religion of the Islamic world, followed the diplomats, and also the merchants who travelled to Persia for silk and precious stones. The Roman Pietro della Valle travelled through Egypt and Syria, stayed longer in Persia (1619–26) and depicted the conditions of the Ṣafavid kingdom. The doctor François Bernier (1620–88) brought back from Syria, Egypt and India sharp observations about society and economy. Adam Olearius (Ölschläger, 1603–71) accompanied a trade mission from Holstein and not only described this in his *Muscovitische und Persische Reyse* covering the years 1633–35 and 1635–39, but was also the first to translate examples of Persian literature into German. Then Jean-Baptiste Tavernier and Jean (Sir John) Chardin gave thorough and many-sided accounts of their Persian travels and experiences—Chardin even became court goldsmith of the Shāh—in the 1660s and 1670s.

3. The beginnings of Islamic studies

Travel accounts, political writing and practical handbooks on Turkey and other Islamic countries satisfied a contemporary interest—an interest which was certainly aimed more at the self-image, even self-criticism, of the Europeans, than at unbiased knowledge. On the other hand, the scientific study of Islam, its languages and literatures—to a large extent within the sphere of theology and Semitic philology—remained restricted to the Koran and the Arabic language. The Reformation had directed attention to the text of the Bible and its oriental versions; people had also begun to appreciate (and soon also to over-estimate) the value of Arabic linguistic studies for an explanation of cognate Semitic roots in the Hebrew Old Testament. Among them was Thomas Bedwell (1563–1632) in Cambridge, who introduced the study of Arabic into England. Few went further. The incumbent of the first Arabic Chair at Oxford, Edward Pocock (1604–91), himself also a theologian, made the pre-Islamic history of Arabia and the dogmatic theology of Islam better known through his *Specimen Historiae Arabum* (1650), and his Arabic-Latin edition of the concise *History of the Dynasties* of Barhebraeus (1663), admittedly a compilation by a Christian writer, nevertheless added to the few sources then known a significant summary of Arab history until the Mongol invasion. It also provided abundant information on literature and science from the best Arab historians.

Towards the end of the seventeenth century the power of the Ottomans began to wane sharply—the attempt to storm Vienna in 1683 had proved abortive—and Europe began to confront Islam more calmly. At the same time the Enlightenment in France opened the way to an undogmatic confrontation with the world of the Orient; a general enthusiasm about Asia also encouraged scholarly studies. Bartholomé d'Herbelot (1625–95) derived from Arabic, Persian and Turkish chronicles the material for his 'Bibliothèque Orientale' (which appeared posthumously in 1697). As the first encyclopedia of the history and culture of the Islamic countries and of the authors and works of their literatures it was a milestone in the history of Oriental studies. Two decades later there appeared the free rendering by Antoine Galland of 'The Tales of the 1001 Nights', soon also translated into English and German from the French version—a European bestseller. Hardly any work of Arabic literature has determined so deeply and definitively the image of the East in the West, and this is not in the best interests of a dispassionate view. The Enlightenment, however, also taught that Muḥammad and the Koran should be viewed more objectively and indeed treated with respect. The Utrecht orientalist Adrianus Relandus in his work *De Religione Mohammedica* (1705) removed old errors, and the English translation of the Koran by George Sale (1734) put the study of the Islamic Book of Revelation on a new basis.

It was, however, Johann Jacob Reiske (1716–74), with whose panegyric of Islamic history we began this chapter, who created a philological basis for these various efforts. His teacher at Leiden, Albert Schultens, had been content to use the study of Arabic in the service of *philologia sacra,* namely Biblical exegesis. Reiske viewed the search for doubtful etymologies of Semitic roots as an idle occupation; and he himself used the Arabic manuscripts of the library in Leiden—for the sake of which he spent arduous years of study in Holland—in order to open new doors for Arabic philology and to establish it as a truly independent scientific discipline. He would, moreover, have been able to achieve still greater things if misfortune, mistrust, and indeed his reputation as a free-thinker had not stood in his way all through his life and prevented his being appointed to a Chair at the University of Leipzig. His wide-ranging works on Arabic poetry, proverbs, medicine, numismatics and Islamic historians remained deprived of the recognition which they deserved. His Latin translation of the *Annals* of Abu'l-Fidā' found no buyers, so that only the first volume could appear; his interpretation of Islamic history as a paradigm of universal history was in advance of his time. So the history of scholarship preserves his memory as a 'martyr of Arabic literature'. Only after the French Revolution had changed the face of the world and the spirit of scholarship could the study of Arabic and Islam be resumed on the same level.

In the meantime, in quite a different way two other researchers of the time enriched our knowledge of the Islamic East: Carsten Niebuhr (1733–1815), a member of the unlucky expedition to Arabia financed by the Danish king, undertook (after the failure of that joint enterprise) further journeys through southern Persia, Iraq, Palestine and Asia Minor (1761–67) and provided valuable descriptions of his findings; and the Frenchman François Volney, who spent the years 1783–86 in Egypt and Syria, observed the society and economy of the Arab world under Ottoman domination. His diagnosis—that the collapse of the economy and culture was brought on by oriental despotism and helped by Islamic fatalism—long moulded the judgement of European historians.

4. The rise of Oriental philology

The word 'orientalist' first appeared in England (in 1779 in an essay about Edward Pocock); in 1791 'orientaliste' appeared in France; in 1838 'orientalisme' was the subject of an article in the *Dictionnaire de l'Académie Française.* At first this term meant the study of the entire Orient, i.e., both Near and Far East. The establishment of the Paris Ecole Spéciale des Langues Orientales Vivantes in the year 1795 was intended to serve the practical demands of economics and diplomacy. The languages of the Near East were of paramount importance; Arabic, Persian and Turkish were represented by professorial chairs. Thus were 'Oriental studies' in a narrower sense established as an academic discipline. In Paris, a whole generation of European scholars in the early nineteenth century either studied under Silvestre de Sacy (1758–1838) or were influenced by his 'school'. De Sacy's Arabic grammar, his Arabic chrestomathy and his textual editions of Arabic and Persian historians and men of letters were important milestones. With his broad interests he exerted an influence on the wide circle of his pupils from all the countries of Europe: Wilhelm Freytag, Gustav Flügel, Heinrich Leberecht Fleischer and others from Germany, Carl Johan Tornberg from Sweden, Don Pascual de Gayangos from Spain and William MacGuckin de Slane from Ireland.

The interests of Austria in the Balkans and those of England in India encouraged Turkish and Persian studies in those countries. In 1784 William Jones had founded in Calcutta the Asiatic Society of Bengal, which promoted not only Indology but also the study of the Islamic culture of India; in Fort William College, where the employees of the East India Company were instructed from 1800 to 1854 in the local languages, native teachers edited grammars and texts. The diplomat Sir John Malcolm produced, with his *History of Persia* (1815), based partly on Persian original sources, a comprehensive work which was not only of historical interest but also served the need for information in view of Anglo-Indian politics and trade.

The versatile Joseph von Hammer-Purgstall (1774–1856) published in Vienna between 1809 and 1818 a scholarly journal entitled 'Fundgruben des Orients'. This linguistically gifted amateur of Islamic literature had studied Turkish and Persian at the Oriental Academy of Vienna (founded in 1754 by Maria Theresa) and had then also learnt Arabic in the East. In his journal—largely filled with contributions from his own pen—he published the widest variety of texts and subjects from the undiscovered treasures of Islamic literature, in collaboration with scholars from the whole of Europe. Today his work arouses admiration more for its abundance than for its philological precision; but his wide-ranging treatment of the history and the governmental system of the Ottoman Empire is still of value and his influence gave a wide circle of people a new image of the East. Goethe read Ḥāfiẓ in Hammer's translation: 'In every part my little book reveals how much I owe to this worthy man', he acknowledged in the 'Notes and Discussions' of the *West-östlicher Divan* (Hamburg edition, Volume 2, p.253). Despite this, he maintained a critical distance towards him—as did the prelate Heinrich Friedrich von Diez (1784–91), the Prussian *chargé d'affaires* at the Sublime Porte and the other source of inspiration for Goethe's encounter with the East.

In Germany Romanticism aroused an interest in the 'differences in the structure of human language', in the 'national character of language' (Wilhelm von Humboldt) and a sense of the specific external and inner form of Oriental poetry. Friedrich Rückert (1788–1866)—who learnt Persian with Hammer-Purgstall and who served first in Erlangen and then in Berlin as Professor of Oriental Languages—created from the very spirit and genius of Romanticism translations, unsurpassed even today, of great works of literature from the Near and the Far East, amongst which was the first translation of the Koran to reflect the rhetorical power of the original.

The growing number of specialists encouraged the idea of union. In the year 1821 the Société Asiatique was founded in Paris (De Sacy was its first president); the Royal Asiatic Society of Great Britain and Ireland followed in 1834, the American Oriental Society in 1842 and the Deutsche Morgenländische Gesellschaft in 1845. They all sponsored (as they still do today) the study of languages and culture of the East in the broadest sense, encompassing the ancient East, the world of Islam, India and East Asia. Their publications made it clear that knowledge of the East was obviously an international branch of scholarship in its own right.

5. *'Historicism' and the opening up of the sources*

The intellectual movement of Romanticism brought in its train a new sensitivity towards the multiplicity and individuality of world literatures; at the same time a new attitude to what constituted the proper study of history gained ground. 'Every era belongs immediately to God, and its value does not depend at all on what results from it but lies in its own existence'; so wrote Leopold von Ranke in 1854 (*Über die Epochen der neueren Geschichte,* new edition Darmstadt, 1954, p.8). To grasp the events, personalities and periods of the past in their uniqueness, variety and richness and to appreciate them with a consciousness that they were of equal value—this was, from the middle of the nineteenth century, the aim of the Islamic historians who dealt extensively with known sources and opened up new ones. It can be asserted that it was only this outburst of historico-critical research which freed scholarship on Islam and its history from all the practical constraints and theoretical considerations which had hitherto imprisoned it. Since then, methods have become more refined. The field of vision has become wider, whilst at the same time, too, the awareness of the relativity and contemporaneity of 'objective' scholarly judgement has become sharpened. Yet even today

Islamic studies are still occupied with the tasks laid down by historicism: assembling, appraising and arranging data and facts to establish a framework to provide a surer interpretation of historical connections and forces.

In this context, then, there appeared the first general work on the period of the Caliphs, by Gustav Weil (*Geschichte der Chalifen*, 1850–51; *Geschichte des Abbasidenchalifates in Ägypten*, 1860–62). Even today, there is no comparable work which gives a detailed presentation of events with constant recourse to traditional sources. (It is true that a sequel would have to reckon with material which has become unmanageable in size; Weil could limit himself to giving an account from the chronicles which were accessible to him.) His biography of Muḥammad (1843) was rapidly overtaken by the more comprehensive work of the Austrian Aloys Sprenger (English 1851, German 1861–65) which even with all the weaknesses of his religio-historical diagnosis (he viewed Muḥammad as a morbid hysteric) for the first time made use of the material of Islamic traditions *in extenso*, giving a witty presentation of it. Like Sprenger, the Scotsman William Muir worked in India and he was active in similar fashion, presenting to the English public a biography of the Prophet (1856–61) based on the sources opened up by Sprenger. Muir's *The history of the Caliphs* (1883) was dependent on Weil. Weil had also prepared *Historisch-kritische Einleitung in den Koran* (1844); most important, however, was the *Geschichte des Qorāns* of Theodor Nöldeke (1860) which is still today a standard work in the extensively revised and re-worked version of Friedrich Schwally (1909–19). Around the same time the Viennese scholar Alfred von Kremer, after extensive journeys in the Orient, began his *Geschichte der herrschenden Ideen des Islams* (1868) and a *Culturgeschichte des Orients unter den Chalifen* (1875–7), unsurpassed synopses of the intellectual and material culture of medieval Islam.

The great chronicles which provided the basis for these first general overviews became universally accessible from the middle of the nineteenth century in printed editions. Ferdinand Wüstenfeld (1808–99) published the classic biography of Muḥammad by Ibn Hishām, the Arabic chronicles of Mecca, genealogical and biographical lexicons and geographical encyclopedias; the Swede Carl Johan Tornberg published the great annals of Ibn al-Athīr; the Dutchman Reinhart Dozy published the historians of the Islamic west—followed by critical studies of the sources and a comprehensive overview. Michele Amari (1806—89) published the Arabic historical sources of his homeland Sicily; in Paris Adrien Barbier de Meynard (with Abel Pavet de Courteille) published the detailed dynastic, cultural and natural history of al-Masʿūdī (1861–77); Michael Jan de Goeje organised in Leiden, with the cooperation of

Dutch, German and Italian Arabists, the monumental edition of al-Ṭabarī (1879–1901)—our principal source for a knowledge of the first three centuries of Islamic history—and soon afterwards Eduard Sachau (director of the Seminar für Orientalische Sprachen founded in Berlin in 1887) published an edition of the *Ṭabaqāt* of Ibn Saʿd, the book on the 'generations' of the Companions of the Prophet and of the men of early Islam. Many of these editions have not yet been replaced or superseded and a good many have been pirated or reprinted in the Arab east.

At the same time a critical analysis of the sources began. Here too, editors achieved important preparatory work. Julius Wellhausen applied methods he had used in his critical study of the Pentateuch—the isolating of layers and tendencies in transmission—to early Arab historians and used the results in his classic work *Skizzen und Vorarbeiten* (1884–99), in a work on *Die religiös-politischen Oppositionsparteien im alten Islam* (1901) and in his most important work *Das arabische Reich und sein Sturz* (1902). In Italy Leone Caetani assembled, in his grandiose *Annali dell'Islam* (1905–27) and his *Chronographia Islamica* which appeared at the same time (1913–22) the sources for a history of the first one-and-a-half centuries of Islam in as complete a form as was possible at that time. The auxiliary disciplines of historical research, archaeology, epigraphy and palaeography were treated more systematically from the turn of the century. As early as 1875 to 1891 Stanley Lane-Poole had published a 10-volume catalogue of the Oriental coin collection of the British Museum, and on the basis of this had compiled a chronological table of the Islamic dynasties. The Russian scholar, Vasilij Vladimirovich Bartol'd (Wilhelm Barthold 1869–1930, the pupil of the Arabist Viktor Rosen) undertook the history of Central Asia and of the Turkish peoples with the aid of numismatic as well as literary sources. In Vienna Joseph von Karabacek (1845–1918) advanced Arabic numismatics and above all papyrology with the aid of the important collection of the Archduke Rainer. The founder of Arabic epigraphy was the Genevan Max van Berchem (1863–1921). His monumental *Matériaux pour un Corpus Inscriptionum Arabicarum* covered a large part of the Arabic inscriptions then accessible in Asia Minor, Syria, Jerusalem and Cairo; this work which appeared from 1894 onwards was continued after his death on the basis of material collected by him and by others, but it has remained incomplete. Amongst those who worked on it were Josef Strzygowski, who was above all active in the field of art history, and Ernst Herzfeld, a pioneer of Islamic archaeology, who brought to light very important material from his journeys in Iraq undertaken with Friedrich Sarre, and above all from the excavation of the ʿAbbāsid Palace at Samarra (1911–14). Alois Musil undertook from 1895 to 1915 a series of extensive research journeys in eastern Syria, North Arabia and Mesopotamia. He discovered the Umayyad castle of Quṣayr 'Amra with its striking frescoes and produced in a series of topographical travel reports the foundation of our knowledge of the historical geography and the ethnography of the Arabian steppe (he accompanied the Rwāla Bedouin on their migrations for a whole year).

During this period the vast number of oriental and above all Arabic literary works which had become known in the manuscript catalogues of the European collections, and also since the middle of the nineteenth century in printed editions from the Orient, grew inordinately. The job of examining and arranging them still remains incomplete; even now, not all the works preserved in the libraries of the east are accessible or have been properly catalogued. The most important tool of Arabic bibliography remains the *Geschichte der Arabischen Litteratur,* which Carl Brockelmann who was then 27 years old published from 1895 onwards ('in order to make it possible for the publisher Felber to publish my edition of Ibn Qutayba's *'Uyūn al-akhbār . . .* by means of a comparatively marketable work', as he was later to remark not without bitterness—the publisher did not keep his promise to him). He enlarged it substantially through supplementary volumes which appeared between 1937 and 1942—a tremendous achievement which moreover could hardly rely on competent earlier work. The most important of such earlier works was the exemplary catalogue of manuscripts in the Berlin Imperial Library—the present-day Staatsbibliothek Preussischer Kulturbesitz—written by Wilhelm Ahlwardt. Edward Granville Browne produced an overall picture of Persian literature in the context of the Islamic history of Iran (*A Literary History of Persia,* 1902–24). He also wrote a fascinating account of a year of study spent in Persia: *A Year Amongst the Persians* (1893). A study comparable to that of Brockelmann on works in Persian was begun in 1927 by Charles Ambrose Storey.

6. Islam as a field of scholarship

Besides historical research in a narrow sense, the study of the religion of Islam became established as a special discipline. More than any other, the Hungarian Ignaz Goldziher (1850–1921) should be mentioned here, who in his seminal *Muhammedanische Studien* (1889–90) and many other works and monographs undertook 'to apply the methods of critical historicism to Islam in its entirety and to view it as a phenomenon of cultural history, the development of which is essentially inspired by religious ideas' (J. Fück [20.01], p.226). Experience of the East gave other scholars the stimulus to study contemporary Islam in its historical context. The Dutchman Christiaan Snouck Hurgronje (1857–1936), a pupil of de Goeje, described the holy city of Mecca from personal experience (1888–9) and—while active as a colonial official in Java and Sumatra—portrayed for the first time the history and society of Islamic Indonesia. In similar fashion, French orientalists contributed to the investigation of French colonial territory in North Africa. Louis Massignon (1883–1962) began his studies with geographical work on Morocco but soon went far beyond a limited geographical framework. Just as the orthodox Judaism of Goldziher was the basis and starting point for his observation of Islam, so too it was Massignon's Catholic Christianity which enabled him to have a deep understanding of Islamic piety and mysticism. In the year 1909 his first important study on the mystic Ḥallāj appeared. Independent in his interpretation of religious phenomena, but also criticised for his drawing of parallels between Islamic and Christian sacred history (the passion of Christ and of Ḥallāj, Mary and Fāṭima) he nevertheless led Islamic scholarship far beyond a historical approach which merely passively observes and compiles. New horizons were also revealed by the Scotsman, Duncan Black Macdonald, who was at the Theological Seminar in Hartford from 1892 and was the first representative of Arabic studies and Islamic scholarship in the United States; he used the methods of the psychology of religion in his works on Islamic theology. At the Seminar für Orientalische Sprachen in Berlin, Richard Hartmann from 1887 onwards produced similar work using sociological methods (following Auguste Comte and Max Weber—who were still at that time viewed with mistrust and indeed attacked) to analyse the law, government and society of Islam. Finally, Carl Heinrich Becker (1876–1933), the first specialist in the history and culture of the Near East in Hamburg, rebelled against the exclusion of the Islamic east from the Western view of history and proclaimed (against Ernst Troeltsch) Islam's role as intermediary between Europe and Asia. He argued that both Islam and Europe had assimilated the classical heritage, despite all the differences between them in the way they chose to interpret it, and that there was continuous exchange between Islam and Europe in all spheres of intellectual and cultural activity. He also showed 'that it was a mistake to view Islam as being totally hostile to economic activity' and to regard Islam as being inherently fatalistic. In this way, he swept away long-standing prejudices ([14.17] p.65).

The abundance of knowledge, perspectives and opinions newly acquired from texts and studies were gathered together in the first great collaborative work of western Orientalism, the *Encyclopaedia of Islam: a geographical, ethnographical and biographical dictionary of the Mohammadan peoples.* This was prepared after a resolution of the Geneva Congress of Orientalists from 1894 by Goldziher, de Goeje and Karabacek, it appeared in Leiden from 1908 in German,

French and English and was completed by the collaborative work of nearly a hundred scholars after thirty years with the appearance of the supplementary volume in 1938.

7. *Research on Islam in East and West: encounter and conflict*

Thus Islam as a field of scholarship began to emerge as a recognised discipline in Europe and America from the end of the nineteenth century, to have independent status through the establishment of Chairs and university institutes, to express itself through journals and the publications of learned societies and also to specialise in the spheres of Arabic, Iranian and Turkish studies. At the same time, in the Islamic countries themselves Islamic research appeared which was no longer primarily motivated by theology or law but which was scholarly in the western sense; this development was brought about by movements of national emancipation, sponsored and not infrequently set up by politicians and scholars who had been students of European scholarship.

One of the great men of the new Egyptian literature, Ṭāhā Ḥusayn —novelist, literary critic and politician of culture, defender of a nationalism which was liberal and open to the West, and champion of a spiritual and scholarly relationship with Europe—wrote about the first phase of fruitful intellectual contacts between European teachers and Arab students. He describes in his personal reminiscences the effect which the lectures of some important European Arabists had on the students of Cairo University, which had been founded in the year 1908. Until that time he had been a pupil of the famous theological college of the Azhar Mosque; and, oppressed by its intellectual narrowness, he was fascinated by the style and content of this new teaching. Here the Egyptian professors not only read the traditional teaching texts of the old curriculum—grammar, law, dogmatics—but opened up vistas of a wide universe of knowledge and historical sources.

> New professors came who completely entranced him [the author presents his autobiography in the third person] and took his fancy. There was Professor Carlo Nallino, the Italian orientalist who gave lectures in Arabic on the history of Umayyad literature [more precisely in 1908–09 on Arabic astronomy, and only in 1909–10 on ancient Arabic literature up to the Umayyad period]. There was Professor (David) Santillana; he also spoke in Arabic with a charming Tunisian accent about the history of Islamic philosophy, especially about the history of (Greek-Arabic) translations. There was also Professor (Gerardo) Meloni, who also lectured in Arabic on the history of the ancient East; he told the students about things which no Professor before him had ever discussed in Egypt—he dealt with the history of Babylon and

> Assyria, he spoke about cuneiform script, and he discussed the laws of Hammurabi. The young man understood everything which the professors said, he found nothing complicated or difficult to understand. Nothing was more displeasing to him than the end of the lectures and he looked forward to nothing more than the next lesson. There was also a German professor, [Enno] Littmann; he spoke primarily about Semitic languages and their relationship with Arabic and then began to teach some of these languages. The young man would have broken away completely from his earlier life had he not spent the rest of the day and part of the evening with his school fellows from the Azhar, from the Dār al-ʿUlūm [a teaching institute which was to teach graduates of the Azhar the modern sciences] and the students of the Faculty of Law.

But mingled with admiration and fascination there was also scorn and amazement; not only certain Egyptian professors,

> but the foreign professors as well were a source of merriment and a target of mockery. Their Arabic made the students laugh; and some of them twisted their tongues in order to imitate the Arabic of this or that Italian or German professor! The young man never forgot the day when the students decided to boycott the lecture of the Italian Professor Nallino because Italy had declared war on Turkey [29.9.1911] and had sent its warships against Tripoli. The students decided to assemble in the lecture room until the professor came and sat down in his chair and then to go out of the room and leave him alone. And so indeed it happened; the students left the teacher alone in the lecture hall and then stood outside the door and waited to see how he would react. The professor remained there for a few moments and then he came out, turned to his students and said to them in pure classical Arabic but with his own peculiar accent: 'You are like a man who castrates himself in order to spite his wife!' The arrow hit the mark and the point went home. From that day onwards no university student contemplated another boycott on lectures. (Ṭāhā Ḥusayn: *al-Ayyām* ['The Days'] Volume 3, Cairo, 1973, chapter 4, p.34; chapter 6, pp.42–3.)

The spontaneous thirst for knowledge, the naive enthusiasm for the sheer novelty of European scholarship, is today a thing of the past. But the conscious withdrawal on the part of young Islamic intellectuals from tradition, the hope for progress through secularisation according to a European model, and the search for national self-expression through a new scholarly observation of the Islamic past have laid the ground for efforts at philological and historical research in the East. Like Ṭāhā Ḥusayn—who later continued his studies in France—a good many writers and scholars from Egypt as well as from other Islamic countries have studied in European and American universities, and academies and universities in the Arab world have been founded as institutions for literary and historical research on the Western model. Muḥammad Kurd ʿAlī, the founder of the Arab Academy in Damascus and its first President from 1922 to 1953 (at the same time an important historian of his home city), acknowledged in a long lecture the role played by European studies since the Renaissance in their effect on the Arabs themselves:

> We should now recognise how this Renaissance has influenced us and our language. That means that we should be aware of how that mighty effort (on the part of the Europeans) to re-awaken the Arab inheritance affects us personally, and we should therefore praise those who have published our books, have given to our beloved language the favour of their endeavour and who have taught us in lectures things about the history of our people and the culture of our ancestors which we did not know. (*Majallat al-Majmaʿ al-ʿIlmī al-ʿArabī* [Journal of the Arab Academy] 7.1927, p.400)

On the other hand, the vigorous attacks of Kurd ʿAlī on the work of the Belgian Jesuit Henri Lammens (1862–1937) then active in Beirut who denied that the traditional sources of early Islam had any truth in them at all show how he could challenge European scholarship.

Yet the closing episode of the passage quoted above from Ṭāhā Ḥusayn contains a lesson which is still valid today. Contempt for the foreigner who will never be able to speak the language of Islam like an Arab, and, above all, anger at the arrogance of power politics for which scholars are given their share of responsibility—these are also factors at work in the scholarly encounter between East and West. Even today, criticism of the political role of the western powers in the Near East invites the judgement that western Oriental research is an 'organ' of colonialism or imperialism.

The European must allow himself to be asked by the representatives of independent and self-assured scholarship in the Islamic countries whether he has mastered the Islamic languages thoroughly enough; whether he has interpreted the sources sensitively enough; and whether he, as a non-Muslim, can understand the religion, history and culture of Islam profoundly enough. Even in the East, however, the classical literary language of medieval sources has become alien and rapidly more difficult of access to people today. Here the rift between the written language and the spoken everyday language also plays a part; only a few Muslims still possess the kind of education which was provided by the traditional theological college (the *madrasa*). In addition, the scholarly methods of philological textual work and of criticism of historical sources which were developed in Europe have first of all been applied here to Islamic literary and historical works and thereafter passed on to the East. The process of assimilation has already begun and is still going on today. Thus the way has been prepared for a fruitful collaboration between Europeans and the scholars of the Islamic world, a collaboration which the East can promote to an ever-increasing extent, but to which Europe can also contribute further by drawing on its ancient and rich scholarly tradition.

The question as to whether philology or sociology is more useful to Oriental and Islamic research is a favourite one today; it is a fairly idle one. As long as many textual sources remain inaccessible, indeed unknown, there is a necessity for philological work. Otherwise, all assertions now made about historical hypotheses have feet of clay. Anyone who cannot read the sources often has to be satisfied with half-baked ideas and half-truths. On the other hand, philological precision can simulate an objectivity which adopts as its own the limited horizon of the medieval reader instead of teaching one to look through it. It often presents to those seeking introduction and orientation nothing more than an overall array of remote facts. Contacts with other disciplines are therefore necessary—with general historical studies, with cultural geography and with social sciences. In this way the field of Islamic history, which is still in its infancy, can answer the vital questions of the present. It can only achieve this aim if it does not capitulate to demands on the part of small-minded bureaucrats that scholarship should produce immediate short-term benefits. Such a capitulation would entail a half-hearted and—in a world of rapid and unpredictable change—vain attempt at modernism. This young discipline can only find itself if it keeps a sense of respect for the individual nature of its partners in the East—a nature which has evolved over many centuries—and at the same time expresses the profound community of shared historical concepts and experiences between Europe and the Islamic world.

Chapter Three

ISLAM: RELIGION AND LEGAL SYSTEM

'God (Himself) is witness that there is no God save Him. And the angels and the men of learning (too are witness). Maintaining His creation in justice, there is no God save Him, the Almighty, the Wise. Lo! religion with God (is) the Surrender (*Islām*). Those who (formerly) received the Scripture differed only after knowledge came unto them, through transgression among themselves. Whoso disbelieveth the revelations of God (will find that) lo! God is swift at reckoning. And if they argue with thee (O Muḥammad), say: I have surrendered (*aslamtu*) my purpose to God and (so have) those who follow me. And say unto those who have received the Scripture and those who read not: Have ye (too) surrendered (*aslamtum*)? If they surrender (*aslamū*), then truly they are rightly guided and if they turn away, then it is thy duty only to convey the message (unto them). God is Seer of (His) bondmen.' (Koran, sura 3, verses 18–20)

Islam is a confession and a mode of conduct; it is the 'exclusive confession' of the One Almighty God; it is 'complete surrender' to His revealed command; for the revelation is God's manifestation and God's command to man. 'Islam' therefore denotes acceptance of the revelation and the implementation of the command, and in a broader sense the historically evolved system of law which regulates both the worship of God as well as the conduct of the believers within the community. Those who profess Islam (*muslimūn*) form a religious and political community (the *umma*) which was founded by His prophet according to God's will. The *umma* is still—even after the break-up of the *Civitas Dei* and the collapse of political unity—the community of people, nations and states who in their belief, in their worship of God, in their private and public behaviour, submit to the law revealed in the Koran. This law is based on revelation; but in its shaping, systematisation and formulation it is the result of historical and political experience; and disputes of faith and law have left their mark on the political history of Islam until today.

1. The Revelation

Anyone who seeks to understand Islam must have recourse to the Koran. The Koran, according to Muslim belief, is the Word of God, the Revelation of His divinity and His command to men; it is the basis of the Islamic religion, a basis which has remained unaltered during the course of history, even if it is constantly experienced and interpreted anew. But the Koran itself is a book which is difficult of access. This is for external and internal reasons: external because in the present arrangement of the texts of the Revelation it is not possible to work out the original chronological sequence; internal because without a knowledge of the historical context it is not really possible to understand either the message in its entirety or many of the details of, and allusions to, its environment. These associations, moreover, have only been preserved for us by the manifold facets and reflections of religious tradition.

Muḥammad, the Prophet, was according to his own belief and that of his community the recipient of the Revelation, God's human instrument. It was his mission to 'repeat' and 'recite' the message of the heavenly Book of Revelation. 'Recite; in the name of your Lord'—with this introduction to the first revelation (sura 96) he found himself called to be a prophet; there then followed the command 'Stand up and warn' (sura 74) which designated him as the messenger of God to His people. Believers gathered around him and they soon began to note down individual revelations; there are in the Koran itself allusions to the fact that a knowledge of writing was quite common in the commercial city of Mecca. For the community of believers these writings soon became an integral part of the worship of God; a text to be recited (*qur'ān* 'recitation'), the Holy Book, which joined the books of the old religions and replaced them. But the task of writing down and collecting of the revelations was not completed during the lifetime of Muḥammad; this occurred only later in the generation of his immediate successors. A recent investigation has tried with penetrating arguments to prove the opposite (John Burton), arguing that it was indeed the Prophet himself who had the Revelations written down and that at a later date Islamic lawyers made a distinction between the Revealed Book of God, and the codified Koran, only so as to be able to use variant readings and apocryphal material, and therefore denied the Prophet the achievement of having assembled the Koran. Yet the tradition is unanimous—and if we wanted to characterise all tradition as being fabrication motivated by bias and pious intention then history could not be written: the tradition is unanimous that it was the third caliph ('Uthmān, 644–56) who first collected the Book of Islam and had it produced in a complete, unified and unchangeable form. Until then individual parts had been transmitted separately, smaller sections had been joined to bigger units,and collections of these shorter and longer texts to be recited, the 'suras' (Arabic, *sūra*), had been assembled in notebook or scroll form by the trusted Companions of the Prophet. After the turmoil of the conquests it seemed essential to ensure that there was unity of belief in the new empire. The caliph therefore ordered that a version of the Koran should be produced which was to be universally valid, 'canonical', and that every other version which was in common use should be withdrawn. The available collections were compared and compiled, and the 114 suras were arranged roughly in order of their length—from the second, which has 286 verses, to the last ones which have between 3 and 6 verses. The opening sura (the *Fātiḥa*), a short prayer which plays an important role in Muslim worship and everyday life, is followed by the long legal texts of the closing years in Medina and then by the numerous prophecies about God, the Creation and Divine History. Only at the end of the book do there appear the short ecstatic messages of the first period, which are full of the overwhelming experience of revelation. Tradition tells us which suras were 'sent down' in Mecca and which in Medina but there is no further information about their chronological sequence and composition. If a relative or absolute chronology can be constructed at all this is only on the basis of allusions in the text. To the mind of the devout Muslim this is a matter of fundamental indifference: all revelations are part of the Divine 'original text', the truth which existed in God's mind before time and creation. But the historian who wants to understand the background, emergence and earliest development of Islam is given a very difficult task. Several researchers on the Koran, such as Theodor Nöldeke, Richard Bell and Régis Blachère, tried to put the suras and parts of suras into their original order according to internal and external criteria, but they came to different conclusions in each case. Absolute certainty is not possible; and yet this remains a problem of great importance.

More than all other extensive traditional sources on the life and work of the Islamic prophet, the Koran provides a firm base: it is a source of unique immediacy and authenticity. If the genuineness and comprehensiveness of the canonical text was questioned at all it was by minorities in the Islamic community who thought that texts which confirmed the legitimacy of their claims had been suppressed by 'Uthmān's editors (but they too were content for the most part to interpret the canonical text for their own ends). The canonical text is also questioned today by some researchers who see in the Koran (as in early Islamic tradition) nothing more than a backward projection of pious fictions and political tendencies; according to them, what Muḥammad originally preached was not the religion of Islam but a Christian or Jewish heresy (M. Cook and P. Crone; G. Lüling). It was the Umayyad caliphs or even later proponents of theocracy who first canonised the Koran, and tradition about the emergence and the activities of the Prophet is mythology (J. Wansborough). There are no convincing proofs to support such hypotheses. It is true that quite a few of the reports about the early period of Islam say more about the tendencies and tensions of the community at the time when the text was written down—a hundred or so years after the death of the Prophet—than about 'how it really happened'. Many questions remain unanswered. But the personality and achievement of the Arab prophet would not be recognisable without his message, without the Koran.

The signs and symbols of the Koran are those of its environment. Otherwise people would not have listened to its message. Islam adopted the ethics, legal concepts and religious rituals of ancient Arabia and drew on the religious paradigms of Judaism and Christianity. It is therefore legitimate to look into the sources—spiritual currents in general and literary 'texts' in particular. European research has made great efforts to isolate and analyse Jewish and Christian elements in the Koran, both Biblical material and other traditions of oriental religious communities. In this way it has produced many important insights but it has also emphasised the wrong issues; the essence and the impact of the Islamic message cannot be explained only in terms of other religions. These religions had spread not only amongst the sedentary Arabs of Syria and Iraq but had also penetrated into inner Arabia. As a young man Muḥammad had become acquainted with Christianity on his trade journeys along the spice route, and after the emigration he met the Jews of Medina. In the course of his religious and political experience he himself came to see his religion as the legitimate continuation of earlier monotheism. But far more important than the paradigms he had inherited was the pragmatic impact of the new message which was revealed through him.

What, then, were the new elements? The society in which Muḥammad grew up was a society in flux; from a nomadic to a sedentary way of life, from tribal collectivism to individualism, from superstitious polytheism to monotheism; a society which could not find a new direction for a way out of its conflicts. The Prophet ordered them to reflect and to change their lives, not by a radical negation of the existing order but by transforming it. He spoke to them in their language—in the widest sense.

He brought the Arabs the Revealed Message in their own language; he drew for that message on the language of the tribal poets who had already transcended the limits of the different dialects; but it was he who really created a common literary language for the Arabs. The form of his speech is related to the language of the ancient

Arabian seer (*kāhin*), as in the form of rhyming prose (*saj'*), which joins the verses of a sura or a shorter group of verses through common end-rhymes. (As the Prophet drew away from the model provided by the pre-Islamic soothsayer, the poetic character of this rhymed prose receded in the course of time, becoming a mere relic in the long-winded legal texts of the later period.) Apart from these ancient and traditional elements we can observe in the Arabic of the Koran an unprecedented richness of religious language and of literary expression in general.

Even before Islam, Allāh (from *al-ilāh 'the* god') was the name of God and the object of worship; individual men and women—they are called *ḥanīf* in the Koran—had already taken the step towards monotheism. The shrine of the deities at Mecca, the *Ka'ba*, remained a shrine and became the spiritual centre of monotheistic Islam; and even the rituals of the old faith were incorporated into the Islamic pilgrimage (the *ḥajj*). But what had previously become an empty shell, and of primary importance because of the markets, the holy months and the truce which was linked with them, now received new meaning: founded by Abraham, the *Ka'ba* became the cornerstone of sacred history, the symbol of the true religion which had been established earlier and was now renewed and completed in the Arabic Koran.

The legal concepts of the pre-Islamic Bedouin are amongst the most important elements which ancient Arabia bequeathed to Islam. They were, of course, revised in the light of social change and under a new dispensation: tribal solidarity and honour (*'irḍ*), norms of a religious dimension in ancient Arabian paganism, collapsed just as the worship of the old gods did; they no longer sufficed to confer unlimited validity on the ideals of manly virtue (*muruwwa*), and it was precisely this which created the malaise which cried out for reform. Insistence on social welfare (alms), the system of private and collective security (*lex talionis* and penal law) and family and inheritance laws in the Koran are proclaimed as the commands of the Divine Judge. In the place of 'ignorance' (*jāhiliyya*, the characteristic of ancient paganism) there appears 'knowledge' (*'ilm*) derived from revelation. The community of the believers (*umma*) transcends tribal society and in many respects replaces it.

The biography of Muḥammad is the biography of a man who sought God and found Him in the experience of the divine summons; it is also the story of the Prophet of Mecca who assembled around him a community of believers; and finally, it is the story of the politician of Medina who founded Islamic theocracy. It is the story of a triumph, but before the years of fulfilment there stretched a long road of conflicts, setbacks and struggles. The leaders of the Quraysh, the Bedouin tribe who had become sedentary in Mecca and taken control of the city, the tribe to which Muḥammad himself also belonged, opposed his cause and defended their way of life with increasingly repressive measures. After the successful emigration to Medina there followed a long series of military encounters, and bitter disappointment when the Jewish tribes refused to recognise him as the spokesman of their own God. The Koran is not only theophany and law; it is also a faithful mirror of this road to God, of the struggles of a man who seeks, goes astray and despairs, who disputes with God, is put back on the right way and consoled by Him and who corrects and justifies himself. The great themes of the Koran can be seen as reflections of this personality. We must, of course, remain aware that with this perspective we grasp only one dimension of 'le fait coranique' (M. Arkoun).

In the early revelations God reveals Himself as the omnipotent Lord, the benevolent Creator and severe Judge. Muḥammad himself is addressed:

> Recite in the name of thy Lord who created, created man from a clot. Recite! Thy Lord is the most bounteous, who teacheth by the pen; taught man that which he knew not. (Sura 96, verses 1–5)

(Erwin Gräf [31.22] points out the Koranic analogy between man's creation and resurrection and translates: 'who has taught you *about* the pen', i.e. about the pen which records man's deeds for the Last Day; others interpret the word, following Muslim tradition, to mean earlier religions with scriptures, or the use of the pen, a symbol of high culture.)

Side by side with praise of God's goodness and creative power there is the threat of judgement; both combine in the warning to convert:

> When Earth is shaken with her (final) earthquake and Earth yieldeth up her burdens and man saith: What aileth her? That day she will relate her chronicles, because thy Lord inspireth her. That day mankind will issue forth in scattered groups to be shown their deeds. And whoso doeth good an atom's weight will see it then and whoso doeth ill an atom's weight will see it then. (Sura 99)

Not only the warning of judgement but also God's beneficence are reminders that one should show compassion and concern for one's neighbour.

> By the morning hours and by the night when it is stillest, thy Lord hath not forsaken thee, nor doth He hate thee, and verily the latter portion will be better for thee than the former, and verily thy Lord will give unto thee so that thou wilt be content. Did He not find thee an orphan and protect (thee)? Therefore the orphan oppress not, therefore the beggar drive not away, therefore of the

> bounty of thy Lord be thy discourse. (Sura 93, verses 1–11)

The demand to give alms—later made officially into the alms tax (*zakāt*)— is also one of the oldest elements of the revelation.

After his public appearance in Mecca, Muḥammad acquired a heightened awareness of his mission by means of meditation, a more exact knowledge of the great scriptural religions and the experience of conflict with the unbelief and attacks of the pagan Meccans. He became aware of his position in God's plan of salvation, he referred to the revealed religions and enunciated a monotheistic faith in God. In the conviction that his God was identical with that of the Jews and Christians he proclaimed the 'Arabic Koran', the 'Clear Book' of his Revelation, to rival the revealed books of other 'People of the Book' (*ahl al-kitāb*). At the same time in his preaching he drew on the religious traditions of his own environment (in the broadest sense); on the Biblical stories of Noah, Abraham, Joseph and Moses, the story of the birth and childhood of Jesus; on post-Biblical—Rabbinical and Christian—material (such as the story of the Seven Sleepers of Ephesus and motifs from the Alexander Romance), religious concepts (the Spirit and Word of God, angels and devils), and indeed popular folk wisdom of Arabia (attributed to the wise man, Luqmān). The literate Meccans accused him of plagiarism:

> Those who disbelieve say: This is nought but a lie that he hath invented, and other folk have helped him with it . . . And they say: fables of the men of old which he hath had written down so that they are dictated to him morn and evening. Say (unto them, O Muḥammad): He who knoweth the secret of the heavens and the earth hath revealed it. Lo! He ever is forgiving, merciful. (Sura 25, verses 4–6)

This Koran, given in 'clear Arabic speech' (sura 16, verse 105 —and elsewhere) can only—according to Muḥammad—be the work of divine mercy.

The conflict with the Quraysh intensified. It developed into social and economic reprisals against Muḥammad's clan, the Banū Hāshim. Recourse to sacred history now acquired a new dimension: Biblical figures as well as ancient Arabian prophets appear as warners in exemplary legends in which unbelief and wickedness receive dreadful punishment. At the same time the conflict led to a theological struggle with polytheism. The concept of Allāh, the Almighty Divine Creator, did not at first preclude the existence of other deities. Only now did the Prophet turn decisively and harshly against the cult of the (female) deities of Mecca and formulate the creed of the one God who has no partner (*sharīk*), who allows no intercessor. Finally, indifference and rejection on the part of the Meccans led to the conclusion that it was God Himself who shut their eyes and hearts to the signs of His creation and the wonder of His revelation: 'He sendeth whom He will astray and guideth whom He will' (sura 16, verse 93).

The activities of Muḥammad in Medina put other themes in the forefront of the revelation. But always the glory and the inaccessible greatness of God remain the fundamental experience of his religion, which includes both strict legal prescriptions and the mystical search for God.

> God is the light of the heavens and the earth. The similitude of His light is as a niche wherein is a lamp. The lamp is in a glass. The glass is as it were a shining star. (This lamp is) kindled from a blessed tree, an olive neither of the East nor of the West, whose oil would almost glow forth (of itself) though no fire touched it. Light upon light. God guideth unto His light whom He will. (Sura 24, verse 35)

'At all times will this simile of the Lord and the mysterious aloofness of his splendour penetrate to the innermost heart' (G. von Grunebaum [14.22], p.88). But 'even as persuasive is the portrayal in the famed "Verse of the Throne" of the Lord in His cool and immovable grandeur' (*ibid.*, p.89):

> God! There is no God save Him, the alive, the eternal. Neither slumber nor sleep overtaketh Him. Unto Him belongeth whatsoever is in the heavens and whatsoever in the earth. Who is he that intercedeth with Him save with His leave? He knoweth that which is in front of them and that which is behind them, while they encompass nothing of His knowledge, save what He will. His throne includeth the heavens and the earth and He is never weary of preserving them. He is the sublime, the tremendous. (Sura 2, verse 255)

The 'emigration' of Muḥammad from Mecca to Medina, the *Hijra*, of the year 622, was no flight; the Muslims left the tribal alliance of the Quraysh and were adopted by the Aws and Khazraj into theirs. Compulsion and favourable circumstances worked together so that from the 'Emigrants' (*muhājirūn*) and 'Helpers' (*anṣār*, the believers in Medina) the core of the Islamic state could grow. Muḥammad showed his political genius for the first time in the pacification of the oasis which had been torn apart by blood feuds. Thereafter he showed the same genius as a military leader in the long conflicts against the economic power of Mecca, which he provoked in calculated fashion, in his successes and failures, and finally in the masterly, cleverly restrained diplomacy which led a good seven years after the *Hijra* to the bloodless conquest of Mecca. The Koran also bears witness to these events, to people's inner response to political happenings, and to the ways in which human destinies are shown to be part of God's design. Thus, after the battle of Badr, the Prophet is given encouragement:

> And remember when thou settest forth at daybreak from thy house-folk to assign to the believers their positions for the battle, God was Hearer, Knower. When two parties of you almost fell away, and God was their protecting friend. In God do believers put their trust. God had already given you the victory at Badr when ye were contemptible. So observe your duty to God in order that ye may be thankful. (Sura 3, verses 121–23)

whereas the defeat at Uḥud is to serve as a test for the believers:

> And was it so, when a disaster smote you, though he had smitten (them with a disaster) twice (as great), that ye said, how is this? Say (unto them, O Muḥammad): It is from yourselves. Lo! God is able to do all things. That which befell you, on the day when the two armies met, was by permission of God that He might know the true believers and that He might know the hypocrites. (Sura 3, verses 165–7)

In Medina the religious institutions of Islam took on the form which—in their broad essentials—they have preserved until today. Muḥammad's relationship with the Jews of Medina was to prove a major development of Islamic ritual. He came to Medina with the conviction that the revelation which he had experienced was identical with earlier ones which had come to the Jews and the Christians; he therefore expected that the Jewish tribes would accept him as the messenger of God. This expectation was disappointed. Before the final break, however, there was an attempt at reconciliation through adaptation: in addition to the morning and evening prayer which had already been established in Mecca, he added a mid-day prayer, and communal Friday worship may well have been instituted as a borrowing from the Sabbath. There then came the order to turn towards Jerusalem at the time of prayer, and the fast of the Jewish Day of Atonement was also made binding on Muslims (the '*Āshūrā*' fast).

Their refusal to follow Muḥammad—which may well have been for political as well as religious reasons—led not only to the banishment and destruction of the Jews of Medina (and later those of Khaybar). It also led to a new direction in the Koranic interpretation of history. Already in the earlier suras Abraham appeared as the representative of the true religion and the ancestor of the Meccans. Muḥammad now came to the conclusion that the Jews must have moved away from the religion of Abraham (*millat Ibrāhīm*) and that they had broken their link with God. Abraham now became the most important predecessor of the Arab prophet; with his son Ishmael he built the *Ka'ba* in Mecca as the shrine of God and the centre of the pilgrimage. Islam, which was founded before Moses and Jesus, before Judaism and Christianity, took precedence over the religions of other 'possessors of scriptures' who had distorted the revelation.

Thus the Ka'ba regained its original significance as the goal of the

Islamic pilgrimage. The direction of prayer (*qibla*) was now also turned towards Mecca, and the number of prayers was later increased to five. It was laid down that there should be fasting during the daytime for the duration of the month of Ramaḍān.

Whether we recognise Muḥammad as the Prophet of God, or whether we regard the Koran as the expression of his personality, the creation of the Islamic state and the unification of Arabia under Islam are his handiwork. The first important sign of this achievement is a document handed down by historians in an apparently authentic form—the regulations or 'Constitution' of the community of Medina. This document, promulgated soon after the *Hijra*, regulated the relationship of the tribes, the Meccan 'Emigrants' and the Medinan 'Helpers' and bound them together in a new larger community which was not based on blood relationships but on religion. From now onwards, there stood above the tribes the *umma*, the community of believers under the authority and protection of God and under the leadership of Muḥammad.

The last years of the Prophet were devoted to the propagation of Islam externally and the legal organisation of the *umma* internally. It had as its central point the mosque (*masjid*: 'place of prostration' before God): the place of communal prayer and at the same time the centre of the community. Solidarity among the believers gave stability to the community. Obligatory and voluntary alms (the *zakāt* which was levied as tax and the *ṣadaqa* which was an act of piety) established a sure financial basis for the community. Communal 'striving in the path of God' (*jihād*), namely the war against unbelievers, served to defend and extend the realm of Islam.

Personal safety within Muslim society remained based on the principle of blood vengeance; but the reforms incorporated in the Koran replaced the sanction of tribal honour by divine command and by the judgement of the Prophet. The principle of apportioning redress and the prohibition of exacting further penalty from the avenger prevented the internecine blood feuds of the past, while the recommendation to accept blood money instead of blood vengeance paved the way for more humane behaviour. The evidence of witnesses was made the basis of contractual law and litigation.

The social system used the individualistic tendencies earlier responsible for the break-up of the old order to build up a new system of marriage, family and inheritance; this system treated the woman as an individual too and guaranteed social security to her as well as to her children. Legally controlled polygamy was an important advance on the various loosely defined arrangements which had previously been both possible and current; it was only by this provision (backed up by severe punishment for adultery), that the family, the core of any sedentary society could be placed on a firm footing.

The large interrelated groups of Bedouin tribes and clans played an important part in the Islamic community for a long time to come. But just as the religion of Islam is the adoration of God by the individual, so too do the social system and the ethics of Islam regulate the corporate life of individuals; each individual is made responsible for his actions. Man's life is not confined within the compass of society in this world but it is given significance by the promise of eternal bliss for all those who by following God's commands deserve such a reward. The state can therefore be no more than a means to this end; it is a religious institution which has the obligation of taking under its protection the worship of God, the maintenance of the law and the propagation of the faith.

Obscured by veneration and hatred, the picture of Muḥammad in history is not easy to discern. The example and precepts of the Prophet became overlaid in Muslim tradition by legend; they were falsified for pious and impious reasons and misused in the struggle for succession and supreme power in the Islamic state. Thus the commentaries on the Koran and the biographies of the Prophet often tell us more about the commentators and transmitters than they do about the original meaning and circumstances of their subject matter. On the other hand, European criticism has all too often imposed concepts and criteria on the personality of Muḥammad which are not appropriate to his time and his milieu. For too long Muḥammad, the Prophet, has been contrasted with Muḥammad, the politician, as if they were two different people; yet there is no separation between religious and political activity either in the ancient East or throughout Islamic history. At the same time as Muḥammad brought to the people of his time and environment a new religion and a new system of communal living, he created the base on which Islam was able to grow into a world religion and the foundation of a world empire.

2. *The development of religious doctrine*

(a) Islamic history and the history of Islam

The Koran is the fundamental document of Islam and, since its codification, the unchangeable basis of Islamic faith and life. To the community of the believers it gave—and still gives today—the basis of communal faith and communal action. It contains the basic duties of the Muslim, namely those fundamentals of communal life which tradition designates as the 'pillars of Islam': prayer, or rather, adoration, the worship of God, which is incumbent on every believer at set times; fasting in the month of Ramaḍān—a communal experience, which determines for one month every year the private and public life of the Islamic world; the pilgrimage to Mecca which, even in the age of the aeroplane, is not possible for every Muslim, but which is the fulfilment of a lifetime for many believers who follow the example of their Prophet in all the details of the ritual; the duty to give alms which also in the form of taxation levied by the state preserves an awareness of social responsibility; and finally, the confession of faith 'There is no God but God, and Muḥammad is His Prophet', and the recitation of the Revealed texts in general which unite all Muslims in communal worship of God, whatever their particular religious persuasion.

The doctrine of salvation in Islam is the doctrine of men being 'rightly guided by God' to temporal and eternal bliss through God's commands. But God's command was not immediately recognisable in every individual case. Here, problems began to manifest themselves early on and conflicts became apparent. In a world of stormy and continuing change the Revealed Book constantly needed to be interpreted anew and, moreover, to be supplemented through experience and transmission. The spread of Islam, political conflicts, social and economic changes—all these gave the impetus; the older religious communities, forms of government and civilisation which the Arabs encountered in the formation of their empire contributed foundation stones, models and methods. With the evolution of political and religious institutions, there developed the various branches of religious and legal doctrine in which the knowledge (*'ilm*) given in the Koran was explained and systematised:

¶ its pronouncements on the duties towards God in jurisprudence (*fiqh*), the doctrine of Revealed law (*Sharī'a*, the 'clear defined way');

¶ its pronouncements on the essence and activity of God in theology (*kalām*, polemic and apologetic 'dialectic') and dogmatics (*uṣūl al-dīn* 'the principles of faith');

¶ its pronouncements on the reality of faith, on the personal relationship of man with God, in mysticism (*taṣawwuf*);

¶ its pronouncements on the life of the Prophet and the first community in historical tradition (*sīra*, i.e. *sīrat al-nabī* 'the normative or model way of life of the Prophet');

¶ the text itself in the study of philology (grammar and lexicography) and in extensive Koranic commentaries (*tafsīr*, 'interpretation').

Islamic doctrine developed out of conflict between the interpreters of the scripture and the forces of change in the community. The very destiny of society and state was experienced and perceived through the prism of conflicts about the interpretation and application of the Revealed Koran, of the 'way' based on the Revelation, model and conduct of the Prophet, the *Sharī'a* of the religious community. From the beginning until the present day, movements and conflicts which are presented as religious in the mirror of the sources —and that means in the minds of the actors themselves—have profoundly affected and indeed shaken state and society.

The expansion of Islam and its formation into a state are only the first and most striking examples of this. At the death of Muḥammad (632) the Arabian peninsula was Islamic; under the four caliphs of the first generation who had belonged to his Companions, Arab armies subjugated the Sasanian empire from Iraq as far as eastern Iran and the Byzantine provinces of the Near East. Under the rulers of the Umayyad dynasty they reached as far as the Atlantic and the Indus (711)—in the name of God and of His message revealed through Muḥammad. The question could be and has been asked—was this not rather a tribal migration and was it not economic necessity which pushed the Arab tribes out of the peninsula? Was it not actually the religions and cultures of the surrounding world which created 'Islam' —as dogma, law, state and culture?

'The Islamic religion did not create a unified civilisation; but the unified civilisation of the caliphal empire which evolved for quite other reasons has been the basis for the expansion and victorious progress of the Islamic religion until the present time.'

So wrote Carl Heinrich Becker with provocative exaggeration in an article on 'Islam as a problem' (1910) [32.03]. But this is only one side. Today we know more about the sources of Islam, including its non-Arab sources—Jewish, Christian, Hellenistic, Iranian. In the period of its emergence and development they gave Islam models of social structure and political order, paradigms of religious expression, the impetus to develop and defend dogma. But the basis of political success, the power which welded the Arabs together and then created a community composed of totally different peoples and cultures, was the religion of the Arab Prophet.

Religion here means the whole of life and experience of the world. Muḥammad gave a disintegrating society both a diagnosis of its malaise and a therapy for it; he was able to answer the fundamental social, economic and ethical questions of the world around him because he saw them as religious and answered them in that way. He was able to create an Arab nation because he brought the Arabs, in the language of the Revelation, a language of communication and literature; because he—the Seal of the Prophets—gave to the Arabs as recipients of the final truth a place in sacred history; because he made a tribal society which was out of joint, into a community of believers under his own guidance, as the messenger of God.

Since unity itself, the formation of a state and the expansion of the Arabs all began under the auspices of a religious mission and under the theocracy of the Prophet, the legitimisation and constitution of the evolving community—and centuries later of the declining community—were viewed and appraised in the light of Revelation. That is also a historical reality. It is true that religion was not only a motivating force but also a provocation: conflicts soon appeared between tribal and communal solidarity and how the community saw itself, between Arabness and the fellowship of Islamic peoples, between autocracy and theocracy, between the claims of charisma and normative tradition. Such conflicts ended in bloody civil wars. Just as the Arab campaigns of conquest may well have been caused by deep material need, so too behind the outbreaks of violence which occurred in the periods immediately after this there may well have been conflicts over the division of pasture and agricultural land, needs dictated by hunger and epidemics, and later on the new migratory movements of Turkish and Mongol nomads. Social oppression and economic exploitation by the rulers led to the outbreak of revolts and to protracted periods of dissension. Many of these conflicts—not only in early Islam—were publicly presented and dealt with as conflicts about the fundamental principles and the institutions of the religious community: about the legitimacy of the caliphs, the successors (*khalīfa*) of the Prophet who as leaders (*imām*) of prayer and the guarantors of the law had to watch over the well-being of the believers; about the relationship of God's omnipotence and justice vis-à-vis human freedom and responsibility; about the relationship of personal inspiration vis-à-vis the eternal and perfect Koran; and about the autonomy of the legal system, which had been revealed and transmitted according to the model laid down by the Prophet, in relation to arbitrary action on the part of individual rulers. For this reason jurisprudence and theology also developed in Islam, both as a result of the internal stimuli of the political, historical process and as a response to external models and influences.

(b) From civil wars to schism

Before his unexpected death, the Prophet had given no indication about succession to the leadership of his community. With the demise of the theocrat who spoke in God's name the preservation of the theocracy itself was called into question. The caliph (*khalīfa*), i.e. the successor and 'deputy' of the Prophet, had to be the most pious person and to rule according to God's will. But how was this to be guaranteed? Unanimity was reached amongst the Prophet's Companions; but it was already a compromise, and had within it the germ of conflict. Only the first two caliphs were brought to power unopposed, on the basis that their legitimacy was assured by the consensus of the community (through election by the *shūrā*) and by their membership of the tribe of Muḥammad, the Quraysh. They were Abū Bakr (632–4), who united the Arabs in the first wars of conquest, and ʿUman (634–44), who created the territorial basis of the Islamic world empire. But these criteria of legitimisation became unusable when dissension amongst the Prophet's companions from the

Quraysh tribe destroyed the unity of the *umma.* The policy of ʿUthmān (644–56) which favoured the family power of the Banū Umayya against the rival clans of the Prophet's house and upheld reasons of state against the rights of the tribal armies which had achieved the conquests, not only created bad blood and social unrest; it was branded as a betrayal of theocracy, as 'innovation' (*bidʿa*) against God's command and the bidding of the Prophet. ('Innovation' became the essence of heresy, just as 'precedent' (*sunna*) became the fundamental concept of true religion.) The murder of ʿUthmān led to the first civil war. The rival parties of the civil war which broke out under his successor, ʿAlī (656–61), embodied at the same time the conflicting beliefs of the first religious schism and these politico-religious views remained in the minds of the theologians as paradigms of the debate about theocracy right up to the disputations of later periods.

The party of ʿAlī (*shīʿat ʿAlī,* known later as the 'Shīʿa'), the Prophet's cousin and son-in-law, had pressed their claims from the beginning. From the outset these claims were based on ʿAlī's special closeness to the Prophet: he had been amongst the first Muslims, he was related to him by ties of blood and marriage and he was the guardian of his inheritance; from this he apparently sought to derive special religious authority. At any rate, it was on these grounds that the Shīʿa justified their claim to legitimate rule when they involved themselves in political opposition and—after fruitless struggle—became sectarian outsiders. Muḥammad, they allege, chose ʿAlī through designation (*naṣṣ*) and personal legacy (*waṣiyya*) as the spiritual leader (*imām*) and head of the theocracy; the 'light' of divine inspiration passed from Muḥammad to him and then to his corporeal and spiritual successors.

With the agreement of the Medinans (Muḥammad's 'Helpers', *anṣār,* after his *Hijra*) ʿAlī was finally made caliph in 656. Yet he lacked the authority to command the precarious situation which developed. Supported by an anti-Umayyad coalition, i.e. by the opponents of ʿUthmān, as well as by the Medinans and above all by the tribes which had settled around Kūfa in Iraq and had opposed ʿUthmān's policies of distribution of wealth, he did not manage to exact vengeance on the murderers of ʿUthmān. In Mecca an alliance of disparate elements was cobbled together in revolt against ʿAlī—old enemies of ʿUthmān amongst the Quraysh grouped around Ṭalḥa, Zubayr, and ʿĀ'isha the influential widow of the Prophet, who were morally responsible for the murder, together with the 'pious' opposition of those who held fast to the ideal of theocracy. The rebels gained Baṣra, the most important garrison in Iraq; but in the Battle of the Camel of 656 (so-called because of the camel from which ʿĀ'isha observed the fighting), Ṭalḥa and Zubayr fell. The outcome divided Islam into the supporters of the Meccan aristocracy, who were finished politically; the party of ʿAlī, which from now on was centred in Kūfa; and the family power of the Umayyads in Syria. Muʿāwiya, the governor of Damascus, emerged as the leader of the Umayyad family, and presented himself as the avenger of ʿUthmān. He forced ʿAlī into a battle at Ṣiffīn (657) and with superb political acumen made himself master of the situation: he avoided the military outcome which threatened to go against him and entrusted the political decision to arbitration 'according to the Will of God'. The pious faction failed when faced with the realities of power: the representatives from Kufa declared that neither ʿAlī nor Muʿāwiya was worthy of the caliphate, while in the meantime the Syrian troops had paid homage to Muʿāwiya. A few months later ʿAlī fell at the hand of an assassin; Muʿāwiya was thus left as the sole if not the uncontested ruler of the empire and Damascus became the new centre of power.

The family to which the caliph should belong was only part of the controversy which was discussed in arbitration and finally decided by military force. That controversy also involved the stability of the Islamic community and the responsibility of the ruler before God and the Muslims. The mismanagement perpetrated by ʿUthmān as whose avenger Muʿāwiya stepped forward had raised the question of responsibility; if it was right to put such a question and if ʿUthmān had transgressed God's commands, Muʿāwiya's claim would be jeopardised. The court of arbitration, in acquitting ʿUthmān, decided against ʿAlī. But was it for a human court to decide such a question? In his readiness to accept the arbitration, ʿAlī had relinquished his right to act. A violent rebellion which rapidly spread in his own ranks was the result.

While ʿAlī in Kufa prepared to march against Syria, a large group of the tribes which were settled in Iraq threw off their allegiance to him and left the garrison town in rebellion. ʿAlī had first to fight against these rebels, on whom he inflicted a decisive defeat at Nahrawān (658); but his murder—an act of vengeance for Nahrawān—assured the caliphate to the Umayyad Muʿāwiya (661). Detailed research on the social background of the Arab tribes who had 'seceded' (*kharaja*), the Khārijites (*khawārij*), has produced very concrete material reasons for their dissatisfaction. Apparently they were not considered to be amongst the earliest conquerors who, according to the register (*dīwān*) of the caliph ʿUmar, received the largest incomes from the conquered land and property; but it was only after the euphoria of the conquests that disagreements over the distribution of wealth began. The opposition of the Khārijites has rightly been seen also as the rebellion of the tribes against any individual assumption of authority: since if the Bedouin had ever acknowledged the authority of anyone at all it was that of the best person in the tribal community as the 'first among equals', and this was always after a unanimous decision and for limited aims and purposes. None of the pretenders who came forward against each other in the fight could bring unity and justice to the Muslims. The bitterness of the Khārijites was directed therefore not only against the Shīʿa but also against the Umayyads, whose control over Iraq and Sistan was seriously endangered by their rebellions in the following decades. The ideology of their opposition was religious fundamentalism: the decision belonged only to God; people should act only according to God's revealed command; and anyone who disobeyed this command should, regardless of his creed, be expelled from the Muslim community. In their view, only the best and most pious person from the community of the just should be chosen as caliph according to their unanimous decision, 'even if he be a black slave'. This was radical Puritanism, then, which could maintain its identity only in opposition and which persecuted with the sword all those who did not share such views. Only later did followers of this doctrine, the Ibāḍiyya characteristically enough, located in Arabia and amongst the Berber tribes of North Africa—manage to establish small, short-lived autonomous states on this basis.

Henceforth the Shīʿa also remained a political and religious party of opposition: political in their rebellion against the Umayyads and religious in their expectation of the just Imām, a doctrine which in the course of two centuries was elevated to a millenarian Utopia. ʿAlī's son, Ḥusayn, was killed during the reign of Muʿāwiya's successor Yazīd, by superior Syrian forces (680); his martyrdom at Karbalāʾ in southern Iraq is still today a commemorative day of the Shīʿa. His brother Ḥasan, the other grandson of the Prophet, resigned. But when ʿAbdallāh ibn al-Zubayr, as the anti-caliph in Mecca, called for war against the Umayyads in Damascus, and a second civil war broke out (683–92) against a background of plague and famine, another claimant of the Shīʿa appeared in Kufa. A respected follower of the family, Mukhtār, persuaded ʿAlī's eldest son, Muḥammad—not from ʿAlī's marriage with Fāṭima, and therefore not even a descendant of the Prophet—to allow himself to be used as the figurehead of the Shīʿite movement. Belonging to 'the house' of the Prophet was the decisive factor (this Arab concept of heredity was used to legitimise the claims of the caliphal dynasties of the Umayyads and later also of the ʿAbbāsids). For the political Shīʿa their claim to leadership was linked to the Arab 'aristocracy' of the Prophet's family and this remained so. Decisive, however, for their religious impact and crucial for the doctrine of Shīʿite Islam were the expectations which its rapidly increasing supporters among the Iranian *mawālī* pinned on it. The *mawālī* were non-Arabs who became the clients of Arab families after conversion to Islam. They had long been settled in Iraq and Persia and were the self-confident transmitters of the old social structure and culture of the towns and of the countryside, but were still of inferior legal status. It was in these circles that the hope of a leader was nurtured, a 'charismatic' leader who would be legitimised through succession in body and in spirit, the impeccable and just Imām, the 'director' of the worship of God and the leader of the community. He alone could exercise the divine leadership of all Muslims, for their well-being in this world and the next. This was 'the rightly guided one', the Mahdī.

Mukhtār's rebellion (685–87) foundered: the offer of alliance with the rebels in Mecca was rejected and ʿAbd al-Malik was able to unite the Arab empire by means of his army of Syrian tribes. But the expectation of the Mahdī remained. It persisted even after the death of the pretender as the hope and mainstay of many opponents of the Umayyad 'kingdom', which in their eyes was illegal.

It was only after the collapse of the political Shīʿa that this expectation became a historical utopia and a religious hope for the restoration of justice at the end of time. At first, for another century after the martyrdom of Ḥusayn and the death of Mukhtār, the supporters of the ʿAlids defended the political claims of the house of the Prophet by passive resistance and militant uprisings. Up to the end of the seventh century disunity amongst the opposition enabled the Umayyad governors, ruling with an iron hand, to keep peace and quiet in Iraq and in the Persian provinces which were governed from there. Continuing bitterness between Shīʿites and Khārijites, and the rivalry between the leaders of the Arab tribes (the *ashrāf*) and the *mawālī* who were struggling for recognition and participation, made it easy for the dynasty to play off one party against another. But deep conflicts and social tensions between different social groups created a ferment of increasing unrest. The internal collapse of the Umayyad state was accompanied by an ever-increasing number of rebellions, amongst which was that of the great-grandson of ʿAlī, Zayd ibn ʿAlī (740).

The successful revolution of the ʿAbbāsids ushered in a new era of Islamic history. (The ideology of revolution obscured, however, the obvious continuity of Arab domination, and the discrepancy between claim and reality was strenuously ignored by the theoreticians of the ʿAbbāsid state.) The ʿAbbāsids too represented the 'house' of the Prophet, and they also took upon themselves the religious expectation of the Mahdī. Abū Hāshim, the grandson of ʿAlī and son of the pretender Muḥammad, died without issue, entrusting his rights to the caliphate to the grandson of the uncle of the Prophet, al-ʿAbbās. Known as the Hāshimiyya, this group began their propaganda in Khurāsān, supported by the Shīʿa in Kufa who thought that their time had come. But it was the ʿAbbāsids who put an end to all political hopes on the part of the Shīʿa. Al-Manṣūr (754–75), the real architect

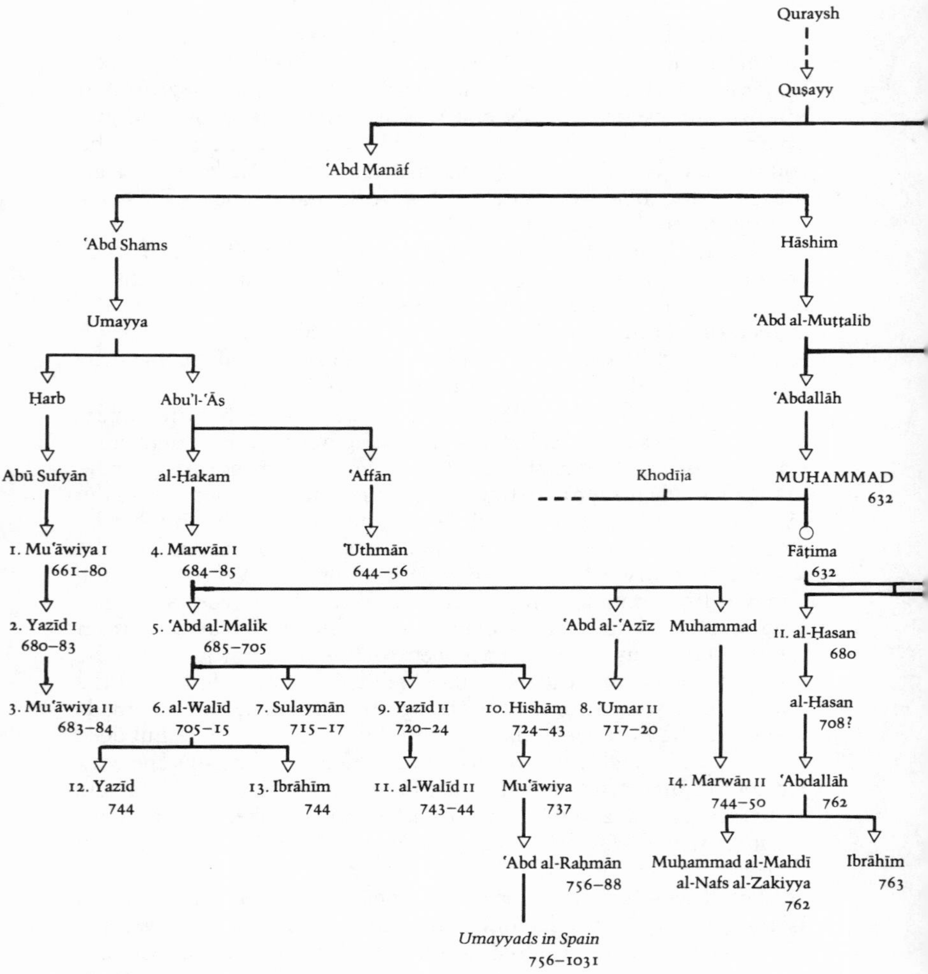

Umayyads

The years given below the names are the years of death, or (with the Caliphs) the years of reign.

1. Genealogy of the Prophet's family and of the caliphal dynasties.

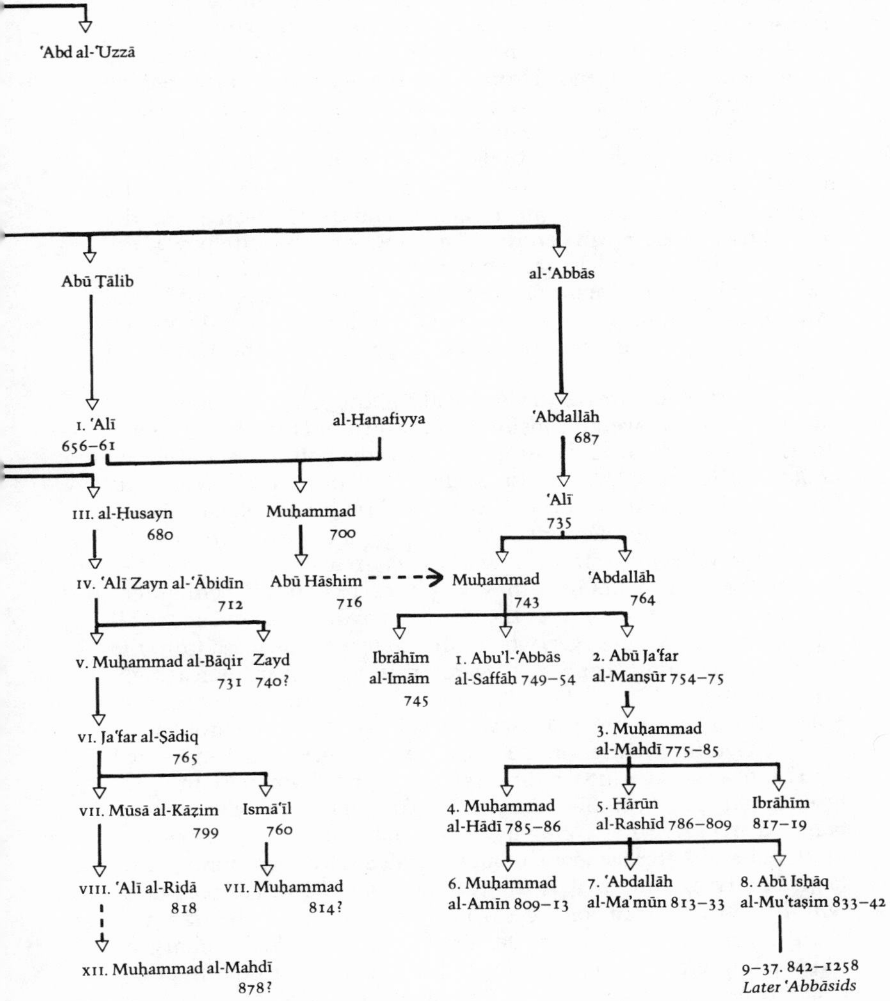

Imāms of the Shīʿa

ʿAbbāsids

of 'Abbāsid power and also the founder of the new capital, Baghdad, got rid of the leading men of the revolution when they stood in the way of interests of state. He replaced religious by dynastic legitimacy, which was made acceptable to the pious by ensuring that his ancestor, al-'Abbās, was surrounded by an aura of panegyric tradition.

After a series of unsuccessful rebellions the Shī'a gathered around Imāms who were descended from Ḥusayn b. 'Alī and who pointed the way through the scholarly tradition of their community to true faith even under illegal rulers. One of the 'Alid lines, the Zaydiyya (named after Zayd ibn 'Alī) developed a theory of government which justified toleration of the ruling régime. This was to become the official doctrine of small states in the Yemen and on the Caspian Sea in the second half of the ninth century. On his way to absolute power the caliph al-Ma'mūn sought reconciliation with the 'Alids once again and proclaimed the Imām of the Ḥusaynids as his successor to the throne (817)—a gesture which remained unfulfilled, as it did not even gain support among the staunchest supporters of the Caliph in Khurāsān.

In the urban centres of the 'Abbāsid empire, Arabs and non-Arabs joined to form an overall Muslim community and together created a flourishing economy and culture in which the political significance of old conflicts receded. The establishment of 'orthodox' law schools based on the Koran and on the recognised traditions of early Islam retained only a dim memory of the struggle of the Khārijites for the absolute validity of scripture and of the consensus of the 'just'; the basis of the authority of the ruling caliph was to be not the enlightenment of the Mahdī but rather the charisma of oriental, and above all Iranian, kingship. However, when caliphal power collapsed from the middle of the ninth century onwards this became an increasingly unimportant problem. The religious expectation of the 'moderate' Shī'a was no longer directed towards rebellion; it became utopian.

The Twelfth Imām from the line of succession of 'Alī disappeared (873) and was taken into 'hiding' (*ghayba*); the chain of Imāms was broken. At the beginning agents (*wakīl*) appeared who, it was believed, received his commands; but in the eyes of the widely-scattered and heterogeneous groups of the Shī'ite community they lacked unifying authority. In the year 940, on the death of the fourth *wakīl*, the theologians of the Shī'a saw the link with the Imām as being at an end: the 'Lesser' Occultation of the Hidden Imām was followed by 'Greater' Occultation, out of which he will return at the end of time as the Mahdī and will re-establish God's authority in an empire of justice.

Until that time it is the task of legal scholars to set out the fundamentals of the law, the Koran and tradition according to 'Alī and the later 'visible' Imāms. They have also to apply these fundamentals, using the insight which has been bestowed on them for the benefit and well-being of the believers and temporal authorities. Scholars and the mass of believers were drawn together by a continuum of painful experience beginning with Ḥusayn's martyrdom at Karbalā'; the certainty of the restoration of justice at the end of time reconciled them to an unjust régime. Not only the belief but also the life of the Shī'ite Muslim was imbued with this attitude; it became a force for social order and for the consolidation of the urban bourgeoisie and the agricultural classes in southern Iraq and Iran. This attitude hardened under the Iranian dynasties of Shī'ite persuasion in the tenth century, and became a critical factor in the continuation of Iranian-Islamic culture in the face of the Turkish and Mongol invasions of later periods. It was only in the sixteenth century, however, that the dynasty of the Ṣafavids elevated the 'Imamite' or 'Twelver Shī'ite' creed to the status of a state religion and made the clergy of their spiritual community into a dominant institution of Iranian government.

Yet while the Shī'a withdrew to the side-lines, gave up any political aspirations and renounced the hope of the Mahdī until the end of time, the movement had become split. The descendants of Zayd ibn 'Alī have already been mentioned. The majority of the party followed Ja'far al-Ṣādiq (d.765), the sixth Imām of the line which began with 'Alī. But disputes arose as to whether Ja'far had passed on the Imamate to his son Ismā'īl who had died before him and through him to his grandson Muḥammad, or to the younger Mūsā al-Kāẓim. A minority, the Ismā'īliyya, recognised Muḥammad ibn Ismā'īl as the seventh and last Imām: he is also 'hidden'.

The early history of the 'Sevener' schism remains shrouded in obscurity. Around the end of the ninth century, however, there arose a militant mission in the name of the seventh Imām, the movement of the Carmathians (*Qarāmiṭa*) (called after their leader Ḥamdān Qarmaṭ) which renewed the revolutionary élan of the old Shī'a. To the farmers in southern Iraq, in the Persian villages around Rayy and later also in Khurāsān, to the Bedouin in Baḥrayn, and to the Berbers of North Africa, they promised the return of the Mahdī or Qā'im 'who would stand up for the cause of God' and bring social justice. Their propaganda also appealed to educated people, since it drew on Greek, neo-Platonic cosmology for its doctrine of the enlightened Imām and it was presented in esoteric circles as a secret doctrine: the cosmic order of the seven heavenly spheres, the seven intellects emanating from the divine spirit, is mirrored in the seven Imāms—or even in the Seven Prophets among the last of whom were Muḥammad, 'Alī and the Qā'im. The rebellions of the Carmathians at the beginning of the tenth century shook the weakened power of the Caliphate, whose authority deteriorated in face of the pressure of the Turkish praetorian guards in their own entourage and of movements for autonomy in the provinces. At the same time a new split inside the Ismāʿīliyya itself led to the establishment of an anti-Caliphate. In the Syrian centre of the movement their leader ʿUbaydallāh had himself proclaimed as the expected Mahdī (899). The Baḥrayn Carmathians and others denied him their allegiance; but in North Africa the ground was already prepared for him. With an army of supporters from Tunisian Berber tribes he pushed the dynasty of the Aghlabids, which was loyal to the ʿAbbāsids, out of Qayrawān (909–10) and became the first caliph of the 'Fāṭimids' (named after Muḥammad's daughter Fāṭima, the wife of ʿAlī and the mother of Ḥasan and Ḥusayn, with whom he sought to establish a blood connection through the Imām Muḥammad ibn Ismāʿīl by means of controversial genealogy). He proclaimed his son as the expected Qā'im.

After a few years the Fāṭimids had become masters of North Africa. After the conquest of Egypt in 969 they founded Cairo (*al-Qāhira* 'the victorious') which was from then onwards their metropolis. They extended their sway to Palestine, Syria, and even the holy cities of Arabia, so that for a century they remained the foremost power of the south and east Mediterranean. For a long time, too, through their continuing missionary activity, they remained a force for spiritual and social unrest in the Islamic east. Even when the political power and religious authority of the Caliphs in Cairo dwindled, new schisms kept alive the revolutionary pathos of the movement: the movement of the Druzes, who revered the deified Fāṭimid Caliph, al-Ḥākim (996–1021); and, more virulent and dangerous still, the Nizāriyya—called after Nizār, the son of al-Mustanṣir, who was bypassed in the succession for the throne (1036–94). Under the leadership of their Persian missionary, Ḥasan ibn al-Sabbāḥ (1090–1124) who established himself in Alamūt in the Elburz mountains, they became a movement of terror in Persia and afterwards in Syria too. Their commanders spread fear and terror amongst orthodox Muslims as well as amongst the Frankish Crusaders by means of religiously motivated murder (allegedly under the influence of hashish, from which comes the name *Ḥashshāshūn*: 'assassins'). The Mongols destroyed the power of Alamūt (1256); yet even today there survive widely scattered groups of the Ismāʿīliyya, such as Nizār's group under the leadership of the Agha Khan in Bombay and others too in Syria, in eastern Iran and in India.

But with these sects of the Shīʿa we have reached the antipodes of 'orthodox' Islam, the heresy of the 'radicals' *(ghulāt)*—radical in that after the revelation and the divinely inspired pronouncements of the Prophet Muḥammad they allowed his inspiration and word to be superseded or even abrogated by other, human leaders. The more stress the sects laid upon this claim, the more firmly the orthodoxy of the legal schools under the 'Abbāsid caliphate and its loyal vassals linked itself to the statutes of the Koran and the transmitted words of the Prophet.

(c) Between theology and tradition: the development of dogma

The political opposition parties of early Islam lived on in the religious sects of the later period, in the large and small groups of the Khārijites and the Shī'a, and in many other movements, which—in a constant convergence of the political and the religious—awaited justice from inspired leaders either in their own lifetimes or on their expected return. Religious scholars erected the edifice of Islamic dogma and pronounced on what was heresy and what was orthodox belief, not in the unrest of the period of expansion and civil wars but under the shelter of stable rule. According to a statement handed down from the Prophet, his community would be split into 73 'divisions' or sects and dogmas. Heresiographers, the authors of manuals on various schisms and sects were busy describing them all; not only the opponents but also the architects of state orthodoxy are covered in this medley of opinions and it is not easy to discern historical reality behind the bias and polemic of later tradition. Indeed, the orthodoxy of the majority, from whose perspective the wide-ranging discussion of the early period is presented to us as a Babel of heresy and error, only formulated its articles of faith three centuries after the revelation of the Koran—three centuries of debate amongst the Muslims and of the defence of their faith against the old religions of different peoples, who were quickly conquered but were united under Islam only after a long process of social and spiritual assimilation.

The schism of the first civil war led to a conflict of opinion about the legitimacy of the Caliphs and their rivals, and more generally about the criteria of orthodox faith. We have just looked at the extreme positions in this dispute: the anti-authoritarian anarchy of the Khārijites and the cult of authority of the Shī'a. If, according to the opinion of the Shī'a, the just Imām was sufficient (and at the same time indispensable) as a guarantor of the well-being of the community, the Khārijites limited the community to a handful of the just. The political reality of the Umayyad caliphate allowed for compromise positions which made it possible to come to an accommodation with the ruling authorities.

The party of 'postponement', the Murji'a, represented such a position: it left judgement on the sinner to God, postponed the verdict on those who aspired to the caliphate and declared that the worship of God, even under a sinful Imām, was valid. When, however, in the last decades of the Umayyad period, one of their leaders in Khurāsān consistently demanded equal rights for all Muslims and—a sign of the social conflicts of the times (cf. p.83)—the removal of land tax and equal pay for all, Arabs and *mawālī*, it became a party of opposition. Amongst the *mawālī*, too, who stood up against the Umayyads but who sought a *modus vivendi*, there were efforts at a compromise solution. The representatives of 'retreat' or 'neutrality' in the dispute between 'Alī and his opponents, the Mu'tazila (as they were later to be called), did not excommunicate the sinner as the Khārijites did. Nor did they treat him as a righteous person, as did the Murji'a. Instead, they viewed him as a member of the community, not as an unbeliever against whom Muslims had to fight.

But these and other positions, attitudes which gradually transpired in the political confrontations of the day, became models of systematic theology only in the course of the decades; only very much later did the Mu'tazila become the name of a dogmatic 'school'. At first it was a matter of open discussion about disputed questions in the community without dogmatic limits. Nor was all the impetus to theological reflection of a political kind; not all discussions were characterised by the divisiveness of schism. Deepened insight—often, it is true, sharpened by political debate—into the image of God in the Koran led to reflection on the stumbling-blocks of monotheistic belief and the justification of man before God.

The preacher Ḥasan of Baṣra (d.728), who is revered because of his ascetic piety as one of the fathers of Islamic mysticism, was one of the first to think about the hypothesis which is embodied in the doctrine of the Khārijites as well as the Murji'a: the concept of a just God who demands virtuous behaviour from man, who punishes the sinner and rewards the pious. He concluded that man, having free will, is responsible for his acts. In the generation of his disciples, discussions about divine justice (*'adl*) and man's free will in the face of God's power (*qadar*) ranged widely; *qadariyya* became the label of theologians (many of them were *mawālī* and harsh critics of the Umayyad caliphate) who could not attribute to God any acts of will which ran counter to the hypothesis of justice, and who could not envisage justice without freedom of choice. Such theologians directed the logic of their arguments against those who advocated unquestioning acceptance of the scriptures, who insisted on the words of the Koran about God's omnipotence and predetermination and who placed God above the alleged necessity of human reasoning. (It was these opponents of theirs who—partly in collaboration with authorities and partly in silent protest—began to develop the statutes of dogma, ethics, and law based on the Revealed Word and on the collection of the established traditions of Islam, the *Sunna* of the Prophet.)

The weapons of theology acquired dialectical brilliance and rationalist edge by discussion with the Hellenised Christianity of the East—experienced in subtle dogmatics—and by the defence of monotheism against the dualism of the Iranian religions, Zoroastrianism and Manichaeism. Missionary zeal, the need for apology and polemic provided the impetus for speculative 'talk' or 'discussion' about God and the world, *kalām*. While jurists practised a pragmatic 'understanding' of revealed ethics (*fiqh*, the Arabic word for jurisprudence) the 'disputants', 'dialecticians' (*ahl al-kalām*, *mutakallimūn*), tried to make the 'knowledge' (*'ilm*) provided in the Revelation accessible to human reason by speculation (*naẓar*). Thus a methodological distinction was drawn between jurisprudence and theology, *fiqh* and *'ilm*. Whereas the casuistry of legal doctrine was based on strict analogy, the *mutakallimūn* used a rational interpretation of the text with the aim of making the doctrine of the faith firm and fast against the attacks of unbelievers and the heresies of sectarians. It is true that they themselves were legally minded enough to justify their reflections as fulfilment of religious duty, the duty of attaining pure knowledge of God. While a rational understanding of divine justice had evolved from the struggle between parties within Islam, the doctrine of divine oneness (*tawḥīd*) had to be refined and defended against non-Muslims, against Iranian dualism and the Christian Trinity. This could not happen without interpreting as metaphor the naively anthropomorphic and all too 'human' picture of God presented in the Koran, thus aiming at a more abstract and spiritual understanding. The Muslims learnt from their Christian opponents Greek dialectical methods and metaphysical ideas. They learned too a transcendent concept of God, stripped of anything visual, a concept which in every predicate and attribute shunned the aberration of *shirk*, polytheism. The rigorous application of this concept led some *mutakallimūn* to propose a 'negative' theology similar to Neoplatonic philosophy (as for example the so-called Jahmiyya—later a term of abuse employed by the opponents of *kalām* for all such tendencies).

The theologians of *kalām* were not philosophers, even though they used concepts and methods of Greek philosophy; they always served the interests of Revealed Law. However, their speculations would not have been possible without their contacts with philosophy; and they themselves prepared the ground for the emergence of philosophy in Islam, a philosophy which was at home in the Hellenistic milieu of the Near East and which became better known from the eighth century onwards amongst the Arabs and Arabic-speaking scientists and scholars through translations of the ancient and late Hellenistic heritage from Greek and Syriac into Arabic. This heritage provided the subject-matter and the starting point for creative progress. Impassioned efforts to explain the relationship between faith and knowledge, between Revelation and the rational cognition of truth and ethical values, also had their effect on philosophy. Thus Islamic philosophy appeared, a philosophy which, drawing on the Neo-Platonic tradition of Aristotle, honoured him as the

First Teacher of a universal and absolute truth which is shown to encompass the specific symbols of revealed religion.

The emergence of rationalism, the formation of a theological scholarly tradition and its increasing political influence all took place before the formation of a new multi-national society of Arabs and non-Arabs to whom the Caliphs of the ʿAbbāsid family promised social equality and just leadership. The zenith of ʿAbbāsid power was also the period of the great teachers of *kalām*—Muʿammar, Abu'l-Hudhayl and his pupil al-Naẓẓām in Baṣra, and Bishr ibn al-Muʿtamir in Baghdad. The principles of their doctrine—embodied in the catch-words 'justice' (i.e. God's justice vis-à-vis human freedom) and 'the profession of oneness' (i.e. purified, spiritualised monotheism)—became the ideology on which the ʿAbbāsid claim to power was based. Why was this? Firstly, because they had proved themselves as *mutakallimūn*, namely as disputants in attack and defence against unbelievers and heretics. *Zandaqa*, 'dualism' or 'Manichaeism', was not only a cheap jibe against political opponents; it was—often in the guise of radical Shīʿism—a real danger and was widespread above all amongst the members of the old Persian aristocracy who rose to the highest positions in the ʿAbbāsid governmental and military establishments.

On the other hand, in the contemporary situation the position of the *mutakallimūn* was important because it could be used in discussing the bases of theocracy, to provide a compromise between conflicting social and political groups. As Muʿtazilites—this label now became the name of rationalist theology—they took as their predecessors those men who had been ready to condemn neither ʿAlī nor ʿUthmān, who had been receptive to the Shīʿa but against its 'radical' direction as well as being against the Khārijites and against the claims of the Umayyads, and who had therefore been the intellectual harbingers of the ʿAbbāsid revolution. The old disputed questions about the caliphate, about ʿAlī and his opponents, had been decided *de facto* by political reality, but behind the subtle disputations about the first schism there were hidden disagreements of contemporary significance. It was no longer a question of which person or family should rule; it was more a question of the general view of the caliphate. Was the caliph a 'charismatic' ruler appointed by God, and therefore the highest lawgiving authority in the State (this was the standpoint of the Shīʿa) or did he also have to submit to the protectors of the *Sunna*, of the exegesis of the Koran as supported by the sanctioned traditions of the Prophet, and to the consensus of the jurists? That was also a question of practical politics. It was a question of whether power—the legislative power and an important part of actual political power—should be in the hands of the scholarly class, the theologians and the jurists; or in the hands of their rivals, the 'secretaries'—the high officials of the bureaucracy set up by the 'Abbāsids.

The question as to whether tradition or charisma should be the basis of legitimacy was the decisive question between the two groups of the social and intellectual elite whom one may (following a suggestion of W. M. Watt [32.40] p.53, 62f) call 'autocrats' and 'constitutionalists'. To the 'autocratic' bloc belonged the secretaries and the descendants of the Persian nobility, the old party of the *mawālī*, who helped to introduce Iranian ideas into the political institutions of the 'Abbāsid caliphate. On the other side there was the 'constitutional' bloc, the transmitters of the scholarly tradition which had developed within Islam; their ideal was not a charismatic leader—the leader had to conform to the Koran and tradition—but rather a charismatic community whose consensus guaranteed the right path. It would appear that the rationalism of the Mu'tazila, already long concerned with the unity of doctrine against extremists and the enemies of Islam, provided a basis for compromise between the 'blocs', by recognising both Imām and scripture as mediators of divine order. The doctrine of the creation of the Koran, an important bone of contention in Mu'tazilite dogma, was the product of absolute monotheism: it distinguished between God's essence—which is eternal and beyond understanding—and His word which is created and accessible to reason. It is difficult to put into their contemporary context fragmentary dogmas which were handed down shorn of their original connotation and were in no way unified. But we can suggest (again with W. M. Watt) that this doctrine also had political implications: it weakened the position of the traditionalists who recognised the text of the Koranic revelation and the practice of early Islam as the sole basis of government order and political behaviour; and it formed a bridge with the Shī'a, who saw the Imām as the authorised interpreter of God's will. Such positions promised to ease tensions and thus appeared politically useful.

This concept was transformed into action by the caliph al-Ma'mūn. We know that he gave important legal posts to a number of Mu'tazilite teachers and that he was very receptive to their speculations. In the year 817 he appointed the Imām 'Alī al-Riḍā as his successor and thus sought to come to an understanding with the Shī'a; however, he provoked a revolt of 'constitutionalists' who appointed the anti-caliph Ibrāhīm ibn al-Mahdī, and after the (violent?) death of the Imām, al-Ma'mūn's move was not followed up. At the end of his reign (827) al-Ma'mūn again tried to fashion a compromise between the conflicting parties and sought further support by forcing through a doctrine agreeable to the moderate Shī'a. The dogma of the creation of the Koran was proclaimed officially as an article of faith. An interrogation of the highest judges was held to ensure that this dogma received universal acceptance. This procedure, which was continued also under the next two caliphs, is known as the *Miḥna,* the 'trial' or also the 'inquisition'—because behind it stood the brutal force of authority. But after two decades, under al-Mutawakkil, reaction set in (848); the policy of compromise had foundered.

It foundered because it sought to find a compromise between groups within the ruling class at a time when the political leadership deeply alienated the people and élitist dogmatism alienated the pious. The traditionist Aḥmad ibn Ḥanbal, a steadfast opponent of this compromise who was long imprisoned, became a martyr of fundamentalist belief who opposed the arbitrariness of human reason and human authority. He also became a hero of a popular movement against the 'innovators'—whether these were theologians, jurists or philosophers. It was no accident that al-Muʿtaṣim (833–42)—who succeeded al-Ma'mūn and continued his policy—removed himself and his Turkish bodyguard from Baghdad, which was becoming more and more disturbed, to the newly-built residence of Sāmarrā. This was not only a traditional manifestation of royal splendour but it was also a move which boded ill for the future. The restoration of 848, which made the codified tradition, the '*sunna* of the Prophet', the constitution of orthodoxy, could not stop the collapse of authority. In vain had the caliph arrogated to himself authority in matters of religious doctrine. From now on the generals of the Turkish bodyguard ruled—until the collapse of the caliphate in the year 945—while the system of orthodox doctrine was developed by traditionists and jurists.

The methods of *kalām,* too, were used to develop a dogma based on literal understanding of the Koran and of tradition 'without asking how?'—i.e. without speculative interpretation. One of the pupils of al-Jubbā'ī (d.915), the systematiser of the Muʿtazila in the wake of the restoration, was al-Ashʿarī (d.*c.*936) who formulated the 'Sunnī' position using the concepts of Muʿtazilite *kalām.* When al-Ashʿarī's doctrine had been systematised by al-Māturīdī (d.941) and al-Bāqillānī (d.1013) there was no more room in Sunnī Islam for a lively discussion of similar theological questions. From now on, the schools of law were in charge of orthodoxy. The Muʿtazila survived—especially in Shīʿite Islam—and its attitudes determined theological issues for a long time to come; but it had finally become devoid of all relevance, the preserve of learned disputation in which well-known opponents indulged in shadow-boxing and attacked well-known losers with arguments which were thought out with more and more subtlety but which were no longer new. 'Anyone who wants to understand properly one of the orthodox doctrines of belief, *ʿaqīda*s, must always be aware that each sentence is a refutation of the dogmatic opponents,

Shīʿa, Khawārij, Murji'a, Jahmiyya and Muʿtazila: only in the fight against the "sects"—they appear as such only after the victory of the *aṣḥāb al-sunna wa'l-jamāʿa* ("people of the Sunna and of the community")—did the orthodox confession of faith become established' (H. Ritter, *Der Islam*, 17, 1928, p.252).

A few sentences from the creed of al-Ashʿarī illustrate this:

> A summary of the views of the followers of tradition and *Sunna*: They profess their belief in God and His angels, His books (of revelation) and His messengers, in that which has come from God and which trustworthy (authorities) have transmitted from the apostle of God—may God bless him and give him peace—without rejecting any of it. They acknowledge that God the Almighty is one God, unique and eternal, that there is no God but Him, that He has taken neither companion nor children and that Muḥammad is His servant and messenger; that paradise and the fire of hell are true, and that the Hour (the Last Judgement) will come without any doubt and that God will resurrect those who are in their graves.
>
> They acknowledge that God—may He be praised—is upon His throne in accordance with His word: 'The Beneficent One is established on the Throne' (Koran, sura 20, verse 5), and that He has two hands—without asking how—according to His word 'I have created with my hands' (sura 38, verse 75) and 'No, His hands are spread out' (sura 5, verse 64)... They acknowledge that the names of God are nothing other than God, as the Muʿtazila and the Khārijites asserted, and that God—may He be praised—has knowledge, according to His word: 'In His knowledge hath He revealed it (his revelation)' (sura 4, verse 166).
>
> ... They confirm that God hears and sees and they do not deny this in respect of God as the Muʿtazila do; and they maintain that God has power, according to His word 'Could they not see that God who created them was mightier than them in power?' (sura 41, verse 15).
>
> They maintain that there is nothing good and nothing bad on the earth other than what God wills and that everything occurs according to the will of God, as He the Mighty and Glorious One has said: 'And ye will not, unless God willeth' (sura 81, verse 29) and as the Muslims say: 'What God wants has happened and what He does not want will not happen.' They maintain that nobody has the ability to perform any course of action before he performs it [enabled to do it by God] and that nobody can escape from God's knowledge or do anything whereof God knows that He will not do it. And they maintain that there is no Creator other than God, that it is God who has also created evil deeds in man, that it is God the Mighty and Glorious One who has created

the deeds of men, and that men can create nothing.

Furthermore, that God—may He be praised—gives help to the believers so that they may obey Him and that He abandons the unbelievers, that He is merciful to the believers, looks after them and allows them to be virtuous and rightly guided; but that He is not merciful to the unbelievers and that He does not let them be virtuous and rightly guided—for if He allowed them to be just they would be just and if He guided them aright then they would be on the right road . . . They maintain that the Koran is the Word of God and uncreated . . . They maintain that God—may He be praised—will be seen with the eye on the Day of Resurrection as one sees the moon in the night when it is full . . .

They declare none of those who observe the direction [i.e. the direction prayer towards the shrine of Mecca—viz. the believers of Islam] to be unbelievers because of a sin which they have committed—such as adultery, theft or similar grave sins—but they all are believers because of the faith which they have even if they commit serious sins. In their view, belief consists in faith 'in God, and His angels, His [revealed] scriptures and His messengers' (sura 2, verse 285). They believe in the predestination of good and evil, sweet and bitter, and they believe that what a person misses cannot meet him and what meets him cannot miss him. Islam consists (according to them) in the confession that there is no God but God and that Muḥammad is the messenger of God—as it is mentioned in the tradition [according to a statement of the Prophet]. Islam [the confession] is in their view something different from faith . . . and they agree that faith consists of words and deeds [. . .] (Al-Ash'arī: *Maqālāt al-Islāmiyyīn. Die dogmatischen Lehren der Anhänger des Islam,* edited by H. Ritter, Istanbul 1929, pp.290–3).

In this credo are revealed three basic attitudes, which gained acceptance in the consciousness of orthodox Islam:

¶ God's being is comprehensible to man only in the signs from God's revealed word, and yet it is actually inaccessible; the text of the Koran is therefore to be accepted without any interpretation.

¶ Man's actions are determined by God's almighty power; his fate in this world and the next is predestined. (Al-Ash'arī, and even more clearly his disciples, seized on a solution of earlier *kalām* in order to remove the contradiction between predestination and just reward: God creates the acts themselves but He also creates for man the possibility of choice, to 'acquire' the acts for himself and thus to take a limited responsibility for their outcome. The reward is just but it always includes mercy too.)

¶ The confession of Islam is not the whole of the faith but is sufficient as a justification for those to whom it is granted by God's mercy as a gift. It is not sinners but only unbelievers and heretics who are damned; for the fallible but believing sinner there is the intercession of the Prophet.

But it was not in *kalām*—even in the 'orthodox' *kalām* of the Ash'ariyya—that Islamic orthodox belief received its definitive expression; this was achieved in the schools of law. It was not in *kalām* that Islamic piety found its certainty of salvation and knowledge of God; this occurred in mystical contemplation. Faced with the consolidation of orthodoxy against a background of social and political change—we will study this development later—the philosophy of the Hellenistic heritage faded into the background. This does not alter the fact that philosophical elements had come into early *kalām* and survived; these originated from living contact with a Hellenised milieu and not from a scholastic continuation by religious thinkers of the heritage transmitted to them.

Nor does this alter the fact that the scholarly tradition of the Ancient sciences found direct continuation and fruitful development in the Arabic language under Islam. But the philosopher's view of the world contained incalculable risks for the faith, risks which Islamic theologians were not prepared to take. This was in spite of the serious efforts on the part of great Islamic philosophers—above all al-Fārābī and Ibn Sīnā (Avicenna)—to ensure harmony by applying the universal insight of philosophy to an interpretation of Islamic prophecy and Revealed Law. The fact that the Shī'a used the neo-Platonic view of the world—the representation of the procession and reversion of the intellect in hierarchical orders, the metaphysics of the intellect and the concept of cosmic sympathy—as an ideology for their doctrine of the Imāmate, deepened the suspicion against Hellenistic philosophy. Nevertheless, the logic and the world view of the Greeks left a deep mark even in orthodox Islam. Even in the course of the rejection of Aristotelian physics (which alleged that the world had no beginning) the followers of al-Ash'arī hellenised the language of systematic theology; and the linking of the Platonic religion of the intellect with the experience of Islamic mysticism is the contribution which Avicenna made to the Persian 'theosophy' of the Ṣafavid period, the last synthesis between Islam and Hellenism.

(d) Asceticism, mysticism and the religious orders

Pious asceticism (*zuhd*), worship of God (*'ibāda*) directed towards the world to come and mystical ecstasy (*fanā'*), simple folk belief as well as esoteric speculation bordering on heresy—all combined in the Ṣūfī movement, so-called because of the coarse woollen garment (*ṣūf*) of the ascetics. *Kalām* had come to the defence of the pure faith but it was not only the mass of believers who remained estranged from its rationalism; clear-sighted intellectuals also turned away from it because to them man's faculty of perception appeared inadequate in the face of God's greatness and unknowability. The orthodoxy of the *ahl al-Sunna* justified the believer who was powerless before God as a member of the community of the faith recognising the law: but not all Muslims were able to contemplate the threat of judgement so easily. As in Judaism and in Christianity, fear of a just God led men in Islam too towards asceticism, escape from the world and painful pangs of conscience. In Islam too, individuals sought to receive enlightenment from God in solitary meditation and encounter, sought indeed spiritual union with God. The piety of the Ṣūfīs does not count on the guarantees of the collective religious community, of public religion—which is such a characteristic, indeed basic, feature of official Islam—but seeks personal certainty of salvation in withdrawal and contradiction. The model of the Prophet, however, could also be used as a yardstick for the way of the Ṣūfīs: he too as a solitary person by ascetic withdrawal from his fellowmen and after his deep search for God had shared in God's theophany; the fear of judgement and the warning to repent were amongst the first and most powerful themes of his message.

The piety and admonitory sermons of the early ascetics can be seen as an imitation of the Prophet; an exemplary case is the work of Ḥasan of Baṣra (d.728, see also above, p.46). In the careful questioning of his conscience by al-Muḥāsibī (d.857) a rejection of possessions and worldly effort went hand in hand with the subtle argumentation of *kalām*. His contemporary Junayd (d.910) was amongst those who prepared the way for real mysticism by striving towards loving union with God. 'The mysticism of love overcomes the severity of God's harsh acts through the love which gives itself up to the will of the beloved and indeed which is made joyful by the expressions of that will even if they are painful. The doctrine of the sole efficacy of God in human activity also accorded with the mystical tendency which had as its aim the disappearance of one's own activity, one's own personality, in that of God, the *fanā'*. From the theoretical point of view, finally, this became a basic tenet in the pantheistic monism developed from mysticism' (H. Ritter [32.55] p.66). In the paradigm of love, in the self-identification of the lover with the beloved object—'I am You', a fundamental theme of Ṣūfī poetry—the mystics bridged the gulf between the religion of the law, of rational knowledge (*'ilm*), and the religion of intuitive gnosis.

From that point onwards different ways of mystical thinking and activity opened up, simple practices of self-denying asceticism and intensive contemplation leading to ecstasy. In the 'drunken' mysticism of Abū Yazīd al-Bisṭāmī (d.874?) and al-Ḥallāj (executed 922) mystical union looked like blasphemy: the ecstatic 'I am God' of al-Ḥallāj brought him to the cross. His successors avoided the scandal of affecting union with God by using the metaphors of gnostic philosophy (Plotinus was amongst their teachers). But al-Suhrawardī, the harbinger of mystical illumination, was also executed as a heretic (1191), and Ibn 'Arabī (1165–1240), the great theoretician of Ṣūfī monism and pantheism—in his thought, lover, beloved and love, God, man and the world all merge together—also remained controversial even amongst those people who felt drawn to the depth and sincerity of his thought. Many mystics were controversial and also accused of heresy, because the rebellion of pious people against the constricting ethics of the law became a platform for popular anti-authoritarian movements.

The Ṣūfiyya became the spiritual bond which united new forms of religious community, ranging from esoteric circles to proletarian vagabonds who wore the ascetic garments of the 'poor' (Arabic *faqīr*, Persian *darvīsh*). In these circles men sought—in new forms of ritualised worship of God, in communal recitation (*dhikr*, the incessant 'naming' of God) and in singing, music and whirling dance (*samā'*, 'listening' to such recitals)—inspiration on the ascent through the stations (*maqāmāt*) of the mystical way towards annihilation (*fanā'*), and unity with God. The Ṣūfīs influenced social life in the border fortresses of the warriors of the faith (*ghāzī*) on the edge of the Islamic world as well as the urban fraternity of the *futuwwa*. Brotherhoods and organised orders emerged. Disciples (*murīd*) assembled around a master (Arabic *shaykh*, Persian *pīr*) of the mystical path, and obtained from him the cloak (*khirqa*) of the initiates in initiation rituals. With the emergence of the orders from the end of the tenth century onwards, the Ṣūfī movement reached its highest degree of social and political importance. In them the individualism of the mystics acquired a social dimension.

The authoritative organisation of the orders had yet another consequence: the authority of the 'path', the 'method' (*ṭarīqa*), which the master revealed to his pupils was founded on the recognised, respected teachers of the early period. Thus the mystical path also became a doctrine transmitted by 'schools' of tradition, validated by an uninterrupted chain (*silsila*) of authentic transmitters—according to the model and the norms of orthodox traditions about the *sunna* of the Prophet—chains which, at the same time, served as a spiritual genealogy. Not only the method but also the spirit of Sunnī tradition dominated the Ṣūfī orders. Influential circles of strict traditionalism—indeed even the strictest, the Ḥanbalite legal tradition—were attached to them. The Ṣūfī orders and the legal schools together created the institutions of orthodoxy which came into their own in the eleventh century. At a time when the authorities—the caliphs and the sultans, engrossed in their struggles for power—had lost spiritual authority, the scholars and the mystics became the trustees of doctrine. The way of the Ṣūfīs became the embodiment of Islamic piety.

In the year 1095 the jurist and theologian, al-Ghazālī (1058–1111), highly respected and at the height of his career, gave up his chair at one of the colleges of law in Baghdad, left Iraq and for eleven years led a life of denial of the world, asceticism and meditation. Later on he gave an account of his reasons for this step in an *apologia pro vita sua*, which he called 'Deliverance from Error' (*al-Munqidh min al-ḍalāl*). This was a recapitulation of his personal experience of faith and life up to this turning point, as well as a critical review of errors and aberrations within the Islamic community in the first five centuries of its history: a review of dialectic dogmatics, Greek philosophy and sectarianism based on blind following of authority. The result of this experience was a crisis which has been compared to the Cartesian Doubt: a scepticism which called into question even the evidence of perception and intellectual certainty. But al-Ghazālī's doubt was not—like Descartes'—directed against tradition. He directed his doubt against the scholasticism of theologians who wanted to make pronouncements on faith and unbelief using reason.

At length, as he wrote, 'God cured me of the malady', but 'this did not come about by systematic demonstration or marshalled argument, but by a light which God most high cast into my breast. That light is the key to the greater part of knowledge. Whoever thinks that the understanding of things Divine rests upon strict proofs has in his thought narrowed down the wideness of God's mercy.' He recognised the way of salvation as following the Ṣūfīs, the mystics: 'I apprehended clearly that the mystics were men who had real experiences, not men of words, and that I had already progressed as far as was possible by way of intellectual apprehension. What remained for me was not to be attained by oral instruction and study but only by tasting [immediate experience] and by walking [in the mystic way]. [. . .] It had become clear to me that I had no hope of the bliss of the world to come save through a God-fearing life and the withdrawal of myself from vain desire. It was clear to me that the key to all this was to sever the attachment of the heart to worldly things by leaving the mansion of deception and returning to that of eternity, and to advance towards God most high with all earnestness' (*al-Munqidh*, ed. by Farid Jabre. Beirut, ^{2}1969, pp.13f., 35f. = transl. by W.M. Watt: *The faith and practice of al-Ghazālī*. London, 1953, pp.25, 55–6).

Five years before his death he again went back into public life and worked at the request of a vizier of the Sultan of Nīshāpūr for a few years more in his native land of eastern Iran as a teacher of law. This he did at the pressing request of the vizier and on the advice of friends, but also because he believed that he had a divine mission. According to a well-known tradition transmitted as the word of the Prophet Muḥammad, at the end of each century God was to send a renewer of His religion. The certainty had grown up within al-Ghazālī that he could be this renewer. His great work *The Revival of the Sciences of Religion (Iḥyā' 'Ulūm al-Dīn)*, composed in the years of his spiritual exile, revealed to the Islamic world that obedience to the *Sharī'a*—the divine law according to the Koran and tradition—was the path to meaningful living and that the worship of God as practised by the mystics was the way of faith in God which brought salvation.

Al-Ghazālī became the voice of renewal (not its initiator—that process had begun before him) because he expressed the predicament of Muslim society in his own time. In his crisis not only personal experience but also the historical experience of Islamic society reached a climax. In the centuries of turmoil which now began, centuries of the turmoil of war and political upheaval, people followed his advice everywhere. From now onwards Islamic society tried to base compromise and rebellion, stability and reform, on traditionalism in the law and in political institutions and on mysticism and fundamentalism in personal piety.

The reconciliation between ascetic, mystical Ṣūfism and orthodox legal tradition had an important effect on the integration of Islamic society. It gave the community of the faith a stability which allowed it to emerge strengthened from the vicissitudes of the Mongol invasion and preserved its spiritual stability in the face of irreversible political disintegration. On the other hand, the uniting of such diverse spiritual attitudes also had its price; it did not occur in the long run without compromises. It is true that a man like 'Abd al-Qādir al-Jīlānī (1077–1166)—a jurist, preacher and Ṣūfī in Baghdad—was able in exemplary fashion to combine mystical practices with the strict traditionalism of the Ḥanbalite school of law. But the 'Abd al-Qādir of legend as he was presented a century after his death in the tradition of his order (the Qādiriyya) was a different person: a fully-fledged saint, a manifestation of divine majesty and a super-human miracle worker. The Ṣūfī community—the Qādiriyya as well as others which gathered in ever-increasing numbers around respected Ṣūfīs—covered the divergences and aberrations of popular religion. It also included sectarian forms and concepts of pre-Islamic and non-Islamic religiosity, veneration of saints and eccentric devotional practices, all of which had continued under Islam but were banned from official worship. The authority of the Ṣūfī master became elevated in the course of time to the status of the spiritual 'pole' (*quṭb*), the secret 'caliph' of the spiritual universe the opposite of worldly authority. The Hanbalite Ibn Taymiyya (1263–1328), who lived in Damascus, then under Mongol threat, felt compelled to direct the force of his criticism against such aberrations of folk-belief. He himself was a follower of the Qādiriyya (admittedly a more moderate group who based their ideas on the writings, and not the mythology, of ʿAbd al-Qādir) and he warned theologians as well as Ṣūfīs to leave God's unfathomable inscrutability to Him.

But the strength of elevated intellectual mysticism continued and experienced its most beautiful flowering in the very midst of devastation, in the Persian poetry of the Mongol period. This included the verse epics of ʿAṭṭār (who died at the beginning of the thirteenth century), the didactic poems of Jalāl al-Dīn Rūmī (1207–73)—the order of the 'Dancing' Dervishes of Anatolia reveres him as Mevlānā ('our Lord')—and the epic and lyric poetry of Jāmī (1414–92). But it was above all the religious orders over the wide expanse of Islamic history that had created a popular impact and were political dynamite. Not even the Ottoman Sultans, masters though they were of the institutionalisation and control of religious and social forces, could effectively combat heterodoxy and rebellion amongst the Anatolian dervish orders. One of the most popular orders, the sectarian Bektāshīs, had numerous followers even amongst the élite Janissary troops. Originally no less heretical—and feared by the Ottomans—were the Turcoman Qïzïlbash (called 'redheads' because of their caps) in Ādharbāyjān, with whose help the Ṣafavid shaykhs conquered and united Iran at the beginning of the sixteenth century. This was, however, in the name of the 'orthodox' Shīʿa who allowed mysticism to stagnate into theosophy in the period which followed. We cannot even mention the most important of the 100 or more other orders, both Sunni and Shīʿite; their number alone indicates their great importance in every Islamic country. Jurists have never tired of attacking their 'innovation' and of refuting the inspiration of their leaders' authority. But right up to our own times many Muslims honour 'the friends of God', saints who are raised to the status of the Perfect Man. They honour them both in their lifetimes and at their tombs and they hope that they will ensure the salvation of the world and will intercede for them on the Day of Judgement.

3. Law and government

(a) The foundation of Islamic law

The Islamic science of law (*fiqh*) developed out of the application and elaboration of Koranic precepts. Its teaching deals with the duties of the Muslim in his worship of God and his activities in public and private life. The law is religious command ('the clear defined way': *Sharīʿa*): the highest lawgiver is God. *Fiqh* is therefore, according to the understanding of the Muslim, 'knowledge of the classification of the laws of God, which concern the actions of all responsible Muslims, as obligatory, forbidden, recommendable, disliked or permissible' (Ibn Khaldūn (1332–1506): *al-Muqaddima*, tr. F. Rosenthal, New York, 1958, vol. 3, p. 9). According to a modern definition it is 'like the *Jurisprudentia* of the Romans, *'rerum divinarum atque humanarum notitia'*, and in its widest sense covers all aspects of religious, political and civil life. In addition to the laws regulating ritual and religious observances (*'ibādāt*), as far as concerns performance and abstinence, it includes the whole field of family law, the law of inheritance, of property and of contract, in a word provision for all the legal questions that arise in social life (*mu'āmalāt*); it also includes criminal law and procedure, and finally constitutional law and laws regulating the administration of the state and the conduct of war' (I. Goldziher in *EI*[1] [13.01], volume 2, article *fiqh*).

The Koran could not answer all the questions that arose in actual practice. Even in situations for which it laid down regulations, it could not be applied immediately as a basis for a unified legal system in the great empire which arose in a few decades after the death of Muḥammad (632). In order to organise the expanding state, the caliphs and their governors had first of all to draw on pre-Islamic government and customary law in the old provinces of both the Byzantine and the Sasanian empires. From the end of the seventh century these different forms of administrative and legal practice were Arabised and Islamicised under the caliphate of the Umayyads—the names of the caliphs 'Abd al-Malik (685–705) and 'Umar II ibn 'Abd al-'Azīz (717–20) should especially be mentioned here. The Umayyads also created, about a century after the Hijra, the office of the Islamic judge, the *qāḍī*. In this way a class of legal specialists emerged and local 'schools' also developed, though not in the sense that they professionally transmitted an established doctrine. The concepts of 'usage' (*sunna*) and previous 'practice' (*'amal*) played an important role in legal reasoning; personal judgement (*ra'y*), supported by analogy (*qiyās*) or again—against such analogy—legal preference (*istiḥsān*) gave a rational pragmatic character to this kind of legal thinking. Differences were removed by recourse to the 'consensus' (*ijmā'*) of the teachers of law. The Iraqi Abū Ḥanīfa (d. 767) and the Medinan Mālik ibn Anas (d. 795) were the authorities for the formative stage of the Islamic schools in this period, authorities to which in the 'Abbāsid period (from *c.* 750) the earliest legal schools *stricto sensu* began to refer.

It would appear that it was the Iraqi lawyers who began to link the doctrine which had emerged from regional use and consensus with the authority of the Prophet, to defend it as 'the *sunna* of the Prophet' —a result of rivalry between the various local movements and indeed of opposition to the government institution. At the same time, however, critics of the prevailing practice, which often appeared to be capricious, argued with ever-increasing urgency—and in steadily more determined opposition to the Umayyad administration—for that *'sunna* of the Prophet' to be placed on a new, authentic basis: namely traditions, precepts and norms of behaviour which were traceable back to the Prophet and to the 'rightly guided' authorities of earliest Islam. Such traditions (*ḥadīth*, 'report', 'tradition') gradually emerged in increasing numbers in legal literature. This development produced in the middle of the ninth century a definitive result: that body of tradition which was regarded as authentic was collected and arranged systematically; and the normative judgement and model of the Prophet and of his most respected companions which was preserved in this corpus—now identified with the *Sunna*—was then, with the Koran, elevated to the status of the authoritative 'root' of *fiqh*. When, in the context of the religion and law of Islam, there is any discussion about 'tradition' (*ḥadīth*), 'traditionists' (*muḥaddithūn, ahl al-ḥadīth*) and 'traditionism' (or, more general still, 'traditionalism') it is about accounts of the words and deeds of the Prophet, the formalised transmission of those accounts and the tendency of teachers to base Muslim belief and actions on the tradition of the earliest community.

The transmission of these accounts poses a problem which is not only a matter of debate in modern research but which has also long been discussed by the Muslims themselves: the problem of authenticity. Are we dealing here with genuine transmission from the time of Muḥammad, or is this a piously naive representation of an old consensus, or tendentious fiction produced by politico-religious parties, the defenders of sturdy material interests? These questions cannot be answered in every case and the answers which do emerge are varied. There is no doubt that traditions from the early period of Islam—which after the first civil wars appeared as a golden age—were already transmitted and written down in the first century. This did not happen because of scholarly motives; it occurred against a background of urgent practical questions and political crises. A society of Arab Bedouin, of old and new settlers in the countries around the peninsula and clients who had converted to Islam from the subject peoples, was ruled with a firm hand by the aristocracy of the Quraysh, but it was not possible to integrate this society; the caliphs of the Umayyad dynasty closed their eyes to the profound social and economic causes of the ever-increasing and ever more violent conflicts that broke out. In places where the memory of the Prophet and of the first four 'rightly-guided' caliphs was preserved most vividly, in the places of their rule, in Mecca and Medina, but also in the old Islamic cities of Iraq, work was begun on the collecting and noting down of such traditions, and here they were used first as a means of establishing the law. However, their themes were not restricted to those of creed and law; *ḥadīth* competed as a literary genre with gnomic wisdom, with history and with stories of secular origin. The compilation of *ḥadīth* which was aimed at placing it next to the Koran as a basis for Islamic legal practice, was met with scepticism and indeed often open opposition on the part of the jurists. The rise of the traditionist movement could not, however, be stopped. The holy cities of the Ḥijāz and the Iraqi provincial towns were also centres of opposition against the governmental policies of the Umayyad caliphs in Damascus which were seen by many as a betrayal of theocracy. Theocracy, the just government according to God's word through His messenger and His legitimate representatives, had been removed at the death of the fourth caliph ʻAlī (who like his two predecessors, ʻUmar and ʻUthmān had come to a violent end). Theocracy had become an ideal for the pious and theoreticians. Recourse to the authorities of earliest Islam—not exclusively, but increasingly to the Prophet himself—was therefore influenced by the contrast between the pious revival and practical politics. It is not surprising that the political institution, the caliphs and their entourage, likewise used the means of legitimisation which was to be found in such accounts. The question of authenticity and its criteria became acute; for it was suspicious that so much contradictory and tendentious evidence came into circulation. The consequence was—from around the beginning of the eighth century—that firm norms were established through which the genuineness of a *ḥadīth* could be verified: the text of each tradition was provided with a 'support' (*isnād*), a chain of witnesses which traced the report in an uninterrupted sequence of personal testimony back to the Prophet; or to another respected authority; or to witnesses who had seen or heard the events.

A good example is the chain of transmitters with which Ibn Hishām (d.828 or 833), the author of the best-known biography (*Sīra*) of the Prophet introduces the tradition about the beginning of the Revelation (cf. above, p.1):

> Ibn Isḥāq (the author of the basic work which was completed by Ibn Hishām, died 767 or 768) said: Wahb ibn Kaysān, the *mawlā* (client) of the Zubayr family (d. between 744 and 747) told me: I heard (personally), how ʻAbdallāh ibn al-Zubayr (son of the Prophet's companion al-Zubayr, anti-caliph in Mecca, 683–92) said to ʻUbayd ibn ʻUmayr ibn Qatāda al-Laythī (d. 687–88): Tell me, ʻUbayd, how it was when the prophecy of the messenger of God began, when Gabriel came to him? Thereupon ʻUbayd said —I myself (Wahb) was present when he informed ʻAbdallāh ibn al-Zubayr and the others present about it—: . . . (Ibn Hishām: *Sīrat Muḥammad Rasūl Allāh*, edited by Muṣṭafā al-Saqqā', Ibrāhīm al-Abyārī, ʻAbd al-Ḥafīẓ Shalabī. Cairo, ²1955, vol.1, p.235.)

Thereafter there follows the account in which variants in subject matter and style from other parallel versions are scrupulously included.

Moreover, efforts were made to test the veracity and probity of the informants in such chains—one of the motivating factors for the flourishing biographical literature from the end of the eighth century.

Ḥadīth became a means of reconciling the differences between schools of law, between jurisprudence and the administration of justice and moreover—this acquired political significance too—between the representatives of apodictic 'traditionism' and the representatives of rationalist theology which had evolved at the same time (cf. above, p.46ff.). To the question of the 'authenticity' of the *ḥadīth* it is possible to give the following reply: We do not know how much has been preserved from the time of the Prophet, but the *ḥadīth* represent an authentic picture of the experiences of early Islam in the first one and a half centuries after the death of the Prophet.

(b) Government, legislation and the administration of justice

Tradition was not the sole nor at first even the most important source of the evolving discipline of jurisprudence. At the beginning tradition was used as a foundation and supplement to rational pragmatic legislation according to the judgement of the jurists. But its importance increased and under the caliphate of the ʿAbbāsids, for whom the outbreak of uncontrollable social conflicts in the middle of the eighth century had paved the way through revolution and the fall of the Umayyads, tradition acquired a completely new dimension. Here again, the articulation of political tendencies played a role. An increasing number of jurists viewed the authentic *Sunna* of the Prophet preserved in *ḥadīth* as the constitution of the religious community, against the claim of enlightened 'charismatic' leadership. This was the claim of the Shīʿite *imāms* but it also revealed itself as an ominous tendency in the absolutism of the ʿAbbāsids.

The ʿAbbāsids promised that they as true *imāms* and commanders of the faithful would establish just rule in succession to the Prophet and that they would do away with any distinction between temporal and spiritual authority. A process of assimilation and integration began (reflected in pro-ʿAbbāsid texts). But with increasing power they created an autocracy which tried to make for itself instruments of absolute power in the institutions of the military, the administration and the law. It is probable that here the model of the Sasanian government of pre-Islamic Iran played a role, transmitted by the 'secretaries' from the circles of the Persian *mawālī* to whom the early ʿAbbāsids accorded great importance.

The Khurāsānian army created the power basis of the dynasty. The destruction of the Umayyads, the suppression of the political

Shīʿa (and the frustrating of all attempts at compromise) were their handiwork. The first ʿAbbāsids developed their local military support into a standing imperial army. Military leaders, *amīrs*, received full powers as provincial governors; next to the amīr was the 'governor' (*ʿāmil*) on whom was placed responsibility for the civil fiscal organisation. With the replacement of the Khurāsānian army by the guard of Turkish military slaves (under al-Muʿtaṣim, 833–44) the decline of the caliphate began. It was increasingly deprived of power by generals who finally combined military and financial control in the office of chief *amīr* (*amīr al-umarāʾ*) and was completely incapacitated when the Iranian dynasty of the Būyids (945) usurped this office.

The civil administration passed into the hands of a centralised bureaucracy. At its head the caliph reigned in inaccessible seclusion. The class of 'secretaries' (*kuttāb*) became the authoritative ruling class of urban society. The increasing involvement of Iranian *mawālī* stamped court protocol and government practice with Sasanian models.

The basic unit of government was the *dīwān* (which originally meant 'list'); other *dīwāns* with increasingly specialised responsibilities had already been added in the Umayyad administration to the early Islamic ministries of the army (*dīwān al-jund* 'army list', established by the second caliph ʿUmar) and of the land-tax (*dīwān al-kharāj*): these new *dīwāns* included the treasury, chancellery and departments for post and intelligence and different aspects of the financial administration and state control. The post of the vizier (*wazīr*, 'helper') at the head was an ʿAbbāsid innovation which was indicative of the centralisation and institutionalisation of the bureaucracy. Full powers were conferred on the viziers of Hārūn al-Rashīd, the Barmecides who had originated from eastern Iran, and had previously been royal tutors. Famed for their omnipotence, they nevertheless fell from grace in 803. The post and status of the vizier as the highest official of the sovereign already reflected the separation between the political and religious institutions of the Islamic state. Towards the end of the ninth century the rivalry between bureaucrats, military men and jurists for political influence over the weakened leadership became increasingly apparent in ever more frequent rise and fall of viziers. The victors were the Turkish generals and their Persian successors (the Būyids) in the office of chief amir. Yet it had been ultimately the apparatus of specialists under the vizier which maintained the functioning of government under foreign usurpers and which preserved Arabic culture among the Iranian amirs of the tenth century and Persian culture in the east under the Turkish and Mongol sultans of the period which followed.

The caliph as *imām* delegated the maintenance of religious law and judgement on controversial issues to the specialists of the *Sharīʿa*, the judges (*qāḍī*). The Umayyads had nominated judges as government officials; the ʿAbbāsids created religious jurisdiction as an institution which was basically independent, answerable only to God-given law. Legislation, in view of the heteronomous nature of Islamic law, was limited to interpretation; in principle the caliph was also subject to the law of the Koran and the precepts of the Prophets, and interpretation was already linked to the scholarly tradition of the legal schools. But the legal apparatus of the lawyers was not sufficient for all the demands of legal practice. The imperial authority of the political administration possessed *de facto* wide-ranging juridical privileges: punitive powers were delegated to the police (*shurṭa*), supervision of trade and public conduct (*ḥisba*) was entrusted to the inspector of markets (*muḥtasib*, comparable to the Byzantine agoranomos). Both institutions had to develop usages in respect of evidence, meting out of punishment and control, which could not be derived from the substance or according to the criteria of jurisprudence in a practicable form and which indeed went against the statutes of the *Sharīʿa*. The ruler in particular acted as sovereign in matters of political leadership (*siyāsa*). Furthermore, the caliphs as a court of appeal took it upon themselves to inspect and correct the decision of judges. The 'inspection of injustice' (*naẓar fi'l-maẓālim*), the prerogative of the sovereign established according to a Sasanian model, examined grievances against encroachments and abuses of government but also against legal decisions. The jurisdiction of the *maẓālim*, which was set up as a court for complaints, competed with the office of judge and impinged on his sphere of competence, for a long time, from the period of the caliphate until that of the Ottomans.

The caliph was not only a political ruler; he was, as the *imām* and Commander of the Faithful, guarantor of the law for the well-being of the Muslims; in the view of the ʿAbbāsids he was not only *Khalīfat rasūl Allāh*, 'the vicegerent of the messenger of God', but also *Khalīfat Allāh*, 'the representative of God on earth'. Al-Manṣūr (754–75) called himself *Sulṭān Allāh fī arḍihi*, 'the authority of God on His earth'. The appointment of judges and the setting-up of a chief judge (*qāḍi'l-quḍāt*; this was also modelled on Sasanian practice) were methods of controlling the exercise of this authority. Nevertheless, the caliph was not a law-giver; the law was given. The decision against the assumption of legislative power was taken early. It is true that the Persian Ibn al-Muqaffaʿ (executed after 756) presented a political programme to al-Manṣūr in which he recommended that he should interpret, unify and codify the religious law according to his own personal inspiration:

> May the Commander of the Faithful also cast his eye on the different and conflicting administration of justice of these two

capital cities [of Iraq: Başra and Kufa—the treatise was written before the foundation of Baghdad] and of other cities and regions . . . If the Commander of the Faithful would deign to order that these different rulings and attitudes should be laid before him in written form, together with the legislative arguments of the individual schools, be they a *sunna* or a [demonstration of proof based on] analogy; if thereafter the Commander of the Faithful would deign to examine these cases, to apply his own divinely-inspired judgement to each case, to make a firm decision and to forbid contradictory rulings and moreover to have this legislation codified in a comprehensive way—then we might hope that God would impose a single correct rule instead of these rules in which right is mixed with error. We might also hope that the unification of legal practice goes hand in hand with unity of authority according to the opinion and verdict of the Commander of the Faithful. (Ibn al-Muqaffaʿ, *Risāla fī'l-Ṣaḥāba*, ed. M. Kurd ʿAlī in *Rasā'il al-bulaghā'*, Cairo, 1946, pp. 126–7.)

But this programme was not put into practice. The caliph must presumably have seen that such a step could bring him increased power but that, in view of the influence of the lawyers who had formulated a juridical basis to his political programme of Islamic justice it could also lose him authority over the Muslims. The jurists themselves were in the process of visibly restricting the judgement (*ra'y*) of scholars by the authority of *ḥadīth* transmission and scholarly tradition. When the chief judge, Abū Yūsuf Yaʿqūb (d. 798) wrote a handbook on land tax for his caliph Hārūn al-Rashīd, he issued a strict warning to the sovereign, the warning to shine as the conserver of the law but of a law which preserves the *sunna* of the ancestors:

God in His mercy, pity and forgiveness has appointed the temporal rulers as caliphs on earth, He has given them light with which they may illuminate for their subjects everything that appears dark in their daily affairs, and with which they make clear those of their rights which are in doubt. The illumination provided by the mighty is the maintenance of legal ordinances (*ḥudūd*) and the guarding of the rights of all through firmness and clear command. The revival of the *sunna*, propagated by a pious generation, takes highest place, because reviving the *sunna* is one of those good deeds which continue and do not perish. (Abū Yūsuf Yaʿqūb, *Kitāb al-Kharāj (Book of land-tax)*, trans. by C. R. Barber and S. M. Stern in I. Goldziher [30.02], vol. 2, p. 73.)

Abū Yūsuf, like his teacher Abū Ḥanīfa, conceded wide judgement to the reasoning (*ijtihād*) of scholars which was proven and supported by consensus. Yet, with the alienation between pragmatic administration and the profession of learned judges, with the increasing gulf between idea and reality in the Islamic state there grew amongst jurists the tendency to base the law on immovable norms. This tendency did not remain restricted to the law; the entire scholarly tradition in the Islamic sciences, even in their external form, was stamped with the norms of *ḥadīth* transmission: the connection of personal authorisation with written records, and the formal authentication of each tradition—of individual accounts or entire literary works—by a coherent *isnād*. The writing of history was also presented in this way in order to serve as a piece of model teaching (quite a few 'historical' reports turn out on closer analysis to be legal instructions). Already, towards the end of the Umayyad and the beginning of the ʿAbbāsid period, traditions were collected (*tadwīn*) and classified (*taṣnīf*) according to the chapters of the *Sharīʿa* for the use of lawyers.

(c) The classical schools of law

Around the turn of the second and third Islamic centuries (eighth and ninth centuries AD) the great jurist al-Shāfiʿī made the decisive step towards a new theory of law: for al-Shāfiʿī *sunna* was no longer idealised practice according to the consensus of the authorities, as had been the case with his Medinan teachers. It was identical with the content of formal traditions from the Prophet, which again were postulated to be identical with the consensus of the community, explicable by strict analogy but not at the disposal of personal judgement:

> Whatever the Apostle has decreed [as *sunna*] that is not based on any scriptural command of God, he has done so by God's command. So God instructed us in his saying: 'And verily thou [Muḥammad] wilt guide [mankind] to a straight path, the path of God' [Koran, sūra 42, verses 52–3]. For the Apostle has laid down a *sunna* [on matters] for which there is a text in the Book of God as well as for others concerning which there is no [specific] text. But whatever he laid down in the *sunna* God has ordered us to obey, and He regards [our] obedience to him as obedience to Him, and [our] refusal to obey him as disobedience to Him for which no man will be forgiven; nor is an excuse for failure to obey the Apostle's *sunna* possible. (al-Shāfiʿī: *al-Risāla,* ed. by A.M. Shākir, Cairo, 1948, pp.88–9 = transl. by Majid Khadduri: *Islamic jurisprudence—Shāfiʿī's Risāla.* Baltimore, 1961, pp.118–19.)

The clash of opinions about the principles of the Sharīʿa developed into an open conflict when the caliph al-Maʾmūn (813–33) tried in a famous and notorious inquisition (the *Miḥna,* see above, p.49f.) to force the highest judges to accept the doctrine of the creation of the Koran. This dogma was the shibboleth of rationalist theologians, who in polemic and apologetic against people of different faiths, and more especially in a dialogue with Hellenised Christianity, had acquired the dialectics and interpretative methods of the Hellenistic tradition. The most important opponent of the inquisition, the traditionist Aḥmad b. Ḥanbal, stood out firmly on the other hand in favour of pious acceptance of the uncreated word of God. Behind him stood the people who were alienated from the caliph, his administration and the speculations of élitist theologians. The turning point came around the middle of the ninth century. The inquisition was ended and a movement against the rationalist interpretation of the Revelation set in: besides the Koran there should only be the *Sunna*, tradition which was sanctioned by the authority of the Prophet and authoritative scholarly transmission, which was the source of the *Sharīʿa* and the constitution of the *Umma* and as such to be recognised even by the caliph. The canonisation of the *ḥadīth* was accompanied by the compiling of collections of texts which were regarded as definitive. Speculative theology also joined in this development and sought compromise formulae which preserved the literal sense of the Koran (see above, pp. 50ff.). But thereafter *taʾwīl*, the 'exegesis' of the Koran which was, however, always accompanied by subjective judgement, remained suspect to the champions of religious orthodoxy. The ancestors, the companions of the Prophet and the transmitters of tradition had not used such a procedure: it was innovation (*bidʿa*) bordering on heresy.

Sunna and orthodoxy therefore became synonyms: orthodoxy, the publicly declared and universally recognised teaching of right belief and right action was not created and formulated by speculative theology (*kalām*) but by the collectors and interpreters of legal tradition. All schools of law, though different in the importance which they attached to the 'principles of law' (*uṣūl al-fiqh*), 'opinion' (*raʾy*) in relation to the Koran, *Sunna* and consensus (*ijmāʿ*) were unanimous in their respect for tradition. These were schools which were attached to the prominent authorities of the formative period and from which four survived: the followers of Mālik (Mālikites), of Abū Ḥanīfa (Ḥanafites), of al-Shāfiʿī (Shāfiʿites) and of Ibn Ḥanbal (Ḥanbalites). The dogmatic 'principles of faith' (*uṣūl al-dīn*) were governed on the basis of traditional sources by the schools of law and in this way theological 'knowledge' (*ʿilm*) and legal 'understanding' (*fiqh*) were both united as disciplines of the *Sharīʿa*. It was only in collaboration with the schools of law that the attitudes of *kalām* survived and continued to influence the positions of politico-religious factions: the Muʿtazila maintained themselves in coalition with Ḥanafite law (which had always reserved a place for rational interpretation); the Ashʿariyya (see above, pp. 50ff.) joined up with the Shāfiʿite school (without thereby finding 'official' recognition as an orthodox dogma as earlier Orientalists would have it).

It has been said that the *Sharīʿa* in the course of history became an edifice of theoreticians, a dead letter which could not take account of changes in society. That is not correct in such a general way. Of course the restricting of the sources of law to the Koran and sacred tradition presented practical difficulties and the character of the law as a doctrine of duties compelled the jurists to conceive of all acts and legal relationships, including all matters of real property, under the categories 'obligatory', 'forbidden', 'recommended', 'disapproved', and a simple 'permissible'. It was possible to respect these principles in the broadest way and for the longest period in the sphere of religious ritual and family and inheritance laws. In government and administrative law, in fiscal law and in penal law, practice in fact went in other directions; in the end the Ottomans placed next to the *Sharī'a* a separate legal body, the *qānūn* (for which the *siyāsa* of the Mamlūks was a precursor) to deal with these legal areas. But it is important to realise that Islamic law was never officially imposed by the body politic. The different interpretations of the four 'canonical' law schools always enjoyed equal status; they differed in the extent and freedom of individual interpretation which they allowed. It is true that al-Shāfi'ī had closed 'the door of *ijtihād*', individual reasoning, by limiting individual judgement to strict analogy according to the *Sunna* and had thereby decisively influenced general development; but the other schools did not follow him with equal strictness. Thus the Ḥanafite lawyers of Iraq, the Islamic country with the most progressive and diverse social structure, created a legal foundation of commercial law by the use of liberal casuistry which nevertheless intelligently preserved the letter of the tradition; this was a commercial law which took account of the flourishing economy of the early 'Abbāsid empire in an appropriate way. And even the followers of Ibn Ḥanbal, the intransigent opponents of all theological speculation and the strictest defenders of traditionalism, who even refused to use analogy, developed their jurisprudence into a flexible instrument of rational pragmatism.

A similar process occurred with the Shī'a: we can confidently class their branches as legal schools alongside the four legal schools of 'orthodox' thought. Before the 'Twelver' Shī'a, the Zaydiyya (cf. p.42) had produced already an early and subtly developed legal system. The doctrine of the occultation of the Imām (see p.42f.) then gave lawyers full powers and an especially wide scope for personal interpretation since in his absence the exercise of *ijtihād* was granted to them. The Shī'a also based their doctrine on *Sunna*, the model and instruction of the Prophet and his companions; but theirs was a different understanding and a different transmission of *Sunna*, which separated them from the consensus and the tradition of the 'orthodox' lawyers who were loyal to the 'Abbāsids: they viewed only 'Alī and his successors as its legitimate and authentic transmitters. It was only amongst the Sunnis that the terms *'Sunna'* and *'Shīʿa'* became used as contradictory concepts and labels for the two big confessional groups of Islam. The 'party'—*shīʿa*—of ʿAlī recognised only him as the successor designated by the Prophet, the bearer of the light which had been sent down to Muḥammad and the bearer of his *sunna*; they saw only his successors as the rightful representatives of the community and expected true guidance to salvation only from these enlightened *imāms.* Furthermore, they sought to legitimise their claims in an interpretation of the 'inner' meaning of Revelation and, the more they claimed esoteric insight, the more they were in opposition to the understanding of the Koran of orthodox traditionalism which was loyal to the letter of the book. But only the 'radical' Shīʿite sect of the Ismāʿīliyya pursued their claim to illumination and leadership by word and sword right up until the time of the Crusades (see p.43f.). The 'Twelver' or Imāmite Shīʿa arrived at peaceful coexistence with Sunni orthodoxy. With the decline of caliphal power, with the disintegration of the empire, with the emergence of Iranian and Turkish dynasties which forced the caliph into their service and involved them in their power struggles, the old conflict about the legitimacy of the ʿAbbāsid caliphal family became meaningless and the spiritual as well as the political authority of the caliph remained only a hypothesis of theoreticians. The political Shīʿa gave up; the twelfth Imām went into concealment and was only to return from hiding as the *Mahdī,* the 'rightly-guided' one, at the end of time. Before his return there was no legitimate authority. When, at the beginning of the sixteenth century, the Ṣafavids conquered Iran on behalf of the hidden Imām, they relied on the prominent jurists of the Shīʿa for their overall authority. These assured their position later on in opposition to the decline of the dynasty and the disintegration of the State. Since the end of the nineteenth century they have acquired independent authority and political influence. Their leaders were then granted the honorary title of *Āyatallāh* 'sign of God', and they formed an increasingly powerful opposition to the reigning dynasties. Authority, both according to the *Sunna* of the orthodox schools and to the *Shīʿa,* is legitimised only when it obeys the judgements of the law.

It is true however that 'the government of Allāh and the government of the Sultan [who was soon no longer identical with the caliph] grew apart', that 'the grandiose dream of a social body operating perpetually under the immutable law which God had revealed in the fullness of time was abandoned' (G.E. von Grunebaum [14.22], p.143). The discrepancy between theory and reality was particularly noticeable in the government of the Islamic empire. From the middle of the tenth century the caliph was only a nominal overlord of a fragmented empire divided up between a number of independent rulers. After the Turkish praetorian guards, the Būyids, Shī'ite condottieri from the Caspian Sea, the conquerors of Western Persia and Iraq, subjected the caliph to their protection and their will; indeed, 'Aḍud al-Dawla (949–983) forced the Commander of the Faithful to crown him as king according to Iranian ceremony (977 or 978). The Ismā'īlī sect of the Shī'a became under the anti-caliphate of the Fāṭimids in North Africa and (from 969) in Egypt a fierce and militant threat to the whole of the Near East. Soon—from the turn of the eleventh century—the nomadic invasion of the Turcomans from Transoxiana to Anatolia ushered in profound social changes. In a period of material threats and political turmoil there arose in the community of Muslims an awareness that the unity and the continuation of the law and thereby the salvation of the believers were to be guaranteed not by the rulers who were locked in power conflicts (whether they were caliphs or the sultans of the invaders) but only by the teachers of the *Sharī'a*, the *'ulamā'*. Only they were viewed as the legitimate preservers of the faith according to the *Sunna*. The rulers also spoke in the name of the *Sunna*, in order to be heard.

The result was a movement which has been called the Sunnī revival—more precisely not a revival but a re-emergence of traditional forces after a long but never dormant activity under the leadership of the Ḥanbalites, a movement which after the decline of the Būyids was also joined by political leaders. The outcome was apparent in the confession which the caliph al-Qādir had publicly proclaimed in the year 1018, a confession directed against the *Shī'a*, against the *Mu'tazila*, but also against the *Ash'ariyya* and therefore against *kalām* altogether. It was a movement of integration uniting different social classes, Arabs and Turks, jurisprudence and mysticism—not, however, without restricting diversity of free intellectual exchange. In the teaching institution of orthodox law, the *madrasa*, a new institution of this movement emerged. In addition to the schools which had long been established in the mosques, whose teachers were appointed by the caliphate or subject to its control, private initiative and endowment founded an increasing number of teaching institutions which were also places to live, in which teachers and pupils were given accommodation and upkeep. The *madrasa* was not a 'university'; the days of the caliph Ma'mūn were over in whose 'house of wisdom' (*bayt al-ḥikma*) philosophy and the sciences were studied and in succession to which, until the tenth century, patrons dedicated libraries and academies to the secular sciences. The *madrasa* was a school of law, of *fiqh*, according to the *madhhab* (doctrine) of the founder—and mostly of one particular *madhhab*, which could be Shāfi'ite, Ḥanbalite and so on—according to his instruction or his caprice (a rapid succession of professors in coveted posts is an eloquent testimony to this). The *madrasa* became the religious and also the political instrument of control in the hands of the orthodox ruling class.

At the same time the teachers of orthodoxy utilised movements of pious awakening in the countryside and anti-authoritarian popular piety in the cities—which had long been in league with Ḥanbalite doctrine. The mysticism of the Ṣūfīs became respectable after it had emerged as an individualistic reaction against authority and collectivity; their teachers—again under the influence of Ḥanbalite traditionalism—linked their doctrine in formal chains of transmission to the ways of early ascetics and pious men. Mystical orders and convents developed under the influence of orthodox missionary zeal into pillars of the *Sunna*. Sectarian and eccentric directions were neutralised in communal life and ritualised worship of God. In the following centuries they acquired also an increasing political and (through wealth from pious foundations) economic importance.

The Turkish sultans also had to make sure of support from the orthodox institutions. When the Seljuq chief Toghrïl had himself crowned sultan (*sulṭān* 'power'—the title itself is a usurpation of the caliphal prerogative) by the caliph of Baghdad, he had legitimised his seizure of power in Baghdad (1055) as Defender of the Faith against its heretical enemies. In their struggle against Christian Byzantium and against the Fāṭimid heretics the Seljuqs showed religious zeal. But that was not all; within their realm they elevated the doctrine of the *Sunna* to a state institution. The number of *madrasas* founded by their viziers—famous above all are the foundations of the Persian vizier, Niẓām al-Mulk (1018–92)—shows that they knew how to use the authority of doctrine as an instrument of political leadership. The Seljuqs were not the 'rescuers' of the caliphate; in reality they remained its lasting rivals. Nor were the Seljuqs the creators of the orthodox movement; but by making it the ideology of their government they assured political stability for it which ensured the intellectual integration of the Islamic world under the banner of the *Sunna*.

(d) The state in the light of legal theory

The last integration of Islamic culture under the leadership of orthodox traditionalism found its highest expression in the work of the jurist and theologian al-Ghazālī (1058–1111, see also p.56). In him scientific logic and mystical piety, philosophical depth and legal pragmatism, strict obedience to the law and dogmatic dialectic were combined. His warning and his advice to abandon everything which did not serve towards salvation appealed to the people of Islam from East to West. God's promise of reward to those who observed the 'true faith' had remained the only assurance of salvation in a political situation which knew Islamic justice under the rule of the most pious person as only a remote ideal. To risk steadfast opposition and militant uprising must have seemed futile in the face of political reality and indeed harmful to the interests of the common weal. Theocracy had already become a fiction of legal scholars. The Sunni tradition became ossified gradually into book knowledge, while the mystical way—which became more and more popular as a retreat and withdrawal in the face of the even greater catastrophe of the Mongol invasion which broke out a century later—degenerated into obscurantism and scholastic theosophy.

It was al-Ghazālī himself who first soberly drew attention to the wretchedness of the political situation. The classical theory of the caliphate, developed under Shāfiʿite lawyers, had recognised two methods by which the ruler could be legitimised as *imām* and by which voluntary homage to him by the Muslims could be justified; either by the consensus of leading teachers of the *Sharīʿa* or by designation through his legitimate predecessor. When, after the decline of the Būyids, and before the Seljuq seizure of power the Baghdad caliphate began once again to hope for a revival of its erstwhile greatness, al-Māwardī (974–1058) once again drew up in a classical treatise 'The Ordinances of Government'. But he already had to pose the question whether the caliph, if 'one of his vassals seizes control of him and usurps the executive power while formally recognising his authority' (*al-Aḥkām al-Sulṭāniyya*, Cairo, 1909, p.16)—this was precisely what the Būyids had done—could still be regarded as the legitimate *imām*. He even had to bear in mind the possibility of an 'emirate by usurpation' (*imārat al-istīlāʾ*) (even if carefully restricted to rebellion in the provinces) and he was forced to concede that only necessity and the interest of the communal good were able to justify the delegation of authority to the usurper. Al-Ghazālī spoke out openly and bluntly in the face of the political reality of Seljuq rule:

> There are those who hold that the Imamate is dead, lacking as it does the required qualifications. But no substitute can be found for it. What then? Are we to give up obeying the law, shall we dismiss the *qāḍīs*, declare all authority to be valueless, cease marrying and pronounce the acts of those in high places to be invalid at all points, leaving the populace to live in sinfulness? Or shall we continue as we are, recognising that the Imamate really exists and that all acts of the administration are valid, given the circumstances of the case and the necessities of the moment?

Faced with a choice between anarchy and inactivity, civil war and bloodshed in futile opposition and the recognition of existing authority:

> the lesser evil is relatively speaking the better, and the reason-

able person must choose the latter possibility'. (*Al-Iqtiṣād bi'l-i'tiqād*, ed. Çubukçu and Atay, Ankara 1962, p.240, trans. G.E. von Grunebaum [14.22], p.168.)

Two centuries later the political situation allowed the lawyers no other alternative but to legally ratify the collapse of the theocratic state:

> As regards the third method (of legitimation, after the other two already mentioned), that by which the allegiance is contracted by compulsion, this arises from the compulsion of the holder of power. At a time when there is no *imām* and an unqualified person seeks the Imamate and compels the people by his power and his armies without any allegiance or succession then his allegiance is validly contracted and obedience to him is obligatory, so as to maintain the unity of the Muslims and preserve agreement among them. This is still so, even if he is barbarous or vicious according to the best opinion. (Badr al-Dīn ibn Jamā'a (1241–1333): *Taḥrīr al-Aḥkām*, ed. H. Kofler in *Islamica* 6, 1934, p.357.)

Even Ibn Khaldūn (1332–1406, a contemporary of the Mongol, Tīmūr), whose practical insight into the social factors of history arouse so much admiration, could not in his grandiose attempt to bring the 'science of civilisation' into the canon of Islamic and philosophical sciences, try anything different from what Islamic lawyers before him had tried: to test the facts of history against the legal ideal of the *Sharī'a* and to warn against the consequences of transgression and despotism.

It is true that the Mamlūk state—under whose authority the above mentioned Ibn Jamā'a worked as chief judge in Cairo and Damascus—installed a successor of the 'Abbāsid family as 'God's vicegerent on earth' in order to present a semblance of legal investiture. In reality they created a monarchy which granted the caliph modest powers only as head of the religious institution, deprived of all real power. The real owners of political authority were the aristocracy of Turkish military slaves (*mamlūk*) from whose number the ruling élite came and which was constantly being replenished from outside by the import of young slaves from the Black Sea and the Caucasus. This aristocracy preferred Jews and Christians at the head of its civil administration and allowed the authority of Arab lawyers to be valid only in the exercise and doctrine of religious law. The Ottomans who in 1516 conquered the Arab east and took over the succession of the Mamlūks followed them in many respects. The Ottoman state too relied on a small ruling class of slaves of the sultan as the officials of the imperial institution (partly recruited by the 'levy of boys', *devshirme*, from amongst the Christian subjects of the Balkans). The Ottoman state also made a distinction between government law (*siyāsa*, codified in the Ottoman *qānūn*) and the *Sharī'a*, and it organised the institutions of the military, of the administration and of religious law (assuring autonomy to every religious community, *millet*) in a wide-ranging and all embracing government system. It was not a puppet caliph but the sultans themselves who took over the title of caliph and of commander of the faithful. But long before the last bearer of this title was deposed (1924) the caliphate as the guarantor of the *Sharī'a* on behalf of all Muslims had become a theoretical fiction.

Yet even today there is current amongst the peoples of Islam the belief that political authority must be legitimised in a religious way. Again and again rigorous, pietistic and fundamentalist movements in Islam have toppled and re-established political power. Whilst pious idealists as well as pragmatists in the East already resigned themselves to the realities of Seljuq power, in the West the Berber Ibn Tūmart (d.1130)—who had perhaps learnt about al-Ghazālī's doctrine in the East—founded the fundamentalist reform movement of the Muwaḥḥidūn ('those who recognise God's unity'), Almohads, who revered him as the promised Mahdī; they fought with spiritual and military weapons against the rigid empty legalism of the Almoravid dynasty and emerged towards the middle of the twelfth century as their successors in Morocco and Spain. The dynasty of the Ṣafavids which conquered Iran at the beginning of the sixteenth century in the name of the Shī'ite Imām emerged from a mystical order there. It was a remarkable repetition of the events in the Near East in the eleventh century in that they accorded the Shī'ite scholarly institution the status of a government authority in order to legitimise themselves (a status which it has recently regained in the Islamic Republic of Iran). As late as the eighteenth century the traditionalism of the Ḥanbalites continued to exert its power in the struggle of Muḥammad ibn 'Abd al-Wahhāb amongst the Bedouin of the Arabian peninsula against the 'heresy' and 'superstitions' of popular religion; and in league with his supporters—the Wahhābīs—the Āl Sa'ūd began their rise to become rulers of Arabia. Even today in the Islamic world, social movements and the struggle for power are clothed in the garb of religion. Contemporary events show Islam to be a religious community which has not yet accepted the split between private belief and secularised public life (a split which is widely accepted in Western society), although it is slowly beginning to realise this painfully and amidst great conflict. Even today, Islam is considered to be a public religion, a community which obeys God's laws in the articles of the faith, professes them in communal worship and makes the government in power responsible for the maintenance of these laws, as well as for the eternal salvation of the believers. Even today, and despite the irretrievable loss of political and spiritual unity, the state and society, civilisation and learning of the Muslim peoples are permeated with this attitude: the quest for the *Civitas Dei*, which through the early conflicts with the religions and cultures of the Hellenistic and Iranian environment fostered the rise and splendour of 'classical' Islam, which afterwards furthered the consolidation of institutions, scholasticism and sclerosis, which in modern times again accompanied the encounter of Islam with the West and its manifold efforts at both reform and restoration, which in the recent past—in the formation of the state of Pakistan, in the overthrow of the state of Iran—has once more proven its political force.

In the social revolution which is gripping the traditional societies of the Islamic east, once again the question of religious legitimacy in government poses itself. How effectively it can be used by the protectors of religious institutions is demonstrated for example in the fall of the Pahlavī dynasty in Iran. But even in places where such legitimacy bears the authority of government—Saudi Arabia, where the Koran is valid as a constitution, is a good example—ineluctable social and economic reforms are undermining traditional society and the traditional foundations of power. There is discussion as to how the foundations of Islam can be interpreted to solve the conflicts of the present. The traditionalism of the old law schools after long ossification could no longer be profitably revived and reused. From the nineteenth century onwards an Islamic modernism has emerged which propagates the spirit, not the letter of the Koran, and seeks to incorporate the legal system of the modern national state, the demands of international trade and the rationalism of enlightened scientific thought into reformed Islam; but it must in the interests of contemporary solutions question the authenticity and validity of the *Sunna* and apply relevant precepts from the Koran to a new society (thus for example, it has used the duty to perform *jihād*, military 'effort' in the cause of Islam, in the service of anti-colonialist nationalism). Here in sharp contrast, often in collaboration with the simple piety of the masses and borne along by malaise of social change, Islamic fundamentalism fights for the establishment of a truly Islamic state on the basis of the *Sharī'a*, calls for a campaign (also called *jihād*) against the satanic forces of secularism inside and outside the Islamic world and denies that there is any separation between religion and politics whether it is in the interest of national or any other pragmatic aims. But it must show itself to be immune to any abuse on the part of ideologists (who have always been clever interpreters of holy scriptures) and demonstrate its ability to solve social questions. If and when the rising flood of secularism reaches the Islamic world, it remains to be seen whether it will obscure the schisms and controversies of the faith—a faith which has become a matter of personal choice, indifferent to the public sphere.

Chapter Four

THE ISLAMIC WORLD: SOCIETY AND ECONOMY

1. Arabia: landscape and history at the beginning of Islam

'We have explained that the cultivated region of that part of the earth which is not covered by water has its centre towards the north, because of the excessive heat in the south and the excessive cold in the north. The north and the south represent opposite extremes of cold and heat. It necessarily follows that there must be a gradual decrease from the extremes toward the centre, which, thus, is moderate. The fourth zone [of the seven climes] is the most temperate cultivated region. The bordering third and fifth zones are rather close to being temperate. The sixth and second zones which are adjacent to them are far from temperate, and the first and seventh zones still less so. Therefore, the sciences, the crafts, the buildings, the clothing, the foodstuffs, the fruits, even the animals, and everything that comes into being in the three middle zones are distinguished by their temperate (well-proportioned) character. The human inhabitants of these zones are more temperate (well-proportioned) in their bodies, colour, character qualities and (general) conditions and religions, even including the various (manifestations of) prophecy that are mostly to be found there, in as much as no historical information about prophetic missions in the southern and northern zones has come to our notice. This is because only those representatives of the (human) species who have the most perfect physique and character are distinguished by prophets and messengers. The Qur'ān says (sura 3, v.110), "You are the best group (ever) produced for mankind". The purpose of this is to have the divine message of the prophets fully accepted . . . The (foregoing statement) is not contradicted by the existence of the Yemen, the Ḥaḍramawt, al-Aḥqāf, the Ḥijāz, the Yamāma, and adjacent regions of the Arabian Peninsula in the first and second zones. As we have mentioned, the Arabian Peninsula is surrounded by the sea on three sides. The humidity (of the sea) influences the humidity in the air (of the Arabian Peninsula). This diminishes the dryness and intemperance that (otherwise) the heat would cause. Because of the humidity from the sea, the Arabian Peninsula is to some degree temperate.' (Ibn Khaldūn (1332–1406): *al-Muqaddima*, tr. F. Rosenthal [33,81], vol. 1, p. 167; n. 214, p. 169.)

Throughout history the earth's form and climate have exercised an influence on human behaviour. Decisive moments of Islamic history have left inextinguishable traces on the face of the earth; landscape and settlement in the East have experienced fundamental changes through the Arab conquests and the expansion of Islam. Conversely, the demands of the landscape have influenced the culture of Islam—its material and spiritual culture: the necessities of life in the dry belt of the Ancient World, the great deserts from the Arabian peninsula to central Asia on the one hand and as far as the Atlantic Sahara on the other, the zones of uncertain equilibrium between sedentary people and nomads, dominated by urban centers in the middle of regions of agricultural settlement. But what sort of relationship is there between landscape and history? Ibn Khaldūn, whose work was quoted at the beginning, was probably the first to see such a relationship, influenced as he was by the historical experience of his North African homeland. Recently his ideas have been re-examined in a penetrating analysis of Islamic anthropogeography: Xavier de Planhol [40.03] found a 'general mechanism of interaction between religion and landscape' which he illustrated by pointing to the 'evident affinity' of Islam with processes of nomadisation. But regional differences and historical diversity in the Islamic world make the historian hesitant to propose rapid generalisations. Only gradually from the great wealth of unexploited sources do the outlines of decisive periods, and the individuality of different regions become sharper. The 'Islamic world'—a concept which already contains a generalisation—has many faces.

The arena for the emergence of Islam was not the desert of the Arabian camel nomads, the Bedouin, but an oasis of the Ḥijāz, the stretch of land on the eastern slope of the chain of mountains above the Red Sea on the North West coast of the Arabian Peninsula. The city of Mecca was one of the natural stopping places on the 'incense route' which followed the valleys of southern Arabia to Syria. Its emergence into a flourishing trading entrepôt in the course of the sixth century AD was the consequence of the economic decline and political collapse of south Arabia—the *Arabia Felix* of the ancient world. The bursting of the great Ma'rib dam (around 570), viewed by the Islamic theology of history as a sign of God's punishment, put an end in spectacular fashion to the ancient high culture of the Yemen. Around the same time the Prophet Muḥammad was born. South Arabia had fallen under Iranian and then under Abyssinian hegemony (Abyssinia was subject to Byzantine control): the Quraysh, the tribe of the rulers of Mecca, entered into the political game of the great powers. With the decline of Persia and its Arab vassals in Iraq the power of the tribes in the north and west of the peninsula grew. The status of the shrine of the Meccan goddesses and the periods of truce during the sacred months stabilised economic prosperity for those who dealt in commerce; at the same time the sacred area became a refuge for the homeless and the persecuted from the Bedouin tribes of Arabia and the surrounding settled area. Marriages between members of the Quraysh and immigrants from different tribes reflected the gradual integration of the immigrants under the traditional leadership of the Meccan aristocracy; but social conflicts were also a result. The ethical norms and legal concepts of the old 'tribal humanism' (W.M. Watt), based as they were on absolute solidarity and strict manly virtue, collapsed in the face of the burgeoning individualism of merchants and traders in families which had become sedentary. The economy around the shrine flourished; but its goddesses became mere figures in a new mixed society of Arabs of different origins, of immigrant Jews and Christians.

The message which Muḥammad experienced as a revelation gave an answer to the moral and social problems of his environment by providing a new religious orientation. The exhortation to care for the poor and the orphans is not the only nor indeed the prime concern of the oldest parts of the Koran but it is nevertheless a crucial part. The way for Muḥammad and his young community to go to Medina (the oasis Yathrib 400 kilometres north of Mecca, which was later called 'the city of the Prophet') was prepared by conflicts in a society in transition: blood revenge was a force for order in the desert where an overall authority was lacking; but amongst sedentary people who could not avoid the vicious circle of revenge and further vengeance, it led—exacerbated by daily problems of subsistence—to self-destructive civil war. In his political leadership Muḥammad revealed talent and willpower and he regulated the law of blood vengeance in a way which was all embracing and adapted to the new circumstances (but not by abrogating it); furthermore, he made the law of marriage and inheritance the basis of a new 'urban' form of family. He also brought to his community unity of faith in the one God whose Revelation he had received—a unity which stood above tribal solidarity and which abrogated it when necessary. The consequences are well known: a century after the *Hijra*, the emigration of Muḥammad from Mecca to Medina, Arab armies had conquered territory from the Atlantic to the Indus for Islam.

2. *Bedouins and sedentary peoples*

'Because of their savagery, the Arabs are the least willing of nations to subordinate themselves to each other, as they are rude, proud, ambitious, and eager to be the leader. Their individual aspirations rarely coincide. But when there is religion (among them) through prophecy or sainthood, then they have some restraining influence in themselves. The qualities of haughtiness and jealousy leave them. It is, then, easy for them to subordinate themselves and to unite (as a social organisation).'

'When there is a ruler in the city, the submissiveness and obedience (of the Bedouins) is the result of the superiority of the ruler. When there is no ruler in the city, some political leadership and control by some of the inhabitants over the remainder must, of necessity, exist in it. If not, the civilisation of the city would be wiped out. Such a leader makes (the Bedouins) obey him and exert themselves on behalf of his interests. He does so either by persuasion, in that he distributes money among them and lets them have the necessities they need from his city, which enables their civilisation to subsist; or, if he has the power to do so, he forces them to obey him, even if he has to cause discord among them so as to get the support of one party, with the help of which he will then be able to overcome the remainder and thus force the others to obey him, since they fear the decay of their civilisation as the result of the unstable situation.' (Ibn Khaldūn: *al-Muqaddima,* tr. F. Rosenthal, vol. 1, p. 305, 309.)

It was not only in the early period of Islam but repeatedly at turning points of its history that migrations of people, periods of nomadic expansion from the steppe, changed the historical map; but regularly—though not to such an extent—it was also changed by the unifying force of religious movements. The strength of pietist reform and heterodox sects in the eleventh century united the Ṣanhāja Berbers south of the Atlas under the Almoravids, around 1500 united the Turcomans of Ādkarbāyjān under the Ṣafavids, and once again in the middle of the eighteenth century in Arabia the Wahhābīs under the leadership of the Āl Saʿūd. It is true that more profound causes for nomadic movements—from the Arab conquests to the catastrophic Mongol invasions of the thirteenth and fifteenth centuries—can be found in ecological and economic changes. Reference has been made to the periodic overflow of nomadic population which 'generates people like locusts regularly and unremittingly' (J. Weulersse, as quoted by X. de Planhol [40.03], p. 14). Some researchers (as for example the Orientalist Leone Caetani and also Arnold Toynbee) have attributed the first expansion of Islam to climatic changes in the peninsula, which caused a search for new pastureland. But the unification of the conquering tribes and the consolidation of the conquests into a permanent state were achieved under the rule of urban centres, centres of religiously legitimated authority, places of common public prayer, focal points of the dynastic exercise of power. Nomads were the conquerors of the Islamic empire but Islamic culture—as were ancient oriental cultures before it—is a culture of cities. The radius of its influence is limited, and at times endangered; for nomadic life is no more economically self-sufficient than agricultural society, nor is it completely dependent: *badw*—the steppe—and *ḥaḍar*—the zone of cultivated land and settlement—live in ancient symbiosis.

The way of life of the Bedouin, the specifically Arab form of camel nomadism, developed in the last centuries before Islam in the NW border areas of the peninsula, in contact with the urban culture of Syria. Constant attacks and assaults on the territory of the sedentary people were a basic part of this way of life; strong tribal unity, given visible shape by genealogy, and the sanction of blood vengeance afforded it the necessary inner cohesion. The lack of respect of the Bedouin vis-à-vis the sedentary peoples was a basic tenet of Bedouin self-awareness, of tribal pride (*fakhr*); and it acquired a mythological character in the accounts of the feuds of the ancient Arabs. This was all the more possible as the ideals of Bedouin life were still preserved in glorified memory by the sedentary Arabs in the old and new centres of Islamic power. For this reason the pattern of 'natural' hostility between the Bedouin and the cities should not be used too sweepingly as a generalisation and it should not be brought out as an explanation of very disparate historical phenomena. Ibn Khaldūn first made it one of the bases of his interpretation of the great movements of Islamic history; but when he speaks of the Bedouin—especially in respect of the North African situation with which he is familiar—he means all those groups of people who were far away from the city and its direct control, nomads as well as farmers (Bedouin and fellahs). In both groups there were nuclei of rebellion and centres of opposition, sustained by anti-authoritarian solidarity (Ibn Khaldūn's *'aṣabiyya*).

There were indeed hotbeds of insubordination and rebellion both amongst the nomadic tribal confederations and in areas of peasant unrest, especially in inaccessible mountainous regions. Such insurrections were often fostered by heretical movements and the dynasty in power had to know how to play off centrifugal forces against each other. This was not always successful; often equilibrium between urban dynasties and the areas of rebellion was only tenuous. Until quite recently the history of Morocco has been characterised by frequent conflict between areas under the control of urban government (*bilād al-makhzan*, 'the land of government treasury', that area subject to taxation by the ruling dynasty) and the 'land of rebellion' (*bilād al-sā'iba, sība*), in this case Berber tribes from the mountain areas. The situation of the Baghdad caliphate towards the middle of the eleventh century, before the fall of the Iranian Būyids and the seizure of power by the Turkish Seljuqs, provides an earlier historical example. The caliphate was almost impotent in the hands of a Shī'ite confederation of Arab Bedouins, the attacks of the Turcomans and the depredations of retreating Kurdish tribes. The orbit of dynastic control was always limited. It could, if means were available, be secured and extended by military and at the same time missionary operations on the frontiers. These outposts of the faith far away from the metropolis became centres of military and religious activity and by gaining both in strength and autonomy, threatened to endanger the dynasty or indeed fundamentally destroy it. The Almoravids, the Berber leaders who took the Maghrib and Islamic Spain in the eleventh century, came from the cloister-like garrisons (Arabic *ribāṭ*, hence the name al-Murābiṭūn, Spanish Almorávides) in the border region towards the Sahara. In the Iranian east and in Turkestan the *ghāzīs*, the fighters for the faith on the borders of Islam (amongst whom there were numerous converted Turcomans) also formed an element of separatism.

Because it was not always possible for declining dynasties to maintain an equilibrium between different forces, phases of Bedouinisation occurred during periods of great upheaval in oriental history. Pre-Islamic Arabia had also undergone such a process. Great waves of nomadic expansion led to the devastation of whole areas: in his chronicle, Ibn Khaldūn speaks of the ravaging 'swarms of locusts' of the Banū Hilāl in North Africa. Having first moved towards Egypt they were then, in the middle of the eleventh century, unleashed on Ifrīqiyya by the Fāṭimid caliphs of Cairo who intended thereby to punish the insubordinate Zīrids. The invasions of Turkish tribes from central Asia into Iran and Anatolia from the eleventh century, and finally the Mongol invasion, as a consequence of which Turkish nomads overran Iranian territory, were in the long run no less portentous. The way in which the expansion of the Turcomans was consolidated politically, not only by military force on the part of the rulers of the Seljuqs and the Īlkhāns but also in the long term by cultural assimilation and the religious legitimisation of their ruling class, is one of the most instructive chapters of Islamic history.

These events were important not only because of the devastations of the advancing armies bringing pillage, arson and murder in their wake; they were still more momentous because the ruined peasantry was forced to revert to nomadism, because migrant tribes who had immigrated or who had long been near at hand took over old agricultural land. The extent of this development is in many places still perceptible today; not only in the wide expanse of the territory occupied by the Turkish nomads in Iran and Anatolia but also in the expansion of Arab Bedouin into the Mesopotamian border zones of the Arabian peninsula. It is true that many Bedouin tribes there—as had already happened before in pre-Islamic times—became sedentary or semi-sedentary, dependent economically on agriculture. But even today the colloquial Arabic of Iraq bears the imprint of the dialects of the Bedouin, who—after the 'classical' period of urbanisation in the first Islamic centuries—as a result of the decline of central power and definitively after the fall of the ʿAbbāsids in Baghdad (1258) were able to penetrate unhindered into the settled territory and were even settled by the Ottoman government in the towns. Remnants of the old sedentary dialects have survived only in the NW border areas, in upper Mesopotamia and Anatolia and in the Jewish and Christian urban population of the south.

In spite of social adaptation and strong discipline, Arab tribalism remained until the late Ottoman period a force of unrest and opposition against those who tried to govern it. Skilfully bolstered up by the European powers, and especially by Britain—not always in the best interests of agriculturalism, when it fell under the sway of powerful tribal leaders—it allied itself with the nationalism of urban intellectuals in the struggle for national independence. Now as ever, the tribal aristocracy of the tribes in places where it has survived—notably in the monarchies of Morocco, Saudi Arabia and Jordan—remains, beside government power and the urban élite, as a very significant third force.

3. Agricultural economy, taxation and land tenure

Nomadism is at home in the steppes; but the basis of oriental economy was agricultural and that remained so under Islam too. The Arab conquerors made no changes in this respect; they did not disturb agriculture overall since they did not allow Bedouinisation of the conquered territories. Arab tribes, which were in Syria and Mesopotamia even before Islam, had moved over to sedentary farming. They submitted not unwillingly to their fellow Arabs and held on to their land with a lighter burden of taxation (the tithe, the alms tax of the Muslims laid down by the Koran). The land too remained in the care of the local farmers; the old territories of the Persian landed aristocracy, the *dihqāns,* also remained—although locked up legally as foundations (*waqf*) at the disposal of the Islamic community—under their care on payment of the land tax (*kharāj*). The former crown land of the Sasanians and the land which had otherwise become ownerless reverted to the Islamic community, the *umma,* but was handed out in 'allotments' (*qaṭāʾiʿ*) to be cultivated by Arab Muslims, who in return for it had to pay the Koranic tithe (*zakāt*). The land tax was therefore at first a tax on the yield from the conquered land which was in the possession of non-Muslims (who also had to pay the poll tax, *jizya*). At the end of the great conquests which brought in great amounts of booty in money and in property, the land tax became the most important source of income for the state; as the land tax was more than the tithe, increasing conversion in the early Umayyad period began to create financial problems for the government exchequer, and above all for the military budget of the central government. These problems combined and were exacerbated by the results of social change: the abrogation of the previous feudal system and of rural slavery freed farmers from being tied to the land and to feudal service for the *dihqāns* or other landowners in Iraq, in Syria and in Egypt.

The more unwillingly the newly converted Muslims were granted exemption from paying the land tax, the more they made use of their freedom of movement. An increasing emigration from the countryside to the rich garrison towns began, where the non-Arab Muslims as clients, *mawālī*, of Arab families vied with the Arabs for social advancement in an urban society. As a counter-move, Arab tribal leaders, the *ashrāf*, seized the empty land and acquired more and more large estates on which they paid only the tithe. The reaction of the Umayyads—in Iraq initiated by the governor al-Ḥajjāj ibn Yūsuf, the dreaded governor of the caliph 'Abd al-Malik, and the architect of the government organisation in the east—was to take measures which were directed at both the *mawālī* and the *ashrāf*. Emigration from the land was curbed and the land—whether it was in the hands of Muslims or unbelievers—was made overall liable to the *kharāj*. The disturbances and rebellions which arose as a reaction to this (amongst which was the serious revolt of Ibn al-Ash'ath in Iraq (701)) could call on the unambiguous injunctions of the Koran, which were, it is true, issued in different circumstances; here too the roots of the reproaches made against the godless rule of the Umayyads can be found. The far-sighted 'Umar II attempted to introduce an egalitarian reform of the land tax and sought by defining cultivated land as the collective property of the Islamic community to place *kharāj* taxation on a Koranic footing and thereby to create unified and stable practice. But he was not able in his all too short period of rule (717–20) to carry out any far-reaching changes. Social differences grew and led to ever increasing tensions not only between Arabs and *mawālī* but also amongst Arabs themselves, between the aristocracy who owned the land and the landless settlers. Militant opposition, frequently established by religious criticism and supported by religious opposition parties (above all the Shī'a, as for example in the rebellion of Zayd ibn 'Alī ibn al-Ḥusayn in 740) undermined the authority of the caliphate of Damascus. Only the 'Abbāsids who were brought to power by rebellious forces in Khurāsān (749) could take into account the transition from an Arab tribal economy to an agrarian society by the creation of a uniform system of land taxation.

The flowering of agriculture in the great period of the 'Abbāsid caliphate is closely linked with the rise of urban economy and foreign trade. Increasing demand led to a stepping up of yield through intensive cultivation and not by the development of hitherto marginal areas for cultivation. The reclamation of the great salt marshes in the delta region of southern Mesopotamia around Baṣra is a famous example, as indeed it is also an example of the fateful abuse of power by the landowners: their negro slaves who had been imported in hundreds of thousands from Africa, the Zanj, organised in 869 a dangerous rebellion and defended an independent state south of Baṣra for around 15 years.

At the same time the power and authority of the Baghdad caliphate began to wane. From the middle of the tenth century *de facto* foreign—Iranian, and then from the eleventh century Turkish—princes ruled in Iraq, and finally in the whole of the Near East. They imposed momentous change on state finances by the introduction of military land tenure: the payment of the army by investiture of the land tax from state-owned land (Arabic *iqṭāʿ*).

In its basic form the *iqṭāʿ*, 'the allotting of the tax income of a piece of land (*qaṭīʿa*) belonging to the state' as a lease to civil and also military licensees was nothing new. The licensee received the land tax (*kharāj*) of a territory; the treasury took from that only the tithe, *inter alia* to cover the costs of the military budget. But the more the increasing influence and independence of the amirs hindered the collection of legitimate taxes from military feudal landowners, the more difficult the situation of the government budget became. When the Būyids, the dynasty of condottieri from Daylam on the Caspian Sea took over power in Baghdad (945), they made a doubtful virtue of necessity: they made direct use of the *iqṭāʿ* to pay the standing army by giving out feudal estates in return for military service. With the extension of the *iqṭāʿ* under the Seljuqs in Iran and Iraq from the eleventh century and under the Ayyūbids in Egypt (second half of the twelfth century) the military land tenure system became the main form of bestowing state-owned land and it remained so under the successor dynasties in Iran (the Mongol Īlkhāns) and in the Near East. The Mamlūk sultans (thirteenth–fifteenth century) in Egypt and Syria made the system the basis of their government while at the same time trying to strengthen the economic autonomy of the ruler by reforms of the land register and by extending crown land. The *tīmār* ('caretakership') of the Ottoman empire is a comparable institution probably also based on Byzantine precedents, and is of comparable importance. In addition, other forms of property allocation were introduced which were more profitable to the exchequer, above all in the Anatolian and Arab provinces: trusteeship (*emanet*), the holder of which had to hand over to the exchequer the income which accrued to them from it while he himself was paid from the treasury, and (increasingly from the sixteenth century) tax farming (*iltizām*).

The transformation of state property into military land tenure assured the letter of Islamic law: the land remained legally the property of the state; the powers entrusted to the licensee were made over to him only temporarily and were restricted to the collection of the income according to the amount and duration of military service. The *iqṭāʿ* therefore did not lead to the formation of a hereditary land-owning military aristocracy. Islamic 'feudalism' is fundamentally different in that respect from European land tenure. It was always only a part—at times of strong dynastic control only a small part—of the government land which was handed over to licensees.

However, the *de facto* founding of the state on a military hierarchy and the financing of the military budget by allotment of the land tax had immediate and also wide-ranging consequences over the centuries for the economy of the Islamic countries. The economy in the period of ʿAbbāsid prosperity had flourished in a blending of government and private initiative, agrarian economy, handicrafts, trade and international traffic in both goods and capital. The new rulers, the Daylamite generals, the Turcoman tribal chiefs and their successors were alien to this economy and its demands. Trade regressed; the monetary economy declined and was replaced by a predominantly natural economy. Finally, agriculture also suffered severe damage not only through the invasion of Turkish nomads from the eleventh to the fifteenth century but also through the shortcomings of the system. The military, and above all its impoverished lower ranks were only interested in the collecting of the revenue, and were not ready or in a position to make long-term investments. Moreover, as the establishment of a theoretical tax evaluation (*ʿibra*) of territories for years in advance did not take account of vacillations in the produce from the harvest, the fellahs were subjected to increasingly unrealisable demands on the part of powerful landlords and subordinate tenants. Only a strong administration could deal with abuses, but had to represent the interests of the exchequer in the evaluation of the land and the allocation of domains. The decline of state power and government led on the one hand to hereditary ownership of fiefs which was not subject to control, and on the other hand by exploiting both people and nature to the ruin of agriculture and the extension of nomadism. This process repeated itself in the periods of Būyid, Mamlūk and Mongol (Ilkhān) decline; the disintegration of the Ottoman empire in the eighteenth and nineteenth centuries was also accompanied by attempts at reform and peasant uprising in the provinces.

In comparison with feudal estates and inalienable government lands, freehold private ownership of land (*milk*) played from early times only a subordinate role. Nevertheless, goods from ownership or usufruct which were endowed as pious foundations (*waqf*, in Egypt and North Africa *ḥabs, ḥubus*) for religious and communal establishments—mosques, *madrasas*, hospices, convents of Ṣūfī orders, frequently also for the use of the family of the founder, played an important economic role. It was not always possible for *waqf* property to escape control and illegal seizure by the state, and mismanagement by corrupt tenants. For all that, the development of the Ṣūfī orders into numerous and authoritative institutions brought about—notably in the Ottoman empire—a concentration of important *waqf* lands outside government and military control which were organised as a profit-making concern by the *darvīsh*s in just the same way as the domains of urban landowners and tenants. Apart from phases of transition under nomadic rule, the institutions and executive bodies of political autonomy and fiscal government were always concentrated in urban centres. The landowners lived in the cities: as for example the land-owning aristocracy of the Umayyad period, and most of the tenants of the ʿAbbāsid domains. The garrisons of soldiers paid out of rural *iqṭāʿs* were stationed in the cities; and the religious institutions which were the beneficiaries of pious foundations were also centred in the cities. Agriculture in rural settled areas always remained under the direct or indirect control of urban rulers. For that reason the peasantry were seldom very active in the political history of the Islamic countries. But here too there were movements of opposition against the authority and oppression of the cities. The rebellion of the Zanj, the negro slaves of the Iraqi estates, has already been mentioned. The sects of the Shīʿa, who promised a just Imām and a kingdom of justice at the end of time, gained a foothold in the town and the countryside; but whilst in the cities of Iraq and Iran, Shīʿites of the 'Twelver' persuasion, estranged from the ʿAbbāsid caliphate, were content with the quiet expectation of the coming of their Imām, the 'radical' element of the Ismāʿīliyya fomented a militant messianic movement in favour of their Imām (who was also in occultation), amongst the rural population of Southern Iraq and in the villages of Northern Iran and Khurāsān. This propaganda presented no small threat to the disintegrating caliphal empire and—intensified by the Bedouin in Baḥrayn and carried by the Fāṭimids to North Africa and Egypt—it had important repercussions. Rebellion arose also against the ruthless exploitation of military land tenure; it could even, as in the rebellions of the fourteenth century against the Mamlūk state of Egypt, bring about a temporary alliance between the fellahs and the Bedouin.

The hegemony of urban landowners over the countryside is the basis of a system which in modern social geography (according to Hans Bobek [40.01]) is called 'rent capitalism'. This concept was derived from an observation of modern developments in the Near East; it has recently been applied also to the circumstances of land law in earlier periods of Islam, but the phenomenon is too complex and has not yet been researched in enough detail to fully justify such a generalisation. It is indisputable that we can already trace the historical conditions of this system in the land tenure system of the Iranian and Turkish military dynasties; this was also a form of economic exploitation of the countryside by the city and it could by misuse lead to an oppressive dependency of village economy on the landlords or on their tenants. Since the Ottoman period we can really observe the characteristics of rent capitalism: the urban landlord creams off the proceeds ('ground rent'); he restricts investments, however, to an amount barely sufficient to maintain productivity and gives the fellahs a share in the harvest which only just achieves the minimum necessary for existence; the peasant pays for the cost of the means of production (land, water, seed, equipment and draught cattle)—especially after years of drought and natural catastrophes—by increased servitude or by the appropriation of the land by urban investors. But this is the culmination of a 700-year-old development: at the outset—in the Būyid period—the relationship of the fief owner with his land was not essentially a commercial one but was restricted to executive care on behalf of government fiscal authority.

'Officers who hold assignments (*iqṭā'*) must know that they have no authority over the peasants except to take from them—and that with courtesy—the due amount of revenue which has been assigned to them to collect': so wrote Niẓām al-Mulk, the Iranian vizier and administrator of the great Seljuqs, in the year 1092 (*Siyāsatnāma*, trans. from the Persian by Hubert Darke. London, 1978, p.32). These conditions were not always contravened, but weakness and decline of centralised control led to abuses, and then heredity of tenure and the transfer to private ownership—against the true principles of Islamic land law—paved the way for 'rent capitalism'. But this did not always happen either in a uniform way or at the same time; and if one wanted to attribute this process to a specifically 'Islamic' combination of natural circumstances, society and economy, it would be difficult to prove.

4. Urban society and economy

The exodus of the Arab Bedouin from the peninsula began Islamic history; but the history of the institutions and culture of Islam was the history of its cities. The leaders of the conquests were the Quraysh of Mecca, experienced politicians and experts in foreign trade (S.D. Goitein [60.02], p.227: 'a victory of business executives over professional generals'); Medina 'the city of the Prophet', was the first Islamic metropolis before it was ousted by Damascus, the old capital of Syria. But other cities of the pre-Islamic, Hellenistic and Iranian east also continued to play a leading role; many ceded to new urban centres of Islamic administration. These were in the first place the garrisons of the conquering armies: for example Baṣra and Kūfa in Iraq—from which the north and east of Iran was conquered and governed—and Fusṭāṭ in Egypt. Later, the foundation of Islamic cities marked important turning points in history: Baghdad, the capital of the ʿAbbāsid caliphate (built in the year 763 by al-Manṣūr) in its siting—near Babylon and Seleucia (Ctesiphon), in a central position between the east and the west of the empire—and in its layout—the Round City, in the centre of which is the palace of the caliph—is in both respects the symbol of an imperial design. Three centuries later, after their conquest of Egypt, the Fāṭimids founded Cairo (al-Qāhira 'the victorious') near the old Fusṭāṭ as the capital of the Ismāʿīlī anti-caliphate. The Mongol rulers of Iran, the Īlkhāns, built their capital Sulṭāniyya (near Qazwīn, founded in 1307) as a symbol of the apogee of their power in close symbiosis with the pastoral economy.

The cities of Islam—as was already the case with the old centres of culture in the Orient—became centres of dynastic power and control, centres of spiritual authority, places of economic production and trade, the repositories of science and literature. There was continuity with the pre-Islamic city also in the external appearance of its Islamic counterpart; the seat of the ruler or of his representative was its central point, and his troops guarded the surrounding walls and their gates. This corresponded to the political status of the cities: they were not autonomous and self governing; their inhabitants were not 'citizens' in the narrower sense of the word which evolved in medieval Europe, members of an urban community with special legal status. They were rather members of the Islamic community (the *Umma*); they were therefore at the same time 'protected subjects' (literally 'flock': *raʿāyā*, Ottoman Turkish *râya*), often directly dependent economically on the sovereign, who safeguarded God's law.

The mosque and the market, the focal points of religious and economic life, were under the religious authority and political supervision of the theocratic ruler. The spiritual focus of the city was the Friday mosque (*jāmiʿ*), the 'cathedral' mosque, in relation to the other mosques (*masjid*) the place of communal public worship, which the sovereign himself or another delegated *imām* led as his deputy. The mosque was also the place where the legal schools carried out their teaching and frequently where they pronounced legal decisions (*fatwā* of the *muftī*), as well as being a social centre, similar in function to the Greek agora and often situated in its place. The centre of urban commercial activities was the market (Arabic *sūq*, Persian b*āzār*)—which had often grown up around the 'great' Friday mosque, whose handicrafts and retail trade formed the basis of urban economy, always divided into branches of trade (but only very much later officially organised into 'guilds'). The market took part in long-distance trade whose stages were the guest houses and warehouses (*khān*) on the outskirts and the caravanserais on the trade routes. Here too the government intervened; administratively through the *ḥisba*, the supervision of trade and public conduct, economically as the employer and the owner of monopolies in certain spheres.

The 'vertical' social structure had its parallels and precedents in the East and also in early Europe. A striking phenomenon of the Islamic city was its 'horizontal' division into ethnic, religious and professional groups, which is clearly apparent in circumscribed quarters. The Islamic city had no regular network of streets, which allowed direct access to all points (except where traces of a Hellenistic city plan have been preserved, as for example in the Seleucid ground plan of the old city of Aleppo); it was an agglomeration of units, living quarters, around a few through roads, accessible at times only at specific points, often only through a gate which could be closed and which led to a labyrinth of blind alleys. There has been talk of the social fragmentation of the Islamic city; its roots stretch far back in history.

The Christian and Jewish population in the ancient and also in the newly flourishing cities preserved from the beginning a narrow social and local identity. Islamic law placed the *dhimmīs*, the 'People of the Book' (*ahl al-kitāb*) of earlier revealed religions, under the protection (*dhimma*) of the Islamic *Umma*, if they recognised its authority. The Zoroastrians, numerous in early Islamic Iraq and southern Iran, were also treated in the same way. (The Ottoman empire institutionalised this practice: every religious community, *millet*, preserved the right to self-autonomy and jurisdiction under its own leader.) As the *dhimmīs* had to undergo no specific restrictions in religious worship (only in its outward expression, such as processions and the use of bells) and no special burdens—the poll tax (*jizya*) levied on the *dhimmīs* was not usually more onerous than the alms tax (*zakāt*) of the Muslims—conditions were laid down which led to tolerant co-existence for centuries. Reprisals and persecution under the banner of orthodox or sectarian zeal or in times of war with Christian powers were the exception. It is true that opportunities for social advancement for non-Muslims were limited. In the early period of the Islamic empire the indigenous officials kept their jobs in the existing government machine; but the subsequent Arabisation and Islamicisation of the chancery and economy deprived them of their offices. Experts were, however, still in demand. Even in Mamlūk Egypt Copts were still in important positions in the civil administration. The ancient scientific tradition of Hellenism was transferred to the Arabs by

Christians and Jews; and long after the acceptance and active continuation of this inheritance within Islam, Christian and Jewish doctors enjoyed a prestige which was seldom accorded to their Muslim colleagues.

As usury was forbidden to the Muslims, people of other faiths dominated the money market (as well as the trade in wine); but most *dhimmīs* lived as artisans. Conversion to Islam decimated their number; the death penalty was exacted on Muslims who apostatised. The old popular languages of the Christian east—Aramaic and Coptic—were ousted by Arabic. But the religious minorities always remained sharply divided from their environment; even today in the old cities of the Islamic world the quarters of the Jews and the Christians are clearly delineated entities in which special dialects distinct from those of the Muslim environment have been preserved.

Muslims, on the other hand, formed no uniform group. The history of urban settlement reflects the ethnic multiplicity of Islamic society which never totally coalesced into a unified whole. The different tribes of the Arab armies of conquest were settled in separate quarters, which formed administrative units for collective payment and taxation. Old tribal affiliations and conflicts lived on after colonisation. Merit and status in the cause of Islam, recorded in the army list (the *Dīwān*) of the caliph ʿUmar, guaranteed to the descendants of the Prophet's companions and the participants in the great campaigns shares in the booty and permanent pensions. Their leaders, the 'nobles' (*ashrāf*) of the tribes, became the first—transient—urban aristocracy of Islam, the leaders of the armies, the possessors of the highest offices, and of the increasing number of large estates (see p.83). But the Koran said nothing about privileges and prerogatives which differentiated between Muslims. It was not only the Arabs who had come too late and too recently, the new settlers in the countryside and in the towns, who were dissatisfied; it was also the newly converted Muslims from other nations who demanded equal rights.

The consequences of the conflict about land and taxation laws have already been mentioned; they led in the Umayyad period to an increasing emigration from the countryside to the towns. Prisoners of war who were freed after conversion as well as an increasing number of those who sought profit and material security through conversion, attached themselves as *mawālī*, 'clients'—an old Arab legal practice—to Arab families. Their number and also their political influence grew. Amongst the *mawālī* were the landed nobility in Iran, the *dihqāns*, the Byzantine patrikioi, the upper échélon of the old administration, the élite in both birth and education. They participated in the expansion and defence of the faith–*mawālī* were amongst the founders of *kalām*, theological discourse—and they sought equal rank and the highest positions.

Theory favoured these efforts. Tensions in society, tensions also amongst the Arabs themselves, caused the jurists to propagate the Islamic justice of the earliest community—a community of equals under God's law. The ʿAbbāsids, whose revolution settled these tensions, adopted this principle as part of their programme. Under their régime the emergence of the Iranian *mawālī*—the ʿAbbāsids had indeed begun their advance from Iran—in the bureaucracy and in all spheres of economic and spiritual life began. The 'peoples' (Arabic *shuʿūb*, hence *Shuʿūbiyya*, the term used for their movement of literary rivalry) competed with the Arabs for supremacy in religious and secular sciences, in literature and in music. But Arabic remained the medium for their efforts too.

The rise of the *mawālī* and the destruction of ethnic constraints went hand in hand with the emergence of new social hierarchies. It is true that the descendants of the Prophet's family remained especially respected amongst Arab families, but they were only a part and, with the exception of the caliph's family, not the most important part of the new élite. With the help of a ruling class of Arab as well as Persian, Aramaic and Greek origin and education, the great caliphs of the ʿAbbāsids—al-Manṣūr, al-Rashīd, al-Ma'mūn—based their supremacy and their authority on Iranian ideas of government and Hellenistic rationalism. But the élite of the urban society did not only comprise the ruling class of 'secretaries' (*kuttāb*) and jurists; it was neither an aristocracy of birth or possessions nor a professional clique. As well as administrators and lawyers of the theocracy, there was the intelligentsia of the aspiring bourgeoisie, of the mercantile, commercial and artisan classes, the proponents of a flourishing international economy who also knew how to acquire competence in cultivated speech, theological dispute and literary contest and thereby to hold their own with the upper class.

The basis of the prosperity and the variety of the economy and therefore of the well-being of the élite, of the 'special people' (*khāṣṣa*), was the work force of the 'common people' (*ʿāmma*), the small craftsmen and shopkeepers, who looked after mass production and the distribution of goods; at the end of the social scale there were the despised and rejected elements—the debit side socially of the prosperity—the growing mass of hired workers (above all in the complex hierarchy of the textile industry) and the down and outs. An army of house slaves was as natural to the Islamic Middle Ages as it had been to classical antiquity.

The economy of the oriental city was based on agricultural production and the financial yields of the agrarian environment. The countryside did not only provide the daily requirements and the raw materials for subsistence; it was also a source of taxation for the state, for its administration, its tenants, its civil and—above all from the Seljuq period onwards—military fief-holders. Times of good yield and efficient central government created mercantile power and promoted thereby a market economy and traffic in commodities:

> It should be known that all markets cater to the needs of people. Some of these needs are necessities, foodstuffs, for instance, such as wheat and barley; corresponding foods, such as beans, chick-peas, and other edible grains; and wholesome foods such as onions, garlic, and the like. Other things are conveniences or luxuries, such as seasonings, fruits, clothes, utensils, mounts, all the crafts, and buildings. When a city is highly developed and has many inhabitants, the prices of necessary foodstuffs and corresponding items are low, and the prices for luxuries, such as seasonings, fruits, and the things that go with them, are high. When the inhabitants of a city are few and its civilization weak, the opposite is the case. (Ibn Khaldūn (1332–1406), *al-Muqaddima,* trans. F. Rosenthal, vol. II, p. 111.)

With the growth and the prosperity of the cities, handicrafts and individual trades, the basis of their own economic activity, flourished. The centre of this was the market in the centre of the city. Its organisation had remained constant over centuries and can be seen in its outlines even today. The places of production and commerce as well as the individual trades are topographically divided and organised. On the outskirts of the town there are the warehouses and trading centres (which are at the same time inns) for wholesale and long-distance trade; also on the periphery are the markets for agricultural produce. The urban dealers and tradesmen sit in the shops in the bazar in the centre of the city, situated usually near the great mosque. Their arrangement is usually dictated by functional demands and by commercial prestige: thus books and devotional literature as well as fine material, leather goods and perfumes are sold near the main door of the mosque; in their immediate vicinity the money changers, gold- and silversmiths (often non-Muslims and therefore not in sight of the mosque) have their shops; the main street of the bazaar provides essential household requirements, materials and clothes; in the side streets basic needs, food and equipment are on offer, and the louder and dirtier the commercial wares and crafts are, the further away they are positioned from the main roads of public traffic.

Stability, government backing of the currency, and thereby a functioning monetary economy and open frontiers within an orderly empire created the conditions necessary for a surge in trade. The ʿAbbāsid capital, Baghdad (later overshadowed by Cairo) became the first centre of a trading network over the land routes of the Fertile Crescent and the Iraqi seaports on the Persian gulf, a network which stretched from Nīshāpūr to Cordoba, an inter-regional and international traffic which extended far beyond the frontiers of Islam towards eastern Asia and north and west Europe.

> It should be known that commerce means the attempt to make a profit by increasing capital, through buying goods at a low price and selling them at a high price, whether these goods consist of slaves, grain, animals, weapons, or clothing material. The accrued (amount) is called 'profit' (*ribḥ*). The attempt to make such a profit may be undertaken by storing goods and holding them until the market has fluctuated from low prices to high prices. This will bring a large profit. Or, the merchant may transport his goods to another country where they are more in demand than in his own, where he bought them. This (again) will bring a large profit. (Ibn Khaldūn, *al-Muqaddima*, trans. F. Rosenthal, vol. II, pp. 113–13.)

The wholesale dealer (*khazzān*), who stockpiled staple wares, could derive profit from fluctuations in the harvest and trade. But fine and rare wares, spices, drugs, perfumes, silks were the domain of the long-distance trader (*raqqād*). The prosperity of inter-regional trade accompanied the 'international' culture of classical Islam, and it was in many ways its prerequisite. It was not Islam, in its political or ethical attitude, which was responsible for the decline of western Mediterranean trade (as Henri Pirenne argued); the sources suggest the opposite. From the ninth century onwards we have detailed information about trade routes from the itineraries of administrative geography and travel accounts; we also have details about the theory and practice of trade. The actual practice has recently become even better known through the study of papyrus documents from Egypt and by the numerous business letters and trade agreements from the Cairo Geniza (the archive of the Jewish community), from which sources S. D. Goitein and others have presented a picture of the 'Mediterranean society' of the tenth to the thirteenth century (from the Fāṭimid to the Ayyūbid period).

A remarkable testimony of Islamic trading spirit is revealed from the end of the eighth century in the development of Islamic commercial law, especially that of the Ḥanafite school: a law which emerged under the initiative of merchants and which met their needs; it was not a dead letter but a mirror of used and tried practice. It is remarkable because the Koran and the material of early Islamic law which had been collected in *ḥadīth* and formed the canonical basis of the *Sharīʿa* imposed certain restrictions on financial transactions in commerce; but these were tailored to smaller dimensions of commercial enterprise, whereas the political and economic development of the empire opened new horizons. The Koran forbade lending money at interest, and the *Sharīʿa* also prohibited commercial investment in goods because transactions in cash only allowed a fair division of the profit between the partners. But in many cases the legal bases of commercial trade were provided in the *Sharī'a*; it regulated partnership treaties, it regulated in particular the so-called *commenda* (Arabic, *muḍāraba, muqāraḍa*): partnership between capital investors and traders with a specified portion of profit for those undertaking the agreement and at the risk of the investor. The lawyers then developed 'tricks' (*ḥiyal*), 'legal means for extra-legal ends—aims that could not, whether they were in themselves legal or illegal, be achieved directly with the means provided by the *Sharī'a*' (J. Schacht [33.05], p.78)—devices with the aim of formally circumventing the giving or taking of interest, or facilitating capital investments in the form of goods in partnership agreements. Moreover, the lawyers developed formularies (*shurūṭ*) for the written authentication of various commercial treaties; this was also against the legal principle which accorded validity not to the written document but to oral witness only. Experts drew these documents up and became active as public notaries who at the same time could bear personal testimony. Amongst these written documents (Arabic, *ṣakk*, from which we derive the word 'cheque') there were also the documents used for a non-monetary economy, as for example the letter of credit (Persian-Arabic, *suftaja*) which could moreover be used by the owner as a form of capital investment. That such practices were operable over great distances was not, however, only due to the observance of legal formalities—these could not always cover the different casuistry of legal schools; the functioning of foreign trade would have been unthinkable without the element of personal reciprocal guarantee, evident in the sphere of informal personal cooperation in economic and also private contexts between partners who often lived very far away from each other.

In all spheres of economy and trade the government interfered in a guiding and controlling manner. The prosperity and decline of the economy, the development and collapse of the social order were therefore most closely linked with the great political processes.

The state was not only—as the steward of the treasury (*bayt al-māl*)—the customer for trade and commerce and the commercial investor of capital. It also exercised a monopoly in many spheres: as for example in the production of papyrus and paper, brocade (*ṭirāz*) and weapons. In Egypt the state controlled the import of iron and wood and, to regulate the balance of payments, the export of alum. The sovereign had coins minted in his name and controlled their weight and proportion of fine metal by the *jahbadh*, the officially appointed examiner and money-changer. The *jahbadha* also served as bankers. (It would appear that the profit from the exploitation of gold and silver resources was not subject to any monopoly.) Naturally the state also took taxes and custom-duties from the trades of the city and the commerce of imported goods. The organisation and upkeep of urban life and all its professional activities were subject to overall authority. Such authority was imposed not by a city-based principality, but the local governors and officials were appointed by the centralised state of the caliph, by the administrative chiefs with delegated powers, and later by the amirs and sultans authorised by the caliph as well as by the Mamlūk and Ottoman rulers who acted as his legal successors. The state controlled the inspection of markets (*ḥisba*), indeed all inspection of urban trade and commerce, through the office of the *muḥtasib*. Religious establishments and institutions of public welfare—mosques, schools, hospitals, fountains—were founded by rulers and high-ranking officials as a private pious act. Such foundations (*waqf*) were also established by the individual who sought respect in this world and reward in the next; they did not form any specific 'public sector' of the town.

The professions and groups in urban society often formed communities in individual quarters of the city. They were defined as such for fiscal purposes but they were not institutional groups. Professions and crafts are sometimes mentioned as 'guilds' (*ṣinf, ḥirfa*) but these were by no means autonomous nor were they organised into large units. Guilds were only organised systematically in the Ottoman empire—but their main function was then to serve as a framework for tight government control.

The *madrasa*, the law college, and the *ṭarīqa*, the Ṣūfī order—the institutions of legal education and religious social life which had developed from the eleventh century onwards—had no corporate nature (in contrast to European universities and monastic orders of the High Middle Ages); there was no form of corporate life for the upper classes, no urban self-government and no privileges of urban 'freedom'. There was therefore no urban institution which could serve as a political mouthpiece or a forum to resolve conflict. The people in the town were subjects; and the authority of the dynasty waxed and waned with the balance of social forces.

We have already observed that opposition to the autocratic rule of the caliphate on the part of lawyers and traditionists was presented as opposition to the assumption of charismatic authority (see pp.49f., 66). But opposition, expressed by 'intellectuals' as a matter of religion, went deeper. The 'Abbāsids had fulfilled old demands for equality amongst the Muslims but their administration could not resolve social tensions in the new turbulent society of the cities. From the ninth century onwards we read about revolts amongst groups of the urban proletariat, the *'ayyārūn*, against the wealthy élite. Moreover, the people of Baghdad took up the cudgels on behalf of Aḥmad ibn Ḥanbal, who was persecuted in the *Miḥna*, and they rebelled against the measures taken by the ruler against him. From that time onwards historians mention such revolts again and again. Ḥanbalism became the label for anti-authoritarian and anti-élitist protest. The reaction of the caliphs was fateful; the formation of a bodyguard of Turkish military slaves delivered the caliphs more and more into the hands of those with military power. In the tenth century the office of generalissimo (*amīr al-umarā'* 'chief amir') was taken over by foreign forces, at first by the Iranian Būyids. From the Seljuq period onwards, military dynasties of Turcoman tribes were the uncontested autonomous rulers of the Near East. At the same time a caste of military slaves, the Mamlūks, became the ruling élite; the Egyptian-Syrian state of the thirteenth–sixteenth centuries was named after them. This was a state in which a closed ruling class of Turcoman and Circassian slaves belonging to the Sultan (who had also come from their ranks) and constantly regenerated by further imports of slaves, wielded supreme authority. The Ottoman state, which placed all groups of society under centralised control by institutionalising the social order, also adopted this principle; the members of the ruling class, the Osmanlis who were sharply divided from the rank and file (literally 'flock': *râya*) of subjects, were the slaves of the sultan.

From the beginning this development exerted an adverse influence on urban economy. The new dynasties based their financial system on military land tenure (*iqṭā'*, see above, p.84). A buoyant market economy, orientated towards capital, was replaced by a subsistence economy directed towards acquisition and based on agrarian production. When the caliphal state, alienated from the people, delegated its authority and its revenues to the generals of the Iranian and Turkish military élite, it literally squandered its capital. The monetary economy collapsed from the Būyid period onwards (the increasing fluctuations in the fineness of the coins can still be seen in those pieces which have been preserved). Long-distance trade was jeopardised by political unrest and declined in its turn. Under favourable circumstances, however, it took a new direction and received fresh impetus. In Fāṭimid Egypt estates were allotted also to private tax farmers (only the Ayyūbids made the *iqṭā'* on the Seljuq model the privilege of the military élite). Egypt thus became the important trading partner of India and Venice. However, when the Mediterranean trade with the Near East collapsed again as a consequence of the Mongol invasion, Europe sought commercial contacts across the Northern land route with the great empire of the Mongols and with the Far East (contacts which were later monopolised by new routes to the detriment of the Islamic world).

While urban culture, its prime and its diversity, declined in the wake of this development, it also resisted; where the effects of fiscal and economic exploitation evolved late or were alleviated by prudent rule, urban societies even mobilised political forces of their own. Out of the groups of the *'ayyārūn*, there grew up in the towns of eastern Islam 'bourgeois' brotherhoods which represented an ideology of manly virtue (*futuwwa*) and social justice. The influence of Ḥanbalism, Ṣūfism, and the Shī'a gave a religious basis to their bonds of solidarity. Under the leadership of the caliph al-Nāṣir (1180–1225), the *Futuwwa* movement was finally organised into an élite state organisation, the mainstay of the last flowering of the caliphate. The *aḥdāth* militia, the 'young men', were similar groups: these had formed from the end of the eleventh century in the towns of Syria and the Jazīra. (Also modelled on the *Futuwwa* were the *akhī* fraternities which emerged in late and post Seljuq Anatolia in the thirteenth–fourteenth centuries.)

In a situation in which the power of government was uncertain and based on the provinces, the urban élite—the leaders (*ra'īs*) of tightly-knit groups in a particular city quarter—became more and more influential. In many parts of the Near East, as in the Iranian east, also in Andalusia (Seville), after the fall of the Umayyads, families of 'patricians' took power in their own hands; 'patricians' (R. W. Bulliet used this concept in a study of Nīshāpūr [44.02] taking due care not to draw false parallels), who on the one hand protected the economy as the basis of their prosperity, and on the other hand, by nominating *qāḍīs*, arrogated to themselves the legal autonomy of the sovereign. This was only possible in a period of weak central government and it only happened from time to time and in certain places. But in general the urban élite in these centuries of changing foreign rule managed to unite spiritual forces under the banner of Islamic tradition. They forced dynasties to rule with them and not against them, and this meant that rulers had to recognise the religious and ethical concepts of orthodox Islamic law as a vital aspect of government.

This intellectual élite came to be known as 'scholars' (*'ulamā'*) of the *Sharī'a*; a thorough knowledge of *fiqh* and its auxiliary sciences was taken for granted. Yet they did not form a separate class of professional lawyers and teachers of law. Such groups belonged to it but amongst the *'ulamā'* there were also bureaucrats, merchants and artisans. Not all of them were specialists, but by virtue of their wide range of expertise they were guarantors of the Islamic consensus in family matters, communal life, the institutions of divine worship and doctrine, and economic relations. This scholarship of theirs was more than a veneer: it was a continuous personal scholarly tradition which had evolved over generations, and it was the sign of a community with spiritual and political solidarity. The old conflicts about the principles of the *Sharī'a* and of the dogma had been hammered out and resolved after the first three centuries of Islam; but the legal schools—as well as the dogmatic attitudes associated with certain groups—created lasting focal points for political parties. (Our major source for this phenomenon, the increasing number of biographical dictionaries, did not only record consolidated learned tradition; it was also the expression of a new self-awareness, and from the beginning of the twelfth century was not limited to traditionalists and lawyers, but included 'notables' [*a'lām*] from all disciplines). The movements of the ascetic, contemplative and mystical *Ṣūfiyya*—still accused of many a heresy in the tenth century and yet increasingly widespread and influential as the vehicle for popular religion—joined forces with this established orthodoxy. Monastic orders grew and spread, and their refined scholarly tradition became an instrument of the *'ulamā'*, a tool to bind and control popular religious movements (but in its debased form a pious front for mendicant dervish vagabonds: *ḥarāfīsh*).

In this milieu religious knowledge was a mark of distinction and religious munificence was a means of social advancement. Pious bequests (*waqf*) from private means for the building and upkeep of the institutions of religious life and public welfare were from early Islamic times a kind of private participation in public affairs. It is important to mention the increasing number of urban notables who sought to acquire religious prestige by endowing pious foundations. These were not only viziers and high functionaries but also merchants and representatives of other classes of economic life. Deliberate self-interest was a factor in this, since the revenue from a pious foundation was exempt from taxation and could even become the preserve of an individual family (we have already drawn attention to the economic value of pious foundations). On a higher level too the self-interest of the founder came into play: the foundation of teaching institutions of *fiqh*, of *madrasas* and mosque schools, mostly reserved for the doctrine of a particular established legal school, afforded the founder the opportunity of appointing his own professors and choosing his own students. From the Seljuq period onwards this practice increasingly became an instrument of power politics. But in the absence of autonomous corporate institutions the Islamic city could develop no lasting defence against partisan strife and therefore no real resistance to tyranny. The flowering and the variety of urban culture up to the fourth Islamic century was followed in the period of Turkish and Mongol military dynasties, the Mamlūks and the Īlkhāns and their vassals, by a period of stagnation everywhere—a period of impoverishment in material culture and stagnation in the intellectual sphere. It is true that the towns of the east still managed, after the devastations of the Mongol invasions, to preserve small islands of privileged well-being, and of scientific, artistic, and literary activity; this was of course to the detriment of the surrounding agrarian land which was threatened by the Bedouin, and exploited by urban landlords and always dependent on the favour of the ruler. While usurpers, presenting themselves as guarantors of divine law, thus aspiring to be the successors of the caliph, sought to legitimise their rule, at the same time they took over the religious institutions by making the *'ulamā'* into a professional class and subjecting them to central control—as did the Mamlūks and the Ottomans amongst the Sunnīs and the Ṣafavids amongst the Shī'ites. Urban society was therefore welded together not by the indigenous but by the foreign ruling class. The period of military feudalism and government bureaucracy was also a period of government monopoly, central control of the economy and of professional guilds, and of the organisation of religion and spiritual life. Policy was aimed not at developments but at preservation and consolidation; it did not suffer from the tensions and struggles to which early Islam was forcibly subjected. The period of prosperity in international trade was also the period of international scholarly exchange; as political society and economic life in the Islamic world became provincial, teaching and learning were also institutionalised and professionalised on a local basis. Science became a mere assemblage of facts in handbooks and encyclopaedias and literature degenerated into artistic mannerisms. In the meantime, the Islamic countries having no common political focus drew further and further apart from each other; instead of the cultural community of classical Islam, 'national' cultures arose with different linguistic, literary and artistic forms of expression.

The economic and intellectual development of the Islamic world came to a standstill while the aspiring cities of Europe, on the threshold of modern times, developed new sources of wealth not dependent on land ownership and created autonomous bourgeois institutions; while the Renaissance and the Enlightenment in the West ushered in new eras of self-awareness and self-determination. Islam's economy remained an economy of acquisition which was directed to the requirements of the government and aristocracy: 'the idea of promoting trade because of an excess in production, with the aim of ensuring or increasing work and the sources of production or simply of creating a balance between import and export in goods—an idea which is self-understood for every modern state—had probably never arisen in any state in the medieval Near East' (C. Cahen [44.37], p.35). Political successes created an illusion of security and economic autonomy; when European expansionism destroyed this illusion it was too late to change course effectively. In Europe the impetus arising from the lack of monetary resources and then the great discoveries of new trade routes led a new urban society to build up dangerous and ultimately disastrous competition. At first the Italian cities established hegemony over Mediterranean trade, while the friendly relations of the European powers with the Mongols facilitated the creation of a northern transit route to the Far East. But more decisive than this was the discovery of the sea route to India, which secured the Portuguese the monopoly over the Indian and Far Eastern spice trade. Gradually European capital and European trade privileges infiltrated into the Islamic world and rebuffed the belated local initiatives; unprotected by the state, which greedily seized customs dues, local attempts to carve out a foreign market collapsed (in particular the efforts of the Ottomans to promote agriculture).

Alongside the economic influence of Europe its intellectual influence also increased. On the one hand Europe in the nineteenth century had taken under its wing a new urban élite of Muslim intellectuals who led the movements of political autonomy and economic adaptation in a nationalist and, in their interpretation of Islam, modernistic direction (it is one of the ironies of this process that the historical theory of Ibn Khaldūn, who was heralded by Arab reformers of the nineteenth century as the chief witness of an Islamic ideology of progress, was until then read only by Turks and then rediscovered by European orientalists). On the other hand, this uprooted élite could only achieve historical self-awareness as well as support from the masses who had remained medieval in attitude by seeking religious authentication for their ideology. This occurred in different places in very different ways. While the Islamic world struggled with the forces unleashed by these conflicts, the West imposed on it a renewed acceleration in economic and social change. The multi-faceted changes which have been achieved through industrialisation, division of labour and mobility no longer allow a comprehensive definition of 'Islamic society'.

Chapter Five

A REGIONAL VIEW OF ISLAMIC HISTORY

The Arab conquests of the first Islamic century created in a few decades a great empire of unprecedented size. The Prophet himself in his own lifetime had united the Arabian peninsula under a Pax Islamica. The threatening movement of apostasy after his death (632) was stemmed by the first caliph Abū Bakr through the call to wage war against the unbelievers—with the aim of booty in this world and eternal salvation in the next. Not only the Arab tribes but also those of the neighbouring areas of Syria and Mesopotamia (where until the sixth century Christian Arab dynasties had served as the buffer states of Eastern Byzantium and Iran against attacks from Inner Arabia) embraced the new movement and advanced in the name of God against the empires of Byzantium and Sasanian Persia, which were unprepared from both the military and the political point of view. Under Abū Bakr's great successor, ʿUmar, Damascus fell (635), and soon afterwards the other territories of the Byzantine Empire in Syria and Egypt fell too (Alexandria 642). At the same time the Persians in Iraq had to undergo severe defeats (636 at Qādisiyya). The decisive battle of Nihāwand (641) cleared the way across the Iranian plateau. In the year 649 the empire of the Sasanian kings came completely to an end, and two years later the fugitive Yazdagird III was killed in Khurāsān. The caliphs of the Umayyad dynasty (from 661), after emerging triumphant from two civil wars, renewed a policy of expansion. Arab armies poured out of Iraq to the east and the north (as far as Ādharbāyjān), and westwards from Egypt. In the year 711 they finally reached Spain, Transoxiana and India.

The consequences of Islamisation and the effects of Arabisation were very different from region to region; everywhere Islamisation was a very slow-moving process. The centres of power, which were at first determined by military necessity, shifted and multiplied under the pressure of political change: the transition from tribal alliance to a centrally-organised State, and tensions between sedentary, nomadic and newly-settled population as well as between Arab and newly-converted non-Arab Muslims. Everywhere the broad outlines of later disintegration can already be seen in the geographical and geopolitical structure of the emerging empire.

Each of the classic regions of Islam had its own individual history: the Arabian peninsula; the Fertile Crescent: Egypt, Syria and the Jazīra, the 'island' between the upper Euphrates and the Tigris; the Islamic West (*Maghrib*): North Africa and Spain (*al-Andalus*); Iraq and Iran with the provinces in the east: Khurāsān, Khwārazm on the Oxus and Transoxiana, Sīstān and Sind. Even after the collapse of the caliphal empire other areas came under Muslim rule: Anatolia and India, South-East Asia and Inner Africa.

1. The Arabian Peninsula

Arabia was the first home of Islam: Mecca was the place of the shrine and the spiritual focus of the new religion, whilst Medina was the city of the Prophet and of the first Islamic community. But already in the first civil war of succession it was clear that the Ḥijāz had forfeited its role as the political centre of Islam. The capital of the Arab Empire of the Umayyads became Damascus in Syria, an old provincial centre, whose administration continued to function almost without break, and whose new government with its reliable army controlled and continued to control the situation in Egypt and in Iraq as long as the privileged position of the Arabs themselves was maintained. The second civil war (683–92) was unleashed in an attempt by the anti-caliph ʿAbdallāh ibn al-Zubayr in Mecca, with the help of the tribes of Arabia and in league with tribes which had wandered to the Upper Euphrates, to turn the clock back: to restore the primacy of Mecca and of the Meccan aristocracy and to enforce the territorial demands of the tribes who had fought the conquests; this attempt clashed with the dynastic claims of the Umayyads and with their policy of compromise between the sedentary tribes—allies of the occupants—and the Bedouin invaders. The successful counter-coup (684 at Marj Rāhiṭ north of Damascus) was a crucial turning point; the victory of the urban government over the tribalism of the peninsula and the partisan interests of the tribes led to a permanent victory for Islam and for the Arabic language outside Arabia.

Control of the holy cities in the Ḥijāz remained a requirement of caliphal authority, but the leading political role of Arabia was played out. The peninsula, above all in the south, became a backwater of heterodoxy, of the Khārijites and Ibāḍites, the Zaydiyya and the Carmathians. In the eighteenth century a religious movement, that of the Wahhābīs, laid the foundations for the power of the Āl Saʿūd, the dynasty which rules there to this day.

2. Syria and Palestine

In Syria nomadic and sedentary Arabs as well as Aramaeans had received the Muslims as liberators from Byzantine power. The old symbiosis between settlers and Bedouin was only temporarily disrupted by the Islamic invasion. Muʿāwiya, who received the governorship of this area from the caliph ʿUthmān, stabilised his power by forming an alliance with a nomadic group, which had been established in the Syrian Arab buffer zone of Palmyra: the association of the Yaman tribes (under the leadership of the Kalb, its most powerful tribe). When Muʿāwiya had gained the caliphate (661) Damascus became the natural centre of the empire and the tribes which had made an alliance with him became the mainstay of the Umayyad dynasty.

Tensions emerged in places where a struggle for land erupted in the pastures and settled territories of the tribes, a struggle between the early followers of Islam and the incoming armies of conquest of the second generation, above all in the fertile Jazīra, the upper part of Mesopotamia. Thus hostility erupted between the Qays, who had fought in the Jazīra against Byzantium and demanded their own pasture lands (having used up the booty obtained in war) and the Kalb. This conflict was viewed (and established in tradition) as a struggle between the 'North Arabian' genealogy of the Qays and the 'South Arabian' of the Kalb. As bitter opponents of the Umayyads, the Qays joined up with ʿAbdallāh ibn al-Zubayr, the anti-caliph in Mecca, in the second civil war. They were, however, defeated in the battle of Marj Rāhiṭ against the allied forces of the caliph Marwān and the Kalb. In any case, this victory was only the first stage towards the re-establishment of Umayyad supreme power. The foundation of the Dome of the Rock in Jerusalem marked a bold attempt by ʿAbd al-Malik (685–705) to establish a counterbalance against Mecca in this city, which was also sacred to the Muslims. In any case it took a further eight years to pacify Iraq, which was subjected to the struggles of different parties of opposition. ʿAbd al-Malik, the most eminent of Marwān's sons, managed to bring about a compromise between Qays and Yaman and to make the tribal troops the means of promoting order in this great empire. With the decline of the Umayyad caliphate the struggle between the tribes once again became a cause of unrest, weakening political control and jeopardising the strategy against the increasing opposition in Iraq and the eastern provinces. Integration in a permanent way could not be achieved by simple policies of expansionism and occupation.

After the ʿAbbāsid revolution in 749 the geographical centre of the multi-racial empire, Iraq with its new capital of Baghdad, became the political centre too. Syria became a province. The South (with Palestine) remained closely linked with the political destiny of Egypt; the North (the Jazīra around Mosul and Aleppo) was controlled until the middle of the eleventh century by confederations of North Arabian tribes, until 991 under the leadership of the Ḥamdānid dynasty. When the Ḥamdānids, towards the middle of the tenth century, became embroiled in the internal confusion of Iraq and by offering protection to the caliphate gained the office of chief amir, they were pushed back by the Iranian power of the Būyids. Nevertheless they maintained the Islamic western frontier in tedious wars against Byzantium and the great Sayf al-Dawla made the court at Aleppo a centre of literary and scholarly life.

In the second half of the eleventh century the Turkish military dynasty of the Seljuqs, having taken Iraq, also captured Syria and Palestine. During the twelfth century several vassals of the Seljuqs ruled there. They were known as the Atabegs ('tutors of princes', a term which was at first a high position at court). The Zangids, the Atabegs of northern Syria (Aleppo) and the Jazīra (Mosul and Diyarbakr) began the war against the Christian Crusaders, a war which was to last 200 years; their Kurdish general Ṣalāḥ al-Dīn (Saladin), who had set himself up as ruler in Cairo and Damascus after the fall of the Egyptian Fāṭimids and had cut loose from Aleppo, won the decisive victory of Ḥaṭṭīn, which led to the reconquest of Jerusalem (1187). The successes of the Zangids and of the dynasty of Saladin, the Ayyūbids, not only freed Islam from a serious threat; they gave political importance to the Fertile Crescent, while the Baghdad caliphate was recognised only for legal purposes and fell to the status of a provincial power. The rise of the Ayyūbids ushered in a century-long dependence of Syria on Cairo; this ended when in the year 1517 Selim I incorporated the territories of the decadent Mamlūk state into the Ottoman empire.

3. *Iraq*

Iraq (Arabic *al-'Irāq*) was not only the second key area of ancient Arab settlement; it was also the basis for conquests northwards and eastwards, and the garrison towns which were founded by the Arabs, Baṣra (635) and Kūfa (638), became the two poles of the eastern half of the Islamic empire. The governor of Baṣra controlled the provinces which were conquered from that base: Khūzistān (with its capital of Akwāz in south-west Persia), Fārs (the ancient Persis, with Shīrāz near the ruins of Persepolis), further east Kirmān, then Sīstān (with the mountainous area of modern-day Afghanistan), and to the north-west Khurāsān with the cities of Ṭūṣ and Nīshāpūr. The areas governed by Kūfa were, apart from Iraq itself and the Jazīra, the provinces of Armenia and Ādharbāyjān in the Caucasus, and Jibāl, the west Iranian region with a triangle of cities: Hamadān, Rayy (near modern Tehran) and Iṣfahān.

But Kūfa was also the city of the fourth caliph ʿAlī, the base of his activities against his rivals in the Ḥijāz, and later the centre of opposition against the Umayyads. The rebellion of the Khārijites, the tribes who had come too late to obtain their fair share of the government's salaries and endowments from the conquests, was directed first against ʿAlī and then against the Umayyads too. Delegating military power to the governors of Baṣra and Kūfa bound the Iranian provinces to Damascus; but if Iraq fell to the opponents of the régime, the whole east could be lost. The caliph ʿAbd al-Malik, the leading personality of the Umayyad dynasty after its founder Muʿāwiya, and his governor al-Ḥajjāj ibn Yūsuf re-established law and order with the help of the Syrian army, centralised military power in a new garrison (Wāsiṭ, between Baṣra and Kūfa), streamlined and reformed the administration, which until then had been maintained only by Persian officials, and relaunched a movement of expansion towards the north-east (Khwārazm, Transoxiana). But the assimilation of the Arabs who had settled in the Iranian east into the landscape, society and economy of the ancient country of Iran was not achieved and the small élite of Arab adminstrators did not view the integration of the Persians who had converted to Islam in a favourable light. In the first half of the eighth century tensions grew and dissatisfied elements embraced the propaganda for a renewal of theocracy under a descendant of the Prophet's family, until finally the ʿAbbāsids (from the line of ʿAbbās, an uncle of the Prophet) managed from Iraq to raise the banner of rebellion in Khurāsān. Iran was conquered in a few months; in the year 749 the black banner of revolution was planted in Kūfa; soon afterwards (750) the last Umayyad caliph fell in Egypt.

The supremacy of the Arabs outside Arabia was shattered; the empire of Islam continued, but under different auspices. The ʿAbbāsids, supported by their followers from Khurāsān, introduced a strong Iranian bias into the new capital of Baghdad (founded in 763), in position and in layout a symbolic centre of ʿAbbāsid power near the ruins of Ctesiphon. The court etiquette and the administrative hierarchy became stamped with Iranian traditions of political thought which also influenced the division of institutions between government, military and law—a division which caused serious alienation between ruler and ruled. It also showed that the new dynasty could not fulfil its claim to be exercising truly Islamic government over the faithful in true succession to the Prophet and in God's name—theocracy. In his residence of Sāmarrā (founded 836) with a bodyguard of Turkish slaves to protect him, the caliph became the plaything of opposing political forces. Social unrest (often in religious guise) shook the country; the greed of the soldiery disrupted the economy.

The weakness of the caliphate opened tenth-century Iraq, and in the eleventh century the Jazīra and Asia Minor, to forces which were then erupting from Iran and from Central Asia.

When the Mongol invasion had brought the caliphate to an end (1258), Iraq, once the centre of Islamic culture, sank into insignificance. It became a province of the Mongol and Turkish dynasties which ruled it from Iran, was conquered in the sixteenth century by the Ṣafavids, and was finally incorporated (in 1638) into the Ottoman empire.

4. The West

Immediately after the seizure of power by the 'Abbāsids, the Western Provinces of the empire—Spain and North Africa—had slipped out of caliphal control and, when the star of the 'Abbāsids began to sink, had finally cut loose from it. Spain (*al-Andalus* of the Arabs) had been in Arab hands since 711 when the general Ṭāriq ibn Ziyād had crossed via Gibraltar (Jabal Ṭāriq). One of the few members of the Umayyad family who had escaped from the massacre of the 'Abbāsids founded there a powerful and flourishing principality. In Morocco a descendant of 'Alī set up his own independent state amongst the Zenāta Berbers with its capital at Fez. In western Algeria (Tāhart) 'Abd al-Raḥmān ibn Rustam gathered the Berber population in favour of the Ibāḍiyya, a radical movement of protest against the claim of the Arab aristocracy along the lines of the old Khārijites. In Ifrīqiyya (the Byzantine province of Africa, roughly speaking modern-day Tunisia and eastern Algeria) were the Aghlabids; although loyal to the caliph as governors, they were nevertheless largely independent.

(a) Spain

The emirate of the Umayyads of Cordoba (Qurṭuba), founded in 755 by 'Abd al-Raḥmān I, ruled for two and a half centuries the difficult territory of the Iberian peninsula as far as the Duro, the Castilian Meseta and the Ebro. The Umayyad emirate established remarkably stable rule in southern Andalusia (Seville and Malaga), northern Andalusia (Granada) and Murcia. The Umayyads also managed to keep continuous hold of central Spain (Castille and Toledo) in spite of opposition from its increasingly Arabised Christian population. They also ruled in the north-east, the basin of the Ebro (with Zaragoza and Tudela), with support from local rulers who were virtually autonomous. The greatest ruler of the dynasty, 'Abd al-Raḥmān II al-Nāṣir, assumed the caliphal title of 'Commander of the Faithful' in opposition to the threatening claims of his rivals, the Fāṭimids in North Africa, and in his rule of 50 years (912–961) led Cordoba to the apogee of its economic and cultural flowering—the Baghdad of the west.

In the eleventh century al-Andalus disintegrated after the sudden decline of the Umayyads into a number of petty principalities (*ṭawā'if*): 'In the eleventh century the Spanish Muslim destroys the caliphal form of government bound up with his religion and embarks on the adventure of fully developing his personality in the heights and depths of intellectual and political life, and—as our Arab mentor (Ibn al-Khaṭīb) has it—allows himself to be led astray by the prince of darkness into accepting full authority: in this respect, he is to some extent a precursor of the Renaissance; his world of petty principalities from the eleventh to the thirteenth century resembles that of Italy in the fourteenth and fifteenth century.' (W. Hoenerbach [54.05], p.293.)

The peninsula, politically divided into small units, became an easy prey for the Berber dynasties from Morocco, the Almoravids (1086) and the Almohads (1145). For at the same time the Reconquista began; Toledo became Christian in 1085 and remained so also after the victory of the Almoravid Yūsuf ibn Tāshufīn over Alfonso IV of Castille and Leon at Zallāqa (1086). Finally the Almohads had to withdraw after the defeat at Las Navas de Tolosa (1212) and to abandon almost the whole of Spain to the Christian reconquerors (Cordoba fell in 1236, Seville in 1248). Only in the mountainous region of Granada did the Naṣrids (1230–1392) preserve a stronghold of Islam and Spanish Islamic culture; the Alhambra (Arabic *al-Ḥamrā'* 'the red citadel') of Granada is the permanent symbol of this last flowering. In 1492 Ferdinand and Isabella, who had united Christian Spain through their marriage, put an end to the centuries-long confrontation with a last crusade against the Muslims.

(b) North Africa

In the Maghrib—North-West Africa from Cyrenaica as far as the Atlantic—the mountain chains of the Atlas with the adjacent desert areas of the north Sahara offered to the indigenous Berber tribes a bastion of permanent resistance against the Arab ruling class and against the imperial claims of the caliphate. Finally it was Islamised Berber dynasties which appeared as the successors to the Arab governors and amirs and became the rulers of a united Maghrib.

The Zenāta Berbers of Tripolitania were the first to follow 'Abdallāh ibn Ibāḍ, who after the example of the early Islamic 'secession' of the Khārijites against the hegemony of the Arab Quraysh, defended the rights of all orthodox Muslims to be eligible for the position of caliph. Already in the eighth century this doctrine, the Ibāḍiyya, had spread amongst the tribes of North Africa. But only the Fāṭimids, who belonged to the 'radical' Ismā'īliyya and who based their claim to the caliphate on illumination and charisma rather than on mere descent from the Prophet, achieved political hegemony over the whole region. With the help of the Ketāma, the sedentary Berbers of Lesser Kabylia, at the beginning of the tenth century, they defeated in succession the Aghlabids (Ifrīqiyya: Tunisia and eastern Algeria), the Rustamids (western Algeria) and the Idrīsids (Morocco), without it is true being able to exercise *de facto* control from their subsequent capital of Cairo over the extreme west.

In Ifrīqiyya (with its capital Qayrawān) the Zīrids (from the Ṣanhāja Berbers), since 972 vassals of the Fāṭimids, proclaimed around the middle of the eleventh century their allegiance once again to the ʿAbbāsid caliphate (1049). The reprisals taken by the Fāṭimids unleashed a catastrophe which was similar to the Mongol invasion in the East: the Arab tribes of Hilāl and Sulaym were launched from lower Egypt westwards (in 1057 they took Qayrawān) and caused through their ravaging activities the devastation and irreversible Bedouinisation of wide areas of central North Africa, from which only the coastal towns were spared.

At the same time a new power emerged in Morocco: Ṣanhāja Berbers from the Sahara had fought for the faith in the southern border area of Islam, from Mauretania as far as the mouth of the Senegal river in groups which were organised as in convents—Arabic *ribāṭ*, hence their name al-Murābiṭūn (rendered into Spanish as Almorávides). Their general Yūsuf ibn Tāshufīn (who ruled from 1061–1106) led them northwards, conquered Morocco (which takes its European name from their capital Marrakesh at the northern slopes of the High Atlas) and Algeria, and finally in Spain took over the inheritance of the Umayyads after a successful counter-attack against the Reconquistadores (1086). The conservative strictness and stark legalism of the Mālikite legal school, which the Almoravids had established in their dominions, prevented spiritual revitalisation and was in stark contrast to the life-style of the upper class. The dynasty of their successors in Marrakesh, the Almohads, began as a movement of protest and reform. Its founder Muḥammad ibn Tūmart (d.1130) spread among the Maṣmūda Berbers of the Atlas a renewal of pure faith and pious living, and was recognised by them as the promised Mahdī—his followers called themselves the al-Muwaḥḥidūn, those who acknowledge God's unity (the Spanish form is Almohades). Under ʿAbd al-Mu'min (1130–63) they gained not only Morocco and Islamic Spain (1145) but also the whole of the Maghrib as far as Tripolitania.

After the retreat of the Almohads from Spain in the thirteenth century, North Africa again disintegrated. The Banū Marīn (Marīnids, a tribe of the Zenāta) surged northwards from the Sahara into Morocco, made Fez their capital in 1248 and in 1269 took Marrakesh. The Ḥafṣids, the governors of the Almohads, made themselves independent in 1237 in Tunisia and eastern Algeria, and the ʿAbdalwādids of Tlemcen (1236–1554) followed their example (Marīnid interim, 1337–59). Whilst a branch of the Sharīfs (*shurafā'*, the descendants the Prophet's family) ruled in Morocco from 1549 onwards and still rules today, the rest of the Maghrib from the sixteenth century until the French colonial period fell under Ottoman supremacy.

5. *Egypt*

Under Islam Egypt, even though it was conquered and governed from Syria, also continued to lead its own life with its ancient administration which was adapted to the economic demands of the Nile valley. One of its provincial governors in the 'Abbāsid period, Aḥmad ibn Ṭulūn, contrived to disobey instructions from Baghdad and to extend his autonomy as far as Syria. In the following centuries, too, the rulers of Egypt managed time after time to unite Palestine and Syria under their authority.

The Fāṭimids (cf. above, p.107f.) conquered the whole of North Africa from Ifrīqiyya (Tunisia), and in the year 969 they proclaimed a caliphate in Egypt in the name of the Shī'ite Imām of the Ismā'īliyya, founding Cairo near the site of the old garrison of Fusṭāṭ. From there they took Jerusalem, Damascus, Mecca and Medina, pressed on the Ḥamdānids (Arabs from the old sedentary tribe of Taghlib) in Aleppo and Mosul, and finally threatened Baghdad. The counter-attack in the name of the Sunnī caliphate was led by the soldier kings of the Turkish mounted nomads from the east, who had occupied first Iran and then Iraq in the eleventh century and from there moved westwards: the conquerors of Baghdad, the Seljuqs, and their governors pushed the Fāṭimids out of Syria. Nevertheless, in the face of Crusader attacks in the twelfth century internal Islamic quarrels were relegated to the background.

Only the great Ṣalāḥ al-Dīn (Saladin, 1171–93), was able in his capacity as general of the Zangids of Aleppo, to put an end to the authority of the Fāṭimids in Cairo (1171), founded in its place an autonomous Ayyūbid dynasty and in 1187 pushed the Crusaders out of Jerusalem. The peaceful policy of his successors allowed the internal economy and Mediterranean trade to flourish again after long years of war, but internal territorial strife weakened the dynasty as early as the generation of Saladin's grandsons. It was finally the generals of the Ayyūbids, the Mamlūks, who took over their heritage and ruled with a strong hand; they also managed to halt the terrible invasion of the Mongols in southern Palestine (1260) and finally to push the Crusaders out of northern Syria too. Founded as it was on an élite army of Circassian and Kipchaq slaves (Arabic *mamlūk*), which was given a stable economic base through land-tenure (*iqṭā'*, see p.84), the Mamlūk state became the most powerful and flourishing political force in the Near East from the middle of the thirteenth to the beginning of the sixteenth century.

Syrians and Egyptians finally managed to become independent national states in the twentieth century after a period of struggle against the successors of the Mamlūks, the Ottoman Turks; but the short-lived United Arab Republic (1958–61) could still hark back to the old historical community of the Arabs in the Fertile Crescent.

6. Iran

Iranian territory was only superficially Arabised. This was due not only to its wide expanse but also to the fact that the dromedary of the Arab Bedouin could not survive on the cold high plateau of Iran in the winter. From the beginning the conquerors had to exercise their authority in alliance with the local landed nobility. As early as the ninth century there emerged provincial governors and usurpers who assumed autonomous power. Those who had settled in Khurāsān had helped the ʿAbbāsid revolution to victory; in the same province the caliph al-Ma'mūn (813–33) prepared the downfall of his brother and rival al-Amīn and his return to Baghdad; but a few years later its governor Ṭāhir (821–2) achieved *de facto* independence. As long as the power of the caliphate remained unbroken, the rebellions which constantly erupted, and in which social unrest was combined with Islamic sectarianism of an Iranian type, could still be put down. But in the second half of the ninth century the caliphs lost the requisite authority even in Iraq. It was not long before the bands of the 'coppersmith' Yaʿqūb ibn Layth conquered Sīstān and took Khurāsān in 873. The Iranian dynasty of the Sāmānids ruled in Bukhārā (the capital of Transoxiana), Farghāna and Samarqand, and also (from 900 onwards) Khurāsān, as loyal yet independent followers of the Caliph. They fostered the expansion of Islam and defended it against the Turkish peoples of the Asiatic steppe. It was here that the revival of the Persian language and Persian literature began. The powerful family of the Būyids emerged from amongst the condottieri of the mountainous land of Daylam on the Caspian Sea. The three sons of Būya divided up amongst themselves western Persia and the central high plateau (Jibāl, Fārs, Khūzistān, Kirmān) and launched themselves successfully into the power struggles of Iraq (945); his grandson ʿAḍud al-Dawla (949–983) established an Iranian monarchy which lowered the caliph of Baghdad to the status of a mere puppet. The division of the Islamic empire into an eastern and a western sphere, into an Iranian and an Arab world, remained irreversible.

But the autonomy of Iranian dynasties in the east was only an intermezzo. Turcoman tribes from Central Asia, held back on the Jaxartes (Syr-Darya) by the Sāmānids, converted to Islam, penetrated in powerful waves towards western Asia, adopted Iranian culture and government organisation and subjugated Mesopotamia, Syria and Asia Minor in the course of the eleventh century. The Qarakhānids took Transoxiana (Bukhārā 992) and defended Islam against the east. Turkish condottieri of the Sāmānids (known as the Ghaznavids) set up a powerful autonomous state in Ghazna (eastern Afghanistan), snatched from their erstwhile masters the lands west of the Oxus in Khurāsān; from the kings of Gurgānj they seized the fertile area of Khwārazm on the Oxus (1017) and from the Būyids they took Rayy and Hamadān in western Persia. But the Ghaznavids were soon expelled by the Seljuqs who came from the tribe of the Oghuz and took western Iran in a few years after the conqest of Nīshāpūr (1038). On their campaigns for plunder the Turcomans advanced into the Caucasus, into eastern Anatolia and upper Mesopotamia, where they found familiar climatic conditions. Political legitimisation of this seizure of land was acquired by Toghrïl, the grandson of the founder of the dynasty Seljuq, who invaded Iraq in the year 1055—ostensibly to liberate the caliph who was being threatened by the activities of the heretical Fāṭimids. In Baghdad, following the example of the Būyids, Toghrïl became the real ruler, and thereafter he moved into the Jazīra and Syria. The victory of the Seljuq sultan Alp Arslan over the Byzantine emperor Romanus IV Diogenes at Malāzgird (Manzikert) in 1071, opened the way to Asia Minor for the Turcoman nomads.

In Iran, unlike the Arabs, the Turcomans found in the summer pastures of the high plateau and in the winter pastures of the deep plains a milieu which suited their way of life, in which their camel (a cross between the Bactrian camel and the female dromedary) was at home. Thus they set in motion a process of nomadisation on which the Mongols finally set the seal. The catastrophe of the Mongol invasion did not only bring about the downfall of the caliphate of Baghdad (1258). It altered the face of the Iranian world for centuries in that it ruined the economic basis of agriculture, except where high mountains—such as the massifs of Afghanistan, the Caucasus and the Elburz near the Caspian made retreat and opposition possible. It was only in such mountainous areas and in urban centres—Iṣfahān, Yazd, Kirmān, Shīrāz, Tabrīz, Bukhārā, Samarqand—that the Persian language and culture remained unchallenged. Mongol dynasties ruled in Iran until the end of the fifteenth century: Tabrīz was governed by the Īlkhāns, the clan of Hülegü (the conqueror of Baghdad, which fell under the authority of one of the vassals in his retinue), by Hülegü's descendants and by various tribal princes in his succession. The family of Tīmūr 'the lame', who unleashed a second Mongol invasion at the end of the fourteenth century and conquered India, Iran and Iraq, ruled in Samarqand.

The decline of the Mongols facilitated the re-emergence of

Turkish tribal confederations which were able to preserve their own territories even under the (intermittent) overall authority of the Tīmūrids: the 'Black Sheep' (Qara-Qoyunlu in Ādharbāyjān and Iraq, and later the 'White Sheep' (Aq-Qoyunlu), who asserted themselves in the Jazīra and in eastern Anatolia, and then (in 1467) conquered the territories of the Qara-Qoyunlu and finally Tīmūrid Persia. In Persia they were only the precursors of the Ṣafavids who under Shāh Ismāʿīl (1501–24), set up a dynasty which lasted more than two centuries. The Ṣafavids also relied on Turkish tribes; originally a dervish order in Ādharbāyjān, they rebelled in the name of the Hidden Imām of the Shīʿa and fomented political unrest in eastern Anatolia. With their Qïzïlbash ('Red caps') followers they overthrew the Aq-Qoyunlu and took the whole of Persia in ten years. They could always defend the Persian heartland against attacks from the Ottomans; thus Persia became and is still today the most important domain of the Shīʿa, and (together with the old Shīʿite centres in Iraq) remained the spiritual bulwark of the Shīʿa against the 'orthodox' Sunna, a cause hitherto propagated by the Turkish Muslims. The successors of the Ṣafavids—the Qājārs in the nineteenth century, who had to tread a difficult path toward constitutional monarchy at the beginning of this century—laid down in accordance with Shīʿite doctrine that their rule would be legitimate only until the return of the Mahdī.

7. *Anatolia*

Asia Minor—modern Turkey—was after Iran and Iraq the last country conquered by the Turkish peoples from central Asia. The Anatolian plateau had been successfully defended by Byzantium against the Arabs for a long time. But it became easy and permanent prey for the Turkish nomads, and patterns of population and settlement were quickly and drastically changed by their invasions. The 'Great Seljuqs' of Baghdad had broken the Byzantine defence (in 1071 at Malāzgird); the 'Seljuqs of Rūm' (the term Rūm means Eastern Rome, Byzantium) pushed further westwards and were able at the end of the twelfth century to set up a fragile authority in eastern and southern Anatolia, around Konya and other urban centres (Sebaste-Sïvas, Caesarea—Kayseri), and to establish permanently the religion and culture of Islam.

The Seljuq empire also fell a victim to the Mongols; a rapid collapse followed the defeat at Köse Dagh (1243). But in the shadow of Mongol rule, the Turcoman family of Qaramān in Cilicia (around Konya) was able to set up an important state; and from the Turkish tribes some of which had been pushed westwards into Anatolia by the Mongols and some of which had fought in the Mongol armies there emerged a number of small principalities which fought a religious war against Byzantium. Soon the Ottomans (the sons of ʿOsmān) gained the upper hand; they established their first capital in 1326 in Bursa, a town a few days journey from the Bosphorus.

The Ottomans began their conquests in the Balkans in the year 1354. After the decisive battle at Kosovo (1389) they led their élite European troops (the *yeni cheri*, the Janissaries), driven by necessity and helped by favourable circumstances in an advance on Asia Minor. In the course of one year (1390–91) Bāyezīd Yïldïrïm ('The Thunderbolt') had occupied not only the small Turcoman principalities of Western Anatolia but also conquered the principality of the Qaramānids, who had—long unopposed in the south—become his most dangerous rivals. It is true that the Mongol Tīmūr defeated the growing empire of the Ottomans (1402) and temporarily re-established the autonomy of the Anatolian principalities; but in 1453 the Ottoman Muḥammad (Meḥmed) II ('The Conqueror') took Constantinople and in 1475 toppled the last Qaramānid. With the conquests of Selīm, who took Syria and Egypt in 1517, and his successor Sulaymān, who with the invasion of Hungary (battle of Mohács 1526) brought the whole of the Balkans under Turkish authority, the Ottoman empire was founded—the last great empire of Islamic history. Able to withstand the advance of European powers and the nationalist movements of the Arab countries in the nineteenth century, the Ottoman empire finally fell because of the events of the First World War.

8. The further lands of Islam

The Arab conquests of the Umayyad period had produced the widest expansion of the empire under the central control of the caliphate. The battle of Tours and Poitiers against Charles Martel (732) marked the end of expansion westwards; the confrontation with the Chinese on the Jaxartes (the Muslim victory of 751 on the Talās prevented further penetration into Islamic territory) brought the expansion in the east temporarily to a standstill. The spread of Islam progressed; but further conquests were not the work of the Arabs; and they were the work of dynasties which were no longer or which were only nominally subordinate to the Caliph. It was the Turkish Seljuqs who ended the century-long border war against Byzantium in the Jazīra by the invasion of eastern Anatolia; two centuries after the end of the Caliphate the Ottomans completed their work with the destruction of the Eastern Roman empire of Constantinople.

Traders and seafarers from the Persian Gulf had colonised the coasts of the Indian and the Pacific Oceans as far as China since the early 'Abbāsid period. Northern India was finally conquered from Sīstān by the dynasties from Ghazna and Ghūr. From the thirteenth to the fifteenth centuries their successors, the Sultans of Delhi, established and expanded the authority of Islam in India and from the sixteenth until the eighteenth century the Mughal emperors brought the power and culture of Indian Islam to its highest peak (see below p.135f.). From India (Gujarāt) trade and religious movements carried Islam into southeast Asia. The rulers who became Muslim in that area set up Islamic states in Indonesia and in the Malaysian archipelago. Here is not the place to assess the importance of Indian Islam. Even in our own century revivalist movements in the sub-continent found political realisation in the foundation of the Islamic state of Pakistan (1947).

In East Africa too it was seafaring traders, Arabs and Persians from the area of the Indian Ocean, who settled on the coasts, united with the indigenous population and founded in Somalia and in Zanzibar a series of Islamic principalities; the Bantu language of the 'coastal dwellers' (Arabic *sawāḥila*), Swahili, became the *lingua franca* of East Africa. The Berber tribes who expanded Islam south from the Atlas over the Sahara as far as Senegal have already been mentioned (see p.107f.). From the eighth century onwards the number of Muslims in the kingdoms of west Africa expanded: in Ghana (actually the title of its ruler, but then the name of its capital), the centre of the gold trade, which was taken in 1076 by the Almoravids; in Mali, which was governed by Islamic princes from the thirteenth to the fourteenth century; further east in the Sudan in the kingdom of Songhai (with Gao and Timbuktu on the Niger) from the middle of the fourteenth century until the Moroccan conquest (1591). West African pastoral tribes from the Fulbe spread Islam further towards central Sudan. Towards the end of the eighteenth century the Hausa were converted and Islamic reform movements shaped a series of new governments. In the first half of the nineteenth century the prince of Sokoto ruled the territory between the Niger and Chad; soon afterwards, around the middle of the century, a militant follower of the Ṣūfī order of the Tijāniyya, al-Ḥājj 'Umar (d.1864), set up a short-lived state after religious wars and pushed western Sudan into anarchy. In the last quarter of the nineteenth century the Mahdī of eastern Sudan, Muḥammad Aḥmad ibn 'Abdallāh (d.1885), and his caliph 'Abdallāh Abū Bakr defied the troops of Egypt and the English colonial power, until the battle of Umm Durmān (1898), which destroyed the state of Khartoum although it did not destroy the ideas of the Mahdī.

The further away we move from the ancient heartlands of Islam, the looser their links are with the institutions, the political processes and the cultural influences of the classical Islamic centres. In Ghana and Zanzibar, in Indonesia and Vietnam, we are still dealing with Islamic religious and cultural history but one can surely no longer speak of Islamic history in a general sense nor are the political realities in question exclusively Islamic ones. All the same, Muslims in those areas lived and still do live with an awareness that they also are part of the *Umma Muḥammadiyya,* the community established by the Prophet.

Chapter Six

PERIODS OF ISLAMIC HISTORY

For the Islamic chronicler of the Middle Ages the revelation which came to Muḥammad was the decisive event which marked the turning point of sacred history. The didactic concept of early historiography links the experience of history to God's call and command. History is thus a model for the use and edification of believers, a model and a warning; it links the temporal with the eternal. Everything historical is only a prelude. The medieval historian knows no periodisation, only simple categories for dividing up the material. This may be according to years (the annalistic format), according to the periods when rulers were in power, and also in the biographical literature according to 'classes', i.e. the generations of scholarly transmission. The modern historian tries to describe the events of particular regions coherently, whilst at the same time bearing in mind relations and reciprocal influences with neighbouring territories and bringing to light overlapping processes; in this he is searching for a structure, for the 'universal' in the multiplicity of data and facts. In the course of Islamic history, however, it becomes progressively more difficult to define periods of the whole Islamic world by important events or by developments which were common to Islam in general. The west (Spain and North Africa) and the Iranian east—even if formal loyalty to the caliph was maintained—led a life of their own from as early as the middle of the ninth century onwards.

In all periods there were external movements and internal developments which wide areas of the Islamic world experienced communally; but there were always regions, too, which remained untouched. Thus, for example, the processes of nomadisation which began in the eleventh century, and which were unleashed in the east by the invasion of the Turcomans and in the west through the irruption of the Hilāl Bedouin into the Maghrib, are striking parallels but they have no deeper relationship with each other. On the other hand, the simultaneous return to doctrinal traditionalism in the west and in the east has a common basis, namely the decline of the religious authority of the caliphate and of its vassals. There is no doubt too that the Mongol invasion of the thirteenth century and the expansion of the Ottoman empire in the fifteenth and sixteenth centuries are events of wide-ranging importance and for that reason are really epoch-making.

Every broad division into periods can therefore be no more than an aid towards the arrangement of general synopses, and in order to achieve its aim must combine chronological and geographical divisions. Such definitions are questionable, since every period contains the beginnings of the following one and in the face of every crisis there is also continuity; but they are nonetheless useful. The following outline has above all the aim of illustrating the patterns and divisions usually drawn up by historians of Islam.

1. Arabia before Islam (until c.610 *AD)*

In the area of the Arabian peninsula, the 'Arabia Felix' of the south and the border states of Syria and Mesopotamia belonged to the sphere of Hellenistic and Iranian civilisations. The political collapse of the ancient super-powers brought profound disruption to the whole region.

¶ From around the second century AD Arab camel-based nomadism extended over the peninsula after the collapse of the border states and the decline of south Arabian culture. The Bedouin advanced into areas which were hitherto settled; the use of writing regressed. The society was formed to which the Koranic revelation was directed, whose ethics and concept of justice were to become the sub-stratum of the Islamic order, and from which there finally were to arise the motivating forces for Islamic expansion outside Arabia.

¶ From the fourth century AD Arabia was drawn into the wars between Byzantium and Sasanian Persia. Situated as it was in the sphere of interest of the buffer states of the sixth century—the Kingdom of the Lakhmids in Iraq, the phylarchy of the Ghassānids in Syrian territory, the Yemen under Abyssinian rule—the trading city of Mecca was also affected by the political game of the two great powers.

¶ The pre-Islamic shrine of Mecca, its economic importance, the rise of trade (along the incense route) and the emergence of an urban society from a Bedouin milieu were behind the social conflicts which the Koranic revelation sought to solve.

*2. Muḥammad: the mission of the Arab Prophet and the first Islamic state (*c.610–32*)*

The activity of the Prophet of Islam in Mecca and in Medina established the religion, law and state of Islam.

¶ With the revelation of God the Creator as the benevolent almighty judge, a revelation given in the Arabic language, he founded Arab monotheism—a world view, a code of values and a social order—and the Arab nation.

¶ Above the solidarity of individual tribes he placed the solidarity of the community (*Umma*) which was sanctioned by the duty of every individual towards God, and thus gave new direction to a society in transition.

¶ It was the revelation of the Medinan period above all (after the *Hijra*, emigration, of 622) that laid the foundation of the legal and governmental system of the empire which was to come.

¶ With the subjugation of the Arab tribes in the last years of his life Muḥammad created the military and—by converting the community to faith in Islam—the spiritual basis of an expansion which was to begin after his death.

3. *The caliphate until the end of the Umayyads (632–750)*

In the first century after the death of Muḥammad the tribes of Arabia, having converted to Islam, conquered an empire from the Atlantic to the Indus. The institutions of the Islamic state were established and formulated; through the medium of the Arabic literary language the Muslims created the foundations of classical Islamic culture.

(a) The period of the 'orthodox' caliphs (al-Rāshidūn, 632–61): the emergence of the Arab state.

After the death of the Prophet four men who in his lifetime had been amongst his companions ruled in his city of Medina as his 'deputies', caliphs. In the eyes of the majority of Muslims they are deemed to be orthodox guardians of his theocracy, legitimised by the consensus of the community.

¶ Abū Bakr (632–34) and 'Umar (634–44) united the Arab tribes through successful campaigns of conquest, thereby strengthening Islam and preparing the way for it to become a world religion.

¶ In three decades the Arab conquerors took the Sasanian empire (Iraq and Iran) and the Byzantine territories of Syria, Egypt and northern Mesopotamia.

¶ The 'city of the Prophet', Medina, was the political centre of the empire; the garrisons of the armies of conquest became provincial centres. The indigenous governmental systems and the existing organisation of land ownership and taxation remained the basis for provincial administration.

¶ The distribution of land and booty from the conquests produced social tensions. Misappropriation and economic exploitation of state funds by 'Uthmān (644–56) led to

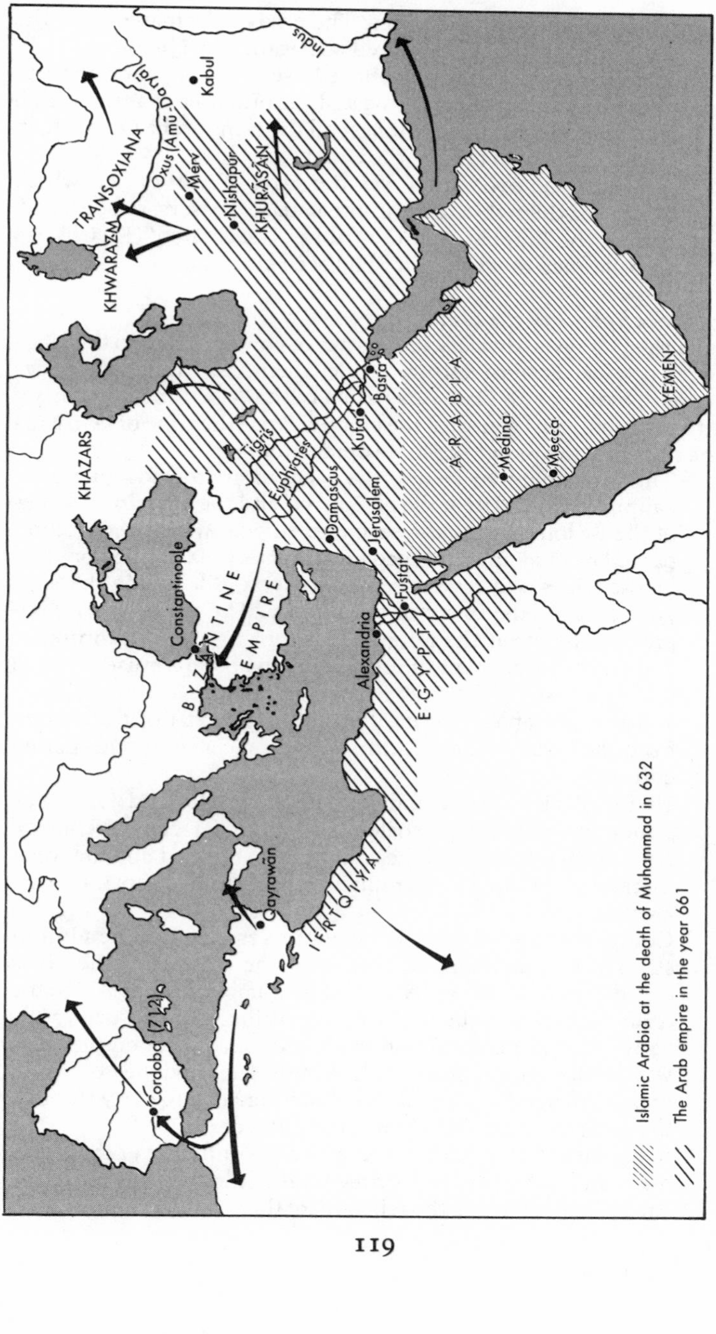

2. *The Arab conquests in the 7th century.*

rebellion amongst the tribes. The crisis culminated after the murder of 'Uthmān in the civil war against 'Alī (656–61).

¶ The victor, Mu'āwiya, established a secular pragmatic concept of the Islamic state and abrogated the principle that the caliph should be elected from amongst all the clans of the Quraysh, in favour of his own family, the Umayyads.

¶ Amongst the opposition was the party (*Shī'a*) of 'Alī which fought for the rights of his immediate successors, the descendants of the Prophet, and the tribes of 'secession' (Khārijites), who claimed that theocracy had been betrayed.

(b) The caliphate of the Umayyads (661–750)

Under the Umayyad dynasty the centres of power shifted to the lands of ancient Near Eastern culture. Under their first caliph, Mu'āwiya (661–80), Syria—with Damascus as its capital—became for nearly a century the political centre of the empire. From the time of 'Alī, Kūfa in Iraq became the refuge of Shī'īte opposition.

¶ The movement to restore the Meccan aristocracy (the anti-caliphate of 'Abdallāh ibn al-Zubayr) and the anarchical forces of the Bedouin led to the second civil war, which was accompanied by epidemics and economic crises (683–92). Supported by the tribes which were settled in Syria, 'Abd al-Malik (685–705) secured the unity of the Empire. The price was a compromise between the religious ideal of the 'just' community and a secular concept of unity. But this compromise allowed the revelation of the Arab Prophet to become a world religion and brought about the intellectual integration of the empire from the Oxus to the Atlantic by means of a pervasive Islamic culture.

¶ Under 'Abd al-Malik and his successor al-Walīd (705–15), strong governors kept strife-torn Iraq under central control. Arab armies completed the conquests in the east and the west, thereby expanding the empire under caliphal control to its greatest size.

¶ Comprehensive governmental reforms established the administrative and financial autonomy of the state after the crisis decade of the civil war. 'Abd al-Malik 'arabised' and unified the chancelleries and the coinage; 'Umar ibn 'Abd al-'Azīz (717–720) adapted taxation and state economy to circumstances which had changed through the Islamisation and the expansion of land ownership. He was not, however, able to carry through the work of reform before his premature death.

¶ In the last phase of the Umayyad state, conflict over the legitimacy and 'justice' of the regime weakened the solidarity of the Arabs. The strife and the rebellion of the tribes, combined with the many criticisms of the pious, the Khārijites, and the Shīʿa about the secular 'kingship' of the dynasty, led to the decline of the Umayyads. They finally came to grief because of conflicts which resulted from the problems of the social assimilation and economic integration of the non-Arabs into the Islamic empire.

4. The caliphate of the ʿAbbāsids and its successor states from 749 until the middle of the eleventh century

The third civil war in Islam—the ʿAbbāsid revolution—brought to power another dynasty from the tribe of the Quraysh, the Banu'l-ʿAbbās (749–1258); they were nearer in their relationship to the Prophet, and nearer also to him in their claim that they were establishing the theocracy of a truly Islamic state. Their claim that they would create an Islamic government and equal justice for all Muslims failed; but from the conflict of religious, political, social and economic forces there emerged a classical Islamic culture which was based on the participation of all Muslims, both Arabs and non-Arabs.

(a) The first century of the ʿAbbāsids (749–847)

In the first century of their power the ʿAbbāsids completed the work of their predecessors: they ensured the hegemony of the Arabs under the leadership of the Quraysh; they kept at bay the politico—religious sects which threatened the unity of the empire and of the faith; and they strengthened the borders of Islam and established bridgeheads for its further expansion. Finally the Arabic language, at first the language of the conquering class, became the language of the empire, and the medium of Islamic culture for all its proponents, of whatever origin. In the same period the process of selection and collection of religious and legal traditions finally was completed. It was a process whose beginnings stretched right back into the Umayyad period, and it culminated in the codification of the *Sunna* (in *ḥadīth*) and in the scholarly transmission of Islamic doctrine in the 'orthodox' legal schools.

¶ The political and cultural centre moved to the East (where the opponents of the Umayyads had assembled their forces and fomented rebellion), to Iraq and the provinces of Iran linked to it geographically and politically, in particular Khurāsān. The foundation of Baghdad (763) as the new capital by al-Manṣūr (754–75) underlined this shift.

¶ The caliphs of Baghdad organised the empire as a multinational centralised state. Non-Arabs, above all Persians, participated more and more in its administration and its culture; the model of Sasanian Iran left its imprint on the institutions of the empire. 'Classical' Islamic culture developed out of the active adoption of the Hellenistic and Iranian literary and scientific traditions, preceded by a period of passive reception.

¶ If the only political institution in the Umayyad empire had been the power of the state, the first 'Abbāsids—who according to their own understanding of the caliphate were charismatic guardians of theocracy—based their rule on Iranian models, created instruments of their spiritual and worldly authority in the institutions of the law, the administration and the army. They tried to follow the command 'to ordain what is right and to forbid what is wrong' (*al-amr bi'l-ma'rūf wa'l-nahy 'an al-munkar*)—the slogan of opposition to the Umayyads—with reforms of the land and taxation laws and thus to take account of social change (Islamisation and urbanisation).

(b) The decline of the caliphate (ninth–tenth centuries)

The theocratic claim of the 'Abbāsids became mere theory. Inner contradictions in society sharpened under the pressure of social change; the military and administrative institutions slipped from the control of the sovereign. Centrifugal forces in the provinces of the great empire led to the break-up of the weakened caliphate and finally to autonomy for a large number of regional principalities, both Arab and Iranian. In place of the Islamic empire as a political institution there remained an Islamic cultural sphere.

¶ The caliphate tried, and failed, to submit the highest judges to an inquisition—the *Miḥna* ('trial') of al-Ma'mūn (813–33) and his two successors (829–48)—so as to force the religious institution to embrace the doctrines of rationalist theology. This attempt came up against resistance from the traditionalists under the leadership of Aḥmad ibn Ḥanbal; their rebellion, supported by large sections of the populace, succeeded (restoration of al-Mutawakkil in 848).

¶ The caliph al-Mu'taṣim (833–42) established a bodyguard of Turkish military slaves and founded the garrison of Sāmarrā (836) as his new residence. The alienation of the caliphate from the people was now clearly visible. Soon after this, however, the retreat from Baghdad was itself also a sign of disastrous weakness; al-Mutawakkil (847–61) and his successors became a tool in the power politics of their Turkish generals.

¶ Payment of the army by military land tenure led to the ruin of the central exchequer. The approved separation between military and financial administration was abandoned; the chief amir (*amīr al-'umarā'*, the first of whom was Ibn Rā'iq 936–38) acquired wide-ranging powers.

¶ In the year 945 the Iranian Būyids conquered Iraq, which was being fought over by Turks and Arabs alike. While they 'rescued' the caliph they made him entirely their puppet and took over political power with the office of chief amir. 'Aḍud al-Dawla (949–83), the renewer of Iranian kingship and from 978 onwards ruler in Baghdad, had himself crowned king by the caliph.

¶ The administration, which was founded on the traditions of Iranian agrarian society, failed in the task of creating forms of organisation for the rapidly growing towns. Here, social differences and tensions led to the spontaneous formation of militant groups and to the outbreak of unrest. At the same time there were rebellions among the agricultural slave proletariat of the large estates in southern Iraq, culminating in the rebellion of the Zanj (African slaves) in 869–83. In these hotbeds of unrest, and also amongst the Arab Bedouin, the Ismā'īliyya began their propaganda in the name of social justice and in this way started their own rise to political power.

¶ Political quietism on the part of intellectuals and a free interplay of intellectual forces at a time of Arab-Persian rivalry produced a new diversity in Islamic culture in the tenth century. This period has been viewed as a 'renaissance' vis-à-vis the 'classicism' of the first period of the 'Abbāsid Golden Age, and with regard to renewed revival of the classical scientific heritage.

(c) The rise of local autonomous states and the successor states of the caliphal empire (c.850–c.1055)

The disintegration of the caliphal empire into small states had already begun soon after the assumption of power by the 'Abbāsids. First in the west, in Spain, as early as 755, the Umayyad 'Abd al-Raḥmān had founded an independent emirate. A little later a group of 'Alids became independent in Morocco, Khārijites in Eastern Algeria followed suit, and loyal governors in Ifrīqiyya and Egypt became practically autonomous from the middle of the ninth century. A similar process occurred with the governors of Khurāsān, Sīstān and Transoxania in the Iranian east. Under the leadership of the Iranian family of the Sāmānids, at the court of Bukhārā, the Iranian world from the middle of the tenth century onwards regained its political autonomy and at the same time its cultural identity.

¶ In the course of the tenth century the centre of power in Iran moved west. The Daylamites began their rise to power on the shores of the Caspian Sea and in the second half of the tenth century, under the Būyid dynasty in Rayy, Iṣfahān and Shīrāz, became the foremost power in the east, controlling even the caliphate itself. Thus western Iran, the former Sasanian empire, which was so deeply Islamicised and also Arabised in

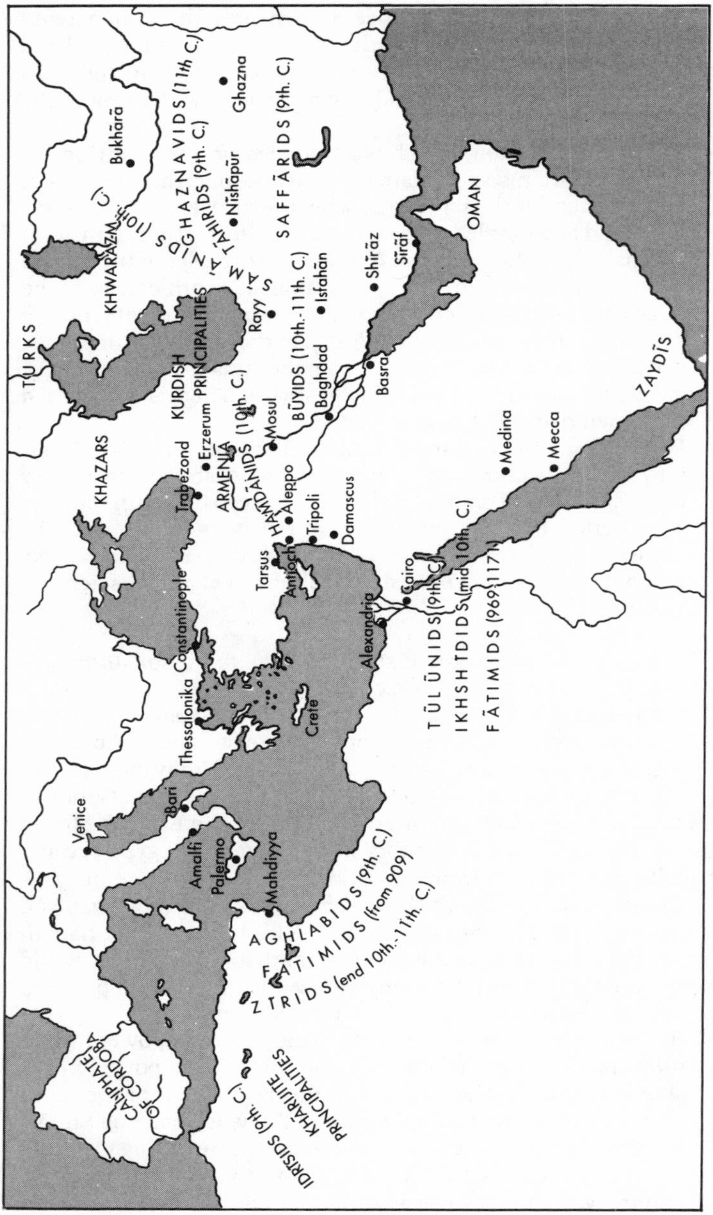

3. *The Islamic world in the 10th century.*

the towns, had a decisive influence on 'new Persian' classical culture.

¶ The economic policy of the Būyids depended on the exploitation of land ownership through military land tenure and prevented social harmony; opposition inside and outside the towns combined with dynastic struggles accelerated their downfall. At the same time the Sāmānids were pushed out of Khurāsān by their Turkish slave generals from Ghazna (999), and Turcoman tribes moved out of the Central Asian steppe towards the Oxus and after a few decades towards Western Persia.

¶ The provinces of the caliphate were reduced to the immediate surroundings of the capital, Baghdad. Just as with the Iranian world, so too the Arab Near East broke away from the caliph. After the political fragmentation of the Islamic empire, the Fāṭimid anti-caliphate also threatened to disrupt the religious unity of the Islamic community. The Seljuqs restored political strength to orthodox Islam but it was only the Mongols who ended the agitations caused by the Nizāriyya (the Assassins) who, after another schism in Cairo, terrified the Islamic east from the eleventh to the thirteenth century.

5. *The Seljuq period* (c.*1055*–c.*1258*)

After inner disintegration there followed an invasion of new forces of nomadism, which shook the world of Islam from the eleventh century onwards. Social disruption, political change and new religious tendencies were consequences.

¶ From the early 'Abbāsid period onwards, Turkish military slaves imported into the Near East from the eastern borders had enjoyed both fame and notoriety and were already in competition with the Iranian dynasties. From the end of the tenth century, however, an invasion of Turkish tribes was unleashed on to the East which fundamentally changed the geographical landscape and—under the leadership of the Seljuq family—the political landscape too.

¶ Movements of Arab Bedouin towards Syria and Egypt reached a high point of devastation with the onslaught of the Banū Hilāl over NW Africa—launched by the Fāṭimids as a reprisal against the rebellious Zīrids (1049).

¶ Likewise, around the middle of the eleventh century Islamicised Berber tribes advanced from the Atlas northwards, took Morocco and from there gained possession of al-Andalus.

(a) The Seljuqs (Iran and Iraq eleventh-twelfth century, in Anatolia until thirteenth century)

The dynasty of the Seljuqs (Selchüqids) from the Oghuz tribe gave political unity and strategic leadership to the forces of Turkish nomads all the way to Anatolia. The subjugation of the Ghaznavids (1040), the occupation of Baghdad by Toghrïl Beg (1055) and the defeat of the Byzantine army by Alp Arslan (1071) were the most important milestones on this route.

¶ After the conquest of Baghdad the Seljuqs took over from their predecessors, the Būyids, investiture by the caliph (who gave them the title *sulṭān*) and they used the model of Iranian-Islamic government as the basis of their authority. Again like the Būyids, they kept a standing army through payment by land tenure (*iqṭāʻ*) and in this way linked the soldiery to the land. The system was now systematically expanded and at first, under strict control, became a means of ensuring stability. After the collapse of the Seljuq central power in the twelfth century, however, local forces became strong; the grants of land which served originally as immediate payment became the hereditary domains of provincial governors (*atabegs*, 'tutors of princes'). The caliph received once again a certain, if regionally limited, freedom of manoeuvre, and in addition to the Seljuq family in Iran independent lines of Seljuqs ruled in Anatolia and Atabegs in Mesopotamia and Syria.

¶ In the face of the rivalry between the caliph and the sultan for political power, religious authority fell to the teachers of law, the transmitters and propounders of the *Sunna* of the Prophet. The Seljuq sultans and their viziers presented themselves as defenders of the *Sunna*, especially in the struggle against the radical Ismāʻīlī Shīʻa; and they tried to legitimise themselves fully by promoting teachers and founding teaching institutions for the recognised schools of law. A process which had continued from the ninth century onwards came to an end with the institutionalisation of the *Sunna*: the traditionalism and pragmatism of the schools of law were recognised as the real orthodoxy of Islam. Ṣūfism, which acquired a structure of 'orders' also turned into an institution and instrument of this orthodoxy. At the same time religiosity was imbued with an anti-intellectual subjective approach.

(b) Syria and Egypt under the Atabegs and Ayyūbids; the Islamic confrontation with the Crusaders; the final phase of the ʻAbbāsid caliphate (twelfth–mid-thirteenth century)

¶ In the twelfth century the Zangids of Mosul and Damascus were appointed as Atabegs of the Seljuqs and soon became

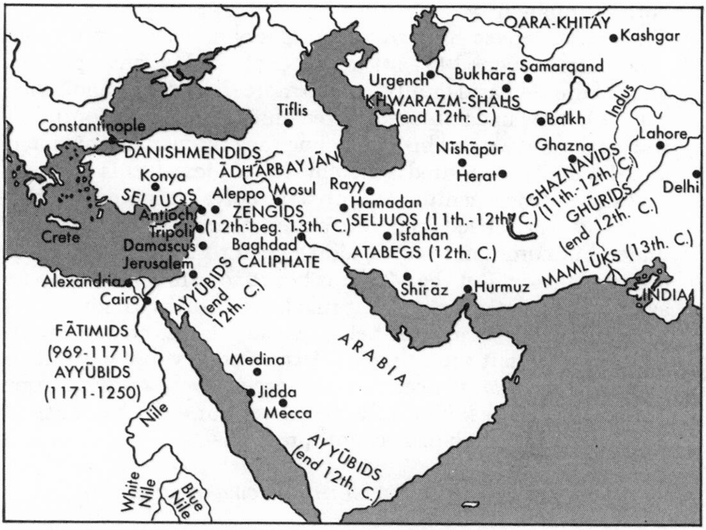

4. *The Islamic world in the 12th century.*

autonomous. The Zangids and thereafter the successors of their Kurdish general Ayyūb led the Holy War to restore Sunnī Islam against the heretical Fāṭimids and the Christian Crusaders. The most important rulers of the two dynasties, Nūr al-Dīn ibn Zangī and Ṣalāḥ al-Dīn ibn Ayyūb (Saladin), were protagonists in the struggle against the Franks. But the crucial events in relation to Islamic history were the ending of the Ismāʿīlī anti-caliphate in Cairo (1171) in the name of the ʿAbbāsid caliph by Shīrkūh and his nephew Saladin. Thereafter the latter, having made Egypt into a new power base, achieved the unification of the Fertile Crescent under his overall authority. The repulsion of the Third Crusade and the conquest of Jerusalem (1187) were prestigious in the eyes of the Muslims but for Saladin they were above all the necessary means of assuring his control over Northern Syria and the Jazīra against the claims of the last Zangids. Here he had achieved his aim. For Europe, the Crusades, which had been launched by a conflict of the revolutionary papacy with political forces, marked an era; for Byzantium they were a lasting catastrophe. For Islam they were a disturbance, and also a regional threat, but in the final analysis only a continuation of the old border struggles with Byzantine Christendom. Even in the face of external danger the political split within Islam could not be cured permanently.

¶ The caliph moved back to the periphery of events even more than before. Even al-Nāṣir (1180–1225), the last great personality of the ʿAbbāsid family, had no more than local importance even when he had managed to free himself from the control of the Turks and extend his power once again towards Khūzistān and Jibāl. The method whereby he achieved this success revealed political genius: he united the chivalric guilds of urban *futuwwa*, revitalised them into a state-controlled organisation under his command and made them into an instrument of political power. But the Muslims hoped in vain for his support against the Crusaders. It is true that he confirmed Saladin in his investiture as sultan (this helped Saladin in his struggle with the Zangids), but the caliph's mistrust of Ayyūbid expansion was stronger than his belief in the necessity of a united front against the Franks. Not only the power but also the political horizon of the caliph had become provincial.

(c) Almoravids and Almohads in North Africa and Spain (1056–1269)

In the period of the Seljuqs and Atabegs in the east, the extreme west was subdued twice by Berber dynasties from the Atlas. Both the Almoravids (*al-Murābiṭūn*) and the Almohads (*al-Muwaḥḥidūn*) conquered Spain and pitted themselves against the Reconquista; but while the Almoravid Yūsuf ibn Tāshufīn achieved a great success against the Christians at Zallāqa (1086), the last Almohads had to retreat to North Africa after the decisive battle of Las Navas de Tolosa (1212).

¶ Both dynasties rose to power under the aegis of religious revival and renewal. But whereas the Almoravids propagated a rigid traditionalism, leading to ossification and isolation through the medium of the orthodox institutions of the Mālikite legal school, the Almohads restored a lively relationship with the eastern centres of Islamic culture by renewed encouragement of spiritual exchange and of the sciences—religious as well as profane.

6. The Mongol period

From the conquest of Baghdad by the Mongols to the establishment of the Ottoman empire in the Near East (1258–1517).

(a) The Mongol invasion and the Mongol period in the Islamic East (thirteenth–fifteenth centuries)

The invasion of Mongol tribes from Central Asia affected and changed a wide area from the Far East to the Balkans. In the Mongol invasion the Islamic world experienced a fundamental threat from non-Islamic enemies. A centuries-old social, economic, religious and cultural order was threatened and in many places definitively destroyed. In that respect the destruction of the Baghdad caliphate at the hand of Hülegü (1258) was an epoch-making date.

¶ The process of nomadisation was renewed and intensified by Turkish tribes who stormed across the Iranian and Anatolian plateaux, either in the Mongol army or displaced by it. The ethnic character of all these regions was permanently changed; the cities and their culture became islands under threat. Within the Mongol realm too, and in places where they encountered opposition, new lines of demarcation were drawn up. Finally the Mongol invasion not only completed the expansion of Turkish tribes over the whole of Western Asia in a very direct fashion but also by causing the collapse of the Seljuq empire indirectly made possible the rise of its successors in Anatolia and finally also the rise of the Ottoman empire.

¶ There now developed a separation more marked than ever before between the Arab world and the Iranian sphere, for after the conversion of the Īlkhāns to Islam (Maḥmūd Ghazan, 1295–1304) Mongol as well as Turkish rulers in Iran, Asia Minor, Central Asia and India adopted eastern Islamic forms of government, Persian language and culture.

¶ While the Mongol rulers in the Far East promoted Buddhism, they were astute enough to embrace the religion of their Muslim subjects in Iranian territory, and also spread Islam in Central Asia (even the Golden Horde in Russia converted to Islam). This frustrated European hopes of strengthening Asian Christianity in lasting fashion amongst the Turks (it had already taken hold amongst the Uighurs) and the Mongols by diplomacy and missionary work. Christianity in Asia was reduced to an isolated minority religion.

¶ Rivalry with the Islamic powers of the Near East led to the establishment of diplomatic relations between Europe and the Mongol empire, opened Asia and the Near East to European traders and travellers and brought about world-wide trade and cultural contacts. These were fostered by Europe on its own initiative and in new ways after the end of the *Pax Mongolica.*

(b) The Mamlūks in Egypt and Syria (1250–1517). The emergence of the Ottoman Empire

The centre of Islamic Arab culture finally moved out of the ruined land of Iraq westwards towards Cairo and Damascus.

By its victory over the Mongol army in Palestine (ʿAyn Jālūt,

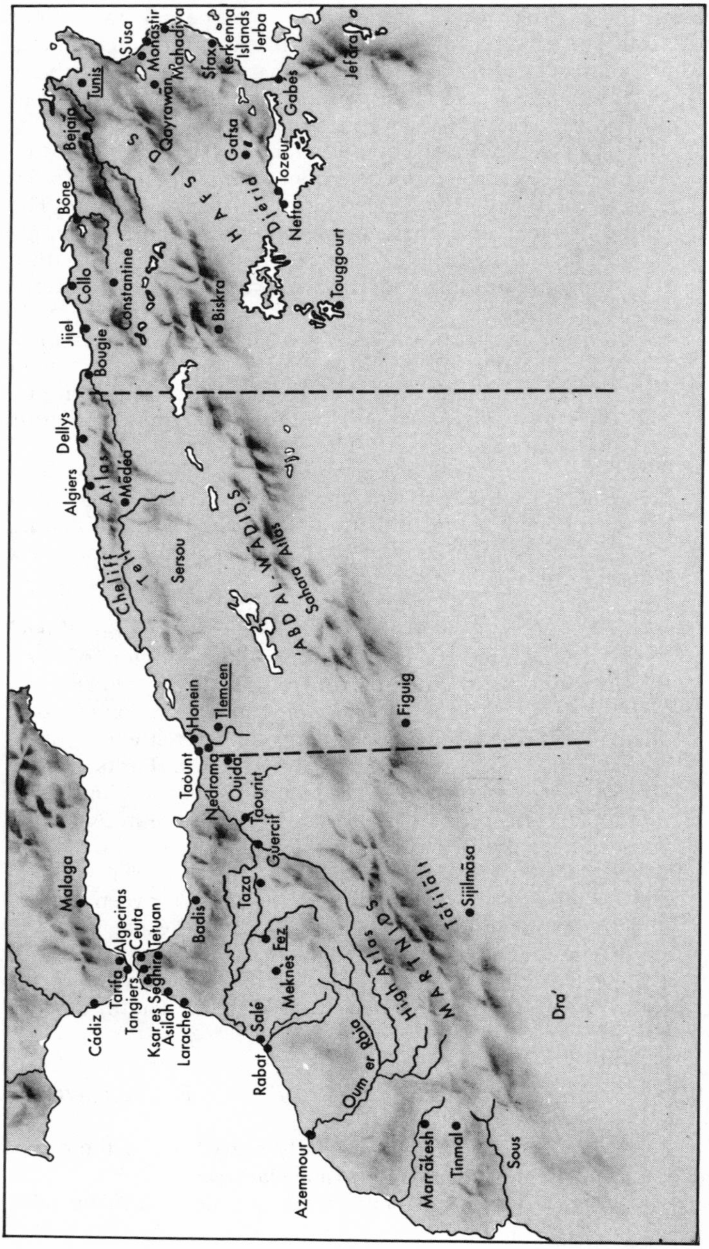

5. *The Maghrib towards the end of the 13th century.*

1260) and the final destruction of the Crusader states on the Syrian-Palestine coast, the Mamlūk state created the conditions for a 200-year-long stable rule in the Near East and for a late flourishing of Sunnī Islamic culture. Admittedly this culture was not creative, but it consolidated tradition and assembled knowledge.

¶ Like the Seljuqs and the Ayyūbids as whose military slaves they rose to prominence in Egypt and Syria, the Mamlūks established their authority on claims to be legitimised by the institution of Sunnī orthodoxy (symbolised in the 'Abbāsid 'puppet' caliphate of Cairo). They based their power on the setting up of a military aristocracy consisting of Turkish military slaves (*mamlūk*), and they based their state budget on the *iqṭā'* system of land tenure.

¶ In the period of its decline the Mamlūk state—at first still victorious (1491)—came up against the expanding power of the Ottomans who after long rivalry took over its domains in the Near East (1516–17). The emergence of the principality of the Ottomans had begun from the fourteenth century in Western Anatolia and in the Balkans. They had been beaten by the Mongol Tīmūr (1402), but had recovered in a few decades. In their early period, the Ottomans were imbued with the spirit of the *ghāzīs* ('fighters' for the faith), which had inspired the Turcomans in central Asia from the time of the border wars on the Oxus and the Jaxartes and now spurred them on in the war against Byzantium and the Christian Balkans. Finally they took over the imperial idea of government and the organisation of their predecessors in the empire of the Arabic caliphate.

(c) The West under the last Berber dynasties (mid-thirteenth–mid-sixteenth centuries)

¶ The Almohad empire, the last great empire of North Africa and Spain in Western Islam, fell in 1269. In Spain the principality of the Naṣrids of Granada remained as a glorious bastion of Islam until it also collapsed under the attack of the united Christian princes (1492).

¶ North Africa was divided between three Berber dynasties: the Marīnids, (1269–1465) in Fez, the 'Abdalwādids (1236–1554) in Tlemcen and the Ḥafṣids (1229–1569) in Tunis. The Ḥafṣids established once again nominal control in North Africa but could not exercise real authority because of a lack of strong central organisation. In the whole of the Maghrib an uneasy equilibrium prevailed between insubordinate tribal groups and the pacified crown lands which were limited to the cities and their environs (between the *bilād al-sā'iba* and *bilād al-makhzan*).

7. The Ottoman period (sixteenth–eighteenth centuries)

(a) The Ottoman Empire

The Ottoman empire had already emerged in the period which is generally called the Mongol period. The principality of 'Osmān, the founder of the dynasty at the end of the thirteenth century, was at first only one of the smallest of the Turkish states of Anatolia. Military successes in the Balkans opened the way to supremacy in Asia Minor; the conquest of Constantinople (1453)—the end of the Byzantine empire—and the conquest of Syria and Egypt (1516–17)—the end of the Mamlūk state—were the phases by which the Ottomans rose to supremacy in the Near East, a supremacy which embraced all the lands of classical Arabic-Islamic culture. The Ottoman state now entered both in theory and in the practical exercise of power into the inheritance of the caliphate.

¶ The ruling hierarchy and government organisation were modelled on their Seljuq and Mamlūk predecessors. Characteristic Ottoman institutions included the caste of ruling élite (the Osmanlïs under the leadership of the Ottoman dynasty), the maintenance of a military élite by purchase and importation of slaves (from the Balkans), a centralised administration under the vizierate and the establishment of a provincial administration based on various forms of land tenure and tax farming, and finally the legal autonomy of the religious communities (*millet*)—and with it the actual abandonment of the idea that the state and the *Umma* were one.

¶ After the high point of power under Sulaymān I (1520–66) the long period of decline began with manifestations of collapse in the internal structure of government. From the second half of the sixteenth century the extension of the power of the Grand Vizier led to the central power being separated from the sultanate, the focal point of loyalty. Then the Turkish aristocracy and, after 1579, also the Grand Vizierate lost their supremacy to the military élite of the āghās of the Janissaries. From the seventeenth century (the peace of Karlowitz, 1699), after a long series of retreats and defeats the empire had to withdraw from most of its territories in the Balkans in the face of the military superiority of Europe.

¶ The development of the empire from the eighteenth century was characterised by the efforts to face the challenge of Europe in economy, technology and culture, by flexibility in the economic sphere and by reforms in the imperial institutions. The 'tulip' period (the vizierate of Dāmād Ibrāhīm, 1718–30) revealed a new openness towards Europe. In 1789 a series of reforms in military government and administration began,

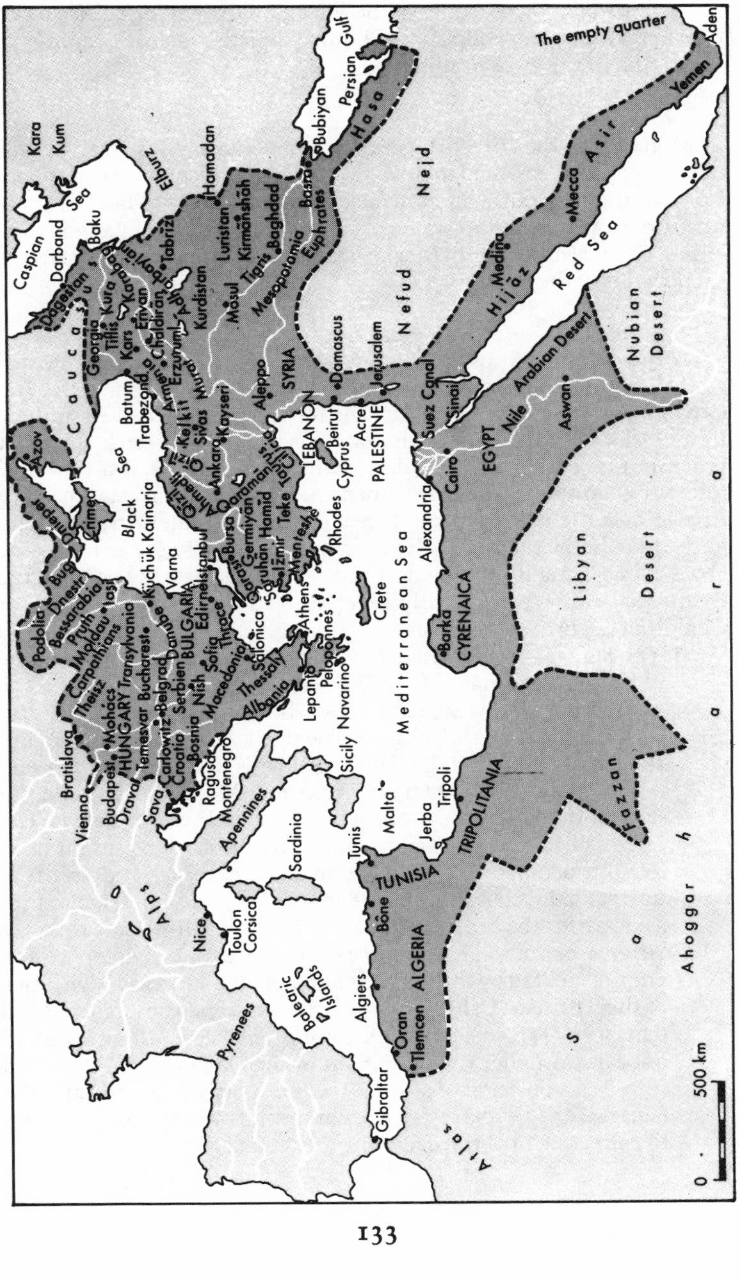

6. *The Ottoman empire.*

reforms which could not, however, halt eventual political and economic dependence on Europe and the gradual disintegration of the great empire.

(b) North Africa

In Morocco in the fifteenth century a new dynasty of Arab Sharīfs (*shurafā'*, 'Alid descendants of the Prophet) emerged triumphant from protracted conflict and managed to extend crown land over the territory north of the Atlas by a skilful policy of alliance with the tribes. Central and eastern Maghrib fell to the Ottoman empire in the second half of the century.

(c) Iran from the Ṣafawid period

After the decline of post-Mongol western Iran, the Turcoman tribal confederations of the Qara-Qoyunlu (1380–1468) and the Aq-Qoyunlu (1378–1508) divided up the territory. The renewed unification of Iran was the work of the Ṣafavids, a dynasty which sprang at first from a sectarian Ṣūfī order, gathered around itself a powerful following amongst the Turcomans of Ādharbāyjān and eastern Anatolia in the course of the fifteenth century (the Qïzïlbash) and with their help conquered the area from Ādharbāyjān as far as the Oxus (Shāh Ismā'īl ibn Ḥaydar, 1501–24). The attacks against the Ottoman empire were finally repelled by the victory of Selīm at Chāldirān (1514).

¶ The Ṣafavids established a theocratic government in the name of the Hidden Imām of the Shī'a; their legitimacy rested on the institution of the teachers of law who exercised personal judgement (*ijtihād*) in the religious law until the return of the Imām, the expected Mahdī. Under the Ṣafavids, Iran—until then predominantly ruled by Sunnī Turks and Mongols—became the land of the Shī'a and, together with the old centres in Iraq, the refuge of its religious and cultural tradition. A common faith led the peoples of Iran to permanent political and spiritual unity. Shāh 'Abbās I (1588–1629) made his capital Iṣfahān into a centre for the brilliant revival of Iranian Islamic culture.

¶ After a century of military conflict and the division of the empire created by the Ṣafavids amongst the successor dynasties of the Turkish Afshār dynasty (1736–95) and the Afghan Zand dynasty (1750–94, with its capital at Shīrāz), Iran acquired once again under the despotism of the Qājārs (1779–1924) an important position of power. It was important also because the Qājārs were partners with the European powers in their politics to gain control of the declining Ottoman empire.

(d) India under the Mughal emperors (1526–1858)

The Turkish sultans of Delhi and a succession of smaller principalities were supplanted by the political heirs of Tīmūr, the leader of the last Mongol invasion of the Muslim world at the end of the fourteenth century. The successful invasion of Northern India (the battle of Pānīpat, 1526) established Tīmūrid rule at first only tenuously but Akbar (1556–1605), the greatest of the Mughal emperors, stabilised Islamic control over north and central India. Under his aegis classical Indo-Islamic culture was formed, moulded by an Iranian government system but also influenced and shaped by indigenous Hinduism. In the *dīn-i ilāhī* ('divine religion') of Akbar himself, a syncretistic universal religion, this culture reached its highest point.

¶ Persian literary traditions, art and architecture and Ṣūfism flourished under the Mughals and developed new forms of expression, also influenced by Hindu and other indigenous currents.

¶ A rapid decline began after the death of Awrangzīb (1658–1707). The invasion of Nādir Shāh from Iran (the occupation of Delhi, 1738–39) and of the Afghan Durrānī led the way to the emergence of Hindu principalities and finally to British colonial power.

8. The emergence of national states. Westernisation and reform (from the beginning of the nineteenth century)

From the turn of the nineteenth century a new development was seen in the course of which the whole Islamic world received new political boundaries and structures.

¶ The political and economic intervention of Europe was decisive for the internal development of the Islamic peoples. Napoleon's invasion of Egypt, 1798–1801, is a highly significant date. It is true that the retreat of the Ottomans in the face of their European opponents and the decline of the imperial government had already begun a hundred years earlier but the encounter with Europe now awakened forces of national consciousness within the Islamic world: at the same time as the Wars of Liberation in the Balkans, Egypt began to revert to autonomous government.

¶ Intellectual confrontation with Europe which was secularised and technologically superior led to critical reappraisal of traditional Islamic values on the part of the Muslims. Islamic reformers showed that development and progress could be achieved from the foundations of the faith and should be envisaged within the spirit of Islam. They began moreover to

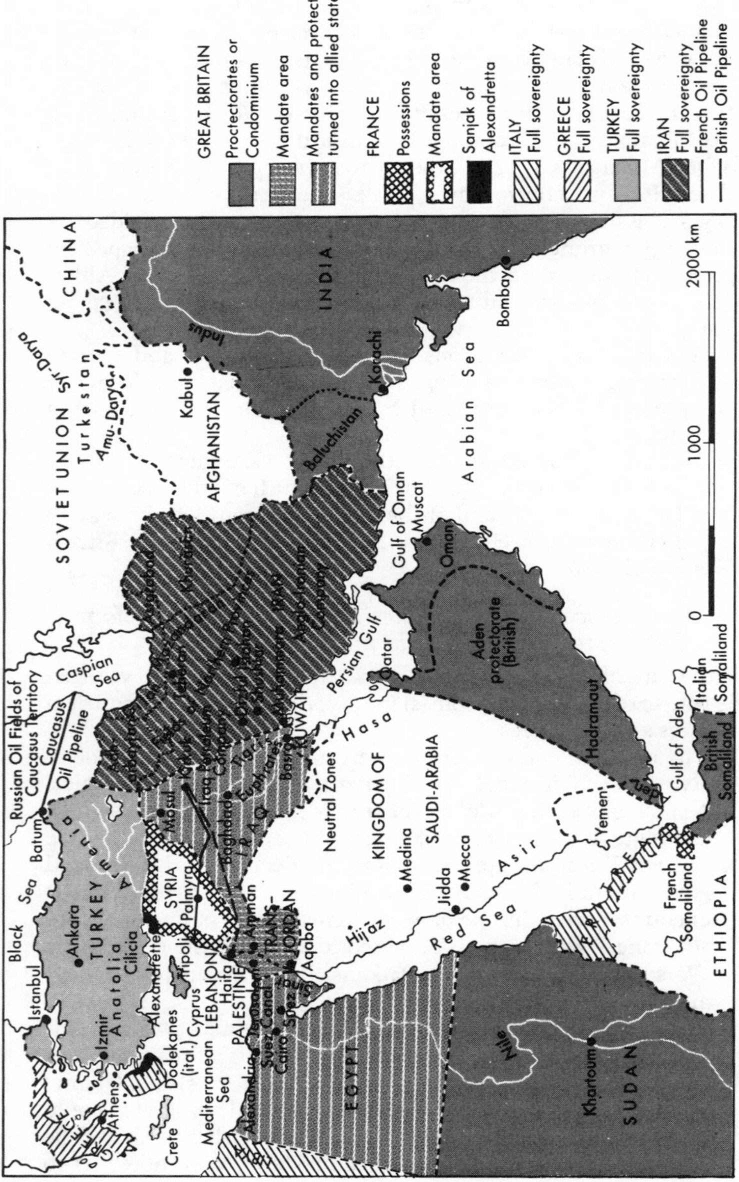

7. *The Near East after the Peace of Lausanne.*

interpret the European concept of nation in an Islamic sense. Traditional lawyers had of necessity accepted the claim of the sultans to authority over the believers (to the caliphate) as legitimate; the concept of national identity within the *Umma*, the community of the believers, was alien to them. With the adoption of the idea of nation the demand for opposition to unjust rule became loud, audible above all in the rebellion against Ottoman oppression amongst the Arabs who began to see themselves—united across borders by the language of the Koran—as the *Umma 'Arabiyya*, 'the Arab nation'.

¶ The forces of nationalism which were awakened by opposition to Ottoman rule directed themselves finally from the end of the nineteenth century—in the Arab world, in Iran as well as amongst the Turks—against European colonialism and imperialism. Their success—the foundation of sovereign states from the end of the First World War—went hand in hand with the secularisation of public and even of private life. With turbulent developments in economics and technology, flagrant social differences and political conflicts within the Islamic world, the idealised unity of religion and of religious culture threatened to become a mere fiction. The movement of fundamentalism in recent times is a reaction to this development; but behind the common slogans—which hark back to the Islamic bases of government and society—there are many different concepts and programmes.

Chapter Seven

APPENDIX: LANGUAGES, NAMES AND THE CALENDAR OF ISLAM

1. Language and Script

(a) Arabic: the language of Islam

Arabic is the language of Islam; it is the language in which, according to Muslim belief, God spoke to the Arabs and through them to the whole world; the language in which the revelation of preceding eras was renewed and transmitted pure and complete to all humanity: 'The Beneficent hath made known the Koran. He hath created Man. He hath taught him [clear] utterance' (Koran, sura 55, verses 1–4); 'And we never sent a messenger save with the language of his folk, that he might make (the message) clear for them' (sura 14, verse 4); The Koran is 'the revelation of the Lord of the world, which the True Spirit hath brought down . . . in plain Arabic speech' (sura 26, verses 192–3, 195).

Arabic, which was carried by the Islamic conquerors beyond the peninsula, was at first only the language of the army and the small ruling class of officers and governors. For the time being, the government apparatus of the conquered empires remained in use as did the official languages of the Sasanian and Byzantine bureaucracies, Persian and Greek. Through the government reforms of the Umayyad caliph, 'Abd al-Malik (685–705), Arabic became the official administrative language of the empire in the 690s. The sources describe this event in the following story:

> In Syria the *Dīwān* ['list', 'state register' of those receiving salaries and of the land tax; in a wider sense, the government financial administration] was written in Greek—until the government of 'Abd al-Malik ibn Marwān, who in the year 81 [700 AD] changed it [to Arabic]. The cause of this was that one of the Greek scribes had to write something and since he could find no water [to moisten the ink powder], he urinated into the ink pot. 'Abd al-Malik heard about it and had him punished; and he ordered Sulaymān ibn Sa'd to translate the *Dīwān*. The latter asked him

> to allocate him (the proceeds of) the land tax of the province of Jordan for one year. That was granted, and before a year was up he had completed the translation and handed it over to 'Abd al-Malik. The caliph called his secretary Sergius to him and presented him with the work; the latter was filled with grief and left him full of sorrow. Outside, he met some of the Greek secretaries and said to them: 'Look for another profession, for God has taken this job away from you'. (Al-Balādhurī: *Futūḥ al-Buldān* ['The Conquests of the Lands'], edited by M. J. de Goeje. Leiden 1866, p.193.)

Similar incidents are recorded from the Iranian provinces which were governed from Iraq.

Yet it was not until the influx and the urbanisation of the Arab tribes and the Islamicisation of the non-Arab population that the indigenous local languages of the Near East were gradually suppressed. Around the turn of the millennium Aramaic (in Syria and Mesopotamia) and Coptic (in Egypt) were spoken only by Christian minorities and kept up as literary languages only by learned theologians. After the Mongol period these languages survived, apart from their use in a few linguistically isolated communities, only in the liturgies of the Monophysite and Nestorian Churches.

The indigenous languages did not die out everywhere; they remained alive in places where the immigration and settlement of Arab tribes after the invasions of the conquering armies were on a small scale only. This was the case, for example, in Iran, in the Caucasus (Armenia) and in North Africa (the languages of the Berber tribes in the Atlas and to the south of the mountain ranges).

In the whole of the Islamic empire, however, Arabic became the language of Islamic government and of classical Islamic culture. As the language of the Koran given by God it was the language of the worship of God, of law and of jurisprudence. As the language of the pre-Islamic poets—these had created from tribal dialects the common language of Arabic, on which the Koran itself drew—it became the language of literature. Finally, as the language of administration, it became the language of the urban political and economic centres—in a word, the language of the exercise of political power. The language of the Arab conquerors thus became a means of social emancipation for everyone who in a narrow or wider sense wanted to have a say. This remained the case even when under the 'Abbāsids, from the end of the eighth century onwards, more and more representatives of the conquered peoples who had converted to Islam took part in the political life of the empire, above all at first the Iranians. These peoples (Arabic *shu'ūb*; it is from this term that the name *Shu'ūbiyya* applied to the social and literary movement of the non-Arabs in the ninth century comes) sought equality and indeed superiority through the medium of the Arabic language. Together with the Arabs who had begun to adopt the culture of their Hellenistic surroundings, they began to translate and develop the antique scientific heritage. Thus Arabic became the language of the sciences in the East after the demise of the Greek and Syriac-Aramaic used by the Christians. One of the great men of Islamic science, al-Bīrūnī (973–*c.* 1050) who was born in Khwārazm, was able to write that he would rather be scolded in Arabic than praised in Persian. The language of the Koran permeated all spheres and became the yardstick of all speech and writing; and the influence of its vocabulary, the themes and forms of its poetry and the style of its prose left a profound influence even in places where political autonomy had once again encouraged respect for, and official use of, the local languages of the provinces.

Arabic belongs to the Semitic group of languages. Three large linguistic families can be distinguished in the Semitic group: (1) Babylonian and Assyrian in ancient Mesopotamia (North-east Semitic); (2) Canaanite—Hebrew, Phoenician—and Aramaic in the Western Orient (North-west Semitic); (3) North Arabian—from the Islamic period Arabic proper; the old 'South Arabian' of the south-west borderlands (until the sixth century), and Ethiopian, which is cognate with it (South-west Semitic). These are all closely linked by numerous common elements of phonology, morphology, vocabulary and syntax. These links are so close that it is plausible to postulate a common origin. A certain structural similarity exists also between the Semitic languages and the 'Hamitic' languages of North and North-west Africa, Egyptian, Cushitic (Sudan, Ethiopia) and, especially obvious, Libyan-Berber.

The sedentary Arab tribes of the northern border states used dialects of Aramaic, the old *lingua franca* of the Near East (as did for example the Nabataeans of the Arab state of Petra and Bosra from the first century BC to the third century AD). Much less well-attested is the language of the North Arabian Bedouin before Islam—known only through a few inscriptions. It seems clear that North Arabian before and after the appearance of Islam was spoken in different regional dialects; the language of the Koran also contains peculiarities which were characteristic of the dialect of the Ḥijāz. On the other hand, it was also important for the subsequent development of Arabic that the language of poets who came together at the festivals and markets connected with the shrines—for example at Mecca—and who there lauded in song the glory and fame of their tribes, converged in the course of the sixth century into a common 'high language'. Of course, the original form of this tongue can no longer be postulated with any certainty. Pre-Islamic poetry was transmitted orally, occasionally written down but only codified and collected in the form that is preserved for us now by Islamic philologists; it must be supposed, of course, that in these collections the normative influence of the Koran was always at work and that some texts were tampered with in this process. Yet there is no doubt that there was one significant phénomenon for the future development of the language: Muḥammad could draw on the common language of the poets and of the pagan seers. This was an important factor in the spreading of the Islamic message and in its impact. The authority of the Koran itself established a norm for language from that time onwards. From the time of the early Umayyads, i.e. from the end of the seventh century, grammarians and Koranic experts made strenuous efforts to establish the *'Arabiyya,* the pure Arabic language in accordance with this norm against the influences of the vulgar language and of foreign languages. To counteract the linguistic effects of the turbulent social change caused by the immigration and mixing of Arab tribes in the course of the conquests, by their settlement and by their living in garrisons and cities both together and with non-Arabs, efforts were made to promote the pure language of the Bedouin dialects. Where the Koran displayed phonetic features of the dialect of Mecca (still discernible in the archaic orthography of the established text), its pronunciation was assimilated to the eastern dialects. Thus a common Arabic literary language arose, namely 'classical' Arabic, which has maintained its integrity according to the laws of normative grammar until the present day.

The literary language was therefore conservative from the beginning; it was an expression of united faith and centralised government. It was also the code of a social hierarchy. Non-Arabs (the *mawālī,* who had become free Muslims through conversion, see p.90) only reached the top of that hierarchy when they adopted this literary language as their own. But the development of the living popular language continued apace. Different linguistic sub-strata of the population and differences of geographical and ethnic structure led, not least in the Arabic spoken by the conquerors, to the formation of different and increasingly independent dialects, above all in the provinces far from the metropolis. At no point was the high language in its 'classical' form spoken in daily life even by scholars, and inevitably it became separated by an ever-widening gulf from the dialects of the everyday language. This process had its repercussions on the literary language; these first manifested themselves in the spheres of writing which were not—like poetry, artistic prose, philological, religious and legal literature—subjected to strict grammatical rules: in the literature of the Greek sciences, in the works of authors from the Christian and Jewish minorities, and in private letters. After the end of the caliphate, that is, after the Mongol invasion, we find phonological and grammatical simplifications of this 'middle' Arabic occurring in chronicles and elevated prose literature too. The development of the literary language, however, did not go further in this direction. On the contrary, after a long phase of stagnation, Arab nationalism in the last hundred years has also promoted linguistic purism—at the price of being unable to express concepts in the spheres of modern science and technology—without, on the other hand, being able to stem the influx of vocabulary and linguistic patterns from European languages.

Thus the Arabic language throughout Islamic history has been characterised by the gulf between the written language (which is used orally only in sermons and speeches and in learned discourse, as for example on the radio today) and the different dialects. The Arabic literary language has remained to this day the unifying bond of the Arab Islamic world; the fact that the Arabic script does not express certain differences of pronunciation—the short vowels and many flexional endings—has helped to maintain this unity. In the meantime the regional offshoots of the old tribal dialects became further removed from the high language as well as from each other, rather as the different Romance languages evolved in relation to Latin. The most important major groupings of the innumerable local dialects are the Bedouin dialects of Central and North Arabia, which after the Mongol period also penetrated into Mesopotamia (with a few pockets of old sedentary dialects on the Upper Euphrates and in Anatolia); the dialectal group of Syria, Palestine and Egypt; and the wide spectrum of Maghribī—the dialects of North-west Africa—which have been influenced in a particular way by contact with the Berber languages. Within individual regions, too, the dialects of special social groups in cities, amongst sedentary rural dwellers, and the Bedouin, vary. When in the year 1301 the Mamlūk army put down a rebellion of Egyptian rural origin, the peasants and the Bedouin (who had united in an alliance which threatened the régime) could be distinguished by their dialect. Today, growing social homogeneity and mobility of population are gradually leading to a certain linguistic convergence; education and the media are beginning to remove regional differences, above all of vocabulary, and to bring the literary and popular language closer together. But the basis of Arab unity still remains the *ʿArabiyya*, the language of the Koran—an important factor in the religious, cultural and political spheres.

(b) The other languages of Islam

The declining political power of the caliph and the disintegration of the empire after the emergence of provincial rulers with *de facto* autonomy ushered in new cultural developments. National languages became once again the languages of the court: Iranian dynasties relied on the traditions of Iranian kingship, promoted Persian literature at their courts and once again used Persian in their government chanceries.

The language of the Sasanian empire (Pahlavī, 'middle Persian', to be distinguished from the Old Persian of the Achaemenid period), which was still the language of government in the east under the first caliphs, was used after the official introduction of Arabic only in the religious traditions of the Zoroastrians. In the meantime, the Persian colloquial language experienced a very gradual development which had begun in the late Sasanian period and was accelerated when under Arab domination the vernacular was liberated from the bonds of a conservative literary language, in a way similar to Anglo-Saxon under the Normans. The disappearance of morphology, the emergence of dialectal peculiarities (above all in Eastern Iran), and the adoption of Arabic elements characterised the 'New Persian' which emerged in this way. As a literary language—the script was now the Arabic one—it appeared first in places where the first independent Islamic Iranian states emerged: in Khurāsān and Transoxiana. From the ninth century Persian literature emerged once again from the ancient and still surviving tradition of poetry, heroic epic and didactic and entertaining tales, and it maintained constant dialogue with the mature poetic and stylistic traditions of Arabic. Under the Sāmānids of Bukhārā it experienced its first blooming towards the end of the tenth century. Here, Firdawsī revived the epic tradition of Iranian heroic and kingly sagas in his 'Book of Kings', using a new poetic form; and doctors, astronomers and geographers produced practical works in the language of the country. Finally, here and at the court of the Turkish princes of Ghazna in Sīstān (who like the Sāmānids before them had Persianised the administration) Persian historical writing began. At the same time, Persian poetry and prose emerged in Western Iran under the dynasties from Daylam—whose most important ruler, the Būyid 'Aḍud al-Dawla, had himself crowned with the Iranian title of Shāh by the humiliated caliph; even in Arabic-speaking Baghdad the Būyids employed a special secretary for court correspondence in Persian. In Iṣfahān, Avicenna (Ibn Sīnā), the great doctor and philosopher from Bukhārā (who like most scholars of his time usually wrote in Arabic) laid the foundations of philosophical literature in Persian by writing a little encyclopaedia in that language.

Throughout Iran the popular language once again became a general means of expression, gradually unified by written interchange; up to the middle of the eleventh century the new high language ousted the older dialects in the larger cities of Iran. Dialectal peculiarities from the east, including archaisms, which continued to survive there—in Khwārazm, Soghd and Khurāsān—were superseded by those of the north-west. They were above all overlaid with the increasing influence of Arabic which deeply and permanently impregnated the vocabulary of Persian and indeed dominated it. The classical literature of Iran has been called a literature in two languages, so powerful was the Arabic 'super-stratum' in Persian, both in vocabulary (as is still perceptible today) and also in the forms of literary expression.

Iranian hegemony in the east of the Islamic world appeared only as an intermezzo between Arab control and the first Turkish incursions. The Oghuz tribes which penetrated westwards in the eleventh century spoke Turkish dialects, but they were not literate. The Seljuq princes who had toppled the power of the Ghaznavids and the Būyids around the middle of the century, and who entered Baghdad in the year 1055, therefore had to use Persian, the language of commerce and government in Iran—as indeed the Arabs had done before them. While Turkish nomads on the Iranian plateau pushed back the sedentary population and their language, their upper class took over Iranian government and culture. The uninterrupted flourishing of Persian literature in the cities was clear testimony of this. Not even under the heavy devastations of the Mongol invasions did it wither away completely. Only the centres shifted: to the south-west which was less affected (Shīrāz) and to Ādharbāyjān (Tabrīz became the capital of the Īlkhānids). Only in the sixteenth century did the centre of gravity return towards the centre, to the Ṣafavid capital of Iṣfahān. Under the Anatolian Seljuqs of the twelfth and thirteenth centuries, Persian was also the language of the court at Konya and the language of its poets and chroniclers, as was the case under the Turkish sultans of Delhi and (after the conquest of India by the Tīmūrids in the sixteenth century) under the Mughal successors until the beginning of the nineteenth century. Under the heavy influence of Persian, which in its turn passed on the Arabic script and Arabic vocabulary, there developed at the same time—away from the big cities—the Islamic variant of the modern Indian literary language, Urdū. In concert with the Islamic religion, the Arabic-Persian linguistic and literary heritage (again transmitting the Arabic script) spread from India into Indonesia. It was influential above all in the Malay language of the Islamic kingdom of Malacca (late 14th–15th century) and of the sultanate of Atjeh in Sumatra (16th–19th centuries).

Just as in the case of Arabic, the Persian literary language—though found in a geographically smaller framework—embraces a wide spectrum of dialectal areas (including Afghanistan, with its ancient dialect of Pashto). Only the eastern (Central Asian) variant began a separate life as a literary language through the introduction of the Cyrillic script in Soviet Tadzhikistan. The language of the Kurds in the mountains of Western Persia, Iraq and eastern Anatolia must also be mentioned briefly; the fate of Kurdish (an Iranian language like Persian) mirrors, however, the political divisions and vicissitudes of this unfortunate people which has had a powerful impact on Islamic history. Only in most recent times has it been used as a literary language, using the Latin alphabet.

Turkish emerged as the third 'great' Islamic language through the government of the Ottomans. The Ottoman imperial language, which lies at the base of the modern Turkish spoken in Turkey today, is only one of the various Turkic languages which grew up from the dialects of the Turkish nomads. They are related to Mongol and other linguistic groups which like them have their home in Central Asia. The earliest testimonies of these are to be found outside the Islamic world from the end of the seventh century onwards and are written in old Turkish 'runes', and then (eleventh–twelfth centuries) in Uighur script. In Islamic territory, for the most part in Arabic script, we find the first literary documents with the Qarakhānids of eastern Turkestan in the second half of the eleventh century: in Kāshghar—on the north side of the Pamirs—there appeared a 'middle Turkish' didactic poem, and the author of an Arabic-Turkish dictionary composed in Baghdad came from that area. Descendants of eastern Turkish literary dialects developed in the thirteenth century in the dialect of Khwārazm, and then—under the Mongols—in Transoxiana, between the Oxus (Amū Darya) and the Jaxartes (Syr Darya): there the court poets of the Tīmūrids in fifteenth-century Samarqand and Herat created a literature which was inspired by Persian models but written in the Chaghatay dialect, the literary language into which the Turkish dialects of the Islamic east had coalesced. Today various Eastern Turkish languages are spoken in the Central Asian Soviet Republics and are written mostly in Cyrillic script.

The Turkish dynasties of the west formed a Turkish literary language later than in the east. The Great Seljuqs who had established themselves in Iran and Iraq in the eleventh century adopted, as already mentioned, Persian as the language of administration along with the Iranian government system, as indeed did the Anatolian branch of the dynasty. But the Turkish-speaking element in the population steadily increased and was substantially enlarged by the Turkish peoples who moved westwards with the Mongol incursions. Even today there still exist in South-west and Central Persia descendants of these tribes, whose dialects have remained at a particularly archaic stage of linguistic development. From the thirteenth century literary monuments of 'middle Turkish' survive from Asia Minor and the Volga area. The Qaramānids in South and Central Anatolia raised Turkish to the status of the government language in the fourteenth century, and they were followed shortly afterwards by the Ottoman sultans in the west. With the Ottoman victory over the Byzantines and their own Turkish rivals, Ottoman (which belonged to the linguistic group of the Oghuz) spread through Asia Minor and the

Balkans. For quite a time it continued to compete with Persian, above all in belles-lettres, and it developed by adopting Persian and Arabic elements of vocabulary and syntax into a mixed language with very substantial foreign borrowings. A distinction should be drawn between this language, Ottoman in a narrower sense (which was written in the Arabic script), and modern Turkish which since the nationalist Turkish reforms (Atatürk introduced the Latin script in 1928) was purged of many Arabic-Persian loan words and was characterised by a return to the middle Turkish linguistic heritage.

(c) The Arabic script

When the triumphal progress of Islam spread the Arabic language, it also spread the Arabic script over the Near East to North and Central Africa, and eastwards through Iran and India as far as Indonesia. The Arabic script was used by Muslims in the most diverse linguistic communities and adapted to a great number of other languages.

The Arabic alphabet consists of 28 signs which represent the consonantal phonemes and long vowels of Arabic. They are written from right to left; some of them are joined up on both sides and some only to the preceding letters. Short vowels, the absence of vowels and doubling of consonants are generally not indicated. They can, however, when necessary—as for example in the establishment of canonical religious texts (especially the Koran) and in order to make a text clearer—be represented by additional symbols added to the basic letters. As in other Semitic languages, the basic roots of words consist of consonants (mostly three); the distribution of vowels used in the derivation and inflection of nouns and verbs is based on specific, regularly constructed morphemic types. A correct reading is therefore discernible from the consonantal form of an individual word, but it is often clear only from the context of the sentence. This is even more so in cases where the Arabic language is applied to non-Semitic languages such as Persian and Turkish. Here a correct reading of rare words, and above all proper names, cannot always be established with certainty in old texts.

The Arabic script is—as indeed is the Greek script and the Latin one we use—an offshoot of the North-west Semitic alphabet which appeared for the first time in Phoenician-Canaanite inscriptions from the beginning of the second millennium BC. The further development of this alphabet can be traced in the first millennium BC in Phoenician, Hebrew and Aramaic (mostly in inscriptions). The Arab Nabataeans of the state of Petra used the Aramaic language—which under the old Persian empire of the Achaemenids had become the *lingua franca* of the Near and Middle East—and they also used the Aramaic script. After the Roman conquest (106 AD) this Nabataean script remained in use in the area of the *Provincia Romana*, with its capital at Bosra. A later, cursive form—which may have been influenced by the Syro-Aramaic script of Mesopotamia—was finally used for writing Arabic too. It replaced the variants of the 'South Semitic' script of the Yemen which was then in use in other Arab states in the northern part of the peninsula, and developed further into the Arabic script proper, which became the vehicle of the classic Arabic literary language.

The phases of this development cannot be traced in a continuous fashion on the basis of the sparse pre-Islamic evidence. Two centuries separate the Nabataean inscription of Namāra (328 AD), in which a certain Imra' al-Qais is described as 'King of the Arabs', from the first datable Arabic inscription from the North-west Arabian border zone fringing the settled lands of Syria. Here, in the sixth century, the graphic elements of the Arabic script can clearly be traced in their basic outline. It is not certain how this alphabet reached the Ḥijāz and Mecca, where in the second decade of the seventh century it became the vehicle of the Islamic revelation. It may, however, be postulated that knowledge of the script spread along the same caravan routes which linked the trading city of Mecca with some of the places where proto-Arabic inscriptions have been found.

The culture of Islam, the last of the great religions with a scripture, is to a very special extent a culture of the script and of the book. With the spread of the Islamic faith and of the Koran—which received its definitive textual form under the caliph 'Uthmān (644–56)—with the Arabisation of the government (from 697) and with the flowering of legal, religious and historical tradition in all cities of the empire, the script developed rapidly. A further development of the script was vital because the Arabic letters as they had developed before Islam were not adequate to represent the range of Arabic phonemes. Some phonological distinctions in Arabic were lacking in Aramaic, and were therefore not represented in the Aramaic predecessor of the Arabic alphabet; on the other hand, some symbols which were originally different had in the course of their development acquired the same form. In order to produce an unambiguous script these 'homographs' were soon differentiated by diacritical marks consisting of one, two or three dots. Towards the end of the seventh century this system of diacritics became fully developed, thereby producing the Arabic alphabet with its 28 letters. Around the same time the governors of the Umayyads in Iraq made great efforts to consolidate the Koranic text, including its orthography and pronunciation; for this purpose a system of reading marks for short vowels, vowellessness and doubling of consonants was introduced which is still in use today in the form which was established by grammarians towards the middle of the eighth century.

Stylish forms of calligraphy began early too. The cursive character of the script with its simple geometrical basic elements, whose ligatures were written in one flourish, affords especially good opportunities for this. The surviving examples of such calligraphy dating from an early period are sparse; but already in the second half of the first century after the Hijra different styles of writing are found in the papyri from Egyptian chancelleries, and similar styles characterise the oldest Koran fragments. The length and slant of the vertical downward groundstrokes, the dimensions of the horizontals, the geometry of the loops and of the curves which billow out at the end of a word, and the harmony of these elements—all these are developed in Arabic calligraphy. In the lapidary script—the ductus used in inscriptions and on coins—the inflexibility of the material but also a deliberate stylisation led to an emphasis on the horizontal, the vertical and basic geometrical forms (circle, rectangle, triangle, rhombus). The earliest building and funerary inscriptions reveal an individual monumental development (already mature in the building inscriptions in the Dome of the Rock in Jerusalem, dating from 691 and in the name of the caliph ʿAbd al-Malik). The tendency to geometrical stylisation and monumentalisation noticeable here also influenced the script of the Koranic codices towards the end of the first Islamic century. This trend apparently began in Iraq, since while the ductus used in the Korans from Mecca and Medina was characterised by high elongated letters inclining to the right, this more compressed style, which stressed the horizontal lines, took its name from Kūfa. It did not remain restricted to Iraq but spread also the Ḥijāz and other provinces. For centuries to come it became the hieratic script *par excellence*; 'Kūfic script' thus became the term used for all geometric and monumental forms of the old type of script.

New developments of calligraphic form were generated by the chancelleries of the ʿAbbāsid caliphate. The Muslims had learned about rag paper from Chinese prisoners of war in Turkestan and had started to produce it in Samarqand after 751. From there this flexible material which was easy to fold and to bind and was moreover economic and relatively cheap, above all in comparison with parchment, gained supremacy in the Islamic east within a century and replaced papyrus in the course of the eleventh century even in Egypt and in the West too. Easier to write on than brittle papyrus, rag paper was also a material well suited to calligraphic forms. Just as the older calligraphy was influenced by the material and technique of the stonemason, so too the new type of fine writing revealed the influence of the reed pen (*qalam*), whose sharpened and flattened edge determined the sizes and proportions of strokes and dots. The revival of calligraphy in chancery writing achieved by the secretaries of the ʿAbbāsid government from the first half of the tenth century (a revival associated with the name of the vizier Ibn Muqla, d.940) elevated the ductus called *naskh* (or *naskhī*), 'copy script', to the status of a Koranic script which stood on a par with 'Kūfic' and ultimately replaced it. Increasing use was made of this ductus (with its monumental form, the *thuluth*, which also developed from a chancellery script), in luxury illuminated Korans as well as in secular codices. The norms created by the calligraphers had their impact not only in the formation and proportion of graphic elements in the cursive book script and the common script but also in lapidary inscriptions: the stonemason imitated the characteristic strokes of the reed pen.

From the older forms of cursive writing there thus developed a wide variety of 'rounded' calligraphical styles which conquered the Islamic east from the eleventh century onwards. A number of regional styles also evolved with the political and cultural independence of the provinces; thus Iran, for example, developed *ta'līq* and *nasta'līq*, with their 'hanging' garlands. A special development manifested itself very early in the West, where the characteristic ductus of the Maghrib emerged from the 'Kūfic' script.

The provenance and analysis of regional and chronological developments in palaeography are only beginning. So far the script of the papyri and inscriptions has been best researched and published (above all through the pioneer work and manuals of Adolf Grohmann [15.11, 15.14–15]); but work on the palaeography of manuscripts—which should help editors in the reading and dating of medieval manuscripts —still needs to be done.

The Arabic script also remained in use in the lands of Islam in places where the language of the inhabitants or (as in the case of Turkey) of the immigrants gained dominance as a government and literary language. In Iran it was used for New Persian, in Anatolia for Turkish (in this case replaced in 1928 in the reforms of Atatürk by the Latin script), in the case of the Muslims of India (Northern India, especially Pakistan and Bangladesh) for Urdū, in Indonesia for Malay and Bahasa Indonesia (now generally ousted by the Latin script), and also for the various languages of Islamic Africa. The range of graphic elements of the script was completed by the use of diacritical points to represent sounds which were not shown in Arabic. While the Jews and the Christians of the Syrian churches in the Arab lands also used Hebrew and Syriac script to write Arabic, the linguistic minorities of the Muslim population always wrote in the Arabic script. Examples include the Spanish dialects of the Iberian peninsula in the Islamic period, the Aljamía (from the Arabic *al-'ajamiyya*, 'non-Arab'); today similar phenomena are called Aljamiado literature, as for example the Serbo-Croat literature of the Turkish period which was written in the Arabic script. Thus the Arabic script is the external symbol of the Islamic cultural community and has remained so until today.

2. *Names and Titles*

(a) Islamic personal names

'Civil' surnames, i.e. surnames which are hereditary and shared by all the members and descendants of a family, appeared in the Islamic east only in recent times. In the Middle Ages and in some Arab countries even today the origin of an individual is indicated by naming his father, grandfather and so on in patronymical sequence; there follow other details as to tribal affiliation, place of origin or residence, profession, and additional nick-names and honorifics which are often used as personal names.

1. In most cases, the personal name (*ism*) is chosen from a relatively small repertoire—a repertoire which has been sanctioned by Islamic tradition. The names and epithets of the Prophet, his companions, Biblical figures who appear in the Koran, and compounds using the names of God are especially popular and widespread in all Islamic countries. Quite a few of these names were already in use in pre-Islamic Arabia and they remained popular firstly because they were thought to bring good luck; but more especially because they had belonged to one of the companions of the Prophet. These include names like Ḥasan, Ḥusayn (from the root *ḥsn* 'good, beautiful'), Saʿd, Saʿīd, Masʿūd (*sʿd* 'luck'), ʿAmr, ʿUmar (*ʿmr* 'life'), Zayd, Yazīd (*zyd* 'to grow'), Thābit ('firm'), Asad ('lion'); some of them are made from adjectives, participles (with the prefixed *ma-*, *mu-*, such as in Muḥammad 'praised', Masʿūd 'blessed with good fortune') and verb forms used as a wish (Yaḥyā, 'may he live', Yazīd, 'may he grow'). Adjectival and generic terms when used as names often retain the Arabic definite article *al-*, as for example al-Ḥasan 'the beautiful', al-ʿAbbās 'the grim-visaged (lion)', al-Ḥārith 'the ravening (lion)'. By far the most common Islamic name became that of the Prophet, Muḥammad, and other variants of the root *ḥmd* ('praise'): Aḥmad, Ḥāmid, Maḥmūd, and the Prophet's surname Muṣṭafā ('the purified one [by God]'). Common female names are those of his mother Āmina, his wives, 'Āʿisha', Zaynab and so on, and his daughter Fāṭima. Similarly, the names of ʿAlī, his sons Ḥasan and Ḥusayn and the names of the Imāms: Jaʿfar, Riḍā (Persian Reẓā), and Mahdī are popular amongst the Shīʿa. The names of Biblical figures who are mentioned in the Koran and revered as prophets became widespread in Islam: Ibrāhīm (Abraham), Ismāʿīl (Ishmael), Isḥāq (Isaac), Yaʿqūb (Jacob), Yūsuf (Joseph), Mūsā (Moses), Hārūn (Aaron), Dāʾūd (David), Sulaymān (Solomon), ʿĪsā (Jesus), Maryam (Mary). Finally there are numerous two-part names connected with the name of God which designate the bearer as the slave of God, ʿAbd Allāh; instead of Allāh, one of the Koranic 'beautiful names of God' can be used: ʿAbd al-Raḥmān, 'slave of the Merciful', ʿAbd al-Malik, 'slave of the King',

ʿAbd al-Qādir, 'slave of the Powerful'.

With the emergence of Persians and Turks into Islamic history, Iranian and Turkish names also appeared; many Persians adopted Arabic names when they converted to Islam and fabricated Arabic genealogies, but many an important man became known by his Iranian name such as the grammarian Sībawayh and the historian Miskawayh (originally Sēbōye and Mishkōye). The generals and commanders of the Seljuq and Mamlūk period were also known by their Turkish names, as for example Alp Arslan ('lion-hero'), Alp-Tegin ('unique hero'), Aq-Sunqur ('white falcon'), Toghrïl ('falcon'), Baybars, Barqūq and others. They have recently become popular again through Turkish nationalism, as have the names of pre-Islamic kings and heroes in Iran—Khusraw, Bahrām, Rustam and more besides.

2. In front of the *ism* there is a personal name (*kunya*), which indicates the bearer of the name as 'father of so and so' (*Abū* . . .) or as 'mother of so and so' (*Umm* . . .). Originally the *kunya* contained the name of the eldest son. Until the early ʿAbbāsid period it was the privilege of 'pure' Arabs and was given to non-Arabs who after their conversion became clients (*mawālī*) of Arab tribes only as a special sign of honour. Later on, even people without children received a *kunya* and the name was also given to a boy who had come of age as a sign of his maturity. It is used in polite and direct speech amongst friends and equals and in respectful indirect reference (for example when an author mentions his teacher).

In this way the caliph ʿUmar had the *kunya* Abū ʿAbdallāh, the daughter of Muḥammad was called Umm Kulthūm, the Prophet himself was called Abu'l-Qāsim. Instead of the name elements, later on there was an extended use of the *kunya* with a noun which suggests a quality or an attribute of the bearer; the *kunya* has then the function of a surname or a nickname (*laqab*): Abu'l-Barakāt, 'the father of blessings', i.e. 'endowed with blessings', Abu'l-Maʿālī, 'man of high virtues', Abu'l-Maḥāsin, 'man of beautiful qualities', or else Abū Shāma, 'the man with the black mole', Abū Hurayra, 'the man with the little cat', Abū 'l-ʿAtāhiya, 'the father of tomfoolery' (a poet). The *kunya* Abu'l-Fidā' (*fidā'* 'ransom, sacrifice') is commonly used with Ismāʿīl: according to widespread Islamic belief Abraham offered not Isaac but Ishmael as a sacrifice.

3. The patronymic, the name of the father, and the preceding affiliation (*nasab*) follow the personal name. In front of each of the names of one's forefathers there is the word *ibn* 'son (of) . . .' (abbreviated *b.*); in front of the patronymic of a woman there is *bint* 'daughter (of)'. Names which are linked with the name *banū* (the plural of *ibn*) denote Arab tribes and tribal groups just as those with *āl* 'family' denote the clans and ruling houses of the Arab Bedouin. Two examples: Muḥammad ibn ʿAbdallāh ibn ʿAbd al-Muṭṭalib ibn

Hāshim ibn ʿAbd Manāf ibn Quṣayy (the Prophet), Fāṭima bint Muḥammad ibn ʿAbdallāh etc. (his daughter). In most Arab countries (except for Arabia and North Africa) the word *ibn* today is omitted (Aḥmad Amīn, Ṭāhā Ḥusayn); in the Persian linguistic area the particle of annexation *-i* is used in its place—Nāṣir-i Khusraw 'Nāṣir (son) of Khusraw'. Sometimes—frequently in Spain—there is at the end of a chain of names the name, surname or title of an ancestor which is used for several generations of his descendants as a kind of family name: Ibn al-Furāt (the family of viziers of the ninth–tenth centuries), Ibn Rushd (Rushd was already the name of the grandfather of the famous philosopher, rendered into Spanish as Averroes), Ibn Khaldūn (the historian was the descendant of an old Spanish Arab family of Banū Khaldūn), Ibn al-Shiḥna (after an ancestor who held the post of *shiḥna*—chief of police), Ibn al-Qūṭiyya (the Spanish historian whose ancestor had married a Gothic princess, Qūṭiyya). Persian patronyms ending in *-zāda* (like English family names which end in -son, -s) have the same function, as also Turkish names which end in *-oghlu* (here put in front of the personal name).

4. After the affiliation comes the *nisba,* a name which denotes the origin or place of residence derived from names of tribes, towns and countries, and formed in Arabic (as in Persian) with the suffix *-ī.* It originally denoted the tribe to which one belonged: al-Kindī 'from the tribe of Kinda', al-Qurashī 'the Qurayshite'; then—in an urban milieu—the place of birth or residence: al-Dimashqī 'the Damascene', al-Maqdisī or al-Muqaddasī 'the man from Jerusalem' (Arabic al-Bayt al-Muqaddas or Bayt al-Maqdis), al-Karkhī 'from the Baghdad suburb Karkh', al-Marwazī 'from Marw', al-Rāzī 'from Rayy', al-Ṭabarī 'from Ṭabaristān'.

A *nisba* could also indicate an affiliation to a legal school or a religious group:: al-Ḥanafī 'belonging to the legal school of Abū Ḥanīfa', al-Shīʿī 'the Shīʿite'; sometimes a profession: al-Ṣayrafī 'the money changer', al-Qalānisī 'the hat maker', al-Bāqillānī 'the bean seller', al-Māwardī 'the dealer in rose water'. The *nisba* form is often used as a *nom de plume* (*takhalluṣ*) for Persian and Turkish poets, for example Firdawsī 'the paradisiacal'. In Turkish the *nisba* has the ending *-li* (or *-lu*) and comes before the other parts of the name—Izmirli 'from Izmir', Konyalï 'from Konya'.

5. Finally we can add to the already mentioned regular elements in nomenclature various surnames (*laqab*). To this category belong titles such as al-Ṭawīl 'the tall one', al-Aʿshā 'the man who is night-blind', al-Aṭrash 'the deaf one', al-Jāḥiẓ 'goggle-eye', and also honorific titles such as al-Ḥāfiẓ 'the one who knows the Koran and *ḥadīth*'; indications of profession are common—a study of them often provides interesting conclusions on the social background of scholars and authors—as for example al-Zajjāj 'the dealer in glass', al-Farrā'

'furrier', al-Ṭaḥḥān 'the miller', al-'Aṭṭār 'the dealer in spices, chemist', al-Warrāq 'the paper and book dealer, copyist', al-Khaṭīb 'the preacher'.

In the Ottoman empire people of non-Muslim origin such as the Janissaries who had no *nasab* often received a *laqab* as a title (put at the beginning). Sultans with the same names were also differentiated in that way: Fāṭiḥ Muḥammad 'the conqueror' (Meḥmed II) was differentiated from Awjī Muḥammad 'the zenith' (Meḥmed IV).

Also called a *laqab* but put in front of the other names are the honorific titles of rulers and the court which designate the bearer as support, upholder etc. of a dynasty (*dawla*) or of religion (*dīn*) (see below). Those which were formed with *dīn* have sunk since the Ottoman period to an additional *ism* and now enrich the repertoire of personal names.

If all or several elements of the nomenclature are used they appear in an established sequence: *laqab* (honorific name)—*kunya* (Abū ...)—*ism*—*nasab* (ibn ... ibn ...)—*nisba* (al- ... ī)—*laqab* (surname).

An example: 'Imād al-Dīn (*laqab*) Abū 'Abdallāh (*kunya*) Muḥammad (*ism*) ibn Ṣafī al-Dīn (*laqab* of the father) Abi'l-Faraj (*kunya* of the father, the form Abī is the genitive) Muḥammad (*ism* of the father) ibn Nafīs al-Dīn (*laqab* of the grandfather) Abi'l-Rajā' (*kunya* of the grandfather) Ḥāmid (his *ism*) ibn Muḥammad (the great-grandfather) ibn 'Abdallāh ibn 'Alī ibn Maḥmūd ibn Hibatallāh al-Iṣbahānī (*nisba* 'from Iṣfahān') al-Kātib (*laqab* 'the secretary').

Historical personalities—and this was already the case with their contemporaries—were known and made famous only by one or two characteristic elements of this chain of names. Thus in the example just quoted above, the secretary and court chronicler of Saladin is usually known only as 'Imād al-Dīn al-Iṣbahānī. Many authors are known by their *nisba* (as for example the historians al-Ṭabarī, al-Mas'ūdī), others are known by their *kunya* (as for example the poets Abū Nuwās, Abū Tammām), by the *nasab* (as for example the historians Ibn Isḥāq, Ibn Qutayba) or by a nickname (such as the writer al-Jāḥiẓ 'goggle-eye'). In the *nasab* there appears instead of the *ism* often the paternal *kunya, nisba* or other forename of the father: Ibn Abī Uṣaybi'a, Ibn al-Jazarī, Ibn al-Khaṭīb, Ibn al-Qalānisī. A popular feature is a combination of *kunya* or honorific title with the *nisba*: Abu'l-Faraj al-Iṣbahānī, Tāj al-Dīn al-Subkī.

(b) The titles of rulers and honorific titles

Since the time of 'Umar, the second holder of the office, the term 'caliph', *Khalīfat Rasūl Allāh* ('successor, representative of the Prophet of God') was the title of the head of the Islamic theocracy. Since the time of 'Umar, in government documents, on inscriptions and coins, the caliph also bore the title *amīr al-mu'minīn* 'Commander of the Faithful'. Apart from that, the caliphs of early Islam and the Umayyad dynasty bore no personal titles. It was only the 'Abbāsids who took regnal titles which marked them off from the 'kingship' of the Umayyads and from the claims of the Shī'a as truly Islamic rulers: as representatives of theocracy, as *imāms* of the Islamic community, who had been set in office by God and ruled with His support, who indeed styled themselves *Khalīfat Allāh* 'representative of God'. The first 'Abbāsid caliph was still named after the revolutionary hope which opponents of the Umayyads pinned on the 'rightly guided' Imām, the Mahdī from the house of the Prophet: al-Saffāḥ 'the shedder of blood'. The next titles designated the caliph as charismatic ruler: al-Manṣūr (in full: al-Manṣūr bi-Allāh) 'the one to whom God gives victory'; his successor al-Mahdī 'the rightly guided (by God)' (a title which the Shī'a, forced into opposition, also gave to the awaited renewer of the faith and commander of the faithful), al-Rashīd 'the one led on the right path (by God)', al-Ma'mūn 'the one who is entrusted (by God with leadership)', al-Mutawakkil 'the one who trusts (in God)', al-Nāṣir 'the victorious one (through God's help)'.

The rivals of the 'Abbāsids also held the title *amīr al-mu'minīn* and corresponding regnal titles denoting authority; thus the Fāṭimids called themselves caliphs when they established their rule in North Africa and Egypt in the tenth century and assumed the epithets of the expected Imām: al-Mahdī, al-Qā'im bi-amr Allāh 'the one who represents God's command (on earth)', al-Ḥākim bi-amr Allāh 'he who judges according to God's command'. In consequence the Spanish Umayyads too adopted the title of caliph ('Abd al-Raḥmān III, from 928). Their successors paid homage once again to the caliph of Baghdad after the end of Fāṭimid rule in North Africa. The Almoravids called themselves *amīr al-muslimīn* 'commander of the Muslims' from the end of the eleventh century—a title which had similar pretensions but appeared more unassuming. But their opponents and conquerors, the Almohads, presented themselves once again as 'caliphs' of the Mahdī Ibn Tūmart and styled themselves once again *amīr al-mu'minīn* with universal claims. Their successors bore the title as a sign of regional hegemony in North Africa, while the Mamlūks—after the fall of Baghdad (1258)—installed an 'Abbāsid 'puppet caliphate' in Cairo. Finally the Ottomans arrogated to themselves the office of Caliph. Even today the kings of Saudi Arabia and Morocco bear the title *amīr al-mu'minīn* as a sign of religious legitimacy.

The executive bodies of the earlier caliphate were established under the 'Abbāsid caliphs as independent institutions: the administration of the 'secretaries' (*kuttāb*) was put under the vizier (*wazīr*), the legal institution was organised under the chief *qāḍī* (*qāḍi'l-*

quḍāt), the army was organised under amīrs (amir, later under a chief *amīr al-umarā'*, the officer commanding); the administration of the provinces was put under an 'agent' (*'āmil*—originally a 'governor', later on an official of the financial administration who was put under the authority of an *amīr*). At first, officials would adopt only the simple title of the office. In the tenth century, however, when the power of the caliphs receded, and the empire became fragmented, the bestowing of certain honorific titles on military leaders and provincial princelings became a political tool—devoid of effective sanctions and rapidly devalued by an inflationary increase of their number. This process is, however, a valuable historical testimony of the distribution and shifting of power in the period of political turmoil until the caliphate was finally brought to an end.

A contemporary complained about this development in the following scornful, outspoken terms:

> 'When the Banī-'Abbās had decorated their assistants, friends and enemies indiscriminately, with vain titles, compounded with the word *dawla* [dynasty]—their dynasty perished'—wrote al-Bīrūnī around the year 1000 in his *Chronology*—'for in this they went beyond all reasonable limits. This went on so long till those who were especially attached to their court [as chief *amīrs*] claimed something new as a distinction between themselves and the others. Thereupon the Khalifs bestowed double titles. But then also the others wanted the same titles, and knew how to carry their point by bribery for lack of legitimate reasons. Now it became necessary a second time to create a distinction between this class and those who were directly attached to their court. So the Khalifs bestowed triple titles, adding besides the title of Shāhinshāh [Persian "King of Kings"]. In this way the matter became utterly opposed to common sense, and clumsy to the highest degree, so that he who mentions them gets tired before he has scarcely commenced, and he who writes them loses his time and writing space, and he who addresses them runs the risk of missing the time of prayer' [. . .] 'Also the Wazīrs of the Khalifs have received certain titles, compounded with the word *Dhū* ["possessor of", "endowed with"], as e.g. *Dhū-al-yamīnain* ["the one with two right hands"], *Dhū-al-ri'āsatain* ["the one with two principalities", i.e. military and administrative authority], *Dhū-al-Kifāyatain* ["the one with two abilities", i.e. for the sword and for the pen, in the same sense as the preceeding title], *Dhū-al-saifain* ["the one with the two swords"], *Dhū-al-Ḳalamain* ["the one with two pens"] etc.
>
> The Buwaihi family, when, as we have mentioned, the power passed into their hands, imitated the example of the Khalifs; nay, they made it still worse, and their title-giving was nothing but

one great lie, when they called their Wazīrs, e.g. *Kāfī-al-Kufāt* ["the most able of the able"], *Alkāfī Al'auḥad* ["the only one amongst the able"] . . . [After further examples:] Some of them, however, have gone beyond this limit, calling themselves '*Amîr-al-'ālam* ["prince of the world"] and *Sayyid-al-'umarā* ["lord of the princes"]. May God inflict on them ignominy in this world, and show to them and to others their weakness!' (Al-Bīrūnī: *al-Āthār al-bāqiya* ['Chronology of Ancient Nations'], edited by C. E. Sachau. Leipzig 1878, pp. 132, 134, cf. transl. by C. E. Sachau. London 1879, pp. 129, 134)

Already in the second half of the ninth century the chief commanders of the Turkish praetorian guard at the caliphal court had taken over the real political power in Baghdad. Towards the middle of the tenth century this development reached a significant turning point: when the caliph al-Muttaqī fled in 942 from strife-torn Baghdad to Mosul and sought the protection of the Ḥamdānid al-Ḥasan, he gave him the title of Nāṣīr al-Dawla together with the post of chief amir (*amīr al-umarā'*), a title which means 'helper of the dynasty', and he gave al-Ḥasan's brother 'Alī the title Sayf al-Dawla ('sword of the dynasty'). Previously, titles of this kind, genitive combinations with the element *dawla* 'dynasty' (literally 'cycle', 'period' of rule) had been given to a few viziers; the bestowing of such titles on governors formally symbolised the handing over of political power to the 'princelings' of provincial dynasties. The victors in the struggle for Iraq were the Iranian Būyids: 'the liberators' of the caliph who eventually humiliated him into becoming their puppet. When in 945, Aḥmad ibn Būya as the new chief amir received a title which marked him out as the 'glorifier of the dynasty', Mu'izz al-Dawla, his brothers in Shīrāz and Iṣfahān also received the titles of 'support' and 'pillar', 'Imād al-Dawla and Rukn al-Dawla. In contrast to the full political power of the ruling princes which is expressed in this titulature, the competence of the caliph became rapidly limited to religious sanction and jurisdiction. The bestowing of titles was used by the Būyids in their foreign policy vis-à-vis rivals and allies, and the caliph became their tool. Such titles were also an expression of a revival of Iranian court tradition. This tradition had influenced the institutions of the 'Abbāsid caliphate from its very beginning. But the Būyids like other preceding and contemporary smaller Iranian royal houses attached themselves consciously and in many externals to Sasanian court ceremonial, and the titles with *dawla* were also modelled on Sasanian court titles. Soon they also used the Iranian royal title. In Iran, Rukn al-Dawla called himself 'King of Kings' (Shāhanshāh); 'Aḍud al-Dawla, the most important ruler of the dynasty, accepted from the caliph himself a second *laqab* Tāj al-Milla 'crown of the religious community'—a clever combination of a Persian symbol with an

Arab-Islamic element. He had himself crowned, and, in addition to the simple title, *malik*, 'king', he used the title of Shāhanshāh. Although this took place in open contempt of the caliph, he had to bestow on a later Būyid, Bahā' al-Dawla, the Arabic title Malik al-Mulūk (1002).

With the power struggles after the death of 'Aḍud al-Dawla the inflation of titles about which al-Bīrūnī complained began. After the eastern rivals of the Būyids, the Sāmānids, had begun to use titles with *dawla* for their governors in Khurāsān, the Būyids regularly adopted titles using the terms *milla* 'religion' and—at first as a privilege of the chief amir—*umma* 'community'. Even more crucial was the fact that in 1002 Bahā' al-Dawla was raised to the rank of Qawām al-Dīn, 'foundation of the faith'. A precedent for this had been the epithet Nāṣir al-Dīn wa'l- Dawla which was awarded to the Kurd Ḥasanwayh, for his services to the Holy Cities and his protection of the pilgrim routes. The Būyids, however, although they left the caliph in office for political reasons, were Shī'ites, members of the opposition party which expected the true, righteous Imām to come from the ranks of the 'Alids. Only when the caliph had regained his freedom of movement after internal weakness within the Būyid family did the ruling princes become concerned to be regarded as 'the True Friend of the Commander of the Faithful', Ṣafī Amīr al-Mu'minīn—another innovation of Bahā' al-Dawla. Titles with *dīn*, 'faith', 'religion', were awarded without such misgivings to the orthodox Ghaznavids, as indeed was the case in the eleventh century with the Seljuqs and their vassals, in addition to the plethora of titles of the Iranian tradition, notably those of 'King' and 'King of Kings'.

The Ghaznavids made no such claim to royal dignity; but when Maḥmūd of Ghazna (998–1030) began to use the title *sulṭān*, 'authority', this symbolised the similarly grandiose claims of the new power in Sīstān. Indeed, the Ghaznavids, who were threatening the Sāmānids in the east and the Būyids in western Persia, were making no less a claim than that of absolute authority, authority symbolised in the title Sulṭān which was originally due only to the caliph. But the Seljuq Toghrïl who entered Baghdad in 1055 as the successor to the Būyids was also given the title Sulṭān by the caliph himself. In addition, the Seljuq state also took over Iranian and Arabic-Islamic administrative practices as well as their predecessors' titulature. The rows of titles became so long that the twelfth-century Damascene historian, Ibn al-Qalānisī, apologises in giving certain excessively prolix titles *in extenso* that he cannot always provide the full honorific names of princes and dignitaries (it is therefore not chronicles but coins and above all inscriptions that are the richest source for the history of titulature). Atabegs in the posts of governor in the Seljuq provinces, officers and court officials (viziers and others) received such a gradation of titles. Even the Islamic scholars under the last Būyids had already become worthy of such distinction. Following the names formed with *dīn*, were those with *Islām, dawla, milla, umma* and finally those with *amīr al-mu'minīn*. The title of King of Kings (Shāhanshāh al-a'ẓam) and at first also double epithets with the genitive *al-dunyā wa'l-dīn* '(helper etc.) of the world and of religion' remained the prerogative of the sultans. (But Saladin too—Ṣalāḥ al-Dīn—was able after his famous victories against the Crusaders to call himself Ṣalāḥ al-Dunyā wa'l-Dīn). Governors had the simple title of King with different epithets (al-Malik al-'Ādil 'the just king' etc.) and the Ayyūbids in Egypt and Syria and also the Mamlūks followed this custom. As well as these, some of the older honorary titles continued to denote Islamic authority, as for example with the later Mamlūks who always took the title Sayf al-Dīn 'Sword of the Faith'. Here and with other Turkish and Mongol dynasties as well as with the Ottomans, the title of Sulṭān remained after the end of the caliphate as an expression of sovereignty which was no longer bestowed by the caliph but was arrogated by his self-styled successors.

The hierarchy of honorific titles which had been built up by the Baghdad caliphate and its provincial princes had its parallels with their rivals in the west, in Cairo (under the Fāṭimids) and in Cordoba. The richer the titulature of the highest offices became, the more abundant the repertoire of titles used by the lower échélons of the court and the military became also. If one wanted to go into this in more detail, one would indeed become 'tired before one has scarcely begun'. It should be noted, however, that increasing use was made of Persian and—under the Turkish and Mongol rulers—Turkish titles for government offices and rulers and for honorifics. At first this was restricted to the military ranks of the armies of conquest but with the consolidation of the government organisation such titles also penetrated the civil hierarchy. Above all, the divided hierarchical structure of the Ottoman empire created a multiplicity of titles for the offices of the palace, the military and the government.

3. *The Islamic Calendar*

The era of the *Hijra* (emigration) of the Prophet Muḥammad from Makka to Madīna is based upon Lunar years, in which the commencement of the months are determined by the appearance of the New Moon, not by (astronomical) calculation. It is used by the whole Muhammadan world. The circumstances under which this very point was adopted as an epoch, and not the time when the Prophet was either born or entrusted with his divine mission or died, were the following: Maimūn ibn Mihrān [tax-collector in the Jazīra] relates that 'Umar ibn al-Khaṭṭāb [the 2nd caliph, 634–44], when people one day handed over to him a cheque payable in the month Sha'bān, said: "Which Sha'bān is meant? That one in which we are or the next Sha'bān?" Thereupon he assembled the Companions of the Prophet, and asked their advice regarding the matter of chronology, which troubled his mind.' [According to other traditions, an enquiry from Abū Mūsā al-Ash'arī, the governor of Kufa, induced 'Umar to consider this problem. The use of older eras—such as the Seleucid or the Sasanid calendar—was rejected for practical reasons. But the exigencies of the administration pressed for a quick decision:] 'Umar had already organised the registers [*Dīwān*, see p.109], had established the land taxes and regulations, and was in want of an era, not liking the old ones. On this occasion he assembled the Companions, and took their advice. Now the most authentic date, which involved no obscurities nor possible mishaps, seemed to be the date of the *Hijra* of the Prophet, viz. of his arrival at Madīna on Monday, the 8th of the month Rabī' I [20th September 622], whilst the beginning of the year was a Thursday [1st Muḥarram = 15th July 622]. Now he adopted this epoch, and fixed thereby the dates in all his affairs. This happened in the year 17 after the *Hijra*. (Al-Bīrūnī (973–*c.*1050): *al-Āthār al-bāqiya* ['The Chronology of Ancient Nations], edited by C. Edward Sachau. Leipzig 1878, pp.29–30, transl. by C.E. Sachau. London 1879, pp.33–4.)

The Islamic calendar, according to the account given above by the astronomer al-Bīrūnī and other sources was introduced in the year 638 AD and remained thereafter the official calendar in all Islamic countries. Today it is gradually being superseded by the Gregorian calendar of the West in economic spheres and also in daily use, but it nevertheless plays now as ever before an important role as the basis of the Islamic festival calendar as well as in public life.

The Islamic year is a 'lunar year': the basic astronomical unit is the synodic month, the period between one new moon—*hilāl*, the first sighting of the crescent—and the next. Medieval astronomers however dated the beginning of a month, and accordingly the beginning of the era, from the real new moon (the conjunction between the moon and the sun during which the moon is still not visible), and therefore from the preceding day. An exact conversion of Islamic dates to our calendar is therefore only possible if the day of the week is known. In most cases however the historian has to presuppose calculation from the day of the first sighting. It should be noted that the calendar day begins with the setting of the sun and ends with sunset on the following day.

The precise length of a lunar year of twelve synodic months amounts to $29.5306 \times 12 = 354.367$ days. Neither the month nor the lunar year is therefore an exact multiple of complete days. As a compromise, months of 30 and 29 days alternate and an intercalary day (*yaum kabs*) is added 11 times in a cycle of 30 years (i.e. at the end of the 2nd, 5th, 7th, 10th, 13th, 16th (or also 15th), 18th, 21st, 24th, 26th, and 29th year):

al-Muḥarram (30 days)
Ṣafar (29 days)
Rabīʿ I (30 days)
Rabīʿ II (29 days)
Jumādā I (30 days)
Jumādā II (29 days)
Rajab (30 days)
Shaʿbān (29 days)
Ramaḍān (30 days)
Shawwāl (29 days)
Dhu'l-Qaʿda (30 days)
Dhu'l-Ḥijja (29, and in leap years 30 days)

The last month of the year is the month of the pilgrimage (*ḥajj*) to Mecca; the tenth of Dhu'l-Ḥijja, the sacrificial festival of the pilgrims to Mecca, is the most important Muslim festival (*ʿīd al-aḍḥā*, also called *al-ʿīd al-kabīr*, Turkish *büyük bayram* 'the big festival'). The second canonical festival day is the feast of the breaking of the fast (*ʿīd al-fiṭr*, which is also called *al-ʿīd al-ṣaghīr* 'the little festival', in Turkish *küçük bayram*, or *şeker bayramï*) on the first of Shawwāl, with which the fasting of the month of Ramaḍān comes to an end—an especially joyful occasion. A popular festival, which appeared locally and was developed only in the course of the Middle Ages is the birthday of the Prophet (*mawlid al-nabī*) on the 12th of Rabīʿ I.

The starting point, the 'epoch' of the Islamic era is the first of Muḥarram of the year in which Muḥammad with his followers emigrated from Mecca to Medina. This day is calculated in astronomical chronology to be on the 15th July 622 AD. Because of a slight shift in the real phases of the moon vis-à-vis the moon calendar the starting-point of calculation was changed in the Ottoman period from the 15th to the 16th July. In cases of doubt, only information on the day of the week, as already mentioned, can provide the answer. The *Hijra*, the emigration itself, ended on the 21st September 622 with the arrival of the Prophet in Medina. The first Islamic community was set up in Medina and legal and political institutions were established; here also new indications were given for how to reckon the time: 'He it is who appointed the sun a splendour and the moon a light and measured for her stages, that ye might know the number of the years and the reckoning' (Koran, sura 10, verse 6). In pre-Islamic Arabia—as with all Semitic peoples of the ancient east—a lunar-solar calendar was used: a moon calendar which through the intercalation of a whole month in certain intervals was adjusted to the calendar of the sun year. The prohibition of the intercalation of the leap month, the *nasī'*, in the Koran (sura 9, verse 37) sprang above all from reasons of religious policy: the old practice was bound up with the festival and market calendar of ancient Arabian paganism; moreover, its organisation was the privilege of certain families. Before Islam, memorable events were used to establish dates in the distant past. Thus, Muḥammad was said to have been born in the 'year of the Elephant', the year in which the Abyssinian governor of the Yemen came to Mecca with an army which had also African elephants in it. This was reckoned to be the year 570 AD but a precise calendar date was not transmitted, nor indeed was there any written historical tradition. On the other hand, the *Hijra* was not only a significant date but also the first precisely fixed date of Islam. The *Hijra* was an obvious starting-point of the era also because from that time onwards the Prophet had become the unopposed political head of the community. The old eras of the Orient also dated from the coming to power of a dynasty or—in Iran—of each individual ruler. The *Hijra* era was introduced only, as we have already said, under the caliph 'Umar (634–44); the date given by al-Bīrūnī and others (17 AH = 638 AD) is testified by a coin of that same year minted in Damascus. The government of the growing empire demanded a unified dating system for issuing decrees, documents and coins; at first the Arab conquerors had used the government apparatus, the taxation and coinage system of the conquered lands as well as local calendars. Those eras were all reckoned according to sun years and were used for a few decades after the introduction of the new era for practical reasons as well as for maintaining continuity. The reforms of the Umayyad caliph 'Abd al-Malik (685–705) led to unification, Arabisation and Islamisation of the administration and soon helped the Islamic calendar to gain overall acceptance.

Amongst the eras which were used at the beginning was the Yazdagird era in Iran (after the accession to the throne of the last Sasanian king Yazdagird III, 632 AD); the Seleucid era, also called in Arabic the 'Alexander era' (which began on 1st October 312 AD) in the Hellenistic Near East; and above all in Egypt the Diocletian era (after the accession to the throne of Diocletian on the 29th of August 284 AD). The Hellenistic eras remained in use amongst the Christians of the Islamic world for the calendar of the Church year and for internal contacts between religious minorities: the Copts reckoned according to the Diocletian era (which because of the persecution of the Christians by Diocletian was also called the 'Era of Martyrs'). In the rest of the Near East the Julian year was maintained with the Seleucid calendar (as well as the Aramaic names of the months, which are still used in modern Arabic to denote the months of the sun year).

In the lunar calendar the year which has 354.367 days is shorter by 10.875 days than the tropic or sun year which has 365.2422 mean solar days. Therefore the beginning of the Islamic year annually falls behind the year in the solar calendar by about 11 days; then after 33 years it falls on roughly the same solar date. In other words, 33 Lunar years correspond to about 32 sun years. For an approximate conversion of *Hijra* years (H) to Christian years (C) the following equations can be obtained from this ratio and from the beginning of the Muslim era (622 AD):

$$H \cdot \frac{32}{33} + 622 \simeq C \qquad (C - 622) \cdot \frac{33}{32} \simeq H$$

For a rough estimate it should be noted that the difference for 100 lunar years is about 3 sun years, for example 1400 AH = 1400 − (3 × 14) + 622 ≃ 1980 AD. Precise calculation reveals that the year 1400 of the Islamic calendar had already begun on the 21st of November 1979 and ended on the 8th of November 1980; by far the majority of *Hijra* years fall in two successive years of our calendar. In order to make precise conversions, tables have been drawn up which allow a convenient calculation of each date and its day of the week to be made. The most reliable and comprehensive of those which are available are the *Vergleichungstabellen* of F. Wüstenfeld and E. Mahler [73.03]. In the latest edition of this work, tables of other Oriental calendars are also provided. Historical dates are usually given in a form where the *Hijra* date is followed by the corresponding Christian year or years (e.g. 132/749–50).

The regular falling behind of the lunar calendar in relation to the seasons of the sun year made it inappropriate for use in financial administration—the times to collect the taxes on the harvest had to be adjusted constantly. Already in the Middle Ages there were various attempts (for the first time in the 4th/10th century) to bring about a reform of the fiscal calendar. The Seleucid calendar also remained in use for this reason, just as the Persian solar calendar did in Iran, newly regulated by the Seljuq Malikshāh (called the Jalālī calendar, from 1079). In the Ottoman Empire a so-called financial year (*māliyye* year) was introduced for the levying of tax in 1677 AD, and officially in 1789, which began on the first of March and in all other respects corresponded to the Julian calendar. The year dates followed those of the lunar calendar after the *Hijra* (according with the lunar year in which the first of March fell) and in compensation skipped every 33rd year in the numerical sequence.

Whilst Turkey introduced the Gregorian calendar on the first of March 1917, Riḍā Shāh Pahlavī in Iran reverted in 1925 to the old Persian solar year which begins at the Spring Equinox (*Nawrūz*, 21st March). The calculation of the new Persian calendar accords with the

Gregorian; the numbering, however, begins with the year of the *Hijra*. The conversion of these 'solar Hijra years' (*hijrī shamsī*, H. Sh.) into years AD is simple: H.Sh. + 621 = C (for dates between 21st March and 31st December); H.Sh. + 622 = C (1st January to 20th March).

CHAPTER EIGHT

CHRONOLOGICAL TABLE

Prepared with the collaboration of Annegret Ellerichmann and Esther Peskes

Our framework for the dating of Islamic history is based on a wide range of sources. But not every historical date has been handed down precisely and reliably in primary sources or by contemporary historians. Some uncertainties have their origin in the Islamic lunar calendar (the dating after the *Hijra* of AD 622, cf. chapter 7 above): variations in the assumed starting-point of the Muslim era, in the observation or the calculation of the new moon and in the dating of the hours after sunset. The statements in the sources are often enough lacunary or imprecise. The annalistic format of many of the older chronicles of imperial or provincial history is not always an advantage since it entails certain dating constraints and its accuracy is therefore more apparent than real. On the other hand, reigns which from the standpoint of the annalist are peripheral are often considered only when they come into the ken of the ruler, following revolutionary and portentous events: only then are the events of preceding years supplied in a condensed form. The interest of the ruler, territorial concerns and other priorities compel the court chronicler (from the end of the tenth century the majority of historians) to present events from the ruler's viewpoint; that is not always history as it really was. Here too there is a need for the auxiliary sciences which open up the study of primary sources. Hardly any original documents have been preserved from the period before the Mongol invasion; they have been preserved in greater number only from the sixteenth century (with the exception of the Egyptian papyri). On the other hand, we have a wealth of inscriptions from the early period (a catalogue of dated inscriptions is the *Répertoire chronologique d'épigraphie arabe* [15.12]) and innumerable coins with information on those who minted them and when they were minted. Coins provide often the only information on the dates of the reigns of smaller local dynasties and the periods of office of provincial governors and other high officials. For this reason chronological tables of the rulers of Islamic dynasties have been produced mostly by numismatists, as for example the comprehensive tables of E. Zambaur [60.07]. New discoveries and research continue to produce corrections; the most recent research was incorporated into the little handbook by C.E. Bosworth [60.04]. For the dates of literary and cultural history the old biographical lexica of the indigenous tradition (and from the twelfth century the obituaries in historical annals) provide rich material but mostly give only the dates of death of scholars and literary men.

The following chronological survey draws on a number of smaller and bigger chronological tables in various general works and monographs. As well as the work by Bosworth already mentioned [60.04], we have gratefully used the tables in Brockelmann [14.01], Cahen [14.11], Duri [40.12], Grunebaum [14.09, 14.11], Hodgson [14.10], Inalcik [67.07], Lewis [15.73], Setton [65.21] and Spuler [66.14] and (especially for the history of the Ottoman empire) the detailed outline of Kissling [14.13]. For the period after 1918 only dates of the establishment and proclamation of independent states in the Near and Middle East have been given.

1. Arabia before Islam

4th-6th c.	Arabia in the foreground of the wars between Rome/Byzantium and Persia and the conflict of their vassals in Abyssinia and South Arabia. Arab buffer states:
End of 3rd c.-602	The Lakhmids of al-Ḥīra, vassals of the Sasanians in Iraq.
502-614	The Ghassānids, phylarchs of the Byzantines on the Syrian border.
6th-7th c.	Bedouinisation and economic collapse of South Arabia. Byzantium and Persia attempted via Abyssinia and South Arabia to bring the Arabian peninsula and the transit trade under their control. Rise of the trade of Mecca. Emergence of the merchant aristocracy of the Quraysh tribe.
until 528	Al-Ḥārith b. ʿAmr (Arethas) king of the Kinda at the apogee of their power in North Arabia.
503-54	The Lakhmid al-Mundhir III ibn al-Nuʿmān of al-Ḥīra.
525	Death of the Jewish king Dhū Nuwās of Yemen; South Arabia became an Abyssinian colony.
529-69	The Ghassānid al-Ḥārith IV b. Jabala, Byzantine patricius and phylarch of the Arabs, defeated Mundhir III in 554.
570 (?)	Third breaking of the Ma'rib dam; end of ancient South Arabian high culture. The Abyssinian governor of Yemen, Abraha, led an unsuccessful attack on Mecca ('Year of the Elephant'), directed at the authority and economic power of the shrine. Birth of Muḥammad from the tribe of the Quraysh in Mecca.

575	The Yemen became Sasanian province (from 598 under Persian satraps).
602	End of the Lakhmids of al-Ḥīra.
610 (?)	Arab tribes defeated an Arab-Persian army at Dhū Qār in Iraq.

2. *Muḥammad*

610 (?)	Muḥammad experienced the first revelation and appeared in Mecca as the Prophet of Islam.
613 (?)	Beginning of public preaching.
615 (?)	Emigration of a group of Muslims to Abyssinia.
616-19	Boycott of the Quraysh against Muḥammad's clan (the Banū Hāshim).
620-22	Members of the Aws and Khazraj tribes of Yathrib (Medina) converted to Islam and negotiated with Muḥammad with the aim of making him leader of their strife-ridden tribal community.
622	The *Hijra*: emigration of Muḥammad and his followers to Yathrib (now: Madīnat al-Nabī, al-Madīna, 'the city of the Prophet'). Foundation of the first Islamic community; social and economic reforms. Starting point of the Islamic calendar.
624	Expedition of Badr: victory of the Muslims over the Quraysh of Mecca.
625	Defeat of Muḥammad against the Meccans at the mountain of Uḥud. Expulsion of the Jewish tribe of the Banū Naḍīr.
626	Expedition to Dūmat al-Jandal against tribes in the Syrian border area.
627	Unsuccessful siege of Medina by the Quraysh (the 'Battle of the Trench', al-Khandaq). Destruction of the Jewish Banū Qurayẓa. Subjugation of the Kalb at Dūmat al-Jandal.
628	Treaty of Ḥudaybiyya opened access to the shrine of Mecca to the Muslims (first pilgrimage 629). Conquest of the Jewish oasis, Khaybar.
629	Unsuccessful expedition against Byzantine territory (Mu'ta).
630	Bloodless conquest of Mecca.
630-32	Subjugation of the tribes of the Arabian peninsula. Battle of Ḥunayn. Siege of al-Ṭā'if. Campaign against Tabūk (Ghassānids, vassals of Byzantium).
632	Farewell pilgrimage and death of the Prophet Muḥammad.

3. *The Caliphate until the End of the Umayyads*

(a) The period of the 'orthodox' caliphs. The emergence of the Arab state

632-34	Abū Bakr, the first caliph (*khalīfa*) reimposed after the rebellion of the tribes the authority of the Islamic government in the whole of Arabia and sent Arab armies of conquest against Mesopotamia and Syria.
633	Conquest of southern Mesopotamia.
634	Victory at Ajnādayn (Palestine) against the Byzantines.
634-44	The caliph 'Umar b. al-Khaṭṭāb. The Muslims subjugated Egypt, Palestine, Syria, Mesopotamia and Persia. Military

	settlement and beginnings of Islamic government and financial organisation in the conquered lands.
635	Damascus submitted to the Muslims.
636	Battle on the Yarmūk: defeat of a powerful Byzantine army surrendered Syria to the Muslims. Definitive occupation of Damascus.
636 (?)	The Arabs under Saʿd b. Abī Waqqāṣ defeated a Sasanian army in the battle of Qādisiyya (near Ḥīra), gaining Iraq west of the Tigris and through the victory at Jalūlā the capital Seleucia / Ctesiphon.
638	Council of Jābiya (Syria): ʿUmar conferred with the Prophet's companions on the division and organisation of the domains acquired in the conquests; thereafter the setting up of the *Dīwān* (army lists, basis of pensions) around 640.
	Conquest of Jerusalem.
	The garrison towns of Baṣra (founded 635) and Kūfa became centres of military government of Iraq and the starting point for further campaigns of conquest east and north.
639-42	Conquest of Egypt (642 taking of Alexandria) by ʿAmr b. al-ʿĀṣ.
640	Taking of the sea port of Caesarea in Palestine; end of the Byzantine presence in Syria.
640-42	Conquest of Persia (640 Khūzistān; 641 decisive battle of Nihāvand in the Zagros).
641	Conquest of Mosul (upper Mesopotamia) and of Babylon in Egypt (Arab garrison Fusṭāṭ south of the future Cairo).
642	Conquest of Alexandria. Campaign to Barqa (Tripolitania, 642-43).
643	Campaigns to the coast of Makrān and SE Iran.
644	Murder of ʿUmar.
644-56	Caliphate of ʿUthmān. Continuation of the conquests in north and east Iran and North Africa; inner conflicts of the Islamic state about privileges of leadership and property.
from 645	Beginnings of Arab sea-power, directed against Byzantium.
645-46	Alexandria reconquered by the Byzantines, retaken by the Muslims.
647	Conquest of Tripolitania.
	First Arab campaigns in North Africa.
649	Beginning of war at sea against Byzantium and the conquest of Cyprus.
649-50	Conquest of Persepolis, capital of Persis (Fārs) and centre of Zoroastrianism.
651	Yazdagird III, the last Sasanian king, murdered on his retreat to Khurāsān.
652	Subjugation of Armenia. The Byzantine fleet pushed back before Alexandria. Attack on Sicilian harbours. Conclusion of a treaty with Nubia.
*c.*653	ʿUthmān authorised collection and official establishment of the text of the Koran.
655	Muslim sea-power destroyed the Byzantine fleet before Asia Minor.
656	Murder of ʿUthmān, caused by movement of protest against his personal and financial policy.

656-61	Caliphate of 'Alī, cousin and son-in-law of the Prophet; seat of government in Kūfa. Civil war between the party (*Shī'a*) of 'Alī and his opponents from the Quraysh.
656	'Alī victorious in the 'Battle of the Camel' at Baṣra over political opponents (Ṭalḥa, Zubayr, 'Ā'isha).
657	Battle of Ṣiffīn between 'Alī and Mu'āwiya.
658	Arbitration judgement of 'Adhruḥ between 'Alī and Mu'āwiya refused to pronounce 'Alī legitimate caliph. Syrian troops proclaimed Mu'āwiya caliph. Protest in 'Alī's camp against arbitration decision and 'departure' from Kūfa: party of Khārijites (*Khawārij*) defeated by 'Alī at Nahrawān, but spread among Arab Bedouins and settled tribes. Growing danger through social tensions in Iraq.
661	Murder of 'Alī by Khārijites; his son Ḥasan renounced claims to the caliphate. Beginning of the rule of the Arab Umayyad dynasty (until 750).

(b) The caliphate of the Umayyads

661-80	Caliphate of the Umayyad Mu'āwiya ibn Abī Sufyān. Damascus became the new capital. Beginning of the second major period of expansion.
662-75	Ziyād b. Abīhi governor in Iraq (Baṣra) and governor of the former Sasanian provinces.
667	The Arabs occupied Chalcedon, threatened Byzantium and took Sicily.
670	Beginning of operations against the Berbers and of the conquest of North Africa by 'Uqba b. Nāfi'. Foundation of Qayrawān (Kairouan).
672	Beginning of the 'seven year' Arab siege of Constantinople.
680-83	Caliphate of Yazīd I, son of Mu'āwiya.
680	Ḥusayn b. 'Alī led the uprising of the 'Alid party in Kūfa and was killed at Karbalā'. His martyrdom made him a central figure of the Shī'a.
683-92	The second civil war. After the death of Yazīd (683-84 caliphate of Mu'āwiya II) 'Abdallāh b. al-Zubayr set up an anti-caliphate in the Ḥijāz. Under Marwān I the Umayyads regained Syria at the battle of Marj Rāhiṭ (684). Mukhtār tried in Kūfa to set up the authority of the 'Alids. 'Abd al-Malik (685-705), Marwān's son, re-established control over all Islamic provinces.
684-85	Caliphate of Marwān I. Sharpened tribal conflicts led to the battle between the tribal confederations of the Kalb (allies of the caliph) and the Qays at Marj Rāhiṭ (684).
684-86	Epidemic of plague in Mesopotamia, Syria, Egypt.
685-87	Religious and socially motivated uprising of the Shī'a under Mukhtār in Iraq in the name of the 'Alid Muḥammad b. al-Ḥanafiyya.
685-705	Caliphate of 'Abd al-Malik. Period of administrative reforms.
691	Building of the mosque of 'Umar (Dome of the Rock) in Jerusalem. Muṣ'ab b. al-Zubayr, the brother of the pretender 'Abdallāh b. al-Zubayr and his governor in Iraq, murdered. 'Abd al-Malik conquered Iraq.

692	Capture of Mecca by al-Ḥajjāj b. Yūsuf. End of the anti-caliphate of ʿAbdallāh b. al-Zubayr.
694-714	Al-Ḥajjāj b. Yūsuf, governor in Iraq, pacified the province disturbed by sectarian uprisings and revolts. Administrative and economic reorganisation.
698	Final removal of the Byzantines from Carthage.
From 698	Monetary reform: replacement of Sasanian and Byzantine coinages by coins with Arab-Islamic legend. Introduction of Arabic as language of government.
701	Revolt of Ibn al-Ashʿath in Southern Persia and in Iraq.
705	Rebuilding of the church of St John in Damascus and transformation into the Umayyad mosque.
705-15	Caliphate of al-Walīd I. Consolidation and biggest expansion of the empire.
711	Ṭāriq b. Ziyād attacked southern Spain; beginning of the conquest of al-Andalus. Destruction of the Gothic army under King Roderick at Wādī Bakka. Conquest of Sind (Mulṭān) by Muḥammad b. al-Qāsim.
712	Qutayba b. Muslim, Arab governor of Khurāsān, conquered Khwārazm and Transoxiana. The Islamisation of Central Asian centres of culture (Bukhārā, Samarqand) began.
715-17	Caliphate of Sulaymān. Unsuccessful siege of Byzantium.
717-20	Caliphate of ʿUmar II. Tax reform to remove social tensions and prevent emigration from the countryside; converted non-Muslims (*mawālī*) exempted from the poll-tax (*jizya*) but not from the land-tax (*kharāj*).
719	Cordoba became the residence of the Arab governors of al-Andalus.
720-24	Caliphate of Yazīd II.
724-43	Caliphate of Hishām. Policy of exploitation in Transoxiana and North Africa favoured opposition movements.
725	First tax rebellion of the Copts.
728	Death of the preacher and theologian Ḥasan of Baṣra.
732	Battle of Tours and Poitiers (Charles Martel). The Arabs withdrew to the Southern Rhône valley; 737 second campaign of Charles Martel, unsuccessful siege of Narbonne (relinquished in 759).
734-46	Rebellion of al-Ḥārith ibn Surayj in Khurāsān: demand for fiscal equality, and equal pay for Arabs and *mawālī*.
740	Uprising of Zayd ibn ʿAlī in Kufa. Berber revolts under Khārijite leadership.
743-44	Caliphate of al-Walīd II. Quarrels and fights in the Umayyad dynasty.
744	Caliphate of Yazīd III. Abū Muslim began public anti-Umayyad agitation in favour of the ʿAbbāsids in Khurāsān.
744	Caliphate of Ibrāhīm.
744-47	Anti-Umayyad revolt of ʿAbdallāh ibn Muʿāwiya with strong *mawālī* support.
744-50	Marwān II, at first pretender against Yazīd III and Ibrāhīm, emerged from the succession struggles of the Umayyads as the last caliph of the dynasty; attempted consolidation by reform of the army, succumbed, however, to the ʿAbbāsid revolution.

745	Epidemic of plague in Iraq, upper Mesopotamia and Syria.
746	Uprisings of the Kalb in Syria and of the Khārijites in Iraq.
747	The revolutionaries under Abū Muslim unfurled in Khurāsān the black banner of the 'Abbāsids.
748	Qaḥṭaba defeated the Umayyad governor of Khurāsān.
749	All Persia under 'Abbāsid authority; occupation of Kūfa.
749-50	The 'Abbāsid revolution ended the caliphate of the Umayyads; 749-1258 caliphate of the 'Abbāsid dynasty (Banū 'l-'Abbās).

4. The caliphate of the 'Abbāsids and its successor states until the middle of the eleventh century

749-54	Caliphate of Abū 'l-'Abbās al-Ṣaffāḥ. The last Umayyad caliph Marwān II was defeated in the decisive battle on the Great Zāb and fell in Egypt (750). Massacre of the Umayyad family and its high officials.
751	Battle of Aṭlakh on the Talās: the Arabs defeated a Chinese army in Central Asia and became acquainted with paper from prisoners of war. The production of paper began at Samarqand.
754-75	Caliphate of al-Manṣūr. Break with the radical Shī'a; uprisings of 'Alid pretenders. Establishment of a standing army of Khurāsānians. The post of Minister of Post and Information (*ṣāḥib al-barīd wa'l-khabar*) was made into an instrument of government control.
755	Al-Manṣūr had Abū Muslim murdered.
755-88	'Abd al-Raḥmān I, since 756 amir of Cordoba, established the Spanish Umayyad dynasty (755-1031). At first the rulers bore the title *amīr*, but from 929 they took the title of *caliph*. Persistent unrest through the mutual rivalry of Arab tribes and with newly-converted Muslims.
756 (?)	Execution of the Iranian writer 'Abdallāh b. al-Muqaffa', the translator of Persian literature (*Mirror for Princes*, historical and philosophical works) into Arabic.
762-63	Al-Manṣūr founded Baghdad as the capital city of the 'Abbāsid empire, the commercial and cultural centre of the Islamic world. 'Alid uprisings in Iraq and Medina (Muḥammad b. 'Abdallāh).
765	Death of Ja'far al-Ṣādiq, Imām of the Ḥusaynid line of the Shī'a; the division of the Shī'a began after his death.
767	Death of Abū Ḥanīfa, the authority of the Iraqi school of law of the Ḥanafites, named after him.
767 (768?)	Death of the historian Ibn Isḥāq, the author of the classical biography (*Sīra*) of Muḥammad.
775-85	Caliphate of al-Mahdī; the Iranian Barmecides as viziers (until 803); campaign against new Mazdakite and Manichean sects.
776-79	Uprising of al-Muqanna' in Khurāsān.
777-909	Khārijite kingdom of the Rustamids in Tāhart (Western Algeria).
778	Failure of the expedition of Charlemagne in the Basque country and the destruction of parts of his army under Roland at Roncesvalles.
785-86	Caliphate of al-Hādī. The building of the Great Mosque at Cordoba.

786	Death of al-Khalīl b. Aḥmad (also dated 776 or 791), grammarian, lexicographer and prosodist. His pupil Sībawayh produced the first systematic grammar of Arabic.
786-809	Caliphate of Hārūn al-Rashīd. The post of chief judge (*qāḍī 'l-quḍāt*) was created. Abū Yūsuf Ya'qūb wrote the *Book of Land-Tax.* Apogee of the caliphate and flourishing of Arabic literature and science.
789-926	The Idrīsids, 'Alid dynasty of Morocco.
795	Death of Mālik ibn Anas, jurist in Medina, authority of the Mālikite law school.
796-822	Al-Ḥakam I in Spain; rebellions in Cordoba, city-state in Toledo.
798	Death of the jurist Abū Yūsuf Ya'qūb, beside Muḥammad al-Shaybānī (d.805) the most important disciple of Abū Ḥanīfa.
800	Islamic merchants in China (Canton). Foundation of a paper factory in Baghdad.
800-12	Ibn al-Aghlab governor of Ifrīqiyya (Tunisia, capital Qayrawān). Aghlabids 800-909.
803	Fall of the Barmecides, viziers of Hārūn al-Rashīd.
806	Conquest of Tyana; Arab advance as far as Ankyra.
808	Foundation of Fez by the Idrīsids.
809-13	Caliphate of al-Amīn. After the death of Hārūn al-Rashīd the empire was divided between his two sons. Al-Amīn was defeated by al-Ma'mūn who, supported by Khurāsānian troops, reunited the empire (813).
from 810	The jurist al-Shāfi'ī, pupil of Mālik b. Anas, in Baghdad; systematisation of sources of law.
813	The Khurāsānian army under Ṭāhir b. al-Ḥusayn besieged and conquered Baghdad for al-Ma'mūn. Murder of al-Amīn.
813-33	Caliphate of al-Ma'mūn. Cultural and scientific heyday. Promotion of translations of the works of Greek philosophers and scientists ('academy' of *Bayt al-Ḥikma*). Suppression of the traditionalist piety of the *ahl al-ḥadīth* in favour of the rationalistic dogmatics of the Mu'tazila. Tendencies towards independence in the provinces.
814 (815?)	Death of Abū Nuwās, representative of new themes and forms in Arabic poetry.
816	Death of the Ṣūfī Ma'rūf al-Karkhī.
816-37	Revolts of Bābak (Mazdakite sects of the Khurramiyya; dualism and transmigration of souls) against landed nobility and Arabs in Ādharbāyjān, from 827 also in Western Persia.
817	Al-Ma'mūn designated in Marv the Shī'ite *imām* 'Alī al-Riḍā (d.818) as his successor: short-lived attempt at reconciliation with the 'Alids.
817-19	Anti-caliphate of Ibrāhīm ibn al-Mahdī in Baghdad. After the overthrow of the pretender, al-Ma'mūn returned to Baghdad.
820	Death of al-Shāfi'ī, authority of the law school of the Shāfi'ītes.
821-73	Eastern Iran under the Ṭāhirids as governors became *de facto* independent.
822-52	'Abd al-Raḥmān II of Cordoba.
823	Death of the historian al-Wāqidī.
825 or 826	Death of the poet Abū 'l-'Atāhiya.

827	Beginning of the conquest of Sicily. Al-Ma'mūn ordered the *Miḥna* (Inquisition, continued by his successors until 848): the authority of the state supported the theological teaching of the Mu'tazila, especially the dogma of the 'createdness' of the Koran. The traditionalist Aḥmad ibn Ḥanbal (780-855) was persecuted as the representative of the opposition of the *ahl al-ḥadīth* to rationalist theology.
829-30	Uprising of the Copts in Egypt.
831	Fall of Palermo after Arab siege (under Islamic authority until 1072).
833-42	Caliphate of al-Mu'taṣim. Formation of a bodyguard of Turkish as well as other élite troops to protect the caliph.
836	Al-Mu'taṣim founded the residential and garrison city of Sāmarrā.
837	The rebellion of the Khurramiyya under Bābak (from 816) in Ādharbāyjān was put down by the army of the caliph under the general al-Afshīn.
841	The general al-Afshīn died in prison (accusation of apostasy to Zoroastrianism).
842-47	Caliphate of al-Wāthiq, last representative of strong 'Abbāsid political power.
844	The Normans attacked Spain and occupied Seville.
847-61	Caliphate of al-Mutawakkil. End of the *Miḥna*; the doctrine of the *ahl al-ḥadīth* was recognised as orthodoxy; anti-rationalist reaction. Persecution of the Shī'a. First caliph who was murdered by his bodyguards.
*c.*847	Death of the mathematician and geographer al-Khwārazmī.
852-86	Muḥammad I of Cordoba.
855	Death of Aḥmad b. Ḥanbal, the teacher of *ḥadīth* and the authority of the law school of the Ḥanbalites.
857	Death of al-Muḥāsibī, an important teacher of Islamic piety and theology.
861-62	Caliphate of al-Muntaṣir. A decade of domination by Turkish soldiery began.
861-945	Collapse of the 'Abbāsid political power; the provinces gradually slipped away from the caliphate.
862-66	Caliphate of al-Musta'īn, like his two successors completely in the hands of the Turkish guard.
865	Party struggles of the Turkish generals. The population of Baghdad defended the city under the caliph against the Turkish army from Sāmarrā.
866-69	Caliphate of al-Mu'tazz. Overthrow and murder of al-Musta'īn.
867-911	Ya'qūb al-Ṣaffār (867-79) and the Ṣaffārids ruled independently in Sīstān, and towards the end of the ninth century controlled most of Iran.
868	Death of the author al-Jāḥiẓ, master of Arabic prose and of anecdotal encyclopaedic *adab* literature.
868-905	Aḥmad b. Ṭūlūn (868-83) and the Ṭūlūnids independent as governors in Egypt. Egypt broke away from the caliphate.
869	Death of Muḥammad ibn Kar(r)ām, teacher of the Karrāmiyya sect popular in Khurāsān (around Nīshāpūr).
869-70	Caliphate of al-Muhtadī. Uprising of Negro slaves (*Zanj*) in

	Southern Iraq under the ʿAlid leader ʿAlī b. Muḥammad; foundation of an autonomous state (869-83).
870	Death of al-Bukhārī, author of the most respected canonical collection of *ḥadīth*.
870-92	Caliphate of al-Muʿtamid. His brother al-Muwaffaq, as regent, restored caliphal power in the territory between Syria and Khurāsān.
870 (?)	Death of al-Kindī, the first great Muslim Arab philosopher and scientist.
873	Yaʿqūb al-Ṣaffār of Sīstān took Khurāsān from the Ṭāhirids.
	Death of the Nestorian Ḥunayn b. Isḥāq, who led the most active phase of translating medical, scientific and philosophical works from Greek into Arabic.
	Disappearance of the twelfth *imām* of the Shīʿa, who according to Shīʿite belief acts as 'Lord of the Age' in occultation (*ghayba*) and is awaited as the *Mahdī* at the end of time.
874 (?)	Death of the Ṣūfī Abū Yazīd al-Bisṭāmī.
875	Naṣr b. Aḥmad (864-92) from the family of the Sāmānids (governors of Khurāsān since 819) received from the caliph the province of Transoxiana (Bukhārā, Samarqand). Independent government of the Sunnī Sāmānids in eastern Iran until the end of the tenth century. Cultural flowering, awakening of Iranian national awareness and of New Persian literature.
	Death of Muslim b. al-Ḥajjāj, the author of a canonical collection of *ḥadīth*.
876	Al-Muwaffaq defeated Yaʿqūb al-Ṣaffār at Dayr al-ʿĀqūl on the Tigris.
877	Aḥmad b. Ṭūlūn, governor of Egypt, occupied Syria. Beginning of the construction of the mosque of Ibn Ṭūlūn in his garrison town of al-Qaṭāʾiʿ (part of modern Cairo).
878	Fall of Syracuse; the Arabs snatched Sicily from the Byzantines.
879	Destruction of the important Islamic trade settlement in the Chinese sea-port of Canton (*Khānfū*).
879-928	ʿUmar b. Ḥafṣūn and his sons disturbed the Spanish Umayyad state.
883	The army of the caliph put an end to the state of the rebellious Zanj.
888-912	ʿAbdallāh, Umayyad caliph of Cordoba. Fight against the rebels around Ibn Ḥafṣūn.
889	Death of the philologist, historian and theologian, Ibn Qutayba.
c.890	The Carmathians, Arab partisans of the Ismāʿīlī Shīʿa, under the leadership of Ḥamdān Qarmaṭ active in Iraq and Syria. The growing militancy of the radical Shīʿa accelerated the collapse of the caliphate.
892	Death of the *ḥadīth* scholar Muḥammad al-Tirmidhī; formulated rules for assessing the reliability of *isnāds* (chains of transmission).
892-902	Caliphate of al-Muʿtaḍid. Religious and political unrest.
894	Founding of a Carmathian state in the east of the Arabian peninsula.
897	Establishment of the Zaydī state in the Yemen.

900	The Sāmānids under Ismāʿīl (892-907) pushed the Ṣaffārids out of Khurāsān. Promotion of the Persian language.
902-08	Caliphate of al-Muqtafī. Stabilising of the power of the caliphate in the territory between Egypt and northern Iran. North Africa under the Aghlabids and eastern Iran under the Sāmānids were autonomous provinces. Struggles with the Carmathians.
905-91	The Arab dynasty of the Ḥamdānids ruled (929-79 independently) in the Jazīra (upper Mesopotamia, capital Mosul), 945-1004 also in northern Syria (capital Aleppo), carried on border warfare against Byzantium.
908-32	Caliphate of al-Muqtadir after struggles for the throne and the death of his rival ʿAbdallāh b. al-Muʿtazz. Increasing loss of power of the caliphate to the viziers and military.
909-72	The Ismāʿīlīs pushed the Aghlabids out of Ifrīqiyya (Tunisia) and established the Fāṭimid caliphate with the capital Mahdiyya (ʿUbaydallāh al-Mahdī 909-34).
910	Death of the mystic Junayd.
912-61	ʿAbd al-Raḥmān III of Cordoba. Struggles against the Fāṭimids and the Berbers in the Maghrib. The Spanish Umayyad empire at its peak.
913-42	The Sāmānid Naṣr II promoted Arabic and Persian culture. The Sāmānid territory reached its greatest size with centres in Khurāsān and Transoxiana.
922	Crucifixion of the mystic al-Ḥallāj in Baghdad.
923	Death of the Koran commentator, lawyer and historian al-Ṭabarī (born 838); his annals incorporate the most important sources for early Islamic history.
925	Death of the physician and philosopher Abū Bakr Muḥammad b. Zakariyyā al-Rāzī (Rhazes).
929	ʿAbd al-Raḥmān III of Cordoba adopted the title of caliph. Death of the astronomer al-Battānī (Albatenius).
929-69	Emirate of the Ḥamdānid al-Ḥasan Nāṣir al-Dawla in Mosul (upper Mesopotamia).
930	The Baḥrayn Carmathians in Mecca: massacre of pilgrims, theft of the Black Stone of the Kaʿba. Conquest of Oman.
932-34	Caliphate of al-Qāhir.
934-40	Caliphate of al-Rāḍī. The power of the weakened caliph was usurped by the chief amir (*amīr al-umarāʾ*) of the army (936). The Shīʿite military clan of the Būyids from Daylam on the Caspian Sea rose to power in western Iran.
935-69	The Ikhshīdids, a dynasty established by the Turk Muḥammad b. Ṭughj (935-46), in Egypt and Syria.
936 (?)	Death of the theologian al-Ashʿarī who systematically established the traditionist dogma of the *ahl al-ḥadīth* with methods of *kalām*.
936	Muḥammad b. Rāʾiq in the post of chief amir at Baghdad, united the office of commander-in-chief of the army with financial and administrative control of the empire.
939	ʿAbd al-Raḥmān III was defeated by Ramiro of León at Simancas.

940	Rūdakī, court-poet of the Sāmānid Naṣr II in Bukhārā, first important representative of New Persian poetry.
940-44	Caliphate of al-Muttaqī.
from 941	Plague epidemic in Iraq.
941	Al-Māturīdī died in Samarqand; after his teacher al-Ash'arī the second great theologian of the *Sunna*, who defended orthodox teaching by means of *kalām* methods.
942	The Ḥamdānid al-Ḥasan of Mosul, protector of the caliph after the murder of Ibn Rā'iq the last Arab chief amir, received the title Nāṣir al-Dawla.
	Beginning of the decline of Sāmānid authority in Iran, brought about by palace revolutions and uprisings.
944-46	Caliphate of al-Mustakfī. The Būyids took over military and administrative power in the caliphal territory (945-1055).
944-47	Revolt of Berber tribes against the Fāṭimids.
945-1003	The Ḥamdānids of Aleppo. Sayf al-Dawla (945-67) took Aleppo and Ḥims from the Ikhshīdids and fought against the Byzantines. He received at his court the poet al-Mutanabbī, the historian and littérateur Abū 'l-Faraj al-Iṣbahānī and the philosopher al-Fārābī.
945	The Būyids occupied Iraq, Mu'izz al-Dawla took over as chief amir in Baghdad the control of the caliphate.
946-74	Caliphate of al-Muṭī'.
949-83	'Aḍud al-Dawla, the most important ruler of the Būyid dynasty in Iran (from 977 also in Iraq); restorer of Iranian kingship.
950	Death of the philosopher al-Fārābī, commentator of Aristotle, interpreted Islamic prophecy and theocracy using concepts of Greek philosophy.
from *c.*950	Conversion to Islam of Turkish tribes east of the Jaxartes (Qarluqs and Qarakhānids).
954-61	The Sāmānid 'Abd al-Malik I.
956	Death of al-Mas'ūdī, world traveller and historian, author of an encyclopaedia on history, geography and sciences.
961-76	Al-Ḥakam II of Cordoba; after his death internal collapse of the Spanish Umayyad caliphate.
961-63	Alptigin, Turkish general of the Sāmānids, established autonomy in Ghazna (Sīstān—Afghanistan, until 999 in the name of the Sāmānids).
965	Death of al-Mutanabbī, the last great representative of the art of classical Arabic poetry.
	Rebellions of the *aḥdāth* in Antioch and Aleppo.
967	Death of Abū 'l-Faraj al-Iṣbahānī, historian and man of letters; his 'Book of Songs' is a major source for ancient and classical Arabic poetry.
968	Byzantium reconquered Sicily and Northern Syria.
969	The Fāṭimids conquered Egypt; the taking of Fuṣṭāṭ and the founding of Cairo (*al-Qāhira*). The Fāṭimid dynasty became the major Mediterranean power.
972-1152	The Berber dynasty of the Zīrids in Ifrīqiyya and eastern Algeria (until 1049 as vassals of the Fāṭimids).
973	Cairo became the capital of the Fāṭimid caliphs. The mosque

and college of al-Azhar (founded 970, completed 972) was the spiritual centre of the Ismā'īlī Shī'a.

c.974 Death of the Sāmānid vizier Bal'amī, the translator of the Annals of al-Ṭabarī into Persian.

974 Death of the Christian Arab theologian and philosopher, Yaḥyā b. 'Adī in Baghdad.

974-91 Caliphate of al-Ṭā'i'. Struggle of the caliph with the Būyid amirs for autonomy in Iraq.

977 The Būyid 'Aḍud al-Dawla took over the chief emirate in Baghdad; had himself crowned king by the caliph.

977-97 Sebüktigin, the slave general of Alptigin, founder of the Ghaznavid dynasty in Afghanistan, norther India and Khurāsān.

c.980 *Letters of the Ikhwān al-Ṣafā'* ('Brothers of Purity') of Basra, a philosophical-scientific encyclopaedia influenced by the Ismā'īlī Shī'ite ideology.

Death of Daqīqī, the court poet of the Sāmānids, as the author of a Persian royal epic the predecessor of Firdawsī.

983 After the death of 'Aḍud al-Dawla the beginning of the decline of Būyid authority; autonomy in the provinces.

991 Venice sent embassies to the Arab Mediterranean princes.

991-1031 Caliphate of al-Qādir after the deposition of al-Ṭā'i'. Support of traditionalist orthodoxy.

until 992 Turkish tribes of the Oghuz (Ghuzz) advanced from the Kirghizian steppe towards Transoxiana and Khurāsān.

The clan of Seljuq (Selchüq), a chief of the Oghuz, having converted to Islam, supported the Sāmānids against the Qarakhānids in the fight for Bukhārā (Qarakhānid conquest 992).

992-1124 The Turkish Qarakhānids (or Ilek-Khāns) in Transoxiana (Bukhārā) and eastern Turkestan. End of Sāmānid authority; the Oxus became the dividing-line between the Qarakhānids and the Ghaznavids. Oghuz in Transoxiana and Khwārazm (Jand, on the Syr Darya/Jaxartes), condottieri of the Seljuq clan in the service of the Qarakhānids.

994 Death of the Baghdad chief judge and man of letters al-Tanūkhī.

995-1017 Khwārazmshāhs of the Ma'mūnids in Gurgānj.

996-1021 The Fāṭimid al-Ḥākim saw himself as the incarnation of the divine intellect; persecution of Jews and Christians.

998-1030 Reign of Maḥmūd of Ghazna; led campaigns into NW India (Punjab, 1001-21) and put the conquered territories under Islamic authority in the name of the 'Abbāsid caliph. Annexation of Khurāsān (999), Khwārazm and western Persia.

1000 Death of al-Muqaddasī, world-traveller and geographer, author of a 'cultural geography' of the earth.

1002 Death of the philologist Ibn Jinnī, who systematised Arabic grammar.

1006 Maḥmūd defeated the Qarakhānids of Turkestan.

1008 Death of Badī' al-Zamān al-Hamadhānī, founder of the literary genre of the *maqāma* (tales of social satire in rhymed prose).

c.1010 Firdawsī of Ṭūs completed the Persian national epic of the *Shāh-nāma* ('Book of Kings'), dedicated to Maḥmūd of Ghazna.

1013	Death of al-Bāqillānī, jurist and theologian of the school of al-Ash'arī.
1016	Naval victory of Pisa and Genoa pushed the Muslims out of the Tyrrhenian Sea.
1017	The Ghaznavids in Khwārazm; defeat of the Ma'mūnids.
c. 1020	Death of the Persian poet Firdawsī.
1021	Death of the Ṣūfī al-Sulamī, who composed a mystical commentary on the Koran and a biographical lexicon of the Ṣūfī teaching tradition.
1023	Death of the man of letters, philosopher and Ṣūfī Abū Ḥayyān al-Tawḥīdī.
1023-79	The Arab dynasty of the Mirdāsids in Aleppo.
1023-91	The 'Abbādids of Seville.
1927-31	Hishām III, last Umayyad of Cordoba.
1029	Maḥmūd of Ghazna conquered Rayy and Jibāl: the Ghaznavids on the west Persian plateau.
1030	The book on India completed by the scientist and cultural historian al-Bīrūnī (973-c. 1050).
	Struggles between *futuwwa* guilds and the Turkish garrison in Baghdad.
	Death of the philosopher and historian Miskawayh: wrote works on philosophical ethics and history ('The Experiences of the Nations').
1030-41	Mas'ūd (after the interregnum of his brother Muḥammad) sultan of Ghazna.
1031	End of the Umayyads of Spain; break-up of al-Andalus into small states.
1031-75	Caliphate of al-Qā'im; last phase of freedom of action on the part of the caliph before the coming of the Seljuqs. Al-Māwardī (d. 1058) formulated the classical theory of the caliphate.
1032	Plague in Iraq, upper Mesopotamia and Syria.
1036-37	The Seljuqs Toghrïl Beg and Chaghrï Beg conquered Khurāsān.
1036-94	The Fāṭimid al-Mustanṣir; high point of the power and the beginning of the political and religious dissolution of the Fāṭimid caliphate.
1037	Death of Ibn Sīnā (Avicenna), universal scholar, the most influential philosopher and physician of the Islamic east in the Middle Ages, interpreted Greek metaphysics in the framework of Islam.
1038	Toghrïl Beg, sultan in Nīshāpūr, Chaghrï Beg in Marv.
1039	Death of Ibn al-Haytham, astronomer, mathematician and optician, sponsored by the Fāṭimid al-Ḥākim.
1039-40	Death of 'Unṣurī, panegyrical poet at the court of Maḥmūd of Ghazna.
1040	Battle of Dandānqān: the Seljuqs Toghrïl and Chaghrï overcame Mas'ūd of Ghazna. End of Ghaznavid power in Khurāsān and western Persia; Ghaznavids survived in Ghazna (Sīstān) and in NW India.
1041	The Seljuqs under Toghrïl occupied Khwārazm.
1043	Toghrïl conquered Ṭabaristān (Elburz mountains) and the Persian city of Rayy. Negotiations with the caliph; Toghrïl

declared himself 'protector of the commander of the faithful'. Syria slipped from Fāṭimid control.

1045-55 Campaigns of the Seljuqs against eastern Anatolia and Armenia; threatening of the Byzantine eastern frontier.

1049 Death of the Persian Ṣūfī and preacher Abū Sa'īd ibn Abī'l-Khayr of Nīshāpūr.

The Zīrids of Qayrawān withdrew allegiance to the Fāṭimids. Cairo unleashed the Hilāl Bedouin against Ifrīqiyya as a reprisal measure (from 1050).

from 1050 Expansion of Arab tribes of the Banū Hilāl and Sulaym in NW Africa; devastation of parts of the Maghrib, century of anarchy.

c. 1050 The Murābiṭūn (Almoravids), warriors for the faith of the Ṣanhāja Berbers, spread Islamic revival movement in West Africa (Senegal estuary, Mauretania, Ghana, West Sudan).

after 1050 Death of Iranian astronomer and polymath al-Bīrūnī (b. 973).

1051 Toghrïl conquered Jibāl (capital Iṣfahān, until then under the Kākūyids).

Advance of Turcoman tribes to Ādharbāyjān and to upper Mesopotamia.

5. *The Seljuq period*

The Seljuqs in Iran, Mesopotamia and Anatolia. Syria and Egypt under Atabegs and Ayyūbids. The Islamic confrontation with the Crusaders. The final phase of the 'Abbāsid caliphate. Almoravids and Almohads in North Africa.

1055 Toghrïl Beg seized power in Baghdad, was recognised by the caliph al-Qā'im as 'Sultan of East and West' and put an end to the principality of the Būyids. The sultanate of the 'Great Seljuqs' in Iran and Iraq takes over control of the caliphate.

1056-61 Ṣanhāja Berbers of the Sahara (a tribal group of the Lamtūna) under Abū Bakr b. 'Umar established the power of the Murābiṭūn (Almoravids) in the Moroccan Atlas.

1057 The Banū Hilāl destroyed Qayrawān.

1058 Death of al-Māwardī, author of 'The Ordinances of Government', legal theory of the political institutions of Sunnī Islam.

Death of the blind poet Abū 'l-'Alā' al-Ma'arrī (b. 973), liberal sceptic.

1059-60 Interregnum of al-Basāsīrī (Turkish general of the last Būyid) in Iraq in the name of the Fāṭimid caliph.

1061-91 The Normans conquered Sicily from lower Italy (1072 Palermo).

1061-1106 The Almoravids (al-Murābiṭūn) under Yūsuf b. Tāshufīn conquered Morocco (1062 founding of Marrākesh) and Spain (1086). Rigid legalism according to the doctrine of the Mālikite legal school.

1063-72 Alp Arslan, Seljuq sultan. In succession to his father Chaghrï Beg (from 1061) and—after the removal of other claimants (battle of Dāmghān)—to his uncle Toghrïl, he became the ruler of all Seljuq domains. Campaigns against the Fāṭimids and the Byzantines.

1064 Death of Ibn Ḥazm, Spanish politician, theologian and man of letters.

1064-68	Attacks by Alp Arslan on Armenia and central Anatolia (1067 Caesarea/Kayseri, 1068 Iconium/Konya). Romanus IV Diogenes prepared for campaign against Armenia (1069).
1065-72	Famine in Egypt.
1065-92	Niẓām al-Mulk, Persian vizier of the Seljuqs Alp Arslan and Malikshāh. Centralised organisation of the empire in Iranian tradition; expansion of the *iqṭā'* system of military land tenure; consolidation of urban and rural economy.
1067	Niẓām al-Mulk founded important school of Shāfi'īte law in Baghdad (*al-Madrasa al-Niẓāmiyya*).
1069-70	Yūsuf of Balāsaghūn wrote in Kāshgar (Turkestan) an allegorical poem in Eastern Turkish: beginnings of *belles-lettres* in Turkish.
1071	Alp Arslan met the Byzantine invasion in Armenia and destroyed its army at Malāzgird (Mantzikert); capture of the emperor Romanos Diogenes. Opening of Anatolia to Turcoman occupation.
	Rise of Malik Dānishmand as leader of an autonomous principality of Turcomans in north and east Anatolia.
1072	Normans under Robert Giscard conquered Palermo (Sicily).
	Death of al-Qushayrī, author of a classical handbook of Ṣūfism.
	Death of Alp Arslan on campaign against the Qarakhānids in Transoxiana.
1072-92	The Seljuq sultan Malikshāh.
1073-94	Badr al-Jamālī, amir and vizier of the Fāṭimid state.
1075 (?)	Death of the Ṣūfī al-Hujwīrī, who wrote the first systematic treatment of the life and teaching of the Ṣūfīs in Persian.
1075-94	Caliphate of al-Muqtadī.
1076	End of Fāṭimid domination in Syria: the Turkish general Atsïz occupied Damascus; request for help from the Seljuqs.
1077-78	Sulaymān b. Qutalmïsh (Qutlumush) established in Nicaea (Iznik) the Seljuq house of Anatolia (the Seljuqs of Rūm until 1307, from 1243 under Mongol authority).
1078	The Seljuq Tutush, brother of sultan Malikshāh, maintained full authority over Syria and Palestine and supplanted Atsïz. Line of Seljuqs in Syria until 1117.
1082	The leader of the Almoravids Yūsuf b. Tāshufīn (1062-1106) controlled an extensive territory in North Africa.
1083	Alfonso VI of Castille and Leon defeated al-Mu'tamid of Seville.
1085	Conquest of Toledo by the forces of the Reconquista under Alfonso VI.
	Death of the theologian al-Juwaynī, teacher of al-Ghazālī (d.1111).
1086	Yūsuf b. Tāshufīn defeated the Spanish Christians under Alfonso VI in the battle of Zallāqa at Badajoz. Supremacy of the Almoravids in al-Andalus until 1148.
1088 (?)	Death of Nāṣir-i Khusraw, Ismā'īlī theologian and poet of Balkh, who wrote substantial travel account (1045-52).
1089	The Fāṭimids took Acre, Tyre and other ports on the Palestinian coast.
	Death of 'Abdallāh al-Anṣārī, Ḥanbalite Ṣūfī, writer of Persian poetry and prose.

1090-1124	Ḥasan b. al-Ṣabbāḥ, Grand Master of the militant 'Assassins' (Nizārī sect of the Ismāʿīlīs) in the fortress of Alamūt in the Elburz mountains.
1090	The Almoravid Yūsuf b. Tāshufīn after suppressing the petty rulers of al-Andalus (*mulūk al-ṭawāʾif*) became sole ruler of Muslim Spain.
1091	The Seljuqs made Baghdād their capital.
from 1092	Numerous uprisings of popular militias (*ʿayyārūn*) in Baghdad.
1092	The Seljuq vizier Niẓām al-Mulk murdered by the Assassins. After the death of Malikshāh dividing up of the Seljuq empire in the Near East.
1092-1107	Qïlïch Arslan I renewed in Nicaea (Iznik) the authority of the Seljuqs of Rūm in Anatolia (after an interregnum 1086-92). Struggles with the Turkish Dānishmendids in eastern Anatolia and with the Crusaders.
1094-1118	Caliphate of al-Mustaẓhir. Death of the amir Badr al-Jamālī and of the Fāṭimid al-Mustanṣir; beginning of the collapse of Fāṭimid authority.
1095	The Seljuq Tutush fell in the war for succession against Berkyāruq (1094-1105 sultan in Baghdad). His sons Riḍwān (until 1113) in Aleppo, Duqāq (until 1104) in Damascus. The Fāṭimids took southern Palestine. The Byzantine emperor Alexius sought help against the Seljuqs from the Pope. Council of Clairmont: Pope Urban II preached the Crusade to Jerusalem.
1095-1106	The jurist and theologian al-Ghazālī gave up his chair at the Niẓāmiyya at Baghdad and wrote in years of seclusion his principal work 'The Revival of the Sciences of Religion
1095-1153	The al-Ṣūfī family provided the *raʾis* of Damascus
1096	Beginning of the First Crusade to conquer Jerusalem, instigated by Pope Urban II.
1097	Victory of the Crusaders over Qïlïch Arslan I at Dorylaeum (NW Anatolia). The Crusaders under Godfrey of Bouillon took Nicaea (Iznik), Tarsus under Tancred and besieged Antioch. The Anatolian Seljuqs made Konya their capital. Baldwin of Boulogne Duke of Edessa.
1098	The Crusaders (Bohemond of Tarentum) took Antioch. The Fāṭimid vizier al-Afḍal took Jerusalem from the Artuqids.
1099	The Crusaders conquered Jerusalem; Godfrey of Bouillon guardian (advocatus) of the Holy Sepulchre. Defeat of the Fāṭimids (al-Afḍal) before the sea fortress of Acre. End of the First Crusade.
from 1100	Urban families monopolised the post of *raʾīs* in Syria and upper Mesopotamia: the Nīsān family ruled in Āmid, the Badīʿ family in Aleppo.
1100-18	Baldwin I, King of Jerusalem (Latin kingdom 1100-87, in Acre until 1291).
1101-30	Rule of al-Āmir, last strong Fāṭimid caliph.
1104	Tughtigīn, atabeg of the Seljuq Duqāq, ruler of Damascus on the latter's death.
1105-18	Reunification of the Seljuq empire under Muḥammad I ibn

	Malikshāh. His brother Sanjar ruled eastern Persia (from 1097).
1106-43	'Alī b. Yūsuf b. Tāshufīn, ruler of Islamic Spain and North Africa.
	Decline of power of the Almoravids, from 1120 in conflict with the Almohad movement.
1107	Registration and redistribution of land concessions in Egypt.
	The Seljuq Qïlïch Arslan I fell by the Khābūr (upper Mesopotamia) in a battle with the Seljuqs of Iraq. The power of his successors remained restricted to central Anatolia (capital Konya).
1109	Agreement of Christian princes before Tripoli on territorial claims in the Orient. Tripoli under siege fell to the Crusaders.
1111	Death of al-Ghazālī, critic of speculative theology and of philosophy (especially also of the militant Shī'ite Ismā'īliyya). Renewer of the faith in the spirit of the Sunnī tradition and Ṣūfī piety.
1113	Death of the Seljuq Riḍwān of Aleppo, succeeded by his son Alp Arslan (until 1114). 1114-29 Aleppo under the rule of various lines of Seljuqs and Artuqids.
	Saragossa fell to Christian Aragon.
1118	After the death of Muḥammad I b. Malikshāh, the Seljuq empire broke up finally into independent small states of the sultans of Nīshāpūr (Khurāsān), Baghdad (Iraq and western Persia) and Konya (Anatolia) and independent principalities of the Atabegs ('princes' tutors') in Syria, upper Mesopotamia and Ādharbāyjān).
1118-57	Sanjar, the son of Malikshāh, 1097 ruler of eastern Persia (Khurāsān) became, after the death of his brother Muḥammad I, supreme sultan of the Seljuq house.
	The Ghaznavids became tributaries of the Seljuqs.
1118-35	Caliphate of al-Mustarshid.
1120-21	Muḥammad b. Tūmart (d. 1130), founder of the religious reform movement of the Muwaḥḥidūn (Almohads), was recognised as Mahdī by the Maṣmūda Berbers and from the Atlas began with his general 'Abd al-Mu'min the struggle against the Almoravids of Marrākesh.
1122	Death of al-Ḥarīrī, philologist and master of the literary genre of the *maqāma* (prose poem).
c. 1131	Death of 'Umar Khayyām, Persian mathematician, astronomer, philosopher, poet of epigrammatic quatrains (*rubā'iyyāt*).
1124	The Frankish and Venetian fleet took Tyre.
1126	Death of Aḥmad al-Ghazālī, brother of Muḥammad al-Ghazālī (d. 1111), popular Ṣūfī teacher.
1127-46	'Imād al-Dīn Zangī b. Aq-Sonqur (atabeg of the Seljuq Mughīth al-Dīn Maḥmūd II) governor of Mosul and from 1129 of Aleppo; propagated *jihād* (Holy War) and opened the offensive against the Crusader states.
1127-56	The Khwārazm-Shāh Atsïz, at first governor of the Seljuq Sanjar, from 1141 independent in Gurgānj.
1130 (?)	Death of Sanā'ī, first great poet of Ṣūfī mysticism in the Persian language.
1130-63	After the death of Ibn Tūmart, his 'caliph', 'Abd al-Mu'min,

pushed the Almoravids out of Morocco (1147 conquest of Marrākesh) and led the Almohad movement to supremacy over North Africa (until 1269) and Spain (1145-1225).

1132 Building of the Palatina of Monreale at Palermo by Roger II (until 1140).

1135-36 Caliphate of al-Rāshid. Numerous *'ayyārūn* uprisings in Baghdad.

1136-60 Caliphate of al-Muqtafī.

1137-75 Shams al-Dīn Eldigüz, atabeg of the Seljuq sultans of Baghdad, established independent state in Ādharbāyjān and NW Persia (until 1225). The power of the sultans declined in the face of independent atabegs and the renewed authority of the caliphs.

1138 The Kurdish generals Ayyūb b. Shādhī (father of Saladin) and his brother Shīrkūh entered the service of Zangī.

1139 Death of the Andalusian vizier, physician and philosopher Ibn Bājja, in Fez.

1141 Defeat of the Seljuqs under Sanjar in the battle against an uprising of Turkish tribes of the Qara-Khitāy. The Khwārazm-Shāh Atsïz (1127-56) sought independence from Sanjar, was forced, however, to recognise the suzerainty of the Qara-Khitāy.

1144 Zangī reconquered Edessa from the Crusaders (Count Joscelin II): prompted the Second Crusade (1147-49).
Death of al-Zamakhsharī, philologist and Mu'tazilite commentator of the Koran in Khurāsān.

1145 The Almohads set foot on the Iberian peninsula.

1146-74 Nūr al-Dīn Maḥmūd b. Zangī, successor of his father in Aleppo and (from 1154) in Damascus, 1146-49 beside his brother Sayf al-Dīn Ghāzī in Mosul, brought the whole of Islamic Syria under his command and fought in the spirit of Holy War and of orthodoxy against Crusaders and Fāṭimids; brought the Crusade to a standstill and pushed the Franks back to the mountainous area west of the Orontes and the Jordan.

1147 The Almohads under 'Abd al-Mu'min conquered Marrākesh; end of the Almoravid dynasty. The court became a centre of arts and sciences.

1147-49 Second Crusade. Defeats of the German Crusaders (under Conrad III) at Dorylaeum, of the French (Louis VII) at Laodicaea (1148) at the hands of the Anatolian Seljuqs.

1148 The Second Crusade failed with a futile siege of Damascus.
Sayf al-Dīn Ṣūrī from Ghūr (central Afghanistān) conducted a campaign of vengeance against Ghazna.

1149-69 The Zangid Quṭb al-Dīn Mawdūd of Mosul.

1149 Nūr al-Dīn defeated the forces of Antioch (Raymond of Poitiers) at Inab (Ḥiṣn Innib).

1150-51 The Ghūrid 'Alā' al-Dīn Ḥusayn (1149-61) destroyed Ghazna. The power of the last Ghaznavids (until 1186) was limited to the Punjab.

1152 Raymond III of Tripoli murdered by Assassins.
Ṣalāḥ al-Dīn b. Ayyūb (Saladin) entered the service of Nūr al-Dīn at Aleppo.

1153 Ascalon fell to the Franks (King Baldwin III of Jerusalem).

Death of the theologian and heresiographer al-Shahrastānī.

1154 Nūr al-Dīn annexed Damascus.
The Fāṭimid caliph accorded Pisa trade privileges.
Al-Idrīsī completed his universal geography at the court of Roger II in Sicily.

1156-92 Qïlïch Arslan II extended the authority of the Seljuqs in central Anatolia; displacement of the Dānishmendids.

1157 Death of Sanjar; collapse of the Seljuq sultanate.
The Khwārazm-Shāhs gained authority over the east from Khurāsān to Anatolia (ended by the Mongol invasion from 1220).

1160-70 Caliphate of al-Mustanjid.

1162 Death of the physician Ibn Zuhr (Avenzoar), court physician and vizier of the Almohad ʿAbd al-Muʾmin.

1163-68 Attacks by the Franks (King Amalric, 1163-74) on Egypt shaken by internal unrest; treaty of alliance with the Fāṭimid vizier Shāwar. Nūr al-Dīn despatched in 1164 and again in 1167 the Kurdish general Shīrkūh and his nephew Ṣalāḥ al-Dīn (Saladin).

1163-84 The Almohad Abū Yaʿqūb Yūsuf I, successor of ʿAbd al-Muʾmin; defender of Islam against the Reconquista in Portugal and Spain; patron of poets, philosophers and physicians at the courts in Seville and Marrākesh.

1164 Ḥasan II, Grand Master of the Persian Nizāriyya (Assassins) of Alāmūt had homage paid to himself as Imām at a 'festival of ressurection' and proclaimed the abrogation of Islamic law.

1166 Death of the preacher and Ṣūfī ʿAbd al-Qādir al-Jīlānī in Baghdad, reconciled the traditionalist legalistic school of the Ḥanbalites with the ecstatic individualism of the mystics. The rule of the order of the Qādiriyya was named after him.

1168-69 At a request for help from the Fāṭimid al-ʿĀḍid, third campaign of the Ayyūbid generals Shīrkūh and Saladin to Egypt. After the retreat of the Franks and the death of Shāwar, Shīrkūh, and after his death, Saladin, became vizier of al-ʿĀḍid.

1169 (?) Death of the Persian poet Anvarī, master of panegyric.

1170-80 Caliphate of al-Mustaḍīʾ.
Construction of the Almohad mosque in Seville with its minaret, the present-day Giralda.

1171 Nūr al-Dīn occupied Mosul.
Saladin proclaimed the ʿAbbāsid caliphate in Egypt.
With the death of the last Fāṭimid al-ʿĀḍid the Ismāʿīlī anti-caliphate ended; Saladin broke with the Zangids and established the sultanate of the ʿAyyūbids (until 1250).

1171-93 Reign of Saladin. Rebuilding of the Egyptian fleet. Exclusion of the Europeans from trade through the Red Sea; support for the Egyptian trade with India. Promotion of Sunnī institutions of learning.

1172 The Almohads under Abū Yaʿqūb Yūsuf I unsuccessfully besieged Huete.

1173 Pisa retained trading privileges in Alexandria.

1174 Death of Nūr al-Dīn. Saladin occupied Damascus and opened the offensive against the Zangids of northern Syria.
The leper Baldwin IV king of Jerusalem.

1175 The caliph al-Mustaḍī' granted Saladin the sultanate of Egypt, Palestine and Syria. Truce with Jerusalem.

1176 Battle of Myriocephalon: destruction of the Byzantine army under Manuel I Comnenos by the Seljuqs of Rūm.

1176-81 New registration of land in Egypt, redistribution in the form of military land tenure (*iqṭā'*) and crown privileges.

1179 Resumption of the *jihād*: Saladin (after a defeat at Tall al-Ṣāfiya [Mount Giscard near Ramla] in 1177) defeated a Crusader army under Baldwin IV at Marj 'Uyūn. Egyptian naval attack on Acre. 1180, new truce.

1180-1225 Caliphate of al-Nāṣir; he united and revitalised the *futuwwa* movement (chivalric guilds) into an official organisation under his control and with its help led the Baghdad caliphate to its last flowering.

1182 Offensive of Saladin against Mosul.

1183 Reginald of Châtillon (Lord of Karak and Shawbak) led an attack directed at Mecca on ports on the Red Sea and was decisively defeated by the Egyptian fleet. Saladin pushed the last Zangids out of Aleppo.

Ibn Rushd (Averroes) became as successor to Ibn Ṭufayl court physician of the Almohad Abū Ya'qūb Yūsuf I and chief *qāḍī* of Cordoba.

1184 The Almohad Yūsuf I fell after an unsuccessful siege of Santarem (Portugal). His successor Abū Yūsuf Ya'qūb al-Manṣūr (1184-99).

1185 Truce between Saladin and Raymond III of St Gilles (Tripoli and Tiberias), which left Saladin free to move against Mosul; by a treaty in 1186 he became lord of the Jazīra.

Death of Anvarī, master of the panegyric *qaṣīda* in the Persian language.

Death of the physician and philosopher Ibn Ṭufayl, precursor and patron of Ibn Rushd in Cordoba.

1187 The Ghūrids destroyed the Ghaznavids in the Punjab and took over their domains in eastern Afghanistan. Ghiyāth al-Dīn Muḥammad (1163-1203 in Ghūr) led expansion to Khurāsān, his brother Mu'izz al-Dīn Muḥammad (1173-1206 in Ghazna) conquered northern India.

Saladin decisively defeated the Crusader army at Ḥiṭṭīn (west of Lake Tiberias), took King Guy of Jerusalem prisoner and executed Reginald of Karak. After a victorious campaign through the Palestinian-Lebanese littoral, siege and capture of Jerusalem.

'Aṭṭār, Persian mystical poet (died 1190 or later) wrote the allegorical verse epic *Manṭiq al-ṭayr.*

1188-92 Third Crusade, provoked by the fall of Jerusalem.

1190 The German Crusaders under Frederick I Barbarossa defeated the Anatolian Seljuqs and conquered Konya. Barbarossa drowned in the Calycadnos (Gök Su) in Cilicia.

1191 Richard I of England and Philip II of France conquered Acre after a three-year siege by the Crusaders.

Yaḥyā al-Suhrawardī, Ṣūfī and teacher of a gnostic cosmology

	and philosophy of illumination (*ḥikmat al-ishrāq*) was accused of heresy and executed on the orders of Saladin.
1192	The Ghūrids took Delhi.
1193	Saladin died in Jerusalem; division of his realm.
1194	The Khwārazm-Shāh Tekish defeated the last Seljuq sultan of Persia.
1195	The Almohad Abū Yūsuf Ya'qūb al-Manṣūr won an important victory at Alarcos over the Castilians.
1196-1549	The Berber dynasty of the Marīnids of Morocco (until 1269 beside the Almohads).
1198	Death of Ibn Rushd al-Ḥafīd (Averroës), Andalusian *qāḍī*, physician and philosopher in the Aristotelian tradition, author of important commentaries on the works of Aristotle.
1199-1214	The Almohad Muḥammad al-Nāṣir in North Africa and Spain. Successes of the Reconquista.
1200-20	Under the Khwārazm-Shāh 'Alā' al-Dīn Muḥammad his empire experienced its greatest flourishing (restoration of the Iranian monarchy, conflict with the caliph al-Nāṣir) before the collapse through the Mongol invasion.
1200-18	Saladin's brother al-Malik al-'Ādil sultan of Egypt and Syria.
1201-02	Plague in Egypt; sharp decline in the population.
1202-04	Fourth Crusade: Latin emperorship in Constantinople.
1203-27	Temujin—Genghiz Khan after 1206—established the Mongol empire.
1204	Conquest of Constantinople by the Crusaders.
	The Jewish-Arab physician, philosopher and religious teacher Maimonides from Cordoba died in Fusṭāṭ near Cairo.
1206-10	Quṭb al-Dīn Aybak, general of the Ghūrid Mu'izz al-Dīn, established the sultanate of Delhi ('Slave-kings', until 1290).
1206	Temujin was acknowledged as supreme chief of the Mongols and received the title Genghiz (Chingiz) Khan.
1208	Sultan al-'Ādil of Egypt accorded Venice trading privileges. Commercial treaty between Venice and the Ayyūbids of Aleppo.
1209	Death of the theologian Fakhr al-Dīn al-Rāzī, defender of the *Sunna* and of the methods of al-Ash'arī, in Herāt.
	Death of the Persian poet Niẓāmī of Ganja, important author of romantic verse epics.
1212	Peter II of Aragon defeated the Almohads in the battle of Las Navas de Tolosa. The Reconquista led to the retreat of the Almohads from Spain (1225).
1215	The Mongols invaded northern China and conquered Peking.
1218	Mongol invasion to Turkestan (Semirechye).
	The Khwārazm-Shāh 'Alā' al-Dīn Muḥammad had the envoys of Genghiz Khan killed in Otrār on the Jaxartes. Retaliatory measures brought Khwārazm and Transoxiana into the hands of the Mongols (1219-20) and began the Mongol invasion of the Middle and Near East.
1218-38	After the death of al-Malik al-'Ādil, division of the Ayyūbid empire; al-Malik al-Kāmil Sultan of Egypt: policy of co-existence with the Franks.

	Threatening of the Ayyūbids of the north (al-Jazīra) by Seljuqs of Rūm and the Khwārazm-Shāhs.
1219	Damietta fell to the Crusaders, reconquered in 1221 by al-Kāmil.
1219-37	'Alā' al-Dīn Kayqubādh I. Heyday of Konya as the capital of the Seljuqs of Rūm.
1220-21	The Mongols conquered Khurāsān and Khwārazm. The last Khwārazm-Shāh Jalāl al-Dīn (1230-31) was pursued to India and spent his last years in flight to the west until his death in Ādharbāyjān.
1221	Death of the Ṣūfī Najm al-Dīn Kubrā (in the Mongol attack on Khwārazm), pupil of 'Abd al-Qāhir al-Suhrawardī (d. 1168); spiritual authority of the Kubrāwiyya order.
1222	Badr al-Dīn Lu'lu', after the death of the last Zengid atabeg of Mosul.
1223	The Mongols under Jebe defeated Russians and Qumāns on the Kalka.
	Civil wars and wars of succession brought about the collapse of the Almohad dynasty.
	Rise of competing dynasties in North Africa.
1225	The Almohads left the Iberian peninsula; Islamic Spain was reduced to the small kingdom of the Naṣrids of Granada (1230-1492).
1225-26	Caliphate of al-Ẓāhir.
1226-42	Caliphate of al-Mustanṣir.
1227	Death of Genghiz Khan and division of the empire: Ögedey (1229-41) became Great Khan of the Mongols in Qaraqorum; completed the conquest of northern China. Batu (1227-55, Khan of the Blue Horde, the core of the later Golden Horde) in Khwārazm and the Qïpchaq steppe (southern Russia); Orda (1226-80, White Horde) in western Siberia; Chaghatay (1229-41) in Transoxiana and eastern Turkestan; Toluy in Mongolia.
1228	Frederick II (1212-50), excommunicated by Pope Gregory IX, began Crusade.
1228-1574	The Ḥafṣids, heirs of the Almohads in Ifrīqiyya (Tunisia and eastern Algeria), Abū Zakariyyā' Yaḥyā I, 1228-49 (from 1237 independent).
1229	Al-Malik al-Kāmil relinquished Jerusalem to the Franks through a treaty with Frederick II.
	Death of the Baghdad scholar Yāqūt, wrote a biographical and a geographical lexicon of great value.
1230-72	Muḥammad I b. al-Aḥmar established in Granada the House of the Naṣrids (Banū 'l-Aḥmar), the last Islamic dynasty in Spain (until 1492). Building of the Alhambra ('Red Castle').
1233	Death of the Mosul historian Ibn al-Athīr, author of a monumental world history.
1234	Death of Abū Ḥafṣ 'Umar al-Suhrawardī, Ṣūfī teacher of the caliph al-Nāṣir, founder of the mystic order of the Suhrawardiyya.
1235	Death of Ibn al-Fāriḍ, the most important Ṣūfī poet in the Arabic language.
1236	Cordoba capitulated to the Castilians under Ferdinand III.

1236-1554 Dynasty of the ʿAbdalwādids in Tlemcen.

1237-41 Most of Russia conquered by the Mongols (1240 fall of Kiev).

1238 Death of al-Malik al-Kāmil; succession struggles amongst the Ayyūbids.

1240 Dervish revolt of Bābā Isḥāq against the Seljuqs in Anatolia. The Spanish Ṣūfī Ibn al-ʿArabī from Murcia died in Damascus; created theory of mystical illumination (*ishrāq*) on the basis of pantheistic monism.

1240-55 Batu, a grandson of Genghiz Khan, ruler of the Golden Horde.

1241 Battle at Liegnitz in Silesia; Mongols of the Golden Horde defeated an army composed of Teutonic knights and Poles and devastated Hungary; summoned home because of the death of the Great Khan, Ögedey.

1242-43 Mongol invasion of Anatolia. Defeat of the Seljuqs of Rūm at Köse Dagh (1243).

1242-58 Caliphate of al-Mustaʿṣim, the last ʿAbbāsid caliph.

1244 An army of Khwārazmian Turks (forced to retreat to Mesopotamia by the Mongols) was summoned to Syria by the Ayyūbid al-Malik al-Ṣāliḥ Najm al-Dīn to fight against his rival ʿImād al-Dīn, plundered Jerusalem and ended Frankish domination.

1246-49 Güyük, Great Khan of the Mongols.

1248 The Castilian Christians took Seville.

1249-50 Crusade of St Louis IX; the French Crusaders took Damietta, had to retreat to Acre, however, after heavy defeats.

1250 The Ayyūbid sultan of Egypt, Tūrān Shāh, murdered by Turkish soldiery. The Mamlūk ʿIzz al-Dīn married the widow and sultana, Shajar al-Durr, and founded the Mamlūk state in Egypt and Syria (1250-1517).

1251-59 Möngke, Toluy's son, Great Khan of the Mongols in Qaraqorum. His brother Hülegü led a new offensive against western Asia.

1253-56 William of Rubruck, a Franciscan from Lower Germany, envoy of the Pope and of St Louis of France at the court of the Great Khan at Qaraqorum.

1256-59 Hülegü, a grandson of Genghiz Khan, conquered Transoxiana, Iran and Iraq, destroyed in 1256 the Assassin fortress of Alamūt in the Elburz mountains. Mongol dynasty of the Īlkhāns in Iran (until 1353).

1256 Batu, Khan of the Golden Horde, died.

1257-66 His successor, Berke, the brother of Hülegü, became a Muslim; agreement with the Mamlūks in Egypt, opposition to the Buddhist Īlkhāns.

6. The Mongol period

From the conquest of Baghdad by the Mongols to the establishment of the Ottoman empire in the Near East. The Mamlūks in Egypt and Syria. The West under the last Berber dynasties.

1258 Hülegü conquered Baghdad; murder of the caliph, demise of the ʿAbbāsid caliphate. Capital of Īlkhān empire became Tabrīz. Death of al-Shādhilī, founder of a Ṣūfī order.

1260 The Mongols besieged and destroyed Aleppo and conquered Damascus (under General Kitbughā).
Death of Möngke; Hülegü went back to Qaraqorum. Qubilay became Great Khan (conqueror of China, 1279-80).
The Mamlūks under Baybars (1260-77) defeated the Mongols at ʿAyn Jālūt (Goliath's Spring, north of Jerusalem) and stopped the Mongol invasion.

1261 Commercial treaty between Egypt and Byzantium about the transit of military slaves from the Black Sea to the Mamlūk empire.

1261-1320 Seljuq Anatolia broke up into independent emirates and slipped out of the control of the Mongol Īlkhāns: Ghāzī principalities in Karia (Menteshe Bey, 1261); around Qaramān (Laranda/Lykaonia) in central and southern Anatolia (Qaramān Turks from the sixties); around Kütahya and Denizli in Phrygia (Germiyan Turks, end of the thirteenth century); in Bithynia (ʿOsmān, 1281); around Aydïn (Tralleis) and Birge (Pyrgion) in the Lydian Menderes valley (Aydïn Turks, 1308); around Manisa (Magnesia) in Gediz (Hermos) valley (Ṣarukhān Bey, 1313); in Mysia (Qarasï Turks).

1265-71 Mamlūk offensive against the Crusades led to the end of most of the Frankish possessions in Palestine and Syria.

1265-82 After the death of the Mongol Hülegü, his son Abāqā established the dynasty of the Īlkhāns in Iran. Struggles with the Golden Horde and the Mamlūks.

1267-80 Möngke Temür, after the Muslim Berke again follower of tribal Shamanism, became Khan of the Golden Horde.

1268 Mamlūks under Baybars took and plundered Antioch.

1269 Death of the Andalusian philosopher and Ṣūfī Ibn Sabʿīn.

1269-1465 The dynasty of the Marīnids (south of the Atlas from 1196; capital Fez from 1248) pushed the Almohads out of Morocco (1470-1549 line of the Waṭṭāsids).

1270 Campaign of Louis IX with the French Crusaders against Tunis. Attack on Carthage; after Louis' death drawing up of treaty and withdrawal.

1270-72 Crusade of Edward of England to Tunisia and Palestine.

1271 Baybars besieged and conquered Krak des Chevaliers, the citadel of the Knights of St John.

1273 Death of the Ṣūfī Jalāl al-Dīn Rūmī in Konya, author of mystical didactic poems in Persian. The Mevleviyya order (the order of the 'Dancing Dervishes') was founded according to his doctrine.

1274 Death of the Andalusian poet and historian Ibn Saʿīd.
Death of Naṣīr al-Dīn al-Ṭūsī, philosopher, Shīʿite theologian and eminent astronomer; he served the Assassins and after their fall (1256) the Mongols.

1277 The Mamlūk Baybars defeated army of Seljuqs and Mongols in Asia Minor (Elbistan); capture of Caesarea (Cappadocia).

1280-90 Qalāwūn sultan of the Mamlūks; completed the explusion of the Franks from Syria.

1281 Mamlūks under Qalāwūn defended Syria at Ḥims against the Mongols.

1281-1326 ʿOsmān I b. Ertoghrïl (ʿOsmān Ghāzī) established the Ottoman principality in Bithynia.

1282 Death of Ibn Khallikān, author of a biographical dictionary of famous men of Islamic history and culture (completed 1274).

1284-91 The Īlkhān Arghūn, the son of Abāqā, tried to impose Buddhism in Iran; died during a popular rebellion.

1286 Death of the *qāḍī* of Shīrāz, al-Bayḍāwī, wrote a popular 'orthodox' revision of the Koranic commentary of al-Zamakhsharī (d. 1144).

1289 The Mamlūks siezed Tripoli from the Crusaders.
Death of the Ṣūfī ʿIrāqī, author of mystical poetry, influenced by Ibn al-ʿArabī.

1290 Qalāwūn died on campaign against Acre; succeeded by his son al-Ashraf Khalīl (1290-94).

1290-1320 Khaljī sultans of Delhi; after them Tughluq-Shāh and his immediate successors (1320-51) extended the authority of the sultanate of Delhi over most of northern and central India.

1291 Acre, the last European stronghold in Palestine, was reconquered by the Mamlūks under Khalīl; end of the kingdom of Jerusalem and the remaining Frankish possessions in Syria.

1292 Death of the Persian poet Saʿdī of Shīrāz, master of lyrical and ethical-didactic poetry and rhymed prose.

1293 Murder of Khalīl; struggle for the Mamlūk throne. Successor al-Nāṣir Muḥammad, Qalāwūn's son (ruled 1294-95, 1299-1309, 1309-40).

1294 Attempt to introduce paper money by the Īlkhāns led to the collapse of the Iranian economy.

1295-1304 Ghazan, Arghūn's son, became a Sunnī Muslim in 1295; the Īlkhāns became a national dynasty of Iran. Order and revival of economic life. Programme for reform by his minister, the physician and historian Rashīd al-Dīn Faḍlallāh (1247-1318).

1296-1316 Sultan ʿAlāʾ al-Dīn Muḥammad of Delhi conquered western and southern Deccan.

1298 Redistribution of Egyptian military land tenure in favour of crown land miscarried because of a rebellion of the Mamlūks; 1299 murder of the Sultan Lājīn (1297-99).

1299 Mongol invasion and temporary occupation of Syria.

1301 ʿOsmān besieged Iznik (Nicaea) and defeated a Byzantine army at Baphaeon. Growing numbers of Turkish warriors of the faith around ʿOsmān in the coastal areas of Asia Minor by the Sea of Marmara; the Ottomans became a threat to Byzantium and for the Mongol authority in Anatolia.
Shaykh Ṣafī al-Dīn established in Ādharbāyjān the dervish order of the Ṣafavids.

1303 The last Mongol invasion to Syria was repulsed by the Mamlūks.

1304-16 The Īlkhān Öljeytü, brother of Ghazan; in 1307 he built the new capital of Ṣulṭāniyya. In 1310 he became a Shīʿite Muslim.

1308 The Aydïn Turks conquered Birge (Pyrgion); rule in western Anatolia as far as Izmir (Smyrna).
Death of the last Seljuq Masʿūd III.

1310 Death of the Ḥanafī lawyer and theologian al-Nasafī.

1311	Death of Quṭb al-Dīn Shīrāzī, astronomer and collaborator with Naṣīr al-Dīn Ṭūsī; revision of the Ptolemaic planetary theory.
1312	Waṣṣāf became court historian of the Mongol Öljeytü in Ṣultāniyya.
1313	Ṣarukhān Beg conquered Manisa (Magnesia); independent principality in the Gediz valley.
1313-41	Özbeg, Khan of the Golden Horde, adopted Islam. Spread of Islamic culture in the capital Saray.
1315 (1316?)	The missionary Raymond Lull stoned to death in Bougie (Algeria).
1315	Registration and distribution of Egyptian military land tenure (*iqṭā'*) by the Mamlūk sultan al-Nāṣir; increase of the crown land and removal of power from the Mamlūk soldiery.
1316-35	The Īlkhān Abū Sa'īd, an adherent of Sunnī Islam.
1318	Death of Rashīd al-Dīn, vizier of the Mongol Ghazan; in his 'Universal History' gave a general picture of the Islamic empire, the Christian west, India and China as well as Judaism.
1320-25	Ghiyāth al-Dīn Tughluq Shāh sultan of Delhi, reimposed Muslim control over the Deccan.
1320	Death of Yūnus Emre, Turkish Ṣūfī and writer of vernacular folk poetry. Death of the astronomer and optician Kamāl al-Dīn al-Fārisī, pupil of Quṭb al-Dīn Shīrāzī (1236-1311). Death of Nizārī, Shī'ite panegyric poet and traveller.
1323	Peace between Mamlūks and Īlkhāns.
1325	Death of the theologian and philosopher al-'Allāma al-Ḥillī, pupil of Naṣīr al-Dīn al-Ṭūsī, respected theologian who systematised the Shī'ite doctrine of the Imāmate. Death of Amīr-i Khusraw of Delhi, founder of Indo-Persian poetry. Death of Niẓām al-Dīn Awliyā' of Delhi, Ṣūfī and principal founder of the Chishtiyya, the most widespread Ṣūfī order in India.
1325-51	Muḥammad b. Tughluq sultan of Delhi; fiscal and political experiments and military adventures led to the weakening of authority in the Deccan.
1325-53	The traveller Ibn Baṭṭūṭa of Tangier visited the Near East, eastern and central Africa, Asia Minor and the territories of the Golden Horde, Transoxiana, India, SE Asia and China.
1326	Death of 'Osmān after the conquest of Bursa by his son Orkhan. His successor Orkhan (1326-61) formed the Ottoman principality around the capital Bursa into a state and began the Ottoman expansion towards Europe (1354).
1326-34	The Chaghatayid Tarmashīrīn converted to Sunnī Islam. Spread of Islam in Central Asia. In the period which followed (1334-60) Central Asia divided into an Islamic western half (Transoxiana) with a predominantly feudal structure and an eastern half under a monarchy and little Islamic influence.
1328	Death of Ibn Taymiyya, Ḥanbalite lawyer and theologian, major exponent of traditionist orthodox Islam.

1331	Orkhan occupied Nicaea (Iznik) and extended his authority as far as Scutari near Constantinople.
1332-45	Campaigns of the Aydïn Turks under Umur Bey in the Balkans.
1333-40	The Moroccan dynasty of the Marīnids in Spain; 1347-49 temporary occupation of the western Maghrib.
1333-54	The Naṣrid Yūsuf I; building of the Alhambra in Granada, completed by his son Muḥammad V (1354-91).
1335	Death of Īlkhān Abū Sa'īd; 1335-53 disintegration of the state of the Īlkhāns under rival local dynasties.
1336-1412	Military hegemony of the Mongol Jalāyirids in Iraq and Ādharbāyjān; conflicts with the Muẓaffarid family until 1393 in Fārs and Persian Iraq.
1336-1576	Kings of Bengal independent; most of eastern Bengal converted to Islam.
1337	First unsuccessful landing attempt by the Ottomans in Thrace.
1337-81	The Sarbadārs—a popular Shī'ite movement—opposed the authority of the Kurt dynasty of Herāt in western Khurāsān; both were destroyed by Tīmūr.
1340	Death of the Mamlūk al-Malik al-Nāṣir Muḥammad.
1341	Jānī Beg, Khan of the Golden Horde, experienced the collapse of the Īlkhān empire in Iran; unsuccessful attempt to take Ādharbāyjān for the Golden Horde.
1345	The Ottomans annexed the principality of Qarasï on the west coast of Asia Minor.
1346	Marriage of Orkhan to Theodora, daughter of the Byzantine pretender John VI Cantacuzenos.
1347-50	Plague epidemic in the entire Mediterranean area (Europe, North Africa, Near East).
1347-58	'Alā' al-Dīn Ḥasan Bahman Shāh founded the kingdom of Bahmanids of Madura (northern Deccan), until 1527 independent of Delhi. Campaigns of the Bahmanids (1347-1527) against the Hindu kings of southern India.
1348	Defeat of the Marīnid Abū 'l-Ḥasan (1331-51) against a confederation of Arab Bedouin tribes at Qayrawān (Kairouan).
1351-1413	The dynasty of the Tughluqids of Delhi, limited to northern India (followed by the Sayyids [1414-51] and the Lōdīs [1451-1526]); development of national variants of Islam under different Indian dynasties.
1352 (1361?)	Death of Khwājū, court poet of the last Īlkhāns, Muẓaffarids and Jalāyirids.
1353	Orkhan's son, Süleymān Pasha supported John Cantacuzenos with Ottoman troops at Adrianople.
1354	Ottoman-Genoese understanding.
1354-57	Beginning of the Ottoman invasion of the Balkans under Süleymān Pasha. 1354 conquest of the Gallipoli peninsula.
1359-61	The Ottomans occupied Thrace.
from 1359	Disintegration of the Golden Horde in civil wars.
1361-89	Murād I, Ottoman ruler, took for the first time the title of sultan. Ottoman expansion in western Anatolia against Byzantium and in the Balkans against the declining power of Serbia.
	Formation of the Janissary corps (*yeni cheri*, 'new army'), élite

troops of the sultan from the conquered Balkan countries (*devshirme*, 'levy of boys').

1361 Ankara became Ottoman.

1362 Murād took Adrianople (Edirne), 1366-1453 Ottoman capital.

1363-66 Ottoman conquests in Bulgaria and Thrace as far as the southern slopes of the Balkan mountains.

1365 Crusaders under Peter I of Cyprus plundered Alexandria.

1370-1405 The Mongol leader Tīmūr (Temür) from 1360 gained ground in Transoxiana; conquered eastern Iran (1379-85), western Persia and Mesopotamia (1395-1400), the Qïpchaq steppe (1395), northern India (1398-99) and Anatolia (1402). Capital Samarqand; outstanding architecture.

1371 The Ottomans defeated the Serbs at Černomen on the Maritsa and gained Serbian Macedonia.

1375 The Mamlūks toppled the Armenian kingdom of Cilicia (Little Armenia) with Turkish support. Growing importance of the Mamlūk empire for trade between Europe and India.

1376-1405 Toqtamïsh united the Golden Horde for the last time; he was twice conquered by Tīmūr.

1378-1508 The Turcoman tribal confederation of the Aq-Qoyunlu ('White Sheep') in Diyār Bakr and eastern Anatolia, after defeating the Qara-Qoyunlu (1467) and the Tīmūrids (1469), became masters of Ādharbāyjān and Persia.

1379-85 The Mongol Tīmūr crossed the Oxus and conquered eastern Persia (Khwārazm, Khurāsān).

1380-1468 The Turcoman tribal confederation of the Qara-Qoyunlu ('Black Sheep') in Ādharbāyjān (capital Tabrīz); struggles against the Jalāyirids (conquest of Baghdad 1412) and expansion in western Persia until defeat by the Aq-Qoyunlu (1467).

1381-86 Ottoman territorial expansions in Anatolia (1381 annexation of the territory of the Germiyan Turks, 1388 victory over the Qaramān Turks at Konya).

1382 Toqtamïsh united the White and Golden Hordes of the Mongols and took Moscow.

1382-99 al-Malik al-Ẓāhir Barqūq (interregnum 1389-90), first sultan of the Circassian Burjī Mamlūks (until 1517).

1385-86 The Ottoman Turks conquered Sofia and Nish.

1387 The Ottomans took Salonika.

1388 Coalition of Serbs, Bosnians and Bulgars defeated the Ottomans at Pločnik.

1389 Battle of Kosovo. By their victory over the Serbian Balkan army the Ottomans secured their conquests south of the Danube (Rumelia).
Death of Sa'd al-Dīn al-Taftazānī, Persian historian and philologist at the court of Tīmūr.
Death of the Ṣūfī Bahā' al-Dīn Naqshband, teacher of the Naqshbandī order.

1389-1403 The Ottoman Bāyezīd I Yïldïrïm (the 'Thunderbolt') extended the power of the Ottomans across Anatolia, until they were pushed back by Tīmūr's Mongols, and consolidated Ottoman control over the Christian peoples of the Balkans.

1389-90	Bāyezīd annexed the Turkish emirates in western Anatolia: Menteshe, Aydïn, Ṣarukhān, Germiyan, Ḥamīd.
1390	Defeat of the Qaramānids at Aq-Chay gave central Anatolia to the Ottomans. Conquest of Philadelphia, the last Byzantine possession in Asia Minor. Death of the Persian poet Ḥāfiẓ, the master of the *ghazal*, in Shīrāz.
1392	The Ottomans took over Kastamonu and Amasya (northern Anatolia).
1393	Bulgaria lost Tirnovo and the Danube territory to the Ottomans.
1394	Bāyezīd had himself invested by the 'Abbāsid puppet caliph in Cairo with the title of 'Sulṭān of Rūm'. Ottoman conquest of Thessalonika. Beginning of the blockade of Constantinople (until 1402).
1395-1400	The Mongol Tīmūr conquered western Persia and Iraq.
1395	Tīmūr invaded the Qipchaq steppe and destroyed the power of his rival Toqtamïsh, the Khan of the White and the Golden Hordes; advance to Moscow and Astrakhān.
1396	Battle of Nicopolis: the Ottomans defeated the army of the Venetian/Hungarian/Byzantine Crusade under Sigismund of Hungary.
1397	The Ottomans took Argos; the Peleponnes in Turkish hands.
1397-8	Bāyezīd annexed Qaramān, Qaysariyya and Sïvas.
1398-99	Tīmūr conquered northern India: plundering of Delhi. Collapse and demise of the Sultanate of Delhi.
1400-01	Tīmūr advanced to Georgia, Anatolia, Syria and Iraq; conquest of Baghdad, Aleppo and Damascus, devastation of Syria.
1402	Battle of Ankara: the Ottoman army was decisively defeated by Tīmūr. Bāyezīd committed suicide in captivity (1403). Tīmūr took Smyrna (Izmir) from the Hospitallers (Knights of St John).
1403	Destruction of Ottoman power: Tīmūr restored the autonomy of the Anatolian principalities and relieved Byzantium once again from Ottoman pressure.
1403-13	After the death of Bāyezīd, interregnum and wars of succession amongst his sons Süleymān (1403-11 in Edirne/Rumelia), 'Īsā (in Bursa), Meḥmed (in Amasya, then Bursa/Anatolia) and Mūsā.
1403	Plague epidemic and famine in Egypt.
1405	Tīmūr died in Otrār on the way to China.
1405-17	Tīmūr's son, Shāhrukh, ruler in Khurāsān, later also in Transoxiana, western Persia and Iraq. Flowering of Iranian culture in the cities (literature in Persian and Turkish, painting, science).
1406	Division of Ottoman domains; fratricidal strife between Süleymān (in Europe) and Meḥmed (in Anatolia, supported by Mūsā). Death of the historian Ibn Khaldūn, statesman and jurist from the Maghrib; he gave in the 'Introduction' (*Muqaddima*) to his Annals a theory and system of history as a political science.
1407	End of civil war in Egypt (1405-07) against Sultan Faraj.

1408 The Qara-Qoyunlu under Qara Yūsuf (capital Tabrīz from 1406) defeated the Tīmūrid Mīrānshāh.

1411 Mūsā defeated Süleymān and besieged Constantinople.

1412 Agreement between Meḥmed and the Byzantine emperor Manuel against Mūsā.
The Qara-Qoyunlu took Baghdad.

1413 Meḥmed defeated his rival Mūsā and became sole ruler of the Ottoman state (1413-21). Efforts at the political and religious unification of the state.
Death of ʿAlī al-Jurjānī, theologian and philologist at Tīmūr's court.

1415 Portuguese expansion, Ceuta conquered.

1416 Ottoman conflict with Venice for supremacy in the Aegean. Victory of the Venetian fleet over the Turks at Gallipoli. Rebellion on the west coast of Asia Minor and in Rumelia under the influence of the heretical Ṣūfī Badr al-Dīn ended with his execution.

1418 Death of al-Qalqashandī, chancellery official, author of an encyclopaedic handbook on administration.

1421-44 First period of government of Murād II; defended the Ottoman authority in the Balkans against the Hungarians. Complete re-establishment of Ottoman power in Anatolia.

1422 The Ottomans used firearms in an unsuccessful attempt to conquer Constantinople.

1422-38 Rule of the Mamlūk sultan Bārsbāy; attempt to control currency and to monopolise trade on sugar, pepper and other commodities.

1423 Thessalonika was ceded to Venice by Byzantine princes in face of Ottoman threat: occasion of Turkish-Venetian war (1423-30).

1426 Mamlūks under Bārsbāy defeated the Cypriot army. Cyprus came under Egyptian rule (1427).

1426(?)-1486 Ḥājjī Giray, descendant of Genghiz Khan, founder of the independent Khanate in the Crimea.

1428 Death of the Ṣūfī ʿAbd al-Karīm al-Jīlī, adherent and continuator of the mystical doctrine of Ibn al-ʿArabī.

1429 The Tīmūrid prince Ulugh Beg built an observatory in Samarqand.

1430 Murād II ended Venetian domination in Thessalonika (1423-30).
Death of Ḥāfiẓ-i Ābrū, Tīmūrid historian and much-travelled geographer.

1437 Death of Mamlūk sultan Bārsbāy.

1438-57 Reign of the Mamlūk al-Malik al-Ẓāhir Jaqmaq.

1438 Turkish attack on Hungary: Semendria taken. Plague in Iraq.

1440 Unsuccessful siege of Belgrade by the Turks.

1442 Death of Egyptian historian al-Maqrīzī.

1443 A Crusader army of Hungarians, Poles, Serbs and Rumanians under John Hunyadi defeated the Turks and occupied Nish.

1444 Murād II signed peace of Szegedin with the Hungarian Crusaders: the Danube became the border, Wallachia became a tributary of the Hungarians. Successful campaign against the

	Qaramān Turks in Anatolia. After the breaking of the peace-treaty by the Hungarians, decisive victory over the Christians in the battle of Varna. Murād II abdicated in favour of his son Meḥmed II.
1446-51	Murād II took power again. Resumption of Ottoman war of expansion in south east Europe; devastation of the Peloponnes.
1447-49	The Tīmūrid Ulugh Beg ruler in Samarqand.
1447-88	Shaykh Junayd (1447-60) and his son Shaykh Ḥaydar (1460-88), militant descendants of Shaykh Ṣafī al-Dīn, organised their followers as military troops (Qïzïlbash, 'red caps'), expanded the Shī'ite order of the Ṣafavids in north west Iran, Ādharbāyjān and in eastern Anatolia.
1448	The second battle of Kosovo; Ottomans defeated the Serbs and Hungarians under John Hunyadi and conquered Transylvania.
1451-1526	Afghan Lōdī dynasty of Delhi.
1451-69	The Tīmūrid Abū Sa'īd ruled in Samarqand over eastern Iran, Transoxiana and western Turkestan.
1451-81	The Ottoman Meḥmed II, called Fātiḥ (the 'Conqueror'). Consolidation of hegemony in the Balkans. First Ottoman legal codes. Intense building activity. Reorganisation of the Janissary corps. Endangering of the social equilibrium by devaluation of the currency, state monopolies and confiscations.
1453	Conquest of Constantinople by the Ottomans. End of the Byzantine empire. Constantinople became the capital of the Ottoman empire and new spiritual centre of the Islamic world.
1453-61	Sultanate of the Mamlūk al-Malik al-Ashraf Ināl.
1453-78	Uzun Ḥasan led the Aq-Qoyunlu to the height of their power in Diyār Bakr, eastern Anatolia and the Caucasus, conquered the Qara-Qoyunlu (1467), limited the last Tīmūrid state to eastern Iran and extended his power over Persia, Ādharbāyjān and Iraq.
1455	The Genoese island empire in the Aegean in Turkish hands.
1456	John Hunyadi defended Belgrade against an Ottoman siege. Turks pushed back to Bulgaria, but reprieved by the death of Hunyadi.
1457-58	Death of the Serbian king George Branković. Defeat of Serbia by Maḥmūd Pasha; advance to northern Adriatic.
1458-1519	Conquest of the Atlantic ports of Morocco by Portugal; 1471 Portuguese in West Africa.
1460	Meḥmed II completed the conquest of the Peloponnes; end of the last Byzantine ruling family of the Paleologi.
1463-79	War between the Ottoman empire and Venice. 1463/64 annexation of Bosnia. Arms sent by Venice to the Aq-Qoyunlu (1470).
1465	Line of the Waṭṭāsids toppled the house of the Marīnids in Morocco (ruled until 1549).
1467	Campaign of the Qara-Qoyunlu under Jihān-Shāh against the Aq-Qoyunlu (Uzun Ḥasan) ended with the defeat and end of the Qara-Qoyunlu dynasty (1468). Expansion of the Aq-Qoyunlu into Persia and Iraq.
1467-68	Campaigns of Meḥmed II against Albania; 1468 death of the rebel Iskender Beg.
1468	Meḥmed II annexed the Turkish principality of Qaramān.

1468-96	The Mamlūk al-Malik al-Ashraf Qā'it Bay led Egypt in battles against the Ottomans to military success but to economic ruin.
1469	Death of the Tīmūrid Abū Sa'īd after an unsuccessful campaign against the Aq-Qoyunlu in Ādharbāyjān.
1469-1506	Ḥusayn Bayqara in Herāt (Khurāsān), last important ruler of the Tīmūrid family.
1470	Venice lost Negroponte on Euboea. Treaty with the Aq-Qoyunlu (Uzan Ḥasan).
1473	Battle of Bashkent (Terjān) on the Euphrates; Meḥmed II inflicted a decisive defeat on Uzan Ḥasan.
1474	Ottoman conquest of Cilicia.
1475	Genoese pushed out of Kefe (Kaffa, Theodosia). The Crimean Tartars became vassals of the Ottomans. Definitive annexation of the Turkish principality of Qaramān.
1479	The Ottoman empire forced Venice to make peace by a siege of Scutari (from 1474). Venice gave up Albania and possessions in the Peloponnes.
1481	Civil war between Bāyezīd II, supported by the Janissaries, and his brother Jem (defeated in 1481, fled in 1482 to Rhodes), who threatened the empire until his death (1495).
1481-1512	Bāyezīd II Ottoman sultan. Period of economic and religious consolidation.
1484	Turkish campaign to the Moldau against Polish southern expansion.
1485-91	War between Ottomans and Mamlūks for Cilicia ended with the defeat of the Ottoman at Qaysariyya (Āghā Chāyrī, 1488) and the loss of Adana and Tarsus in the peace of 1491.
1492	Turkish expeditions to Styria, Carinthia, Carniola; the Turks defeated at Villach. Plague epidemic in Egypt. A Christian army under Ferdinand of Aragon and Isabelle of Castille took Granada and ended Islamic rule in Spain. The last Naṣrid retreated to Morocco. Death of the Persian Ṣūfī and poet Jāmī in Herāt.
1497-1503	Building of the Bāyezīd mosque in Constantinople.
1497-1510	Conquest by Spain of the most important Mediterranean cities of North Africa.
1498	Death of Mīrkhwānd, court historian of the Tīmūrids.
1498-1509	Establishment of Portuguese supremacy in maritime trade in the Indian Ocean; 1498 Vasco da Gama sailed with the Arab captain Ibn Mājid from east Africa to India. Establishment of Portuguese trading posts; 1502 victory for the Portuguese against an alliance of the sultans of Gujarāt with the Egyptian Mamlūks in a sea battle before Diu.
1499-1503	Second Turkish-Venetian war; Venice lost possessions in the Peloponnese to the Ottomans.
1500	Muḥammad Shaybānī, Khān of a Siberian Mongol state, conquered the domains of the last Tīmūrids and established the Özbeg dynasty in Transoxiana and Khwārazm.
1501	Death of the vizier 'Alī Shīr Nevā'ī, important poet of eastern (Chaghatay) Turkish at the Tīmūrid court at Herāt.
1501-16	Qānṣawḥ al-Ghawrī, last important Mamlūk sultan.

1501-24	Shāh Ismāʿīl established with the Turcoman Qïzïlbash the Ṣafavid dynasty in Ādharbāyjān (defeat of the Aq-Qoyunlu 1501) and conquered Iran and Mesopotamia. Theocratic rule in the name of the ʿAlid Imām united Persia under Shīʿite faith.
1502	Death of Persian philosopher and theologian Dawānī; philosophical theory of the Islamic state according to al-Farābī and Naṣīr al-Dīn al-Ṭūsī.
1504	The Turk Ẓahīr al-Dīn Bābur from Farghana (Central Asia) occupied Kābul; first raids into India as far as the Indus. Death of the Persian preacher Kāshifī in Herāt, author of edifying artistic prose and poetry.
1505	Death of Jalāl al-Dīn al-Suyūṭī, Egyptian philologist, historian and encyclopaedist.
1506	Death of Ḥusayn Bayqara, Tīmūrid ruler in Khurāsān, poet of Chaghatay Turkish, patron of the poet Jāmī and Nevā'ī, the historian Mīrkhwānd and the painter Bihzād.
1511	The Saʿdī Sharīfs established ʿAlid power in Morocco (1549 end of the Waṭṭāsids of Fez). Defence of the country against Turkish and Portuguese attacks and extension of Moroccan power over West Africa.
1511-12	Civil war between Sultan Bāyezīd and his younger son Selīm.
1512-13	Shīʿite rebellion under Shāh Qulï in Anatolia, stirred up by the Ṣafavids.
1512-20	The Ottoman sultan Selīm I Yavuz ('the Grim'). Bloody suppression of the Shīʿa, exacerbated by the political conflict with the Shīʿite Ṣafavid dynasty of Iran.
1514	The Ṣafavid Ismāʿīl, as protector of the Shīʿa, led a campaign against the Ottomans. Battle of Chāldirān (Ādharbāyjān); Selīm I defeated Ismāʿīl, brought Kurdistan and Mesopotamia under Ottoman rule and definitively pushed back Ṣafavid expansionist efforts.
1515	Destruction of the Dhū 'l-Qadr, the vassals of the Mamlūks, in Armenia by the Ottomans.
1515-16	The Mamlūks conquered the Yemen. Their attempt to take Aden failed.
1516	Selīm defeated the Mamlūk Qānṣawḥ al-Ghawrī at Marj Dābiq and took Syria.
1517	The Ottomans under Selīm conquered Egypt. End of the Mamlūk state. Introduction of the Ottoman system of land tenure into the Arab Near East. Selīm received the keys of the Kaʿba of Mecca and legitimised his control of the Holy Places by taking the title of Caliph.

7. *The Ottoman period*

The Ottoman empire. Iran from the Ṣafavid period, India under the Mughals.

1520	The Turkish pirate Khayr al-Dīn Barbarossa put his conquests in Algeria under the control of the Ottoman sultan Selīm and led naval enterprises against Spain in the southern Mediterranean.
1520-66	Sultan Süleymān, called Qānūnī (the 'Law-Giver', also 'the Magnificent') ruled over the Ottoman empire at the height of its power. The political and social structure of the empire

received its definitive form through reforms of the government system. Involvement in the power games of European politics.

1521 The Ottomans conquered Belgrade and broke through the Danube defence line.

1522 The Ottomans took Rhodes; departure of the Hospitallers (Knights of St John).

1524-76 Shāh Ṭahmāsp I, Ismāʿīl's son, in Iran; campaigned against Özbegs and Ottomans.

1526 Battle of Mohács: victory of Süleymān over King Louis of Hungary, devastation of the countryside. Hungary became a tributary of the Turks.
Battle of Pānīpat: Ẓahīr al-Dīn Bābur (1526-30) defeated the last Lōdī sultan of Delhi and established the dynasty of the Mughal emperors in India.

1527 End of the Bahmanid dynasty. Five local dynasties divided the Deccan until the conquest by the Mughal emperors Akbar and Awrangzīb.

1529 The first Turkish siege of Vienna failed. Khayr al-Dīn Barbarossa entered Ottoman service, began the construction of the Ottoman fleet.
Algiers became Ottoman.

1530-56 The Mughal emperor Nāṣir al-Dīn Humāyūn (1540-55 in exile).

1532-33 Campaign of Süleymān against Austria; conquest of Güns, 1533 peace with the Hapsburgs.

1534 Ottoman campaign against Shāh Ṭahmāsp I of Persia. Süleymān took Tabrīz and Baghdad; thereafter occupied Ādharbāyjān and Iraq.

1534-74 The Turks set foot in North Africa from Algiers; conflicts with emperor Charles V and Spain. Repeated conquest of Tunis (1534 by the admiral of the fleet Khayr al-Dīn Barbarossa, 1570, definitively 1574) until the almost total removal of the Spaniards from North Africa.

1536 Franco-Turkish commercial treaty which had the effect of a political alliance (directed against Charles V).

1536-41 Expedition of Emperor Charles V against Tunis and Algiers.

1536-87 Régime of Ottoman Beglerbegs in North Africa.

1537-57 Expulsion of the Portuguese from southern Morocco by the Saʿdī Sharīfs.

1538 Battle of Preveza: the Ottomans defeated the fleet of the Holy League (Charles V, Venice, the Pope) and gained naval supremacy in the Mediterranean.

1540-55 Interregnum of the Afghans under Shīr-Shāh Sūr and his successors in Delhi.

1541 Naval enterprise of Charles V against Algiers failed.

1541-47 After the death of John Zápolyai of Hungary, Turco-Austrian war over the claims of the Hapsburgs to Hungary. Ottoman supremacy in Hungary. After Turkish conquests, armistice with the Hapsburgs who kept only small parts of Hungary.

1548-55 New Turco-Persian war. In the peace of Amasya the Ottomans kept their conquests in Mesopotamia; division of Georgia.

1549 Saʿdī Sharīfs (*Shurafāʾ*) pushed the Waṭṭāsids out of Fez and took

	control of the whole of Morocco (the dynasty of the Sa'dids until 1659).
1549-54	Repulsing of Ottoman attacks by the Sa'dī Sharīfs of Morocco.
1550	Building of the Süleymān mosque in Constantinople.
1551	The Turkish admiral Pīri Re'īs took Masqat.
	The Hospitallers (Knights of St John) surrendered Tripolis (Libya) to the Ottomans.
1551-62	Resumption of the Hungarian war between Ottomans and Hapsburgs.
1554-56	Dragut (Ṭurghūd), successor to Khayr al-Dīn Barbarossa, completed Turkish conquest of North African coast.
1556	Ottomans toppled the Ziyārid dynasty in western Algeria.
	Ottoman-Portuguese naval war in Indian Ocean.
	Death of Turkish poet Fużūlī.
1556-1605	Emperor Akbar in Delhi, founder of a syncretistic universal religion. Flowering of the Mughal empire in North and Central India.
1558	Death of Zayn al-Dīn al-'Āmilī, Iranian Shī'ite theologian.
1565	Unification of the Muslim dynasties of the Deccan; destruction of the Hindu Kingdom of Vijayanagar in Southern India, the last bastion of ancient Hindu culture.
1565-68	Turco-Austrian war.
1566	With the death of Süleymān the period of the expansion of the Ottoman empire ended. His successor Selīm II, the 'Sot' (1566-74); full governmental powers were in the hands of the Serbian Grand Vizier Ṣoqullu Meḥmed Pasha and the Jew Joseph Nasi.
1568-70	Zaydī rebellion against the Ottomans in the Yemen.
1570	The Ottomans took Cyprus.
	Peace with the Muscovites.
1571	Sea battle of Lepanto: destruction of the Ottoman fleet by the Spanish-Venetian fleet of the Holy League (Don Juan of Austria). After the collapse of the League and the reconstruction of the Turkish fleet Spain was restricted to the western Mediterranean.
1573	Venice relinquished Cyprus to the Turks, after a three-year war.
1574-95	Murād III Ottoman sultan. Increasing influence of the palace (period of 'petticoat rule'). Misuse in the military land tenure system and in the recruitment of the Janissaries; 1589/92 troop revolts.
1577-90	Ottoman war with Persia; taking of Tiflis (1578), Kars and Tabrīz (1585); the principalities of Georgia became tributary vassals.
1578-1603	The Sharīf Aḥmad al-Manṣūr of Morocco; 1590-91 conquest of west Africa (kingdom of Songai with Timbuktu and Gao on the Niger).
1580	Ottoman trade privileges for England.
1583	Death of Waḥshī of Bāfq, Ṣūfī romantic poet.
1587	Creation of the three Ottoman *beyliks*, Algiers, Tunis and Tripoli.
1588-1629	Shāh 'Abbās of Persia; apogee of the Ṣafavid empire. Expansion

of Iranian sphere of influence, expulsion of the Özbegs from Khurāsān and the Ottomans from Ādharbāyjān, Diyār Bakr and Iraq. High point of architecture and painting (Riḍā-i 'Abbāsī).

1588 (?) Death of Sinān Pasha, architect of the Ottoman capitals (Süleymān mosque (1557) in Istanbul, Selīm mosque in Edirne).

1590 Peace between Persia and the Ottoman empire, which by the acquisition of Georgia, Karabag and Shīrwān now reached the Caucasus and the Caspian Sea. The Ottomans gained Tabrīz and Luristān.

1593-1606 Ottoman-Hapsburg war, ended by the treaty of Sitvatorok (1606).

1595-1603 Sultan Meḥmed III.

1596 Shāh 'Abbās made Iṣfahān the capital of the Ṣafavid empire.

1599 Death of the Ottoman historian Sa'd al-Dīn Khōja Efendi.

1600 Death of the Turkish poet Bāqī; his work was the apogee of classical Turkish lyrical poetry.

1602-12 New Turco-Persian war.

1603 The Ṣafavid Shāh 'Abbās regained Ādharbāyjān (Tabrīz) and the Caucasus (Eriwan, Shīrwān, Kars) from the Ottomans.

1603-17 Rule of the Ottoman sultan Aḥmed I.

1605 Persian victory over the Ottomans at Lake Urmia; the Ṣafavids regained Diyār Bakr and Iraq (Mosul, Baghdad).

1605-27 The Mughal emperor Jahāngīr in Delhi.

1606 Peace of Sitvatorok, twenty-year peace treaty between the Ottomans and Austria; territorial losses by the Hapsburgs in Hungary.

1609-14 Expulsion of the Muslims from Spain.

1609-87 After the fall of other Deccan kingdoms the 'Ādil-Shāhī dynasty of Bījapūr and the Quṭb-Shāhī dynasty of Golkonda divided up southern India until conquest by the Mughal emperors.
Rise of Urdu literature.

1612 Peace treaty between Iran and the Ottoman empire, which lost Ādharbāyjān and Georgia to the Ṣafavids.
Ottoman trade privileges for Dutch merchants.

1617-18 After palace revolution Sultan Muṣṭafā I deposed because of imbecility.

1618-22 Sultan 'Osmān II.

1622 (1621?) Death of Bahā'ī (Bahā' al-Dīn al-'Āmilī), Ṣūfī, Shī'ite theologian, mathematician, poet.

1622 England bombarded Algiers in reprisal for piracy (repeated 1655, 1672).
Turkish campaign in the Moldau against Poland (1620-22) ended with losses; after peace agreement Janissary rebellion: 'Osmān II killed.

1622-23 Second period of government of Muṣṭafā I, deposed by a *fatwā* of the Shaykh-ül-Islām.

1623 Conquest of Baghdad by Shāh 'Abbās I of Persia.

1623-40 Sultan Murād IV limited the powers of the Janissary corps. War with Iran with changing fortunes (1623-39).

1628-58 The Mughal emperor Shāh Jahān.

1629-42 With Shāh Ṣafī the decline of the Ṣafavids began.
Murād IV regained Iraq (1638).

from 1631	Reign of the Filālī line of Sharīfs maintained political unity of Morocco.
1633	Rebellion of the Druze prince Fakhr al-Dīn in Lebanon and Syria, in league with Tuscany, the Pope and Spain, was put down by the Ottomans (Fakhr al-Dīn executed 1635).
1635	Death of Nafʿī, poet of Indo-Persian school.
1638	Murād IV reconquered Iraq from Iran (massacre of Shīʿites in Baghdad). In the treaty of Qaṣr-i Shīrīn Murād IV relinquished the Caucasus (Eriwan) and Ādharbāyjān (Tabrīz) to the Ṣafavids; definite drawing up of territorial frontiers between Ottomans and Ṣafavids.
1640-48	Sultan Ibrāhīm I. Influence of harem cliques at its height. Mismanagement led to the ruin of the state finances.
1640	Death of the Persian theologian and philosopher, Ṣadr al-Dīn Shīrāzī (Mullā Ṣadrā).
1645-69	Ottoman-Venetian war for Crete, the last Venetian possession in the eastern Mediterranean.
1648-87	Sultan Meḥmed IV; until 1656 anarchical period with continued party struggles.
1651	Victory of Venetian fleet at Paros.
1656-61	The Grand Vizier Meḥmed Köprülü revitalised the declining Ottoman empire by inner reforms—removal of the influence of harem and Janissaries, restoration of state economy—and military successes.
1657	Restoration of Turkish authority over the Danube principalities.
1658	Death of the Turkish cosmographer and encyclopedist Ḥājjī Khalīfa (Kātib Chelebī).
1658-59	Suppression of revolts in Anatolia by the Ottomans.
1658-1707	The Mughal emperor Awrangzīb prevailed over his brother Dārā Shikōh in succession struggles (1658-59) and stabilised the dominance of Islam in NW India and the Deccan. After his death the decline of the Mughal empire began.
1659-71	Régime of the Āghās of the army corps in Algiers.
1661-76	Aḥmed Köprülü, Meḥmed's son and successor as Grand Vizier wielding *de facto* power.
1663-64	Ottoman offensive against Austria ended with defeat at St Gotthard; 20-year truce.
1665	French bombarded Algiers and Tunis as reprisals for piracy.
1669	The Ottomans conquered Crete from Venice.
1670	Peace of Venice; Crete became Ottoman, except for three strongholds.
1671-1830	Régime of the Deys (*dayī*) in Algiers.
1672-76	Turco-Polish war. King John III Sobieski of Poland had to cede Podolia and the Ukraine to the Ottomans after changing fortunes of war (1676 defeat at Zurawno): the Ottoman empire became immediate neighbour of Russia.
1676-83	Qara Muṣṭafā (brother-in-law of Aḥmed Köprülü) Ottoman Grand Vizier.
1677-81	Turco-Russian war. In the peace of Radzin (1681) Kiev fell to Russia.
1683-99	Turco-Austrian war. 1683 second unsuccessful siege of Vienna

	by Qara Muṣṭafā; defeat at Kahlenberg. 1684 Holy Alliance of Austria with Poland, Venice and the Pope, 1687 also Russia against the Ottomans.
1684	Death of Evliyā Chelebi, author of an important travel account which deals with the Ottoman empire and neighbouring countries in Europe and in the Near East.
1686	Austria conquered Ofen.
1687	The Ottomans defeated at Mohács; loss of Hungary. Mutiny of the Janissaries; deposition of Sultan Meḥmed IV.
1687-91	Süleymān II Ottoman sultan.
1688	The Austrians took Belgrade.
1689	Defeat of the Ottomans at Nish. Muṣṭafā Köprülü Grand Vizier; reorganisation of mutinous army and of finances.
1690	Nish and Belgrade reconquered by the Ottomans.
1691	Muṣṭafā Köprülü fell in the battle of Szalankamen.
1691-95	Aḥmed II Ottoman sultan.
1694	Establishment of the Compagnie d'Afrique, North African territorial and trade concessions to France.
1694-1722	Ḥusayn, the last independent Ṣafavid Shāh in Iran, in danger from internal conflicts, Russian and Turkish interests and anti-Shī'ite autonomy in Afghanistan.
1695-1703	Muṣṭafā II, Ottoman sultan.
1696	Peter the Great took Azov.
1697	Decisive defeat of the Ottomans against imperial army under Prince Eugene of Savoy at Zenta on the Theiss.
1699	Treaty of Karlowitz; first important diplomatic defeat of the Ottomans: Hungary, Transylvania, Slovenia and Croatia fell to Austria; Kameniecz, Podolia, the Ukraine to Poland, and the Peloponnes and most of Dalmatia to Venice.
1700	Death of the Ṣafavid vizier, Muḥammad Bāqir Majlisī, Shī'ite theologian.
1702	The Ottomans lost Azov in peace treaty with Russia.
1703	Janissary revolt against the Shaykh-ül-Islām Feyżullāh and the fall of the sultan Muṣṭafā II. His successor Aḥmed III (1703-30).
1706-1957	The dynasty of the Ḥusaynid Beys in Tunis.
1707	Death of Awrangzīb after heavy losses in 20-year war against the Marāṭhās in the Deccan. Under his successors rapid dissolution of the Mughal empire.
1710-11	Ottoman-Russian war, ended with defeat of Peter the Great and peace at the Pruth; return of Azov to Turkey.
1711-1835	Dynasty of the Qaramānlis in Tripolitania.
1714-18	Ottoman offensive against Venice. The Venetians lost their fortresses on the Peloponnes and their last holdings in Crete. 1716 intervention of Austria.
1716	Prince Eugene of Savoy defeated the Turks at Peterwardein, took Temesvár and conquered Belgrade (1717).
1718	Peace of Passarowicz, second great defeat of the Ottomans against the Hapsburgs; Turkey lost Temesvár, northern Serbia and Little Wallachia to Austria.
1718-30	The 'Tulip era' under Nevshehirli Ibrāhīm Pasha, Grand Vizier of Sultan Aḥmed III: receptiveness to western cultural

	influence, introduction of the printing press. Reforms to stabilise government finances.
1722	Afghan revolts in Persia; Mīr Maḥmūd took Iṣfahān, deposed Shāh Ḥusayn and murdered Ṣafavid princes. Short-lived Afghan rule.
1722-23	Russia reached the Caspian Sea with the expedition of Peter the Great against Darband and Baku. By taking the side of Ṭahmāsp (1722-32) in the Iranian succession struggles, laid claim to further Iranian territories. The Ottomans took Tiflis (1723).
1724	Turkish-Russian treaty on the division of NW Iran. The Turks occupied Hamadān and Tabrīz.
1727	Ibrāhīm Müteferriqa, Ottoman statesman of Hungarian origin, set the first Ottoman printing press in operation.
1729	Nādir, leader of the Turcoman tribe, Afshār, and in the service of the Ṣafavid Ṭahmāsp III, drove out the Afghans from Persia, received the governorship of eastern Persia and a key position of authority.
1730	Nādir pushed the Turks out of Ādharbāyjān (Tabrīz) and Kirmānshāh (Hamadān). Rebellion of the Janissaries forced Aḥmed III to abdicate. Two-year dictatorship of the Janissary leader Patrona Khalīl.
1730-54	Sultan Maḥmūd I. The French renegade Bonneval reorganised govertnent and army.
1736	After a treaty alliance with Russia (1735) Nādir forced the Ottoman empire to hand back lands of the Caucasus, Georgia, Shīrwān and Armenia. After the death of the last Ṣafavid, Nādir had himself proclaimed Shāh of Persia (1736-47).
1736-47	Nādir ruler of Iran. Conquest of Afghanistan (1738), campaigns against India (1738-39), Turkestan (1740), Dagestan (1741-42). Attempt at compromise between Sunnī and Shīʿite Islam through reform of the Shīʿite doctrine of the Imāmate. 1743-46 war with the Ottoman empire about the recognition of the moderate Shīʿa as an orthodox legal school.
1736-39	War of the Ottomans against Austria and Russia. In the peace of Belgrade (1739), Turkey regained northern Serbia with Belgrade as well as naval supremacy over the Black Sea; Azov returned to Russia.
1738-39	Nādir Shāh attacked India and plundered Delhi. The Mughal emperor Muḥammad had to relinquish provinces north and west of the Indus.
1746	Muḥammad b. ʿAbd al-Wahhāb (1703-91), founder of the fundamentalist reform movement of the Wahhābiyya, began the militant expansion of his teaching in Arabia, in league with the Arab tribal leader Muḥammad b. Saʿūd, in Darʿiyya (Najd/central Arabia).
1747	Nādir Shāh murdered by Afshār and Qājār leaders. The empire collapsed into struggles between numerous contenders. Aḥmad Shāh Durrānī established strong autonomy in Afghanistan, expansion towards eastern Iran and India.
1747-1831	Régime of the Mamlūk Pashas of Baghdad.

1750-79	Muḥammad Karīm Khān Zand of Shīrāz ruler of Iran. Period of political and economic stability; trade contacts with England.
1754-57	Sultan 'Osmān III. Internal unrests, régime of intolerance.
1757-74	Muṣṭafā III Ottoman sultan; his Grand Vizier Rāghib Pasha real ruler. In spite of desire for peace, involved in disastrous war with Russia.
1757	Aḥmad Shāh Durrānī (1747-73) of Afghanistan plundered Delhi and Agra and extended his state across NW India (Sind, Balūchistān, Punjab and Kashmir).
1761	Friendship treaty between the Ottoman empire and Prussia.
1768-74	Ottoman-Russian war.
1770	The Russian Baltic fleet destroyed the Ottoman fleet in the battle of Cheshme (opposite Chios).
1774	Peace of Küchük Kaynarjï: the Ottoman empire relinquished authority over the Crimean Tartars (with the sultan preserving his position as spiritual overlord of the Muslims); the Tsarina Catherine II retained protection rights over the orthodox Christians under Ottoman authority. With Russian shipping rights Turkey lost her position in Levantine trade. Internal and external weakness vis-à-vis the European Powers.
1774-89	Sultan Abdülḥamīd I.
1779	Āghā Muḥammad, leader of the Turcoman Qājārs, seized northern Persia (capital Tehrān 1785).
1783	Tsarina Catherine II subjugated the Crimean Tartars.
1784	Treaty of Aynalï Kavak between the Ottoman empire and Russia; the Crimea fell to Russia. The claim of the sultan to the Imāmate over all Muslims became untenable.
1787-92	Ottoman war against Russia and Austria, ended by the treaties of Sistowa (1791) and Jassy (1792): the Turks lost the northern Black Sea coast as far as the mouth of the Dnjestr and the Crimea to Russia.
1788-1840	Bashīr Shihāb II, amir of Lebanon, fought for the autonomy of the country.
1789-1807	Sultan Selīm III: second period of Europeanisation; first Ottoman embassies to European capitals; establishment of the *Niẓām-i jedīd* army. Revolt of the Janissaries against innovations led to the deposition of the sultan.
1794-97	Āghā Muḥammad murdered the last Zand of Shīrāz (1794) and established the authority of the Qājār dynasty over the whole of Persia (1794-1924); crowned *shāh* in 1796.
1797-1834	Fatḥ 'Alī Shāh ruler of Iran. Persia became focus of expansionist interests of Russia (the Caucasus) and England (Afghanistan).

8. The emergence of national states

1798-1801	French expedition under Napoleon Bonaparte to Egypt; military conquest and scientific exploration of the country. Ottoman alliance with England and Russia.
1799-1801	Ottoman expedition corps under Muḥammad 'Alī forced the French to leave Egypt.
1800	Treaty of the English East India Company (ambassador Sir John

	Malcolm) with Fatḥ ʿAlī Shāh of Iran against Afghanistan and France.
1801	The Wahhābīs attacked and plundered Karbalāʾ in Iraq.
1801-05	Power struggle between the Ottoman governor, the Mamlūks and the Albanian brigade of Muḥammad ʿAlī after the departure of the French from Egypt.
1802	Egypt returned to the Ottoman empire in the treaty of Amiens.
1803-06	The Wahhābīs under Saʿūd b. ʿAbd al-ʿAzīz conquered the Ḥijāz (Medina 1804, Mecca 1806) and controlled large areas Arabia until their suppression by Egyptian troops (1812-18).
1804-06	First Serbian rebellion under Karageorgios (Karađorđe); 1805 constitution for Serbia.
1804-13	Iranian-Russian war in the Caucasus.
1805-48	Muḥammad ʿAlī seized control in Egypt, was recognised as governor of the country by the sultan (1806-48, from 1840 as independent hereditary ruler) and led Egypt towards national independence. Army, land and tax reform; efforts to build up a modern educational system and modern industry.
1806-12	Ottoman-Russian war, ended by the treaty of Bucharest.
1807	English naval intervention before Constantinople repulsed; English landing force defeated before Alexandria. Treaty of Finkenstein between France and Iran against Russia and England. The French general Claude-Matthieu Gardane built up the army in Iran.
1807-08	Sultan Muṣṭafā IV came to power after the murder of Selīm III; overthrown by supporters of Selīm.
1808-39	Sultan Maḥmūd II. Reforms under the influence of western European ideas, reorganisation of government administration and the army. Removal of the Janissary corps (1826).
1811	Muḥammad ʿAlī destroyed the Egyptian Mamlūk corps; assassination of Mamlūk leaders. Reorganisation of the army and government on French model. Monopolist economy, confiscation of large estates and pious foundations (1816).
1811-18	Muḥammad ʿAlī's campaigns against the Wahhābīs; his sons Ṭūsūn and (1816-18) Ibrāhīm destroyed the Wahhābī power of the Āl Saʿūd in the Arabian peninsula. The Ḥijāz and the coast of the Red Sea came under Egyptian influence.
1812	Ottoman-Russian peace of Bucharest.
1813	Iranian-Russian peace of Gulistān: Iran relinquished Caucasian provinces (Dagestan, Georgia, Darband, Shīrvān) to Russia.
1814	Iranian-British agreement; consolidation of English influence.
1815-17	Second Serbian rebellion under Miloš Obrenović, 1817 recognised as highest Kuz of the Pashalïk of Belgrade.
1817	Prohibition of piracy in Morocco.
1818	The Egyptian army under Ibrāhīm Pasha took Darʿiyya; end of the first Wahhābī kingdom of the Āl Saʿūd.
	Import of European machines to Egypt. Establishment of colleges of medicine, engineering sciences and chemistry, and military and marine academies.
1820	British treaty with the Shaykhdoms of the Persian Gulf.

1820-22	Muḥammad ʿAlī of Egypt conquered eastern Sudan (1823 founding of Khartoum).
1821	Setting-up of the Egyptian government printing press in Cairo-Būlāq.
1821-29	The Greek war of independence. Philhellenic movement in Europe.
1824-27	Muḥammad ʿAlī joined in the Greek war of independence as commander-in-chief of the sultan. Campaign of his son Ibrāhīm in the Peloponnes; occupation of Crete. 1827 capitulation of the Acropolis.
1826	Bloody liquidation of the Janissaries after mutiny against the army reforms of Maḥmūd II. Abolition of the Bektashī order which was closely linked with the Janissaries.
1826-28	Russo-Persian war in the Caucasus. In the peace of Turkomančai (1826) Iran relinquished Eriwan and Nakhchiwān to Russia. High war indemnity: 'Capitulations' (extra-territorial rights) for Russian representatives in Iran.
1827	English-French-Russian alliance against the Ottomans to support the Greeks. Destruction of the Egyptian fleet in the naval battle of Navarino.
1828	Russia advanced around the Caspian Sea towards Central Asia. Appearance of the first Arabic newspaper, the official gazette of the Egyptian government, *al-Waqāʾiʿ al-Miṣriyya.*
1829	London protocol of European powers about the independence of Greece. Russian conquest of Adrianople (Edirne). In the peace of Adrianople Russia gave up its conquests in European Turkey. Ottoman recognition of the London protocol.
1830	The French occupied Algeria.
1831	Maḥmūd II reconquered Baghdad and abolished the Pashalīk of the Mamlūks.
1831-32	The Egyptian army under Ibrāhīm Pasha conquered Syria. The Qājār prince ʿAbbās Mīrzā conquered Khurāsān.
1832	Appearance of the first Ottoman newspaper, *Taqwīm-i weqāyiʿ* (government gazette).
1832-33	Egyptian invasion of Anatolia; victory at Konya (1832). Russian intervention on behalf of the sultan caused first international Near East crisis; diplomatic counter-moves by England and France. In the agreement of Kütahya the sultan relinquished Syria with Adana to Muḥammad ʿAlī.
1832-47	ʿAbd al-Qādir, amir in Algeria; led war of independence against France.
1833	Support treaty of Hunkar Iskelesi between Ottomans and Russians. Turkey relinquished Syria and Adana to Egypt. Establishment of the Sanūsiyya brotherhood in Cyrenaika.
1834-48	Muḥammad Shāh of Persia. Departure of the British military mission. Military intervention in Afghanistan failed because of British pressure. Religious unrest because of the sectarian movement of the 'Bāb' (1844-50).
1835	ʿAbd al-Qādir defeated the French at the Macta. Reconquest of Tripolitania.
1837-38	Persian siege of Herāt, lifted because of British pressure.

	Muḥammad 'Alī extended the rule of Egypt in Arabia (as far as the Persian Gulf) and in Sudan.
1838	Treaty of Jalta-Liman between Turkey and Great Britain; preferential duty for English products.
1839	England occupied Aden, a measure against Egyptian expansion in Arabia.
	Second Near East crisis, caused by Ottoman-Egyptian war: Ottoman invasion in Syria, defeat in the battle of Naṣībīn. The British occupied Kabul and Kandahar (until 1842) in order to prevent Russian expansion.
1839-61	Sultan 'Abd ül-Mejīd; his Grand Vizier Rashīd Pasha: resumption and expansion of the policy of reforms (*Tanẓīmāt* period). 1839 *Khaṭṭ-ï Sherīf* [decree] of Gülhane: civil rights, abolition of military land tenure and tax farming, formation of the first legislative council (1854, 1861).
1840	The treaty of London ended Near East crisis. Peace offer of Muḥammad 'Alī rejected; defeat of Egyptian fleet against England. Egypt had to implement the treaty of Jalta-Liman and remove protective custom duties. The attempt at industrialisation failed. The European powers intervened in favour of the sultan and forced Egypt to retreat from Syria.
1841	Muḥammad 'Alī was made hereditary viceroy of Egypt; *de facto* independent while recognising Ottoman authority.
1842	Druze revolt in Lebanon, redevelopment of the country. Rebellion of the amir Dōst Muḥammad of Kābul pushed the British out of Afghanistan.
1843	In Morocco, 'Abd al-Qādir, amir of Algeria incited rebellion against the French.
1847	Rebellion of 'Abd al-Qādir failed in Algeria, 'Abd al-Qādir taken captive in Morocco (died in 1883 in exile).
1848	Regency of Ibrāhīm Pasha in Egypt; death of Ibrāhīm and Muḥammad 'Alī in the same year.
1848-50	In Persia uprisings of the supporters of the 'Bāb' Sayyid 'Alī Muḥammad who appeared from 1844 as the receiver of divine revelations. The 'Bāb' was taken prisoner and executed in 1850.
1848-54	'Abbās Ḥilmī viceroy of Egypt. Anti-western spirit against modernisation of the country.
1848-96	Nāṣir al-Dīn Shāh in Iran. The chief amir Mīrzā Taqī Khān made efforts at modernisation (1848-51).
1849	The Wahhābīs under Fayṣal (Āl Sa'ūd) pushed the last Egyptian governor out of the Arabian peninsula.
1850-60	Egyptian peasants were given hereditary right to their land.
1852	First Egyptian railway.
	Attack on Nāṣir al-Dīn Shāh by supporters of the 'Bāb'. Persecution and mass executions amongst the Bābīs.
1853-56	The Crimean war, caused by European rivalry over the protection of Christian minorities in the Ottoman empire; ended with the treaty of Paris (1856).
1854	The Council of the *Tanẓīmāt* became the first Ottoman legislative body.
1854-63	Sa'īd viceroy of Egypt; first European loan.
1856	*Khaṭṭ-ï hümāyūn*: decree to ratify and promulgate Ottoman

reforms; freedom of belief, rights of Christian subjects, reforms of law and taxation.
Peace of Paris at the end of the Crimean war: recognition of the territorial integrity of Turkey, neutrality of the Black Sea, setting-up of the Russian Protectorate over the Danube principalities.

1856-57 Irano-British war as a result of the Iranian conquest of Herāt, ended with the treaty of Paris: Iran left Afghanistan and recognised the independence of the country. Afghanistan became a buffer state between Russia and India.

1857 Constitution for Tunisia.

1858 Ottoman land law.
Foundation of the Suez Canal Company (concession granted to Ferdinand de Lesseps in 1854) using English and French capital; beginning of construction in 1859.

1859 Failure of *Qūleli waq'asï*, the conservative attempt to end Ottoman reform.
Beginning of construction of the Suez Canal.

1860 In Syria and Lebanon reactionary movements against *Khaṭṭ-ï hümāyūn*. Persecution of Christians in Damascus.
Defeat of Morocco in the war against Spain.

1860-61 Druze revolts, civil war and massacre of Christians in Lebanon; military intervention of France to protect the Maronite Christians.
1861 establishment of the autonomous province of Mont Liban; 'règlement organique' laid down the proportions of political representation between the different faiths.

1861 Creation of the *Majlis-i aḥkām-ï 'adliyye*, the new Ottoman law-giving body.

1861-76 Sultan 'Abd ül-'Azīz; continuation of *Tanẓīmāt* reforms (legislation, educational system); financial bankruptcy of the empire through high debt in Europe (1874).

1862 The Sultan recognised the union in 1859 of Moldavia and Wallachia: emergence of Rumania (independent in 1866).

1863 Bahā'allāh, disciple of the 'Bāb', appeared in Iraq as the manifestation of God's will; founding of the religious community of the Bahā'īs. Exiled with his followers to Acre from 1868 until his death in 1892, on orders of the Ottoman government.

1863-79 The viceroy Ismā'īl in Egypt (from 1866 with the title Khedive [Khidīw]). Expansionist foreign policy on the Red Sea and in the Sudan and expensive reforms to Europeanise the country led to high foreign debts. Boom in cotton trade during the American civil war.

1864 Great Britain obtained concession to build telegraph system in Iran.
The *vilāyet* law reformed the Ottoman provincial system.

1865 Establishment of the opposition alliance of the Young Turks under the leadership of Nāmïq Kemāl, Żiyā' Pasha and 'Alī Su'āvī; ideology of Ottoman patriotism and constitutionalism and of Islamic modernism, active until 1870.

1866 Establishment of the American University of Beirut by Protestant missionaries; 'Renaissance' (*nahḍa*) of Arabic literature

	with Syrian Christians, patronised by Buṭrus Bustānī and Nāṣif al-Yāzijī.
1866-68	Rebellion in Crete put down by the Ottomans.
1867	'Abd ül-'Azīz the first sultan to visit Europe. The Ottomans left Serbian fortresses.
1868	Creation of the Ottoman council of state (*shūrā-yi devlet*), a modern representative legislative body.
1868-69	Composition of the *Mejelle*, an Ottoman code of civil law.
1869	Opening of the Suez Canal.
1869-71	Attempt by Midḥat Pasha at reform in Iraq.
1870	Algeria was incorporated into French civil government. Muḥammad Aḥmad b. 'Abdallāh appeared in the Sudan as the first 'Mahdī'; fundamentalist Islamic reforms.
1871	Death of Muḥammad Muqranī in anti-colonial peasant rebellion in Algeria (Kabylia).
1871-79	The Persian religious philosopher and reformer Jamāl al-Dīn al-Afghānī, founder of pan-Islamic modernism, in Cairo; influenced the growing opposition of Egyptian nationalists and constitutionalists against the Khedive and against foreign control of the country. Amongst his disciples were Muḥammad 'Abduh and Sa'd Zaghlūl.
1872	The English baron Julius de Reuter obtained from Nāṣir al-Dīn Shāh comprehensive concession to open up and exploit the economy of Iran. 1873 dismissal of the reforming politician Mīrzā Ḥusayn Khān, annulling of the concessions.
1873	European journey of Nāṣir al-Dīn Shāh (other journeys 1887, 1889); he wrote influential travel accounts in straightforward style.
1873-77	Khayr al-Dīn Pasha Grand Vizier of Tunisia: reforms of the administration, economy measures to restore financial stability.
1873-94	Sultan al-Ḥasan of Morocco.
1874	Financial collapse of the Ottoman empire. Establishment of the *Düyūnu 'umūmiyye* ('General debt commission'), a control consortium of European creditor states. As a result, plot by Midḥat Pasha against Sultan 'Abd ül-'Azīz.
1875	Introduction of mixed law courts in Egypt. Bankruptcy of Egyptian state finances led to the sale of the bonds of the Suez Canal to England (Benjamin Disraeli); formation of an international 'Caisse de la Dette publique' (1876) increasing English influence in Cairo.
1875-76	Rebellions against Ottoman authority in Bosnia and Herzegowina, in 1876 in Bulgaria. 1876 declaration of war by Serbia and Montenegro on the Ottoman Empire, Turkish occupation of Serbia. Armistice through Russian pressure.
1876	Sultan 'Abd ül-'Azīz was deposed (and later murdered) by a palace rebellion under the leadership of Midḥat Pasha; the new sultan, Murād V, was deposed shortly after taking office because of mental illness.
1876-1909	Sultan 'Abd ül-Ḥamīd II.
1876	Midḥat Pasha proclaimed the constitution of the Ottoman

empire: indivisibility of the empire, freedom and equal rights for all subjects, parliamentary government.

1877 The Ottoman parliament was adjourned after a short sitting. Sultan ʿAbd ül-Ḥamīd annulled the constitution and reverted to an absolutist form of government. Persecution of political opposition. Midḥat Pasha was dismissed (murdered in 1883 in exile).

1877-78 Russo-Turkish war. Battle around Plevna and the Šipka Pass. The Russians in Adrianople. Peace of San Stefano: Montenegro, Serbia, Rumania *de jure* independent, Bulgaria autonomous. Russia obtained territories in eastern Anatolia and Transcaucasia. England obtained Cyprus in return for secret offer of help to Turkey against Russia.

1878 Berlin congress. Ratification of the arrangements of San Stefano. Austrian right to have garrisons in Bosnia and Herzegowina. Remaining Ottoman territories in the Balkans were hotbeds of dissension.

Creation of the Cossack Brigade under the command of Russian officers, as part of the Iranian army; Russian influence in Iran was strengthened by this.

1879 Concessions by the Khedive Ismāʿīl to the nationalist opposition to foreign economic control. Ismāʿīl was deposed by the sultan under pressure from European powers. His successor Tawfīq (1879-92). Renewal and extended powers of financial control by Europe.

Expulsion of Jamāl al-Dīn al-Afghānī from Egypt.

1881-82 Rebellion of officers in Egypt under Aḥmad ʿUrābī Pasha, supported by constitutionalists and supporters of Afghānī, forced a nationalist cabinet.

Popular rebellions led to occupation by England (1882): Egypt came under British rule. The 'Mahdī' Muḥammad Aḥmad b. ʿAbdallāh called for Holy War against Egyptian rule in the Sudan; first military successes.

1881-83 French occupation of Tunisia (1881); Tunisia became a French protectorate through the treaty of Bardo (1881) and the convention of La Marsa (1883).

1882-1907 Lord Cromer British pro-consul in Egypt. Economic expansion and stability; increase in cotton production; high rise in population. Creation of statute-labour for feudal landlords.

1883 The Mahdī defeated ʿUbayd and controlled eastern Sudan after the destruction of the Anglo-Egyptian army.

1884 In Paris Jamāl al-Dīn al-Afghānī and Muḥammad ʿAbduh published the Arabic newspaper *al-ʿUrwa al-wuthqā* (for Islamic revival, against British colonialist policies).

1885 Mahdists took Khartoum from Egyptian forces commanded by the English governor Charles George Gordon; death of Gordon. Death of the Mahdī as ruler of the Sudan in Khartoum. His successor (caliph) ʿAbdallāh Abū Bakr; expansion towards Abyssinia.

1885-88 Rebellions in eastern Rumeli; movement for union with Bulgaria. Continual unrest and acts of terrorism in the Ottoman Balkan provinces.

1888	The Mahdists waged war against Abyssinia, destroyed Gondar, subdued the Equatorial Province.
1889	The Mahdists defeated the Abyssinians at Gallabat; Emperor John fell. Students of the medical military academy in Istanbul established first organisation of the liberal opposition movement of the 'Young Turks'. After unsuccessful attempt at revolution (1892), agitation in European exile.
1890-97	Armenian revolutionary movement. Massacre of Ottoman officials by rebel groups.
1891	Masqaṭ and 'Omān under British protection. Jamāl al-Dīn al-Afghānī pushed out of Iran to Turkey, agitated in exile against Nāṣir al-Dīn Shāh.
1891-92	The tobacco revolts in Iran: protest of a religious-radical alliance under the leadership of the Shī'ite *'ulamā'* against foreign tobacco monopoly (concession of 1890) and the selling off of Iran to the Europeans. Recall of the concession (1892) burdened Iran with high foreign debts. Increase of Russian influence at cost of British.
1892-1914	'Abbās Ḥilmī II. Viceroy of Egypt.
1892	Midḥat's reforms given up in Iraq. Muḥammad 'Abduh, the most important Egyptian disciple of al-Afghānī, worked in the college of the Azhar mosque in Cairo (1892-1905), from 1899 also as *muftī* of Egypt, for liberal reforms in the spirit of Islamic modernism. The novelist Jurjī Zaydān (1861-1914) founded with other Lebanese Christians in Cairo the influential literary journal *al-Hilāl*.
1894	Bloody suppression of Armenian revolts with help of Kurdish irregular troops; massacre of Armenians aroused public opinion in Europe.
1894-1907	Sultan 'Abd al-Azīz of Morocco.
1896-97	Greco-Turkish war for Crete. After Turkish success, peace treaty under pressure from Great Powers. 1898 Crete obtained autonomy under Greek governor (1908 union with Greece).
1896	Nāṣir al-Dīn Shāh murdered by a supporter of Jamāl al-Dīn al-Afghānī.
1896-97	Muẓaffar al-Dīn Shāh ruler of Iran; with weak government, further promotion of Russian and British interests, conflict for control of Iran through economic concessions to foreign powers.
1898	British-Egyptian troops under General Kitchener defeated the rebels of the Mahdiyya movement at Umm Durmān. Muḥammad Rashīd Riḍā, disciple of Muḥammad 'Abduh, founded in Cairo the weekly newspaper *al-Manār* to spread his ideas and those of 'Abduh on modern reform harking back to the authority of the 'forefathers' of early Islam (*salaf*, hence *Salafiyya*).
1899	British-Egyptian condominium over the Sudan.
1900-08	Construction of the Ḥijāz railway to Mecca as a pan-Islamic project.

1905	Massacre of Armenians in eastern Turkey.
1905-06	Revolution in Iran against foreign influence and the incompetent Qājār government. Dismissal of the Prime Minister ʿAyn al-Dawla (1903-06); elections for a consultative national assembly (*Majlis-i shurā-yi millī*). The first *Majlis* met in Tehrān and drew up a parliamentary constitution.
1906	Publication of the Iranian constitution. England forced the cession of the Sinai peninsula to Egypt.
1906-07	The Dinshawāy affair caused by encroachments of British officers in Egypt aroused activity of nationalist resistance movements; establishment of Muṣṭafā Kāmil's national party and Luṭfī al-Sayyid's *Umma* party. Resignation of Cromer.
1907	The revolutionary movement of the 'Ottoman society for freedom' (*Osmānlï Ḥürrīyet Jemʿiyyeti*) united in Thessalonika with exile groups of Young Turks into the 'Committee for unity and progress' (*Ittiḥād ve Teraqqī Jemʿiyyeti*). British-Russian entente on the division of Iran into spheres of influence: British influence in the area of the Persian Gulf and in the south-east, Russian area of influence in north and central Iran, a neutral area in the south-west remained open for concessions to both powers.
1908	The autocratic Shāh Muḥammad ʿAlī (1907-09) supported by the Cossack Brigade, dissolved the *Majlis* and had leaders of nationalist opposition executed. Rebellion of opposition in Ādharbāyjān (Tabrīz). Young Turks rebellion under the leadership of the 'Committee for unity and progress', supported by rebel government troops. Proclamation of Parliamentary constitution in Thessalonika (Enver Pasha). Sultan ʿAbd ül-Ḥamīd reinforced the constitution of 1876; new election of Parliament with Young Turk majority. Żiyā' Gökalp formulated the fundamental concept of Turkish nationalism. Bulgaria declared its independence from the Ottoman empire; Austria annexed Bosnia and Herzegovina.
1908-09	Civil war in Iran: Russian troops occupied Tabrīz; Bakhtiyārīs and revolutionaries from Ādharbāyjān took Iṣfahān and Gīlān and marched against Tehrān. Flight of the Shāh to Russia.
1909	Failure of the conservative counter-attack in Istanbul. Sultan ʿAbd ül-Ḥamīd deposed, Meḥmed v (1909-18) constitutional sultan. Liberal reform of the constitution.
1909-25	Sultan Aḥmed Shāh ruled under control of constitutionalists in Iran.
1909	Establishment of the Anglo-Persian Oil Company, concession to exploit the south Persian petroleum resources. Tension between English and Russian petroleum interests.
1911	The American Morgan Shuster in Iran took over the reorganisation of Persian finances on the instructions of the *Majlis*. Russia forced the formation of a pro-Russian government and dismissal of Shuster.
1911-12	Ottoman-Italian war for Tripoli; Italy conquered Libya, relinquished by Turkey in the peace of Lausanne.

1912-13	First Balkan war. The Ottomans lost Adrianople and Thessalonika.
	French and Spanish protectorates in Morocco.
1912-25	Marshall Lyautey governor of Morocco.
1913	The Young Turks gained power through a coup d'état; the pro-German triumvirate of Enver, Ṭal'at and Jemāl led the empire into the First World War.
	In the second Balkan war of Serbia, Greece and Rumania against Bulgaria, Enver regained Adrianople; peace treaties of Constantinople (1913) and Athens (1914).
1914-18	First World War.
1914	Turkey entered the First World War on the side of Central Powers (Germany and Austria). Battles on four fronts: Suez Canal, Mesopotamia and Persia, Caucasus, Dardanelles.
	Egypt declared a British protectorate to protect the Suez Canal.
1914-17	Iran sought neutrality, was occupied by British and Russian troops in struggles against Turkey; the government's power was limited to Tehrān.
1916	Sykes-Picot agreement to lay down limits of English and French interests in the Near East, to establish an independent Arab state under European control.
1916-18	Revolt in the Arab peninsula against the Ottoman empire under the Sharīf Ḥusayn of Mecca, with the support of the British (T. E. Lawrence).
1917	Declaration of the English foreign minister Balfour about the establishment of a 'national homeland' of the Jews in Palestine.
	The Ottomans defeated by the British in Mesopotamia and retreated from Iraq. After the Bolshevik revolution, Russian withdrawal from Iran.
1918	British military mission organised the Caucasus against Bolshevik Russia and to ensure English influence in Iran. Front against Turkish invasion (Ādharbāyjān—Kirmānshāh) and against German attack from the Ukraine.
	Lawrence conquered Damascus. Collapse of the Turkish Palestine front. Dismissal and flight of the leader of the Young Turks. Truce of Mudros: demobilisation of Turkey, opening of the straits, thereafter occupation of Istanbul and parts of Anatolia by the Allies.
	Independence of the Yemen; constitution as a Kingdom.
	Short-lived republic of Tripolitania.
	Egyptian delegation (*wafd*) under Sa'd Zaghlūl submitted demands for independence. Beginning of the *Wafd* movement in Egypt.
1918-22	Meḥmed VI Waḥīd ül-Dīn, last Ottoman sultan.
1919	Sa'd Zaghlūl, leader of the *Wafd* party for the national independence of Egypt, arrested by the British authorities; popular rebellion put down by troops of occupation.
	Declaration of the Turkish national pact.
	Irano-British treaty to bolster up the British position signed after bribery of Iranian ministers.
1919-22	After Greek invasion in Anatolia, gathering of nationalist

fighting forces under Muṣṭafā Kemāl (Atatürk); Turkish war of independence against the Allies.

1920 The Syrian national assembly proclaimed independent kingdom of Syria under Fayṣal, son of the Sharīf Ḥusayn.
The conference of the League of Nations at San Remo declared Syria and Lebanon as a French mandate; France occupied Damascus and overthrew Fayṣal's government.
The Ḥijāz obtained independence.
The state territory of Mont Liban extended by the power of the French mandate by annexation of the coastal towns (amongst them Beirut) to Grand Liban.
The Bolsheviks occupied Rasht in Iran. The Soviet republic of Gīlān proclaimed; the British withdrew to Qazvīn.
The terms of the treaty of Sèvres signed by the government in Istanbul; not recognised by Muṣṭafā Kemāl, invalid because of the Greco-Turkish war.

1921 Iraq became a constitutional monarchy under the Hāshimite Fayṣal b. Ḥusayn; 'treaty of alliance' safeguarded British aims.
Battle on the Sakarya: the Turks repelled the Greek invasion.
The Turkish national assembly proclaimed the Constitution in Ankara.
Government of Riḍā Khān, officer of the Cossack Brigade in Iran. New national government. 1921-25 suppression of the autonomy of the tribes (Bakhtiyārīs and South Persian tribes, supported by Britain) and strengthening of military rule.

1921-26 Rīf war in Spanish Morocco, defeat of 'Abd al-Karīm.

1922 Conference of Mudanya: the Allies agreed to the evacuation of Anatolia. The Turks abolished the sultanate; Meḥmed VI fled from Istanbul; 'Abd al-Majīd declared caliph without secular power.
Great Britain proclaimed the formation of an independent Kingdom of Egypt with Aḥmad Fu'ād I as king under British control.

1922-32 Final conquest of Libya by Italy.

1923 Proclamation of the Egyptian constitution.
Peace treaty of Lausanne: Turkey gave up non-Turkish territories, kept eastern Thrace around Edirne, control of Istanbul with the Straits, sovereignty of Anatolia.
Proclamation of the Turkish Republic; Muṣṭafā Kemāl President.
Transjordan recognised as autonomous state under British mandate (capital 'Ammān).
Riḍā Khān became Prime Minister in Iran; the Shāh went to Europe.

1924 Ibn Sa'ūd conquered the Ḥijāz, pushed out Ḥusayn, established a Wahhābī kingdom.
Abolition of the caliphate in Turkey; end of the Ottoman line. Civil instead of *Sharī'a* courts.

1925 End of the Qājār dynasty; Riḍā Khān proclaimed Shāh.

1926 'Abd al-'Aziz b. Sa'ūd proclaimed king of the Ḥijāz after the conquest of Mecca and the fall of the Sharīf Ḥusayn (1925). Independence recognised by Britain in 1927.
Proclamation of the republic of Lebanon under French

	mandate. Constitution laid down proportional representation of the religious confessional groups.
1928	Abolition of Islam as the state religion in Turkey; introduction of the Latin alphabet.
1932	Independence of Iraq and acceptance in the League of Nations. Turkey joined the League of Nations.
1936	End of the English military occupation in Egypt (except for the Canal zone).
1937	Entrance of Egypt into the League of Nations.
1941	Formal removal of the British-French mandate and proclamation of the republic of Syria.
1943	Independence of Lebanon. 'National pact' laid down the distribution of political mandates, above all between Maronite Christians and Sunnī Muslims.
1945	Syria and Lebanon joined the League of Nations. Foundation of the Arab League: Egypt, Syria, Lebanon, Transjordan, Iraq, Saudi Arabia and Yemen.
1946	Jordan, Lebanon and Syria declared independent; retreat of French and British troops. Proclamation of the kingdom of Transjordan.
1947	Establishment of the state of Pakistan and of the Indian Union as successor states of the viceroyship of British India.
1948	End of the British Palestine mandate; the United Nations sanctioned the division of the country and the establishment of the Jewish state of Israel. Arab-Israeli war.
1950	After the annexation of a part of Palestine, Jordan renamed the Hāshimite Kingdom of Jordan.
1951	The kingdom of Libya independent.
1952	Egyptian revolution: putsch of 'Free Officers' under Colonel 'Abd al-Nāṣir (Nasser) and General Najīb, deposition of King Fārūq (1936-52).
1953	Egypt declared a republic.
1954	Recognition by France of the autonomy of Tunisia. Beginning of Algerian war of liberation against France.
1956	Kingdom of Morocco independent under Muḥammad v (1927-61). Independence of Tunisia, 1957 republic.
1958	Revolution in Iraq under 'Abd al-Karīm Qāsim, fall of the monarchy, proclamation of the republic.
1958-61	Egypt and Syria in the United Arab Republic.
1962	Proclamation of the independence of Algeria. Constitution for Morocco. Proclamation of the Yemenite Arab Repubic after the fall of the monarchy.
1967	Proclamation of the People's Republic of South Yemen (since 1970 People's Democratic Republic of Yemen).
1969	Fall of the monarchy in Libya caused by Colonel Mu'ammar al-Qadhāfī; 1977 proclamation of the Socialist Libyan Arab People's Jamāhiriyya.
1979	Revolution in Iran: fall of the Shāh Muḥammad Riḍā Pahlavī; proclamation of the Islamic Republic of Iran.

Chapter Nine

BIBLIOGRAPHY

The division of the bibliography follows the order of the chapters in the book. The first number refers to the chapter, the second to the section. The bibliography of general works of reference, surveys and auxiliary sciences is given a special classification (see below).

Numbers in square brackets [. . .] refer to the item numbers in the bibliography.
EI[1] = *Encyclopaedia of Islām*, 1913-38 [13.01].
EI[2] = *Encyclopaedia of Islam*, 1954ff. [13.02].

I. Bibliographies. Reference works. General surveys. Information on sources

1. Bibliographies
   (a) Bibliographies of bibliographies
   (b) Current bibliographies
   (c) Systematic subject bibliographies
2. Periodicals and collective works
3. Encyclopaedias and biographical reference works
4. General surveys of Islamic history and cultural history
5. Sources
   (a) Coins (numismatics)
   (b) Inscriptions (epigraphy)
   (c) Documents (papyrology and diplomatic records)
   (d) Monuments (archaeology and art history)
   (e) Historiography and biography
   (f) Geography and travel literature
   (g) Belles-lettres
   (h) Philosophical and scientific writing

1. Bibliographies

(a) Bibliographies of bibliographies

11.01 Bestermann, Theodore: *A world bibliography of Oriental bibliographies.* Revised and brought up to date by J. D. Pearson. Totowa, München 1975.
Arranged in alphabetical order according to key words. Updated abstract of Bestermann: *A world bibliography of bibliographies.* 4th ed. Lausanne 1965-66.

11.02 *Arab Islamic bibliography. The Middle East Library Committee guide.* Based on Giuseppe Gabrieli's *Manuale di bibliografia musulmana.* [Ed.] Diana Grimwood-Jones, Derek Hopwood, James Douglas Pearson. Hassocks 1977.
Bibliography, history of book production and auxiliary historical sciences.
11.03 Pearson, James Douglas: *Oriental and Asian bibliography. An introduction with some reference to Africa.* London 1966.

Catalogues of manuscripts:
11.04 Sezgin, Fuat: 'Bibliotheken und Sammlungen arabischer Handschriften'. In: Sezgin: *GAS* [13.10]. 6. 1978, pp.311-466.

(b) Bibliographies
11.05 *Abstracta Islamica.* In: *Revue des études islamiques.* Paris 1927ff.
Annual bibliography, arranged according to subject, with short critical comments. Also includes literature published in the East.
11.06 Behn, Wolfgang H.: *Islamic book review index,* 1982ff. Berlin 1982ff.
11.07 Pearson, James Douglas: *Index Islamicus. A catalogue of articles on Islamic subjects in periodicals and other collective publications, 1906-1955.* Cambridge 1958. [With] Supplement 1ff. 1962ff.
1: 1956-1960. Cambridge 1962.
2: 1961-1965. Cambridge 1968.
3: 1966-1970. London 1972.
4: 1971-1975. London 1977.
5: 1976-1980. Part 1: Articles; Part 2: Monographs. 1983.
Bibliography of the contents of journals, congress proceedings, *Festschriften* and other collective works, arranged systematically.

Supplements:
11.08 Majer, Hans-Georg: Osmanistische Nachträge zum Index Islamicus 1906-1965. In: *Südostforschungen.* München. 27. 1968. pp.242-91.
11.09 Pearson, James Douglas [ed.]: The *Quarterly Index Islamicus.* Current books, articles and papers on Islamic subjects (1-6,2: on Islamic studies). 1-6,2: ed. by J. D. Pearson; 6,3ff.: compiled by G. J. Roper [etc.]. 1ff. London 1977ff.
Quarterly continuation of *Index Islamicus* [11.07], also covers monographs. Five-year series of cumulative volumes [11.07].

(c) Systematic subject bibliographies
11.10 *Bibliographical guide to Iran. The Middle East Library Committee guide.* Ed. by L[aurence] P. Elwell-Sutton. Sussex; New Jersey 1983.
11.11 Cahen, Claude: *Introduction à l'histoire du monde musulman médiéval, VIIe-XVe siècle. Méthodologie et éléments de bibliographie.* Paris 1982. (*Initiation à l'Islam.* 1.)
An introduction to sources and modern studies. Replaces Jean Sauvaget: *Introduction.* 1961 [11.19].
11.12 Ettinghausen, Richard [ed.]: *A selected and annotated bibliography of books and periodicals in Western languages dealing with the Near and Middle East, with special emphasis on medieval and modern times.* (Completed Summer 1951.) With *Supplement* (December 1953). Washington, DC 1954. Repr. New York 1975.

11.13 *Middle East and Islam. A bibliographical introduction.* Ed. by Derek Hopwood and Diana Grimwood-Jones. Foreword by J. D. Pearson. Rev. ed. Zug (Switzerland) 1979. (*Bibliotheca Asiatica.* 15.)

11.14 Kornrumpf, Hans-Jürgen: *Osmanische Bibliographie mit besonderer Berücksichtigung der Türkei in Europa.* Unter Mitarbeit von Jutta Kornrumpf. Leiden, Köln 1973. (*Handbuch der Orientalistik.* Abt. 1. Erg.-Bd. 8.)

11.15 Littlefield, David W.: *The Islamic Near East and North Africa. An annotated guide to books in English for non-specialists.* Littleton, Colorado 1977.

11.16 Martin, Aubert: *Éléments de bibliographie des études arabes.* Paris 1975.

11.17 Meiseles, Gustav: *Reference literature to Arabic studies; a bibliographical guide.* Tel-Aviv 1978.

11.18 Pfannmüller, Gustav: *Handbuch der Islam-Literatur.* Berlin and Leipzig 1923, repr. Berlin 1974. Valuable guide to the older literature.

11.19 Sauvaget, Jean: *Introduction to the history of the Muslim East. A bibliographical guide.* Berkeley, Los Angeles 1965.
Updated English version of Sauvaget: *Introduction à l'histoire de l'Orient Musulman,* éd. refondue et complétée par C. Cahen. Paris 1961. Now replaced by C. Cahen: *Introduction.* 1982 [11.11].

11.20 Schwarz, Klaus: *Der Vordere Orient in den Hochschulschriften Deutschlands, Österreichs und der Schweiz. Eine Bibliographie von Dissertationen und Habilitationsschriften* (1885-1978). Freiburg 1980. (*Islamkundliche Materialien.* Bd. 5.)

11.21 Spuler, Bertold; Forrer, Ludwig: *Der Vordere Orient in islamischer Zeit.* Bern 1954. (*Wissenschaftliche Forschungsberichte. Geisteswiss. Reihe.* Bd. 21 = Orientalistik. T. 3.)
Report on works of research which have appeared during and after the war.

11.22 *The study of the Middle East: research and scholarship in the humanities and the social sciences.* Ed. by Leonard Binder. New York [etc.] 1976.

2. *Periodicals and collective works*

Journals in European languages (selection):

12.01 *Al-Andalus. Revista de las escuelas de estudios árabes de Madrid y Granada.* Madrid 1933-78. – [Continued as:] *Al-Qanṭara. Revista de estudios árabes.* Madrid 1980ff.

12.02 *Annales islamologiques* (1-3: *Mélanges islamologiques*). Le Caire: Institut français d'archéologie orientale. 1940ff.

12.03 *Annali.* Napoli: Istituto Universitario Orientale. 1929ff.

12.04 *Arabica. Revue des études arabes.* Leiden 1954ff.

12.05 *Bibliotheca Orientalis.* Leiden 1943ff.
Review journal. Abbrev.: BiOr.

12.06 *Bulletin of the School of Oriental and African Studies, University of London.* London 1917ff.
Abbrev.: *BSOAS.*

12.07 *Bulletin d'études orientales.* Damas: Institut français d'études arabes 1931ff.
Abbrev.: *BEO.*

12.08 *Les Cahiers de Tunisie. Revue des sciences humaines.* Tunis: Faculté des lettres et des sciences humaines 1953ff.

12.09 *Hespéris. Archives berbères et bulletin de l'Institut des Hautes-études marocaines.* Rabat 1921-59. [Continued as:] *Hespéris-Tamuda.* 1960ff.

12.10 *IBLA. Revue de l'Institut des belles lettres arabes.* Tunis 1937ff.

12.11 *Der Islam.* Straßburg 1910-19; Berlin 1920ff.

12.12 *The Islamic Quarterly. A review of Islamic culture.* London 1954ff.
Abbrev.: *IQ.*

12.12a *Israel Oriental Studies.* Tel Aviv 1971ff.

12.13 *Journal Asiatique.* Paris: Société asiatique 1822ff.
Abbrev.: *JA.*

12.14 *Journal of Arabic Literature.* Leiden 1970ff.

12.15 *Journal of Near Eastern Studies. Journal of the Department of Near Eastern Languages and Civilizations of the University of Chicago.* Chicago 1942ff.
Abbrev.: *JNES.*

12.16 *Journal of Semitic Studies.* Manchester 1956ff.
Abbrev.: *JSS.*

12.17 *Journal of the American Oriental Society.* New Haven 1843ff.
Abbrev.: *JAOS.*

12.18 *Journal of the Economic and Social History of the Orient.* Leiden 1958ff.
Abbrev.: *JESHO.*

12.19 *Journal of the Royal Asiatic Society of Great Britain and Ireland.* London 1843ff.
Abbrev.: *JRAS.*

12.20 *Mélanges. Institut dominicain d'études orientales.* Le Caire 1954ff.
Abbrev.: *MIDEO.*

12.21 *Mélanges de l'Université Saint-Joseph* (1-6: *Mélanges de la Faculté Orientale*). Beyrouth 1906ff.
Abbrev.: *MUSJ.*

12.22 *Le Muséon. Revue des études orientales.* Louvain 1881ff.

12.23 *Muslim World. A quarterly journal of Islamic study and Christian interpretation among Muslims.* Hartford 1911ff.

12.24 *Oriens. Zeitschrift der Internationalen Gesellschaft für Orient-forschung.* Leiden 1948ff.

12.25 *Orientalistische Literaturzeitung.* Berlin 1898ff.
Review journal. Abbrev.: *OLZ.*

12.26 *Revue des études islamiques.* Paris 1927ff.
Abbrev.: *REI.*

12.27 *Rivista degli Studi Orientali.* Roma 1907ff.
Abbrev.: *RSO.*

12.28 *Studia islamica.* Paris 1953ff.
Abbrev.: *SI.*

12.29 *Wiener Zeitschrift für die Kunde des Morgenlandes.* Wien 1887ff.
Abbrev.: *WZKM.*

12.30 *Zeitschrift der Deutschen Morgenländischen Gesellschaft.* Leipzig 1847-1944; Wiesbaden 1945ff.
Abbrev.: *ZDMG.*

Russia and Eastern Europe:

12.31 *Acta Orientalia Academiae Scientiarum Hungaricae.* Budapest 1950ff.

12.32 *Archiv orientální.* Praha 1929ff.

12.33 *Folia Orientalia.* Kraków: Polska Akademia Nauk 1959ff.

12.34 *Narody Azii i Afriki.* Moscow 1959ff.

12.35 *Przeglad orientalistyczny.* Warsaw 1960ff.

12.36 *Rocznik orientalistyczny.* Warsaw 1914ff.

International congresses

12.37 *International congress of orientalists.* 1874ff.

12.38 *Congress of the Union européenne d'arabisants et d'islamisants* (UEAI). 1962ff.

A list of numerous other specialist journals, conference proceedings, *Festschriften*, memorial volumes and other collective works is given in *Index Islamicus* [11.07, 11.09] ('List of sources').

The publications of universities and academic institutions in the Islamic world are becoming increasingly important and authoritative. They have not yet, however, been adequately dealt with in bibliographies.

3. *Encyclopedias and biographical reference works*

13.01 *The Encyclopaedia of Islām. Geographical, ethnographical and biographical dictionary of the Muhammadan peoples.* Volumes 1-4. Leiden, Leipzig 1913-34. Supplement 1938.
Abbrev.: *EI*[1].

13.02 *The Encyclopaedia of Islam.* New edition. Vol. 1- . Leiden 1954- . *Encyclopédie de l'Islam.* Nouvelle édition. T. 1- . Leyde & Paris 1954- .
Abbrev.: *EI*[2].
The most comprehensive reference work for the religion, history and culture of the Islamic world. Signed articles with bibliographical information. The new edition has now reached Vol. 6 (letter M).

13.03 *Shorter Encyclopaedia of Islam.* Edited on behalf of the Royal Netherlands Academy by H. A. R. Gibb and J. H. Kramers. Leiden and London 1953. Repr. 1961, 1964.
Contains those articles from *EI*[1] which are concerned especially with Islam as a religion (with some additions).

13.04 *İslâm Ansiklopedisi. İslâm âlemi coğrafya, etnografya ve biyografya lugati.* Cilt 1-13. Istanbul 1940-87.
Abbrev.: *İA.* Turkish edition of *EI*[1] with numerous new articles about the Turkish peoples, languages, Turkey and the culture of the Ottoman empire.

13.05 Kreiser, Klaus; Diem, Werner; Majer, Hans-Georg [ed.]: *Lexikon der islamischen Welt.* Bd. 1-3. Stuttgart 1974. (*Urban Taschenbücher.* 200, 1-3.)

13.06 Ronart, Stephan & Nancy: *Concise Encyclopaedia of Arab Civilization. The Arab East.* Amsterdam 1959. *The Arab West.* 1966.
Not entirely reliable.

13.07 *Handbuch der Orientalistik.* Abt. 1: *Der Nahe und der Mittlere*

Osten, ed. Bertold Spuler. Leiden 1952- .
Series of introductory and general surveys.

Bio-bibliographical reference works, especially on literature

13.08 *Dictionary of Oriental Literatures*. Vol. III: *West Asia and North Africa*. General editor: Jaroslav Prušek. Volume editor: Jiří Bečka. London 1974.

13.09 Brockelmann, Carl: *Geschichte der arabischen Litteratur. Zweite, den Supplementbänden angepaßte Auflage*. Bd. 1. 2. [With:] *Supplementband* 1-3. Leiden 1943-49; *Suppl.*: 1937-42.
Abbrev.: *GAL*², *GAL S*. Biographical sketches of authors and bibliography (manuscripts, editions) of their works.

13.10 Sezgin, Fuat: *Geschichte des arabischen Schrifttums . . . bis ca. 430 H*. Bd. 1- . Leiden 1967- .
1: *Qur'ānwissenschaften, Ḥadīṯ, Geschichte, Fiqh, Dogmatik, Mystik*. 1967.
2: *Poesie*. 1975.
3: *Medizin, Pharmazie, Zoologie, Tierheilkunde*. 1970.
4: *Alchemie, Chemie, Botanik, Agrikultur*. 1971.
5: *Mathematik*. 1974.
6: *Astronomie*. 1978.
7: *Astrologie und Meteorologie*. 1979.
8: *Lexikographie*. 1982.
9: *Grammatik*. 1984.
Abbrev.: *GAS*. A catalogue of authors and works, modelled on Brockelmann's *GAL* [13.09], the first series covering literature until the beginning of the eleventh century.

13.11 Graf, Georg: *Geschichte der christlichen arabischen Literatur*. Bd. 1-5. Città del Vaticano 1944-53. (*Studi e testi*. 118. 133. 146. 147. 172.)

13.12 Kaḥḥāla, 'Umar Riḍā: *Mu'jam al-mu'allifīn; tarājim muṣannifī l-kutub al-'arabiyya*. Juz' 1-15. Damascus 1376/1957-1381/1961.
An Arabic lexicon of authors.

13.13 al-Ziriklī, Khayr-al-Dīn: *al-A'lām. Qāmūs tarājim li-ashhar al-rijāl wa'l-nisā' min al-'Arab wa'l-musta'ribīn wa'l-mustashriqīn*. Juz' 1-8. Beirut⁴ 1979.
Biographical lexicon of Arab authors and historical personalities.

13.14 Storey, Charles Ambrose: *Persian Literature. A bio-bibliographical survey*. Vol. 1- . London 1927- .
1: *Qur'ānic literature; history and biography*. Part 1. 1927-1939. Part 2. 1953.
2, part 1: *A. Mathematics. B. Weights and measures. C. Astronomy and astrology. D. Geography*. 1958.
2, part 2: *E. Medicine*. 1971.
2, part 3: *F. Encyclopaedias and miscellanies. G. Arts and crafts. H. Science. J. Occult arts*. 1977.
3, part 1: *A. Lexicography. B. Grammar. C. Prosody and poetics*. Leiden, 1984.
An updated Russian version of Vols 1. 11, 1.2 was published by Jurij E. Bregel' and Jurij E. Borščevskij: *Persidskaja literatura*. 1-3. Moscow 1972.

13.15 Babinger, Franz: *Die Geschichtsschreiber der Osmanen und ihre Werke*. Mit einem Anhang: *Osmanische Zeitrechnungen*. Von

Joachim Mayr. Leipzig 1927.
Abbrev.: *GOW.*

4. *General surveys of Islamic history and civilization*

—— Bergé, Marc: *Les Arabes.* 1978 [15.66].

14.01 Brockelmann, Carl: *Geschichte der islamischen Völker und Staaten.* München and Berlin 1939, ²1943; repr. Hildesheim 1977.
Compact, informative survey of events until the Second World War; a good reference work. Updated English translation entitled: *History of the Islamic Peoples.* New York 1944 [re-issued London 1980].

14.02 Cahen, Claude: *L'Islam des origines au début de l'Empire Ottoman.* Paris 1970.
Valuable *inter alia* for a thorough and competent presentation of social and economic history.

14.03 *The Cambridge History of Islam.* Vol. 1: *The central Islamic lands.* Vol. 2: *The further Islamic lands. Islamic society and civilization.* Ed. by P. M. Holt, Ann K. S. Lambton, Bernard Lewis. Cambridge 1970.
Collaborative work by specialists.

14.04 Elisséeff, Nikita: *L'Orient musulman au moyen âge.* Paris 1977.
An especially thorough presentation of the Near East in the Seljuq and Crusader period.

14.05 Gabrieli, Francesco: *A short history of the Arabs.* London 1965.

14.05a *Geschichte der arabischen Welt.* Hrsg. von Ulrich Haarmann unter Mitwirkung von Heinz Halm, Barbara Kellner-Heinkele, Helmut Mejcher, Tilman Nagel, Albrecht Noth, Alexander Schölch, Hans-Rudolf Singer und Peter von Sivers. München 1987.

14.06 *The Muslim world. A historical survey.* Part 1-4. Leiden 1960-1982.
1: Spuler, Bertold: *The age of the Caliphs.* 1960; ²1968.
2: Spuler, Bertold: *The Mongol period.* 1960; ²1969.
3: *The last great Muslim empires.* With contributions by H. J. Kissling [a.o.]. 1969.
4: *Modern times.* Fasc. 1- . With contributions by Helmuth Scheel [a.o.]. 1981- .

14.07 Gibb, Hamilton Alexander Roskeen: An interpretation of Islamic history. In: *Cahiers d'histoire mondiale* 1. 1953, pp.39-62 = Gibb: *Studies in the civilization of Islam* [14.19], pp.3-33.
Analysis of the historical process until the decline of the caliphate.

14.08 Grunebaum, Gustav Edmund von: *Classical Islam; a history, 600 AD to 1258 AD.* Chicago, Ill. 1970.
Puts religion and literature into the context of political developments.

14.09 Hodgson, Marshall Goodwin Simms: *The venture of Islam. Conscience and history in a world civilization.* Vols 1-3. Chicago and London 1974.
1: *The classical age of Islam.*
2: *The expansion of Islam in the middle periods.*
3: *The gunpowder empires and modern times.*
Broad view of political and intellectual development until the modern period.

14.10 *Der Islam.* I: *Vom Ursprung bis zu den Anfängen des Osmanen reiches.* By Claude Cahen [see 14.02]. II: *Die islamischen Reiche nach dem Fall von Konstantinopel*. Edited by G.E. von Grunebaum. Frankfurt a.M. 1968-71 [and reprints]. (*Fischer Weltgeschichte*. Bd. 14.15.)

14.10a Kennedy, Hugh: *The Prophet and the age of the Caliphates*. London 1986. (A history of the Near East, ed. P. M. Holt.)
Supplemented by P. M. Holt: *The age of the Crusades*. 1986 [65.06].

14.11 Kissling, Hans Joachim: Die islamischen Länder am Mittelmeer und im Nahen Osten. In: *Abriß der Geschichte außereuropäischer Kulturen*. Bd. 1. München 1961. (*Oldenbourgs Abriß der Weltgeschichte*.) T. II, pp. 35-83 [with maps and indices, pp.84-110].
Chronological tables of Islamic history arranged according to important periods and regions.

14.12 Lewis, Bernard: *The Arabs in History*. London, New York 1950. Revised ed.: London [4]1958.
Essentially restricted to the pre-Mongol period, with some perspectives on the modern era.

14.13 Saunders, John Joseph: *A history of medieval Islam*. London 1965 [and reprints].

14.14 Sourdel, Dominique: *Medieval Islam* [*L'Islam médiéval*. 1979]. Transl. J. M. Watt. London 1983.

14.15 Taeschner, Franz: *Geschichte der arabischen Welt*. Mit einem Beitrag '*Die arabische Welt in der Epoche des Nationalismus*' von Fritz Steppat. Stuttgart 1964. (*Kröners Taschenausgabe*. 359.)

14.16 Weil, Gustav: *Geschichte der Chalifen*. Bd. 1-3. Mannheim 1846-1851. Bd. 4.5: *Geschichte des Abbasidenchalifates in Ägypten*. 1860-62. Repr. Osnabrück 1967.
Still useful for its constant use of traditional sources.

Cultural history

For specialised literature on the religion, law and institutions of Islam, cf. Ch. III below.

14.17 Becker, Carl Heinrich: *Islamstudien. Vom Werden und Wesen der islamischen Welt*. Bd. 1.2. Leipzig 1924-32.
Bd. 1, pp.1-23: *Der Islam als Problem*; pp.24-39: *Der Islam im Rahmen einer allgemeinen Kulturgeschichte*.
—: *The Cambridge History of Islam*. 1970 [14.03].
Vol. 2 includes contributions on economy and society, religion and law, mysticism, reform movements, literature, art, sciences and other aspects of Islamic culture.

14.18 Gätje, Helmut: Gedanken zur Problematik der islamischen Kulturgeschichte. In: *Die Welt als Geschichte*. Stuttgart. 20. 1960, pp.157-67.

14.19 Gibb, Hamilton Alexander Roskeen: *Studies on the civilization of Islam*. Ed. by Stanford J. Shaw and William R. Polk. London 1962; repr. Princeton, NJ, 1982.

14.20 Goitein, Shlomo Dov: *Studies in Islamic history and institutions*. Leiden 1966.
Collected essays 1929-1964; pp.3-53: The four faces of Islam; pp.54-70: The intermediate civilization. The Hellenic heritage in Islam.

14.21 Gottschalk, Hans Ludwig [a.o.]: *Die Kultur des Islams. Die Kultur der Araber* by Hans L. Gottschalk. *Die Kultur des islamischen*

Ostens by Bertold Spuler. *Die Kultur des Islams in Indonesien und Malaysia und die Kultur der Kapmalaien in der Republik Südafrika* by Hans Kähler. Frankfurt a.M. 1971. (*Handbuch der Kulturgeschichte.* Abt. 2: *Kulturen der Völker.*)

14.22 Grunebaum, Gustav Edmund von: *Medieval Islam.* Chicago 1961.

14.23 —: *Studien zum Kulturbild und Selbstverständnis des Islams.* Zürich and Stuttgart 1969.

14.24 Kraemer, Jörg: *Das Problem der islamischen Kulturgeschichte.* Tübingen 1959.

14.25 Kremer, Alfred von: *Culturgeschichte des Orients unter den Chalifen.* Bd. 1.2. Wien 1875-77.

14.26 Lewis, Bernard [ed.]: *Islam and the Arab world. Faith. People. Culture.* London 1976.

Contributions on faith and law, art, the Islamic city, mysticism, literature, music, science, the conduct of war, Islam in Spain, in Iran, the Ottoman empire, Islam in India and modern Islam.

14.27 Miquel, André: *L'Islam et sa civilization.* Paris 1968.

14.28 Pareja, Felix M.: *Islamologie.* En collaboration avec Ludwig Hertling, Alessandro Bausani, T. Bois. Beyrouth 1957-63.

Original edition in Italian: *Islamologia.* Roma 1951.

14.29 Peters, Francis Edward: *Allah's Commonwealth. A history of Islam in the Near East, 600-1100 AD.* New York 1973.

14.30 Rosenthal, Franz: *Knowledge triumphant. The concept of knowledge in medieval Islam.* Leiden 1970.

14.31 Schacht, Joseph; Bosworth, Clifford Edmund [ed.]: *The legacy of Islam.* Oxford 1974.

The cultural heritage of Islam and its influence on Europe, with contributions by various authors. Also the earlier collection under the same title (edited by T. W. Arnold, A. Guillaume. Oxford 1931) contains still useful contributions.

14.32 Sourdel, Dominique; Sourdel-Thomine, Janine: *La civilisation de l'Islam classique.* Paris 1968.

With contributions on society and economy, archaeology and art.

14.33 *Unity and variety in Muslim civilization.* Ed. by Gustave E. von Grunebaum. Chicago 1955. (*Comparative Studies of Cultures and Civilisations.* [7.])

14.34 Vernet Ginés, Juan: *La cultura hispanoárabe en Oriente y Occidente.* Barcelona [etc.] 1978.

Updated German version: *Die spanisch-arabische Kultur in Orient und Okzident.* Übers. von Kurt Maier. Zürich and München 1984.

14.35 Watt, William Montgomery: *The majesty that was Islam. The Islamic world, 661-1100.* London 1974.

5. Sources

Bibliography of auxiliary historical sources in: *Arab Islamic Bibliography* [11.02], Cahen [11.11] and Sauvaget: *Introduction* [11.19].

15.00 *Grundriss der arabischen Philologie.* Hrsg. von Wolfdietrich Fischer und Helmut Gätje. Bd. 1: Sprachwissenschaft. Bd. 2: Literaturwissenschaft. Wiesbaden 1982-87.

Vol. 1 contains articles on the history of the Arabic language, script, palaeography, epigraphy, numismatics, papyrology and codicology;

vol. 2 gives surveys of Arabic belles-lettres, traditional grammar and literary theory, and the literature of the Islamic disciplines and the Hellenistic sciences.

(a) Coins (numismatics)

15.01 Mayer, Leon Ary: *Bibliography of Muslim numismatics, India excepted.* London 1954. (*Oriental Translation Fund.* 35.)
Supplements in: *Arab Islamic Bibliography* [11.02], pp.211-20.

15.01a Balog, Paul: *The coinage of the Mamlūk Sultans of Egypt and Syria.* New York 1964. (Numismatic Studies. 12.) – Additions in: *American Numismatic Society. Museum notes* 16. 1970, pp.113-71.

15.02 Balog, Paul: Études numismatiques de l'Égypte. 1-3. In: *Bulletin de l'Institut d'Égypte.* Le Caire. 33. 1951, pp.1-42; 34. 1952, pp.17-55; 35. 1953, pp.401-25.
Fāṭimids, Ayyūbids, Mamlūks.

15.02a Broome, Michael: *A handbook of Islamic coins.* London 1985.

15.03 Gaube, Heinz: *Arabosasanidische Numismatik.* Braunschweig 1973. (*Handbücher der mittelasiatischen Numismatik.* Bd. 2.)

15.04 Hazard, Harry W.: *The numismatic history of late medieval North Africa.* New York 1952. (*Numismatic Studies.* 8).

15.05 Lane-Poole, Stanley: *Catalogue of Oriental coins in the British Museum.* Ed. by Reginald Stuart Poole. Vol. 1-10. London 1875-90. Repr. Bologna 1967.

15.05a Miles, George Cable: *The coinage of the Umayyads of Spain.* Vols. 1-3. New York 1950. (*Hispanic numismatic series.* 1.)

15.06 Miles, George C.: *The numismatic history of Rayy.* New York 1938. (*Numismatic Studies.* 2.)

15.07 Zambaur, Eduard von: *Die Münzprägungen des Islams, zeitlich und örtlich geordnet.* Bd. 1: *Der Westen und Osten bis zum Indus mit synoptischen Tabellen,* ed. Peter Jaeckel. Wiesbaden 1968.
Survey of mints of Islamic coins west of the Indus. Sheets of an edition prepared in 1942.

(b) Inscriptions (epigraphy)

15.08 *Répertoire chronologique d'épigraphie arabe.* Publié par M. Cohen [et al.] sous la direction de Étienne Combe, J[ean] Sauvaget et G[aston] Wiet (t. 16: N. Élisséeff, D. S. Rice et G. Wiet; t. 17: établi par Ludwig Kalus sous la dir. de N. Élisséeff, D. Sourdel et J. Sourdel-Thomine). T. 1-17. Le Caire 1931-82.
Repertory of dated inscriptions up to the year 783/1382. [With:] *Index géographique.* Cairo 1975. [Covering vols. 1-16.]

15.09a Berchem, Max van [et al.]: *Matériaux pour un Corpus Inscriptionum Arabicarum.* Partie 1-3. Le Caire 1894-1956.
1: *Égypte.* 1. 1894-1903. 2. 1929-1930.
2[a]: *Syrie du Nord.* 1. 1909. [2:] *Alep.* 1.2. 1954-1956.
2[b]: *Syrie du Sud. Jérusalem.* 1-3. 1920-1949.
3: *Asie mineure.* 1. 1910-1917.

15.09b —: *Opera minora.* Introduction et bibliographie par Anouar Louca. Index établi par Charles Genequand. Publié par les soins de la Fondation Max van Berchem. Genève 1978.

15.10 *Catalogue général du Musée arabe du Caire. Stèles funéraires.* Par

Hassan Hawary et Hussein Rached, [T. 2.4-10:] Gaston Wiet. T. 1-10. Le Caire 1932-42.

15.11 Grohmann, Adolf: *Arabische Paläographie.* T. 1.2. Wien 1967-71. (*Österreichische Akademie der Wissenschaften. Philosophisch-Historische Klasse. Denkschriften.* Bd. 94, 1.2.)
T. 2: *Das Schriftwesen. Die Lapidarschrift.*

For bibliography see Creswell [15.30].

Metrology:

15.12 Hinz, Walter: *Islamische Maße und Gewichte, umgerechnet ins metrische System.* Leiden, Köln 1955; ²1970. (*Handbuch der Orientalistik.* Abt. 1. Erg.-Bd. 1. H. 1.)

(c) Documents (papyrology and diplomatic)

15.13 Abbott, Nabia: *Studies in Arabic literary papyri.* Vol. 1-3. Chicago and London 1957-72. (*The University of Chicago Oriental Institute. Publications.* Vol. 75-77.)

15.14 Grohmann, Adolf: I. *Arabische Chronologie.* II. *Arabische Papyruskunde.* Mit Beiträgen von Joachim Mayr und Walter C. Till. Leiden, Köln 1966. (*Handbuch der Orientalistik.* Abt. 1. Erg.-Bd. 2. Halbband 1.)

15.15 —: *Einführung und Chrestomathie zur arabischen Papyruskunde.* Bd. 1: *Einführung.* Praha 1954. (*Monografie Archivu Orientálního.* 13, 1.)

15.16 Berque, Jacques; Chevallier, Dominique [et al.]: *Les Arabes par leurs archives (XVIe-XXe siècles).* Paris 1976. (*Colloques internationaux du Centre National de la Recherche scientifique.* 555.)

15.17 Busse, Heribert: Persische Diplomatik im Überblick. Ergebnisse und Probleme. In: *Der Islam.* Berlin. 37. 1961, pp.202-45.

15.18 —: *Untersuchungen zum islamischen Kanzleiwesen an Hand turkmenischer und safawidischer Urkunden.* Kairo 1959. (*Deutsches Archäologisches Institut Kairo. Abhandlungen. Islamische Reihe.* 1.)

15.19 Deny, Jean: *Sommaire des archives turques du Caire.* Le Caire 1930.

15.20 Dilger, Konrad: Das osmanische Urkundenwesen in der neueren Forschung. In: *Der Islam.* Berlin. 57. 1980, pp.120-29.
Review of Josef Matuz: *Das Kanzleiwesen Sultan Süleymāns des Prächtigen.* Wiesbaden 1974. (*Freiburger Islamstudien.* Bd. 5.)

15.21 Diplomatic – I. Classical Arabic (W. Björkman). II. Maghrib (G. S. Colin). III. Persia (H. Busse). IV. Ottoman Empire (J. Reychman and A. Zajaczkowski). In: *EI*². Vol.2 (1962).

15.22 Fragner, Bert G.: *Repertorium persischer Herrscherurkunden. Publizierte Originalurkunden (bis 1848).* Freiburg i.Br. 1980. (*Islamkundliche Materialien.* Bd. 4.)

15.23 Goitein, Shlomo Dov: The Cairo Geniza as a source for the history of Muslim Civilization. In: *Studia Islamica.* Paris. 3. 1955, pp.75-91.
See also id.: L'état actuel de la recherche sur les documents de la Geniza. In: *Revue des études juives.* Paris. 118. 1959-60, pp.9-27.

15.24 Lewis, Bernard: The Ottoman archives as a source for the history of the Arab lands. In: *Journal of the Royal Asiatic Society.* London. 1951, pp.139-55.

15.25 Roemer, Hans Robert: Arabische Herrscherurkunden aus Ägypten. In: *Orientalistische Literaturzeitung.* Berlin. 61. 1966, coll.325-44.

15.26 —: Über Urkunden zur Geschichte Ägyptens und Persiens in islamischer Zeit. In: *Zeitschrift der Deutschen Morgenländischen Gesellschaft.* Wiesbaden. 107. 1957, pp.519-38.

15.27 Shaw, Stanford J.: The Ottoman archives as a source for Egyptian history. In: *Journal of the American Oriental Society.* New Haven. 83. 1963, pp.447-52.

15.28 Veselý, Rudolf: Die Hauptprobleme der Diplomatik arabischer Privaturkunden aus dem spätmittelalterlichen Ägypten. In: *Archiv Orientální.* Praha. 40. 1972, pp.312-43.
Gives an overall view of the state of research and a bibliography.

15.29 Zajaczkowski, Ananiasz; Reychman, Jan: *Handbook of Ottoman-Turkish diplomatics.* The Hague 1968.

(d) Monuments (archaeology and art history)

15.30 Creswell, Keppel Archibald Cameron: *A bibliography of the architecture, arts and crafts of Islam to 1st January, 1960.* Cairo 1961. [With:] *Supplement,* Jan. 1960-Jan. 1972. 1973.

15.31 —: *Early Muslim architecture.* Vol. 1.2. Oxford 1932-40.
1: *Umayyads, AD 622-750.* 1932. – 2nd ed. Part 1.2. Oxford 1969. Repr. New York 1979.
2: *Early ʿAbbasids, Umayyads of Cordova, Aghlabids, Tulunids, and Samanids.* 1940. Repr. New York 1979.

15.32 —: *A short account of early Muslim architecture.* Harmondsworth 1958; repr. 1968. (*Pelican Books.* A 407.)

15.33 —: *The Muslim architecture of Egypt.* Vol. 1.2. Oxford 1952-59. Repr. New York 1977.
1: *Ikhshids and Fatimids, AD 939-1171.* 1952.
2: *Ayyubids and early Bahrite Mamluks, AD 1171-1326.* 1959.

15.34 Erdmann, Kurt: *Der orientalische Knüpfteppich. Versuch einer Darstellung seiner Geschichte.* Tübingen ²1960; ⁴1975.

15.35 Ettinghausen, Richard: *Arab Painting.* Geneva 1962.

15.36 Gaube, Heinz: Die syrischen Wüstenschlösser. Einige wirtschaftliche und politische Gesichtspunkte zu ihrer Entstehung. In: *Zeitschrift des Deutschen Palästina-Vereins.* Wiesbaden. 95. 1979, pp.182-209.

15.37 Grabar, Oleg: *The formation of Islamic art.* New Haven and London 1973.

15.38 Gray, Basil: *Persian painting.* Geneva, New York 1961.

15.39 Kuban, Doğan: *Muslim religious architecture.* P. 1: *The mosque and its early development.* 2: *Development of religious architecture.* Leiden 1974-85. (*Institute of Religious Iconography, State University Groningen. Iconography of Religions.* Section 22: Islam. Fasc. 2.)

15.40 Kühnel, Ernst: *Islamische Schriftkunst.* Berlin/Leipzig s.a. [1942]; Graz ²1972. (*Monographien künstlerischer Schrift.* Bd. 9.)

15.41 —: *Die Kunst des Islam.* Stuttgart 1962. (*Springers Handbuch der Kunstgeschichte in Einzeldarstellungen. Kröners Taschenausgabe.* 326.)

15.42 *Die Kunst des Islam.* By Janine Sourdel-Thomine and Bertold Spuler. With contributions by Klaus Brisch [et al.]. Berlin 1973. (*Propyläen Kunstgeschichte.* Bd. 4.)

15.43 Marçais, Georges: *Manuel d'art musulman. L'architecture: Tunisie, Algérie, Maroc, Espagne, Sicile.* 1.2. Paris 1926-27.

15.44 Pope, Arthur Upham; Ackermann, Phyllis [et al.]: *A survey of Persian art from prehistoric times to the present.* Vol. 1-6. London 1938-39. – 2nd ed. Vol. 1-13 (with corrigenda and addenda). 14. London, Tokyo 1964-67. – 3rd ed. Vol. 1-16 (15. 16: Bibliography. Index). Ashiya (Japan) 1977.

15.45 Otto-Dorn, Katharina: *Kunst des Islam.* Baden-Baden 1964. (*Kunst der Welt. Die außereuropäischen Kulturen.*)

15.46 Sarre, Friedrich; Herzfeld, Ernst: *Archäologische Reise im Euphrat- und Tigris-Gebiet.* 1-4. Berlin 1911-20.

(e) Historiography and biography

The most important literary-historical reference works have already been mentioned: Brockelmann: *GAL* [13.09], Sezgin: *GAS* [13.10], Storey: *Persian literature* [13.14], Babinger: *GOW* [13.15].

15.47 Cahen, Claude: L'Historiographie arabe: des origines au VII[e] s. H. In: *Arabica.* Leiden. 33. 1986, pp.133-98.

15.48 Dūrī, 'Abd al-'Azīz: *The rise of historical writing among the Arabs (Baḥth fī nash'at 'ilm al-tārīkh 'ind al-'Arab).* Edited and trans. by Lawrence I. Conrad. Introduction by Fred M. Donner. Princeton, NJ 1983.

15.49 Gabrieli, Francesco: La storiografia araba. In: Gabrieli: *L'Islam nella storia.* Bari 1966, pp.153-71.

—[Engl.:] Arabic historiography. Transl. by M. S. Khan. In: *Islamic Studies.* Islamabad. 18. 1979, pp.81-95.

15.50 Gibb, Hamilton Alexander Roskeen: Ta'rīkh (Historiography). In: *EI*[1]. Suppl. 1938 = Gibb: *Studies in the civilization of Islam.* London 1962, pp.108-37.

15.51 Goldziher, Ignaz: Historiography in Arabic literature. Transl. by Joseph de Somogyi. In: Goldziher: *Gesammelte Schriften.* Hildesheim 1967-73. Bd. 3, pp.359-94.

From the Hungarian original: *A történetirás az arab irodalomban.* Budapest 1895.

15.52 Hillenbrand, Carole: Some medieval Islamic approaches to source material; the evidence of a 12th century chronicle. In: *Oriens,* Leiden 27-28. 1981, pp.197-225.

15.53 *Historians of the Middle East.* Ed. by Bernard Lewis and P[eter] M[alcolm] Holt. London 1962. (*Historical Writing on the Peoples of Asia.* 4.)

Collaborative work with contributions on the Islamic historical writing of the Middle Ages, on the historiography of the Near East in Europe and Russia and on the modern view of history in the Islamic world.

15.54 Rosenthal, Franz: *A history of Muslim historiography.* Leiden 1952. 2nd rev. ed. 1968.

15.55 Somogyi, Joseph de: The development of Arabic historiography. In: *Journal of Semitic Studies.* Manchester. 3. 1958, pp.373-87.

15.56 Spuler, Bertold: Die historische und geographische Literatur in persischer Sprache. In: *Handbuch der Orientalistik.* Abt. 1. Bd. 4: Iranistik. Abschnitt 2: Literatur. Lfg. 1. Leiden 1968, pp.100-167.

Individual periods:
15.57 Haarmann, Ulrich: Auflösung und Bewahrung der klassischen Formen arabischer Geschichtsschreibung in der Zeit der Mamluken. In: *Zeitschrift der Deutschen Morgenländischen Gesellschaft*. Wiesbaden. 121. 1971, pp.46-60.
15.58 Little, Donald P.: *An introduction to Mamluk historiography. An analysis of Arabic annalistic and biographical source for the reign of al-Malik an-Nāṣir Muḥammad ibn Qalā'ūn*. Wiesbaden 1970. (*Freiburger Islamstudien*. 2.)
15.59 Meyer, Egbert: *Der historische Gehalt der Aiyām al-'Arab*. Wiesbaden 1970. (*Schriften der Max-Freiherr-von-Oppenheim-Stiftung*. Heft 7.)
Pre-Islamic and early Islamic tales about the 'Battledays' of the ancient Arabs.
15.60 Noth, Albrecht: *Quellenkritische Studien zu Themen, Formen und Tendenzen frühislamischer Geschichtsüberlieferung*. Teil 1: *Themen und Formen*. Bonn 1973. (*Bonner Orientalistische Studien*. N.S. Bd. 25.)
Deals *inter alia* with the question of whether history can be discerned behind the literary themes and forms of early Islamic chronicles.
15.60a Shatzmiller, Maya: *L'historiographie mérinide: Ibn Khaldūn et ses contemporaires*. Leiden 1982.

Biographical literature:
15.61 Fragner, Bert G.: *Persische Memoirenliteratur als Quelle zur neueren Geschichte Irans*. Wiesbaden 1979. (*Freiburger Islamstudien*. 7.)
15.62 Gibb, Hamilton Alexander Roskeen: Islamic biographical literature. In: *Historians of the Middle East* [15.53], pp.54-58.
15.63 Kellner-Heinkele, Barbara: Osmanische Biographiensammlungen. In: *Anatolica*. Leiden. 6. 1977-78, pp.171-94.
15.64 Lambton, Ann Katherine Swynford: Persian biographical literature. In: *Historians of the Middle East* [15.53], pp.141-51.
15.65 Rosenthal, Franz: Die arabische Autobiographie. In: *Studia Arabica*. 1. Roma 1937 (*Analecta Orientalia*. 14), pp.1-40.

Selections of texts from the original sources in translation (see also [30.17-20], [60.08-35], [65.17-18]):
15.66 Bergé, Marc: *Les Arabes. Histoire et civilization des Arabes et du monde musulman, des origines à la chute du royaume de Grenade, racontées par les témoins. IXe siècle av. J.-C.-XVe siècle*. Paris 1978.
15.67 Lewis, Bernard: *Islam from the Prophet Muhammad to the capture of Constantinople. Edited and translated. Vol. 1: Politics and war. 2: Religion and society*. London 1976. (*Documentary history of western civilization*.)
15.68 Sauvaget, Jean: *Historiens arabes. Pages choisies, traduites et présentées*. Paris 1946. (*Initiation à l'Islam*. 5.)

(f) Geography and travel literature
15.69 Kračkovskij, Ignatij Julianovič: *Arabskaja geografičeskaja literatura*. Moskva, Leningrad 1957. (Kračkovskij: *Izbrannye sočinenija*. T. 4.)
15.70 Kramers, Johannes Hendrik: La littérature géographique classique

des Musulmans. In: Kramers: *Analecta Orientalia.* Vol. 1. Leiden 1954, pp.172-204.

—: L'influence de la tradition iranienne dans la géographie arabe. In: Kramers: *Analecta Orientalia.* Vol. 1. Leiden 1954, pp.147-56.

15.71 Miquel, André: *La géographie humaine du monde musulman jusqu'au milieu du 11e siècle.* T. 1-3. Paris, La Haye 1967-80. (*École pratique des Hautes études. Section 6: Sciences économiques et sociales. Centre de recherches historiques. Civilizations et sociétés.* 7. 37. 68.)
- 1: *Géographie et géographie humaine dans la littérature arabe des origines à 1050.* 1967; ^{2}1973.
- 2: *Géographie arabe et représentation du monde: la terre et l'étranger.* 1975.
- 3: *Le milieu naturel.* 1980.

15.72 Schuster-Walser, Sibylla: *Das ṣafawidische Persien im Spiegel europäischer Reiseberichte (1502-1722). Untersuchungen zur Wirtschafts- und Handelspolitik.* Baden-Baden, Hamburg 1970.

15.73 Scurla, Herbert: *Reisen im Orient. Berichte deutscher Forscher aus dem 18. und 19. Jahrhundert, ausgewählt und eingeleitet. Carsten Niebuhr – Ulrich Jasper Seetzen – Richard Lepsius – Heinrich Brugsch.* Berlin ^{2}1962.

15.74 Tobler, Titus: *Bibliographia geographica Palaestinae. Kritische Übersicht gedruckter und ungedruckter Beschreibungen der Reisen ins Heilige Land.* Leipzig 1867. Repr. Amsterdam 1964.

15.74a Walsh, Ann: Scientific expeditions. In: *Arab Islamic Bibliography.* 1977 [11.02], pp.140-47.

(g) Belles-lettres

15.74 Blachère, Regis: *Histoire de la littérature arabe des origines à la fin du XVe siècle de J.-C.* 1-3. Paris 1952-1966.
The three volumes which have appeared deal with pre-Islamic and early Islamic literature and the literature of the Umayyad period.

15.76 *The Cambridge History of Arabic Literature.* [1:] *Arabic literature to the end of the Umayyad period.* Ed. by A. F. L. Beeston, T. M. Johnstone, R. B. Serjeant and G. R. Smith. Cambridge 1983.

15.77 Gibb, Hamilton Alexander Roskeen: *Arabic literature.* Second ed. Oxford 1963.
Cf. also German edition: *Arabische Literaturgeschichte.* Zürich and Stuttgart 1968, with a second part (pp.187-288) by Jacob M. Landau: *Arabische Literaturgeschichte der neuesten Zeit; 20. Jahrhundert* – the bibliography (prepared by Walter W. Müller, pp.291-319) gives a wide selection of Arabic literary works which have been translated into a Western language.

15.77a Nicholson, Reynold Alleyne: *A literary history of the Arabs.* Cambridge 1907; repr. 1969.

15.78 Browne, Edward Granville: *A literary history of Persia.* Vol. 1-4 (1.2:) London 1902-1906; (3.4:) Cambridge 1920-1924. Re-issued: Cambridge 1928 [and further editions].

15.79 Levy, Reuben: *An introduction to Persian literature.* New York 1969. (*Persian Heritage Series.*)

15.80 Rypka, Jan: *Iranische Literaturgeschichte.* Unter Mitarbeit von

Otakar Klíma, Věra Kubičková, Jiří Bečka, Jiří Cejpek, Ivan Hrbek. Leipzig 1959.
— [Revised English edition:] *History of Iranian literature.* Ed. by Karl Jahn. Dordrecht 1968.
15.80a Schimmel, Annemarie: *Islamic literatures of India.* Wiesbaden 1973. – *Classical Urdu literature from the beginning to Iqbāl.* Wiesbaden 1975. (*A history of Indian literature,* ed. by J. Gonda. Vol. VIII, fasc. 1.3.)

15.81 Bombaci, Alessio: *Storia della letteratura turca.* Milano 1956.
— [Updated French edition:] *Histoire de la littérature turque.* Trad. par Irène Mélikoff. Paris 1967.
15.82 *Turkologie.* With contributions by Annemarie von Gabain [et al.]. Leiden, Köln 1963. (*Handbuch der Orientalistik.* Abt. 1 Bd. 5: Altaistik. Abschnitt 1.)
Pp. 205-41: Literatur.

Poetry and literary prose as a historical source:
15.83 Canard, Marius: Les allusions à la guerre byzantine chez les poètes Abū Tammām et Buḫturī. In: Vasiliev, A. A.: *Byzance et les Arabes.* 1: La dynastie d'Amorium. 1935 [63.15], pp.397-403.
15.84 Latham, J. Derek: Towards a better understanding of al-Mutanabbī's poem on the battle of al-Ḥadath. In: *Journal of Arabic Literature.* Leiden. 10. 1979, pp.1-22.
15.85 Pellat, Charles: *The life and works of Jāḥiẓ; translations of selected texts.* Transl. from the French by D. M. Hawke. London 1969.
On al-Jāḥiẓ, cf. also:
15.86 Enderwitz, Susanne: *Gesellschaftlicher Rang und ethnische Legitimation. Der arabische Schriftsteller Abū ʿUṯmān al-Ǧāḥiẓ (gest. 868) über die Afrikaner, Perser und Araber in der islamischen Gesellschaft.* Freiburg 1979. (*Islamkundliche Untersuchungen.* 53.)
15.87 Stetkevych, Suzanne Pinckney: The ʿAbbasid poet interprets history: three qaṣīdahs by Abū Tammām. In: *Journal of Arabic Literature.* Leiden. 10. 1979, pp.49-64.

(h) Philosophical and scientific writing
15.88 Rosenthal, Franz: *Das Fortleben der Antike im Islam.* Zürich and Stuttgart 1965. – English ed.: *The classical heritage in Islam.* Transl. by E. and J. Marmorstein. London 1975.
15.89 Walzer, Richard: *Greek into Arabic. Essays on Islamic philosophy.* Oxford 1962. (*Oriental Studies.* 1.)
15.90 Corbin, Henry: *Histoire de la philosophie islamique.* 1: *Des origines jusqu'à la mort d'Averroës (1198).* Avec la collaboration de Seyyed Hossein Nasr et Osman Yahya. Paris 1964. (*Collection Idées.* 38)
2: La philosophie islamique depuis la mort d'Averroës jusqu'à nos jours. In: *Histoire de la philosophie.* Paris 1969-74. 3, ed. Y. Belaval, pp.1067-1188. – 2nd ed. [in one vol.]: Paris 1986.
15.91 Fakhry, Majid: *A history of Islamic philosophy.* New York, London 1970; 2nd ed. 1983.
15.92 Leaman, Oliver: *An introduction to medieval Islamic philosophy.* Cambridge 1985.

Science and medicine:
15.93 *Dictionary of scientific biography.* Ed. in chief: Charles Coulston Gillispie. Vol. 1-16. New York 1970-80: repr. 1981.
15.94 Sarton, George: *introduction to the history of science.* Vol. 1-3. Baltimore 1927-48.
On the works of Arab physicians and scientists, cf. Sezgin [13.10], Vols. 3-7. For short accounts of philosophy and the sciences in Islam, see also *Cambridge History of Islam* [14.03]; Lewis [14.26].
15.95 Arnaldez, Roger; Massignon, Louis; Youschkevitch, A. P.: La science arabe. In: *Histoire générale des sciences.* T. 1: *La science antique et médiévale (des origines à 1450).* [Ed.:] René Taton. 2ème éd. Paris 1966, pp.440-525.
15.96 Berggren, J. L.: History of mathematics in the Islamic world: the present state of the art. In: *Middle East Association Bulletin.* Tucson. 19. 1985, pp.9-33.
15.97 Kennedy, Edward Stewart: The exact sciences in Iran. In: *The Cambridge history of Iran* [56.09]. 4: *The period from the Arab invasion to the Saljuqs.* 1975, pp.378-95. – 5: *The Saljuq and Mongol periods.* 1968, pp.659-79. – 6: *The Timurid period.* 1986, pp.568-80.
15.98 King, David A.: The exact sciences in medieval Islam: some remarks on the present state of research. In: *Middle East Association Bulletin.* Tucson. 14. 1980, pp.10-26.
15.99 Nallino, Carlo Alfonso: Storia dell'astronomia presso gli Arabi nel medio evo. In: Nallino: *Raccolta di scritti.* Roma 1939-48. Vol. 5, pp.88-329.
15.100 Ullmann, Manfred: *Die Natur- und Geheimwissenschaften im Islam.* Leiden, Köln 1972. (*Handbuch der Orientalistik.* Abt. 1. Erg.-Bd. 6. Abschnitt 2.)
Zoology, botany, mineralogy, alchemy, astrology, magic, agriculture.
15.101 —: *Die Medizin im Islam.* Leiden, Köln 1970. (*Handbuch der Orientalistik.* Abt. 1. Erg.-Bd. 6. Abschnitt 1.)
15.102 —: *Islamic medicine.* Edinburgh 1978. (*Islamic Surveys.* 11.)
More concise introductory survey.
15.102a Youschkevitsch, Adolf P. [Adol'f Pavlovič Juškevič]: *Les mathématiques arabes (VIIIe-XVe siècles)* [*Istorija matematiki v srednie veka,* partial transl.]. Trad. française de M. Cazenave et K. Jaouiche . Paris 1976. (*L'Histoire des sciences.* Textes et études. 2.)

Musical theory:
15.103 Farmer, Henry George: *A history of Arabian music to the XIIIth century.* London 1929. Repr. 1973.
15.104 Neubauer, Eckhart: Neuerscheinungen zur arabischen Musik. Eine Auswahl an Nachschlagewerken und allgemeinen Darstellungen in europäischen Sprachen. In: *Zeitschrift für Geschichte der Arabisch-Islamischen Wissenschaften.* Frankfurt. 1. 1984, pp.288-311.
For religious and legal literature, cf. Chapter III below.

II. Europe and Islam: the history of a science

20.01 Fück, Johann: *Die arabischen Studien in Europa bis in den Anfang des 20. Jahrhunderts.* Leipzig 1955.

20.02 Barthold, W. (Vasilij Vladimirovič Bartol'd): *Die geographische und historische Erforschung des Orients mit besonderer Berücksichtigung der russischen Arbeiten.* Translated from the Russian by E. Ramberg-Figulla. Leipzig 1913. (*Quellen und Forschungen zur Erd und Kulturkunde.* Bd. 8.)

—— [French ed.:] *La découverte de l'Asie.* Trad. par B. Nikitine. Paris 1947.

20.03 *Historians of the Middle East.* Ed. by Bernard Lewis and P[eter] M[alcolm] Holt. London [etc.]. 1962. (*Historical Writings of the Peoples of Asia.* [4.])

Part II: European (including Russian) historical writing on the Near and Middle East from the Middle ages to the present day.

Part III: Modern Middle Eastern historical writing.

20.04 Kračkovskij, Ignatij Julianovič: *Die russische Arabistik. Umrisse ihrer Entwicklung* [*Očerki po istorii russkoj arabistiki.* 1950, German transl.]. Transl. by O. Mehlitz. Leipzig 1957.

Middle Ages and the early modern period

20.05 Daniel, Norman: *Islam and the West; the making of an image.* Edinburgh 1960; repr. 1962, 1966.

The evolution of the western concept of the Islamic religion from *c.* 1100-1350 and its survival into modern times. Contains good bibliography of source material.

20.06 —: *Islam, Europe and Empire.* Edinburgh 1966.

The image of the Islamic world in Europe from the French Revolution to the end of the 19th century – *vis-à-vis* colonialism, missionary activity and imperialism.

20.07 Hagemann, Ludwig: *Der Ḳur'ān in Verständnis und Kritik bei Nikolaus von Kues. Ein Beitrag zur Erhellung islāmisch-christlicher Geschichte.* Frankfurt a.M. 1976. (*Frankfurter Theologische Studien.* 21.)

20.08 Kritzeck, James: *Peter the Venerable and Islam.* Princeton, NJ 1964. (*Princeton Oriental Studies.* 23.)

20.09 Southern, Richard William: *Western views of Islam in the Middle Ages.* Cambridge, Mass. 1962, ^{2}1978.

20.10 Strohmaier, Gotthard: Johann Jacob Reiske – Byzantinist und Arabist der Aufklärung. In: *Klio.* Berlin. 58. 1976, pp.199-209.

History and criticism of modern Islamic scholarship

20.11 Lewis, Bernard: The study of Islam. In: *Encounter.* London. Jan. 1972 = Lewis: *Islam in history.* London 1973, pp.11-32.

20.12a Rodinson, Maxime: The Western image and Western studies of Islam. In: *The legacy of Islam.* 1974 [14.31], pp.9-62.

20.12b —: *La fascination de l'Islam.* Paris 1980.

20.13 Waardenburg, Jean-Jacques D. J.: *L'Islam dans le miroir de l'Occident. Comment quelques orientalistes se sont penchés sur l'Islam et se sont formé une image de cette religion*: I. Goldziher, C. Snouck-Hurgronje, C. H. Becker, D. B. Macdonald, Louis Massignon. Paris, La Haye 1962; ^{3}1970. (*Maison des sciences de l'homme. Recherches méditerranées. Études.* 3.)

20.14 Said, Edward W.: *Orientalism.* London 1979.

Sharp criticism (not always fair) of Western studies of Islam and the Orient.

Modern Muslim interpretation of Islamic history:

20.15 Ende, Werner, *Arabische Nation und islamische Geschichte. Die Umayyaden im Urteil arabischer Autoren des 20. Jahrhunderts.* Beirut, Wiesbaden 1977. (*Beiruter Texte und Studien.* 20.)
See also *Historians of the Middle East* [20.03].

20.16 Wielandt, Rotraud: *Offenbarung und Geschichte im Denken moderner Muslime.* Wiesbaden 1971. (*Akademie der Wissenschaften und der Literatur. Veröffentlichungen der Orientalischen Kommission.* Bd. 25.)

III. Islam: religion and legal system

General introductions
(in addition to the general surveys of the cultural and intellectual history of Islam already mentioned [14.17-35])

Some 'classics' of Islamic studies still worth reading:

30.01 Macdonald, Duncan Black: *Development of Muslim theology, jurisprudence and constitutional theory.* New York 1903; repr. Beirut 1965.

30.02 Goldziher, Ignaz: *Muhammedanische Studien.* Th. 1.2. Halle a.S. 1889-90.
English transl.: *Muslim studies.* Ed. and transl. by S. M. Stern and C. R. Barber. Vol. 1.2. London 1967-71.

30.03 —: *Vorlesungen über den Islam.* 2. Auflage. Heidelberg 1925. Repr. Heidelberg 1963.
English transl.: *Introduction to Islamic theology and law.* Transl. by A. and R. Hamori. Ed. by Bernard Lewis. Princeton, NJ 1981.

30.04 —: *Gesammelte Schriften.* Ed. by Joseph Desomogyi. 1-6. Hildesheim 1967-73.

Modern interpretations:

30.05 Arberry, Arthur John [ed.]: *Religion in the Middle East. Three religions in concord and conflict.* Vol. 1.2. Cambridge 1969; ^{2}1976.
2: *Islam.* Contributions on Islam in the different countries of the Near and Middle East, Africa and Europe, on groups and sects, as well as on the relationship of Islam with other religions in the spheres of dogma, law, society and culture.

30.06 Brunschvig, Robert: *Études d'islamologie.* T. 1: *Vues générales, histoire, aspects de la pensée religieuse, langue.* T. 2: *Droit musulman.* Avant-propos et biographie de l'auteur par Abdel Magid Turki. Paris 1977.

30.07 Fazlur Rahman: *Islam.* London 1966; ^{2}1979.
A scholarly survey by a Pakistani Muslim.

30.08 Gardet, Louis: *Les hommes de l'Islam; approche des mentalités.* Paris 1977.

30.09 —: *L'Islam, religion et communauté.* 3e éd., revue et corrigée. Paris 1978.

30.10 Gibb, Hamilton Alexander Roskeen: *Islam. A historical survey.*

Second ed. [1949 as: *Mohammedanism*]. Oxford [etc.] 1975.
Concise presentation of the most important themes.
30.11 Grunebaum, Gustav Edmund von: *Medieval Islam.* Chicago 1961.
30.12 Hartmann, Richard: *Die Religion des Islam. Eine Einführung.* Berlin 1944.
—— *Der Islam in der Gegenwart.* Ed. by W. Ende and U. Steinbach. 1984 [68.09].
30.13 Pareja, Felix Maria: *Islamologie.* En collaboration avec Ludwig Hertling [et al.]. (*Islamologia.* 1951 [French ed.]). Beyrouth 1957-63.
P. 2: *Institutions.*
30.14 Sourdel, Dominique: *L'Islam médiéval.* Paris, 1979.
30.15 Watt, William Montgomery: *The formative period of Islamic thought.* Edinburgh 1973.
30.16 —: *Islam and the integration of society.* London 1961.

Anthologies of primary sources in translation (see also [15.66-68]):
30.17 Arberry, Arthur John: *Aspects of Islamic civilization as depicted in the original texts.* London 1964.
30.18 Jeffery, Arthur: *A reader on Islam.* The Hague 1962.
30.19 Schacht, Joseph: *Der Islam mit Ausschluß des Qor'āns.* Tübingen 1931. (*Religionsgeschichtliches Lesebuch,* ed. by Alfred Bertholet. 2. Aufl. 16.)
30.20 Stieglecker, Hermann: *Die Glaubenslehren des Islam.* Paderborn 1962.

1. The Revelation

(a) The Koran

The text of the Koran:

31.01 *Qur'ān karīm (al-Muṣḥaf al-sharīf).* Cairo 1342/1924 (and republished frequently).
The official Cairo edition (prepared by a committee of the theological faculty of the Azhar University) according to the 'reading' (*qirā'a*: pointing and vocalisation) of 'Āṣim ibn Abī 'l-Najūd (d.128/745) in the recension (*riwāya*) of his pupil Ḥafṣ ibn Sulaymān (d.180/796). The text of the Cairo edition and the 'Kufan' (named after the town of Kūfa in Iraq) division of the verses used in it form the basis of all more recent translations and research. The text of Gustav Flügel (Leipzig 1834 and reprints) is still referred to because earlier scholarship quotes according to his division and numbering of the verses. Thus double references are often given: Sūra 3, 180/175 means Sūra 3, verse 180 according to the Cairo edition, verse 175 according to Flügel's.

Indices of words:

31.02 'Abd al-Bāqī, Muḥammad Fu'ād: *al-Mu'jam al-mufahras li-alfāẓ al-Qur'ān al-Karīm.* Cairo 1364/1945 [and reprints].
The Koranic index of 'Abd al-Bāqī gives every word which appears in the Koran (according to the alphabetical order of Arabic roots), with its context, and places where it occurs. It is therefore an excellent tool for tracking down Koranic quotations.

Translations:

31.03 *The Koran interpreted.* By Arthur J[ohn] Arberry. Vol. 1.2. London 1955, ^{3}1971.

31.04 *The Qur'ān.* Translated, with a critical re-arrangement of the Surahs by Richard Bell. Vol. 1.2. Edinburgh 1937-39; repr. 1960.

31.05 *The Meaning of the Glorious Koran.* Explanatory translation by Marmaduke Pickthall. London 1930 [and later editions].

31.06 *Le Coran.* Traduit de l'arabe par Régis Blachère. Paris 1957.

31.07 *Der Koran.* Transl. by Rudi Paret. Stuttgart 1966; [revised ed. in paperback:] 1979; ^{4}1985.

Islamic Koranic exegesis

31.08 Gätje, Helmut: *The Qur'ān and its exegesis* [*Koran und Koran-exegese.* 1971]. Selected texts with classical and modern Muslim interpretations. Transl. from the German and ed. by A. T. Welch. London 1976.
Selected texts in translation.

31.09 Goldziher, Ignaz: *Die Richtungen der islamischen Koranauslegung.* An der Universität Upsala gehaltene Olaus-Petri-Vorlesungen. Leiden 1920. Repr. Leiden 1952. (*Veröffentlichungen der 'De-Goeje-Stiftung',* 6.)

31.10 Baljon, J. M. S.: *Modern Muslim Koran interpretation (1880-1960).* Leiden 1961.

31.11 Jansen, J. J. G.: *The interpretation of the Koran in modern Egypt.* Leiden 1974.

Scholarly introductions and commentaries

31.12 Bell, Richard: *Bell's Introduction to the Qur'ān.* Completely revised and enlarged by W. Montgmery Watt. Edinburgh 1970. (*Islamic Surveys.* 8.)

31.13 Blachère, Régis: *Introduction au Coran.* 2e éd. partiellement refondue. Paris 1959; repr. 1977.

31.14 *Der Koran.* Ed. by Rudi Paret. Darmstadt 1975. (*Wege der Forschung.* Bd. 326.)
Collection of articles surveying modern scholarship on the Koran.

31.15 Nöldeke, Theodor: *Geschichte des Qorāns.*
1: *Über den Ursprung des Qorāns.* Bearb. von Friedrich Schwally. Leipzig 1909.
2: *Die Sammlung des Qorāns.* Völlig umgearb. von Friedrich Schwally. Leipzig 1919.
3: *Die Geschichte des Korantextes.* Von G[otthelf] Bergsträsser und O[tto] Pretzl. Leipzig 1938.
Repr. Hidesheim 1961, 1970.
Still the most comprehensive work on the origin, collection and textual history of the Koran.

31.16 Paret, Rudi: *Der Koran: Kommentar und Konkordanz.* Stuttgart 1971. 2. Aufl. 1977. [Revised ed. in paperback:] ^{3}1986.
Continuous commmentary and concordance of texts with parallel content and language in the Koran.

31.17 Watt, William Montgomery: *Companion to the Qur'ān, based on the Arberry translation.* London 1967.

31.18 Welch, Alfred T.: al-Ḳur'ān. In: *EI*² 5, pp.400-29 (1981). [With:] J. D. Pearson: Translations of the Ḳur'ān, pp.429-32.

A general introduction to the history and theology of the Koranic Revelation is given in the monographs on Muḥammad cited below [31.27-35].

Biblical material in the Koran:

31.19 Masson, D.: *Le Coran et la révélation judéo-chrétienne; études comparées.* 1.2. Paris 1958.

31.20 Speyer, Heinrich: *Die biblischen Erzählungen im Qoran.* Gräfenhainichen 1931. Repr. Darmstadt 1961.

Individual questions:

31.21 Baneth, David Z. H.: What did Muḥammad mean when he called his religion 'Islam'? The original meaning of *aslama* and its derivatives. In: *Israel Oriental Studies.* Tel Aviv. 1. 1971, pp.183-90.

31.22 Gräf, Erwin: Mohammeds Berufung. Eine koranexegetische Studie. In: *Bustan.* Wien. 8. 1967, pp.20-28.

31.22a Neuwirth, Angelika: *Studien zur Komposition der mekkanischen Suren.* Berlin 1981. (*Studien zur Sprache, Geschichte und Kultur des islamischen Orients.* Beihefte zur Zeitschrift 'Der Islam'. N.F. 10.)

31.23 Paret, Rudi: Der Koran als Geschichtsquelle. In: *Der Islam.* Berlin. 37. 1961, pp.24-42 = *Der Koran* [31.14], pp.137-58.

31.23a Wansborough, John: *Quranic studies: sources and methods of scriptural interpretation.* Oxford 1977. (*London Oriental Series.* 31.)

(b) Life and work of the Prophet Muḥammad

31.24 *The life of Muḥammad. A translation of Isḥāq's Sīrat Rasūl Allāh.* With introduction and notes by A[lfred] Guillaume. London 1955.
The classical Arabic biography of the Prophet (*Sīra*) according to the work of Ibn Isḥāq (d.767 or 768), revised by Ibn Hishām (d.828 or 834).

31.25 Sellheim, Rudolf: Prophet, Chalif und Geschichte. In: *Oriens.* Leiden. 18-19. 1965-66, pp.33-91.
About the historical and political background, 'layers' and tendencies of the *Sīra*.

31.26 Rodinson, Maxime: Bilan des études mohammadiennes. In: *Revue historique.* Paris. Ann. 87, t. 229. 1963, pp.169-220.
Excellent bibliographical survey.

31.27 Andrae, Tor: *Muhammed, sein Leben und sein Glaube* [*Muhammed, hans liv och hans tro,* German transl.]. Göttingen 1932; repr. 1977.

31.28 Buhl, Frants: *Das Leben Muhammeds* [*Muhammeds Liv.* 1903, German transl.]. German by Hans Heinrich Schaeder. Leipzig 1930. 2. Aufl. Heidelberg 1955. Repr. Darmstadt 1961.
Full treatment closely linked to the sources.

31.29 Fück, Johann: Die Originalität des arabischen Propheten. In: *Zeitschrift der Deutschen Morgenländischen Gesellschaft.* Leipzig. 90. 1936, pp.509-25 = *Der Koran* [31.14], pp.167-82.
Cf. also Watt: *Muhammad at Mecca* [31.36], pp.72-85.

31.30 Grünebaum, Gustav Edmund von: Von Muhammads Wirkung und Originalität. In: *Wiener Zeitschrift für die Kunde des Morgenlandes.* Wien. 44. 1937, pp.29-50.

31.31 Paret, Rudi: *Mohammed und der Koran. Geschichte und Verkündigung des arabischen Propheten.* Stuttgart 1957; [6]1985. (*Urban Taschenbücher.* 32.)
The best short introduction.

31.32 Rodinson, Maxime: *Mahomet.* Paris 1961; [2]1968. – [English version:] *Mohammed.* London 1971.

31.32a Serjeant, Robert Bertram: The *Sunnah Jāmi'ah*, pacts with the Yathrib Jews and the *Taḥrīm* of Yathrib: analysis and translation of the documents comprised in the so-called 'Constitution of Medina'. In: *Bulletin of the School of Oriental and African Studies.* London. 41. 1978, pp.1-42.

31.33 Wensinck, Arent Jan: *Muhammed and the Jews of Medina (Mohammed en de Joden te Medina.* Leiden 1908 [English transl.]). With an excursus: *Muhammed's Constitution of Medina (Muhammads Gemeindeordnung von Medina.* 1889 [English transl.]) by Julius Wellhausen. Transl. and ed. by Wolfgang Behn. Freiburg i.Br. 1975. (*Islamkundliche Materialien.* Bd. 5.)

31.34 Watt, William Montgomery: *Muhammad at Mecca.* Oxford 1953 [and other editions]. *Muhammad at Medina.* Oxford 1956 [and other editions].
Standard works of recent research on Muḥammad.
A shorter account in one volume is:

31.35 Watt, W. M.: *Muḥammad, prophet and statesman.* Oxford 1961.

31.35a Watt, W. M.: *Muḥammad's Mecca: Quaranic studies.* Edinburgh 1988.

2. *The development of religious doctrine*

See also [30.01-20].

(a) The Islamic religion and Islamic history

32.01 Arkoun, Mohammed: Introduction à la pensée islamique classique. In: *Cahiers d'histoire mondiale.* 11. 1968-69, pp.578-614 = Arkoun: *Essais sur la pensée islamique.* Paris 1973, pp.13-49.

32.02 —: *La pensée arabe.* Paris 1975; [2]1979 (*Que sais-je?* 915.)

32.03 Becker, Carl Heinrich: Der Islam als Problem. In: *Der Islam.* Straßburg. 1. 1910, pp.1-21 = Becker: *Islamstudien* [14.17], 1, pp.1-23.

32.04 *L'Élaboration de l'Islam.* Colloque de Strasbourg, 12-13-14 juin 1959. Paris 1961.

—— Gibb, Hamilton Alexander Roskeen: *An interpretation of Islamic history.* 1953 [14.07].

32.05 —: Structure of religious thought in Islam. In: *The Muslim World.* Hartford, Conn. 38. 1948, pp.17-28, 113-23, 185-97, 280-91 = Gibb: *Studies* [14.19], pp.176-218.

32.06 Goitein, Shlomo Dov: The four faces of Islam. In: Goitein: *Studies in Islamic history and institutions.* 1966. [14.20], pp.3-53.

32.07 *Scholars, Saints and Sufis. Muslim religious institutions in the Middle East since 1500.* Ed. by Nikki R. Keddie. Berkeley, Los Angeles, London 1972.

—— Watt, William Montgomery: *Islam and the integration of society.* 1961 [30.16].

—— —: *Islamic philosophy and theology.* 1962; revised ed. 1985 [32.40].

(b) Civil war and schism

32.08 Laoust, Henri: *Les schismes dans l'Islam. Introduction à une étude de la religion musulmane.* Paris 1965.

32.09 Strothmann, Rudolf: Schiiten und Charidschiten. In: *Handbuch der Orientalistik.* Abt. 1. Bd. 8: *Religion.* Abschnitt 2: *Religionsgeschichte des Orients in der Zeit der Weltreligionen.* Leiden, Köln 1961, pp.476-95.

—— Watt, William Montgomery: *The formative period of Islamic thought.* 1973 [30.15].

32.10 Wellhausen, Julius: *Die religiös-politischen Oppositionsparteien im alten Islam.* Berlin 1901. (*Abh. d. Kgl. Gesellschaft d. Wissenschaften zu Göttingen. Philosophisch-historische Klasse.* N.F. Bd. 5, 2.)
1, pp.3-55: Die Chavârig. 2, pp.55-99: Die Schîa.

The Shīʿa

32.11 Corbin, Henry: *En Islam iranien. Aspects spirituels et philosophiques.* T. 1-4. Paris 1971-72. (*Bibliothèque des Idées.*)
T. 1: Le shīʿisme duodécimain.
T. 2: Sohrawardī et les platoniciens de Perse.
T. 3: Les Fidèles d'amour. Shīʿisme et soufisme.
T. 4: L'école d'Ispahan. L'école Shaykhie. Le Douzième Imām.

32.12 Donaldson, Dwight M.: *The Shiʿite religion: a history of Islam in Persia and Irak.* London 1933.

32.13 Fischer, Michael M. J.: *Iran: from religious dispute to revolution.* Cambridge, Mass. 1980. (*Harvard Studies in Cultural Anthropology.* 3.)

32.14 Madelung, Wilferd: *Der Imam al-Qāsim ibn Ibrāhīm und die Glaubenslehre der Zaiditen.* Berlin 1965. (*Studien zur Sprache, Geschichte und Kultur des islamischen Orients.* Beihefte zur Zeitschrift *'Der Islam'.* N.F. Bd. 1.)

32.15 *Le Shīʿisme imāmite.* Colloque de Strasbourg, 6-9 mai 1968. Paris 1970.

32.16 Strothmann, Rudolf: *Die Zwölfer-Schīʿa.* Leipzig 1926.

—— —: *Schiiten und Charidschiten.* 1961 [32.09].

The Ismāʿīliyya

32.17 Ivanow, Wladimir: *Ismaili literature: a bibliographical survey.* Second ed. of: *A guide to Ismaili literature,* 1933. Tehran 1963. (*The Ismaili Society.* Series A. 15.)

32.18 Poonawala, Ismail K.: *Bibliography of Ismāʿīlī literature.* Malibu, Cal. 1977. (*Studies in Near Eastern Culture and Society.*)

32.18a Halm, Heinz: *Die islamische Gnosis. Die extreme Schia und die ʿAlawiten.* Zürich, München 1982. (Die Bibliothek des Morgenlandes.)
Texts of the Ismāʿīliyya and other sects of the 'extremist' Shīʿa (*ghulāt*), translated with introductions and commentaries.

32.19 Lewis, Bernard: The Ismāʿīlites and the Assassins. In: *A History of the Crusades.* 1955-77 [65.20]. 1, pp.99-132.

32.20 —: *The origins of Ismāʿīlism. A study of the historical background of the Fāṭimide Caliphate.* Cambridge 1940.

32.21 Madelung, Wilferd: Fatimiden und Baḥrainqarmaṭen. In: *Der Islam.* Berlin. 34. 1959, pp.34-88.

32.22 —: Das Imamat in der frühen ismailitischen Lehre. In: *Der Islam.* Berlin. 37. 1961, pp.43-135.

32.23 Stern, Samuel Miklos: *Studies in early Ismailism.* Jerusalem, Leiden. 1983. (*Max Schloessinger Memorial Series.* Monographs. 1.)

32.24 Hodgson, Marshall Goodwin Simms: The Ismāʿīlī state. In: *The Cambridge History of Iran.* 5. 1968 [65.05], pp.422-83.

32.25 —: *The order of Assassins. The struggle of the early Nizārī Ismāʿīlīs against the Islamic world.* 's-Gravenhage 1955.

32.26 Lewis, Bernhard: *The Assassins: a radical sect in Islam.* London 1967.

32.27 Sacy, Silvestre de: *Exposé de la religion des Druzes.* 1.2. Paris 1838. Repr. Paris 1964.

32.28 Bryer, David R. W.: The origins of the Druze religion. In: *Der Islam.* Berlin. 52, 1975, pp.47-84, 239-62; 53. 1976, pp.5-28.

(c) Dogma

32.29 Allard, Michel: *Le problème des attributs divins dans la doctrine d'al-Ašʿarī et de ses premiers grands disciples.* Beyrouth 1965. (*Recherches publiées sous la direction de l'Institut de lettres orientales de Beyrouth.* T. 28.)

32.30 Arberry, Arthur John: *Revelation and reason in Islam.* London 1957; ³1971.

32.31 Ess, Josef van: *Die Erkenntnislehre des ʿAḍudaddīn al-Īcī. Übersetzung und Kommentar des ersten Buches seiner Mawāqif.* Wiesbaden 1966. (Akademie der Wissenschaften und der Literatur. *Veröffentlichungen der Orientalischen Kommission.* Bd. 22.)

32.32 —: The logical structure of Islamic theology. In: *Logic in classical Islamic culture,* ed. by G. E. von Grunebaum. Wiesbaden 1970 (First Levi Della Vida Biennial Conference, 1967), pp.21-50.

32.33 —: *Zwischen Ḥadīṯ und Theologie. Studien zum Entstehen prädestinatianischer Überlieferung.* Berlin 1975. (*Studien zur Sprache, Geschichte und Kultur des islamischen Orients.* N.F. Bd. 7.)

32.34 Gardet, Louis: *Dieu et la destinée de l'homme.* Paris 1967. (G.-C. Anawati et L. Gardet: *Les grands problèmes de la théologie musulmane. Essai de théologie comparée. Études musulmanes.* 9.)

32.35 Gardet, Louis; Anawati, M.-M. [Georges C.]: *Introduction à la théologie musulmane. Essai de théologie comparée.* Paris 1948. (*Études de philosophie médiévale.* 37.)

32.36 Laoust, Henri: *La profession de foi d'Ibn Baṭṭa.* Damas 1958.

32.37 Makdisi, George: Ashʿarī and the Ashʿarites in Islamic religious history. In: *Studia Islamica.* Paris. 17. 1962, pp.37-80; 18. 1963, pp.19-39.

32.38 Patton, Walter Melville: *Aḥmed ibn Ḥanbal and the Miḥna. A biography of the Imām including an account of the Moḥammedan inquisition called the Miḥna, 218-234 A.H.* Leiden 1897.

32.39 Schaeder, Hans Heinrich: Ḥasan al-Baṣrī. In: *Der Islam.* Berlin. 14. 1925, pp.1-75.
On Ḥasan of Baṣra see also Ritter [32.56].

32.40 Watt, William Montgomery: *Islamic philosophy and theology.* Edinburgh 1962. 2nd ed. 1985; paper, 1987. (*Islamic Surveys.* 1.)

—— —: *The formative period of Islamic thought.* 1973 [30.15].
32.41 Wensinck, Arent Jan: *The Muslim creed; its genesis and historical development.* Cambridge 1932. Repr. London 1965.
32.42 Wolfson, Harry Austryn: *The philosophy of the Kalam.* Cambridge, Mass.; London 1976.

(d) Asceticism, mysticism and the Ṣūfī orders

32.43 Anawati, Georges C.; Gardet, Louis: *Mystique musulmane. Aspects et tendances – expériences et techniques.* Paris 1961; ³1976. (*Études musulmanes.* 8.)
32.44 Andrae, Tor: *Islamische Mystiker [I myrtenträdgarden. Studier i sufisk mystik.* 1947]. Stuttgart 1960. (*Urban-Bücher.* 46.)
32.44a Arberry, A. J.: *Sūfism.* London 1950.
32.45 Birge, John Kingsley: *The Bektashi order of dervishes.* London; Hartford, Conn. 1937.
32.46 Drague, G.: *Esquisse d'histoire religieuse du Maroc: confréries et zaouïas.* Paris 1951.
32.47 Ess, Josef van: *Die Gedankenwelt des Ḥāriṯ al-Muḥāsibī, anhand von Übersetzungen aus seinen Schriften dargestellt und erläutert.* Bonn 1961. (*Bonner Orientalistische Studien.* N.S. Bd. 12.)
32.48 Gellner, Ernest: *Saints of the Atlas.* London 1969.
32.49 Goldziher, Ignaz: Heiligenverehrung im Islam. In: Goldziher: *Muhammedanische Studien.* 1889-90 [30.02]. 2, pp.277-378.
32.50 Gramlich, Richard: *Die schiitischen Derwischorden Persiens.* T. 1-3. Wiesbaden 1965-80. (*Abhandlungen für die Kunde des Morgenlandes.* Bd. 36, 1.2. 45,2.)
1: Die Affiliationen. 1965.
2: Glaube und Lehre. 1976.
3: Brauchtum und Riten. 1980.
32.51 Jong, Fred de: *Ṭuruq and ṭuruq-linked institutions in nineteenth-century Egypt. A historical study in organisational dimensions of Islamic mysticism.* Leiden 1978.
32.52 Massignon, Louis: *The passion of al-Ḥallāj, mystic and martyr of Islam [La passion de Husayn ibn Mansûr Ḥallâj.* 1922, ²1975]. Transl. from the French by H. Mason. Vol. 1-4. Princeton, NJ 1982.
1: The life of al-Ḥallāj.
2: The survival of al-Ḥallāj.
3: The teaching of al-Ḥallāj.
4: Bibliography and index.
32.53 Meier, Fritz: The mystic path. In: *Islam and the Arab world.* Ed. by B. Lewis. 1976 [14.26], pp.117-40.
32.54 Nicholson, Reynold Alleyne: *The mystics of Islam.* London 1914. Repr. Beirut 1966; London 1981.
32.55 Ritter, Hellmut: *Das Meer der Seele. Mensch, Welt und Gott in den Geschichten des Farīduddīn 'Aṭṭār.* Leiden 1955; ²1978.
32.56 —: Studien zur Geschichte der islamischen Frömmigkeit. 1: Ḥaṣan al-Baṣrī. In: *Der Islam.* Berlin. 21. 1933, pp.1-83.
32.57 Rosenthal, Franz: 'I am you' – individual piety and society in Islam. In: *Individualism and conformity in classical Islam.* Wiesbaden 1977 (Fifth Giorgio Levi Della Vida Biennial Conference, 1975), pp.33-60.
32.58 Schimmel, Annemarie: *Al-Halladsch, Märtyrer der Gottesliebe.*

Leben und Legende. Ausgewählt, übersetzt und eingeleitet. Köln 1968.

32.59 —: *Mystical dimensions of Islam.* Chapel Hill 1975.

32.60 Smith, Margaret: *Studies in early mysticism in the Near and Middle East.* London 1931.

32.61 Trimingham, J. Spencer: *The Sufi orders in Islam.* Oxford 1971.

32.62 Watt, William Montgomery: *Muslim intellectual: the struggle and achievement of al-Ghazali.* Edinburgh 1963.

3. Law and state

Introductions to Islamic law (fiqh)

33.01 Brunschvig, Robert: *Études d'Islamologie. T. 2: Droit musulman.* Paris 1976.

33.02 *Law in the Middle East.* Ed. by Majid Khadduri and J. Liebesny. Vol. 1. *Origin and development of Islamic Law.* Washington 1955.

33.03 *Orientalisches Recht.* Leiden, Köln 1964. (*Handbuch der Orientalistik.* Abt. 1, Erg.-Bd. 3.)
Contains contributions on Islamic law in Syria, Lebanon, Egypt, Tunisia, Algeria, Morocco and Turkey.

33.04 Spies, Otto; Pritsch, Ernst: Klassisches islamisches Recht. In: *Orientalisches Recht.* 1964 [33.03], pp.220-343.
Bibliographical introduction.

33.05 Schacht, Joseph: *An introduction to Islamic law.* Oxford 1964.
With comprehensive bibliography.

33.06 *Theology and Law in Islam.* Ed. by G. E. von Grunebaum. Wiesbaden 1971. (Second Giorgio Levi Della Vida Biennial Conference, 1969.)

Tradition literature (ḥadīth)

33.07 Brunschvig, Robert: Ibn 'Abdalh' akam et la conquête de l'Afrique du Nord par les Arabes. In: *Annales de l'Institut d'Études orientales.* Alger. 6. 1942-74, pp.108-55.
Early historical tradition serving legal purposes.

33.08 Goldziher, Ignaz: On the development of the Ḥadīth (1890). In: Goldziher: *Muslim Studies.* London 1971 [30.02], Vol. 2, pp.17-251.
A fundamental study. An opposing position is adopted by Sezgin: *GAS* [13.10], Vol. 1. 1967 (authentic, written scholarly transmission from the generation of the Prophet's Companions).

33.09 Juynboll, Gualterus H. A.: *Muslim tradition; studies in chronology, provenance and authorship of early ḥadīth.* Cambridge [etc.] 1983.

33.10 Schacht, Joseph: A revaluation of Islamic tradition. In: *Journal of the Royal Asiatic Society.* London 1949, pp.143-54.

33.11 Ṣiddīqī, Muḥammad Zubayr: *Ḥadīth literature. Its origin, development, special features and criticism.* Calcutta 1961.

33.12 Wensinck, Arent Jan: *A handbook of early Muhammadan tradition, alphabetically arranged.* Leiden 1927; repr. 1971.
Alphabetical subject register of the most important Arabic collections of *ḥadīth*, from the ninth century.

The development of the schools and methods of Islamic law

33.13 Brunschvig, Robert: Considérations sociologiques sur le droit musulman ancien. In: *Studia Islamica.* Paris. 3. 1955, pp.61-73.

33.14 —: Logic and law in classical Islam. In: *Logic in Classical Islamic*

Culture. Ed. by G. E. von Grunebaum. Wiesbaden 1970 (First Giorgio Levi Della Vida Biennial Conference, 1967), pp.9-20.

33.15 —: Polémiques médiévales autour du rite de Mālik. In: *Al-Andalus* 15, 1950, pp.377-435. Repr. in Brunschvig [33.01].
The concept of *Sunna / 'amal* of Mālik b. Anas in the criticism of al-Shāfi'ī and others.

33.16 Fazlur Rahman: *Islamic methodology in history*. Karachi 1965. (*Publications of the Central Institute of Islamic Research*, Nr. 2.)

33.17 Goldziher, Ignaz: *Die Ẓāhiriten. Ihr Lehrsystem und ihre Geschichte. Beitrag zur Geschichte der Muhammedanischen Theologie*. Leipzig 1884.

33.18 Gräf, Erwin: Vom Wesen und Werden des islamischen Rechts. In: *Bustan*. Wien. Heft 2. 1960, pp.10-21.

33.19a Laoust, Henri: *Essai sur les doctrines sociales et politiques de Taḳī-d-Dīn Aḥmad b. Taimīya*. Le Caire 1939.

33.19b —: *Contribution à une étude de la méthodologie canonique de ... Ibn Taimīya*. Le Caire 1939.

33.20 Makdisi, George: *Ibn 'Aqīl et la résurgence de l'Islam traditionaliste au XIe siècle (Ve siècle de l'Hégire)*. Damas 1963.

33.21 —: L'Islam hanbalisant. In: *Revue des études islamiques*. Paris. 42. 1974, pp.211-44; 43. 1975, pp.45-76.

33.22 —: The Sunni revival. In: *Islamic civilization, A.D. 950-1150*. Oxford 1973. (*Papers on Islamic History*. 3.), pp.155-68.

33.23 —: The juridical theology of Shâfi'î; origins and significance of uṣûl al-fiqh. In: *Studia Islamica* 59. 1984, pp.5-47.

—— Patton, W. M.: *Aḥmed ibn Ḥanbal*. Leiden 1897 [32.38].

33.24 Rentz, George: The Wahhābīs. In: *Religion in the Middle East*. 2. 1969 [30.05], pp.270-84.
Cf. also Laoust: *Essai* [33.19a], pp.506-40: 'Ibn Taimīya et la théocratie wahhābite'; Hartmann [68.17].

33.25 Schacht, Joseph: *The origins of Muhammadan jurisprudence*. Oxford 1950.

33.26 —: Zur soziologischen Betrachtung des islamischen Rechts. In: *Der Islam*. Berlin. 22. 1935, pp.207-38.

33.27 Tyan, Émile: Méthodologie et sources du droit en Islam (Istiḥsān, Istiṣlāḥ, Siyāsa šar'iyya). In: *Studia Islamica*. Paris. 10. 1959, pp.79-109.

Institutions and methods of scholarly transmission

See also art. 'Madrasa' and 'Masdjid' in *EI*[1] and *EI*[2].

33.28 Halm, Heinz: Die Anfänge der Madrasa. In: *XIX. Deutscher Orientalistentag, 28. 9.-4. 10. 1975 in Freiburg. Vorträge*. Wiesbaden 1977 (*ZDMG. Suppl. III*), pp.438-48.

33.29 Gilbert, Joan Elizabeth: Institutionalization of Muslim scholarship and professionalization of the 'ulamā' in medieval Damascus. In: *Studia Islamica*. Paris. 52. 1980, pp.105-34.

33.30 Makdisi, George: Law and traditionalism in the institutions of learning of medieval Islam. In: *Theology and law in Islam*. 1971 [33.06], pp.75-88.

33.31 —: *The rise of colleges. Institutions of learning in Islam and the West*. Edinburgh 1982.

33.32 —: Muslim institutions of learning in eleventh-century Baghdad. In:

Bulletin of the School of Oriental and African Studies. London. 24. 1961, pp.1-56.

33.33 Rosenthal, Franz: *The technique and approach of Muslim scholarship.* Roma 1947. (*Analecta Orientalia. 24.*)

33.34 Sourdel-Thomine, Janine: Locaux d'enseignement et madrasas dans l'Islam médiéval. In: *Revue des études islamiques.* Paris. 44. 1976, pp.185-97.

33.35 Sourdel, Dominique: Réflections sur la diffusion de la madrasa en Orient du XIe au XIIIe siècle. In: *Revue des études islamiques.* Paris. 44. 1976, pp.165-84.

Handbooks of the legal schools

33.36 Bergsträsser, Gotthelf: *Bergsträsser's Grundzüge des islamischen Rechts.* Bearb. und hrsg. v. Joseph Schacht. Berlin and Leipzig 1935.

33.37 Bousquet, Georges-Henri [transl.:] *Khalîl ben Ish'âq. Abrégé de la loi musulmane selon le rite de l'Imâm Mâlek.* 1-4. Paris 1956-62.
1: Le rituel. 2: Le Statut personnel. 3: Le patrimoine. 4: Judicature, droit pénal, affranchissements, statut successoral.

33.38 —: *Précis élémentaire de droit musulman mâlékite et algérien.* Alger 1935. 3e éd. [as]: *Précis de droit musulman, principalement mâlékite et algérien.* Alger 1960.

33.39 Fyzee, Asaf Ali Asghar: *Outlines of Muhammadan law.* New Delhi, London 1949, ^{4}1974.

33.40 Juynboll, Theodor Willem: *Handbuch des islamischen Gesetzes nach der Lehre der schafi'itischen Schule nebst einer allgemeinen Einleitung.* Leiden, Leipzig 1910.

33.41 Linant de Bellefonds, Yves: *Traité de droit musulman comparé.* 1ff. Paris, La Haye 1965ff. (1-3: 1965-73). (*Études méditerranées.* 6.9.)

33.42 Sachau, Eduard: *Muhammedanisches Recht nach schafi'itischer Lehre.* Berlin 1895. (*Lehrbücher des Seminars für Orientalische Sprachen.* Bd. 17.)

33.43 Santillana, David: *Istituzioni di diritto musulmano malichita con riguardo anche al sistema sciafiita.* 1.2. Roma 1926-38.

Shī'ite law

33.44 Fyzee, Asaf Ali Asghar: Shī'ī legal theories. In: *Law in the Middle East.* Vol. 1. Ed. by Majid Khadduri and H. J. Liebesny. Washington 1955, pp.113-31.

33.45 Löschner, Harald: *Die dogmatischen Grundlagen des šī'itischen Rechts. Eine Untersuchung zur modernen imāmitischen Rechtsquellenlehre.* Köln [etc.] 1971. (*Erlanger Juristische Abhandlungen.* Bd. 9.)

33.46 Strothmann, Rudolf: Recht der Ismailiten. In: *Der Islam.* Berlin. 31. 1953, pp.131-46.

On Shī'ite law, cf. contributions by R. Brunschvig and Y. Linant de Bellefonds in: *Le Shī'isme imāmite.* 1970 [32.15].

Jurisdiction and administration of justice

33.47 Brunschvig, Robert: Le système de la preuve en droit musulman. In: *Recueils de la Société Jean Bodin.* Bruxelles. 18. 1964, pp.169-86.

33.48 Gräf, Erwin: Gerichtsverfassung und Gerichtsbarkeit im islamischen

Recht. In: *Zeitschrift für Vergleichende Rechtswissenschaft.* 58. 1955, pp.48-78.
33.49 Schimmel, Annemarie: Kalif und Kadi im spätmittelalterlichen Ägypten. In: *Welt des Islam.* 24. 1942, pp.1-128.
33.50 Tyan, Émile: *Histoire de l'organisation judicaire en pays d'Islam.* 2è éd. revue et corrigée. Leiden 1960.
33.51 —: Juridical organisation. In: *Law in the Middle East.* 1955 [33.02], pp.28-56.
33.52 —: *Le notariat et le régime de la preuve par écrit dans la pratique du droit musulman.* Beyrouth 1945; ^{2}1959. (*Annales de la Faculté de droit et des sciences économiques de Beyrouth.*)
33.53 Cahen, Claude [et al.]: Ḥisba. In: *EI*^{2}. 3, s. v. (1967).
Cf. also [44.31-2] on supervision of markets.

Religious duties and ritual

33.54 Bousquet, Georges-Henri: *Les grandes pratiques rituelles de l'Islam.* Paris 1949. (*Mythes et religions.* 24.)
33.55 Gaudefroy-Demombynes, Maurice: *Le pèlerinage à la Mekke. Étude d'histoire religieuse.* Paris 1923.
See also Snouck Hurgronje, C.: *Het Mekkaansche Feest.* 1880 [61.23]; art. Ḥadjdj in *EI*^{2}. 3. 1965 (A. J. Wensinck et al.).
33.56 Grunebaum, Gustav Edmund von: *Muhammadan festivals.* New York 1957. 2nd ed.: Introd. by C. E. Bosworth. London 1976.
33.57 Haarmann, Ulrich: Die Pflichten des Muslims – Dogma und geschichtliche Wirklichkeit. In: *Saeculum.* Freiburg and München. 26. 1975, pp.75-110.
33.58 Lech, Klaus: *Geschichte des islamischen Kultus. Rechtshistorische und ḥadīṯ-kritische Untersuchungen zur Entwicklung und Systematik der ʿibādāt.* Bd. 1: *Das ramaḍān-Fasten.* T. 1. Wiesbaden 1979.

The Islamic state

33.59 Cahen, Claude: The Body Politic. In: *Unity and Variety in Muslim Civilization.* 1955 [14.33], pp.34-46.
33.59a Crone, Patricia: *Slaves on horses: the evolution of the Islamic polity.* Cambridge 1980.
33.59b Crone, Patricia; Hinds, Martin: *God's Caliph: religious authority in the first centuries of Islam.* Cambridge 1986.
33.59c Donner, Fred M.: The formation of the Islamic state. In: *Journal of the American Oriental Society.* New Haven. 106. 1986, pp.283-96.
33.60 Gardet, Louis: *La cité musulmane: vie sociale et politique.* Paris 1954; 4e éd., augmentée d'une préface. 1976 (*Études musulmanes.* 1.)
33.61 Gibb, Hamilton Alexander Roskeen: The evolution of government in early Islam. (1953.) In: Gibb: *Studies* [14.19], pp.1-17.
33.62 —: Government and Islam under the early ʿAbbasids: the political collapse of Islam. In: *L'Élaboration de l'Islam.* Paris 1961, pp.115-27.
33.63 —: Some considerations on the Sunni theory of the caliphate. (1939.) In: Gibb: *Studies* [14.19], pp.141-50.
33.64 —: Al-Māwardī's theory of the caliphate. (1937.) In: Gibb: *Studies* [14.19], pp.151-65.
33.65 Goitein, Shlomo Dov: The origin of the vizierate and its true character. In: *Islamic Culture.* Hyderabad. 16. 1942, pp.255-62,

380-92; Appendix in: *Journal of the American Oriental Society*. 81. 1961, pp.425-6 = Goitein: *Studies* [14.20], pp.168-96.
33.66 —: A turning-point in the history of the Muslim state. (Apropos of the Kitāb al-Ṣaḥāba of Ibn al-Muqaffaʿ.) In: *Islamic Culture*. Hyderabad. 23. 1949, pp.120-35 = Goitein: *Studies* [14.20], pp.149-67.
33.67 Lambton, Ann Katherine Swynford: Quis custodiet custodes: some reflections on the Persian theory of government. In: *Studia Islamica*. Paris. 5. 1956, pp.125-48.
33.68 —: *State and government in medieval Islam. An introduction to the study of Islamic political theory: the jurists*. London 1981. (*London Oriental Series*. 36)
33.69 Laoust, Henri: La pensée et l'action politiques d'al-Māwardī 364-450/974-1068. In: *Revue des études islamiques*. 36. 1968, pp.11-92.
33.70 —: *La politique de Ġazālī*. Paris 1970. (*Bibliothèque d'études islamiques*.)
33.71a Nagel, Tilman: *Rechtleitung und Kalifat. Versuch über eine Grundfrage der islamischen Geschichte*. Bonn 1975. (*Studien zum Minderheitenproblem im Islam. 2 = Bonner Orientalistische Studien*. 27, 2.)
33.71b —: *Staat und Glaubensgemeinschaft im Islam. Geschichte der politischen Ordnungsvorstellungen der Muslime*. Bd. 1.2. Zürich, München 1981.
33.72 Makdisi, George: Les rapports entre Calife et Sulṭân à l'époque Saljûqide. In: *International Journal of Middle East Studies*. London. 6. 1975, pp.228-36.
33.73 Pritsch, Emil: Die islamische Staatsidee. In: *Zeitschrift für vergleichende Rechtswissenschaft*. 53. 1939, pp.33-72.
33.74 Rosenthal, Erwin I. J.: *Political thought in medieval Islam. An introductory outline*. Cambridge 1958, ²1968.
33.75 Sourdel, Dominique [et al.]: Khalīfa. In: *EI²*. 4, s. v. (1977).
33.76 Tyan, Emile: *Institutions du droit public musulman*. 1: *Le Califat*. 2: *Sultanat et Califat*. Beyrouth 1954-56.
See also A. Fattal: *Le statut des non-musulmans en pays d'Islam*. 1958 [42.02].

Ibn Khaldūn and his theory of social organisation:
33.77 *The Muqaddimah. An introduction to history*. By Ibn Khaldûn. Translated from the Arabic by Franz Rosenthal. Vol. 1-3. London, New York 1958; ²1967. (*Bollingen Series*. 43).
33.78 Gibb, Hamilton Alexander Roskeen: The Islamic background of Ibn Khaldun's political theory (1933). In: Gibb: *Studies* [14.19], pp.166-75.
33.79 Mahdi, Muhsin: *Ibn Khaldūn's philosophy of history; a study in the philosophic foundation of the Science of Culture*. London 1957.
33.80 Sivers, Peter von: *Khalifat, Königtum und Verfall. Die politische Theorie Ibn Khaldūns*. München 1968. (*Schriftenreihe zur Politik und Geschichte*. Hrsg. v. Eric Voegelin.)

Administration:
33.81 Ben Sheneb, Aharon: *Taxation in Islam*. Vol. 1-3. Leiden 1965-69.
Texts of the early ʿAbbāsid period in translation, with thorough introductions.

For further literature on taxation, cf. Chapter IV [43.01-10].
33.82 Duri, Abdalaziz [et al.]: Dīwān. In: *EI²*. 2, s. v. (1962).
33.83 Puin, Gerd-Rüdiger: *Der Dīwān von ʿUmar ibn al-Ḫaṭṭāb. Ein Beitrag zur frühislamischen Verwaltungsgeschichte.* Bonn 1969.
On the Ottoman law of government and administration see Gibb, H. A. R.; Bowen, H.: *Islamic society and the West.* 1950-57 [40.13]; Röhrborn, K.: *Untersuchungen zur osmanischen Verwaltungsgeschichte.* 1972 [67.18].

Islamic law and government in modern times

Cf. also [68.01-15].
33.84 Anderson, James N. D.: *Islamic law in the modern world.* New York 1959; repr. Westport 1975.
33.85 Berkes, Niyazi: *The development of secularism in Turkey.* Montreal 1964.
33.86 Bonderman, David: Modernization and changing perceptions of Islamic law. In: *Harvard Law Review.* 81. 1968, pp.1169-93.
33.87 Bousquet, Georges-Henri: *Du droit musulman et de son application effective dans le monde.* Alger 1949. (*Bibl. de l'Institut d'Études supérieures islamiques d'Alger.* 1.)
33.88 Gibb, Hamilton Alexander Roskeen: *Modern trends in Islam.* Chicago 1947.
33.89 Kerr, Malcolm H.: *Islamic reform. The political and legal theories of Muḥammad ʿAbduh and Rashīd Riḍā.* Berkeley, Los Angeles 1966.
33.90 Merad, Ali; Algar, Hamid; Berkes, Niyazi; Ahmad, Aziz: Iṣlāḥ (reform, reformism). In: *EI²*. 4, s. v. (1973).
33.91 Peters, Rudolph: *Islam and colonialism. The doctrine of Jihad in modern history.* The Hague [etc.] 1979. (*Religion and Society.* 20.)
33.92 Rosenthal, Erwin I. J.: *Islam in the modern national state.* Cambridge 1965.
33.93 Schacht, Joseph: Islamic law in contemporary states. In: *American Journal of Comparative Law.* 8. 1959, pp.133-47.
33.94 —: Problems of modern Islamic legislation. In: *Studia Islamica.* Paris. 12. 1960, pp.99-129.
33.95 Smith, Wilfred Cantwell: *Islam in modern history.* Princeton, NJ 1977.
33.96 Tibi, Bassam: *Die Krise des modernen Islam. Eine vorindustrielle Kultur im wissenschaftlich-technischen Zeitalter.* München 1981. (*Beck'sche Schwarze Reihe.* Bd. 228.)
33.96a Tibi, Bassam: *Nationalismus in der Dritten Welt am arabischen Beispiel.* Frankfurt a.M. 1971.
English transl.: *Arab nationalism; a critical enquiry.* Ed. by Marion Farouk-Sluglett and Peter Sluglett. London 1981.
33.97 Vatikiotis, Panayiotis J.: *Islam and the nation-state.* London 1983.

IV. The Islamic World

Cultural geography: landscape and history

40.01 Bobek, Hans: Die Hauptstufen der Gesellschafts- und Wirtschaftsentfaltung in geographischer Sicht. In: *Die Erde.* 90. 1959, pp.259-98.
40.02 Coon, Carleton Stevens: *Caravan: the story of the Middle East.* New York 1951.

40.03 Planhol, Xavier de: *Les fondements géographiques de l'histoire musulmane.* Paris 1968.
—— Miquel, André: *La géographie humaine du monde musulman.* 1967-80 [15.71]. *3: Le milieu naturel.* 1980.

Social and economic history of the Islamic world

40.04 Ahsan, M. Manazir: *Social life under the Abbasids, 170-289 A.H./ 786-902 A.D.* London, New York, Beirut 1979. *(Arab Background Series.)*
40.05 Ayalon, David: On the eunuchs in Islam. In: *Jerusalem Studies in Arabic and Islam.* Jerusalem. 1. 1979, pp.67-124.
40.06 Baer, Gabriel: *Studies in the social history of modern Egypt.* Chicago, London 1969. (*Publications of the Center for Middle Eastern Studies.* 6).
40.07 Cahen, Claude: L'histoire économique et sociale de l'Orient médiéval. In: *Studia Islamica.* Paris. 3. 1955, pp.93-115.
40.08 —: Economy, society, institutions. In: *The Cambridge History of Islam.* 1970 [14.03]. Vol. 2, pp.511-38.
See also Cahen: *L'Islam.* 1970 [14.02], ch.8.
40.08a —: *Les peuples musulmans dans l'histoire médiévale.* Damas 1977. Collected articles.
40.09 *Colloque sur la sociologie musulmane, 11-14 septembre 1961. Actes.* Bruxelles 1962. (*Correspondence d'Orient.* 5.)
40.10 Dols, Michael W.: *The Black Death in the Middle East.* Princeton, NJ 1976.
40.11 Duri, Abdalaziz: Arabische Wirtschaftsgeschichte (*Muqaddima fī l-tārīkh al-iqtiṣādī al-'arabī.* 1969). *Aus dem Arabischen übersetzt von Jürgen Jacobi.* Zürich and München 1979. (*Die Bibliothek des Morgenlandes.*)
40.12 Gellner, Ernest: *Muslim society. A sociological interpretation.* Cambridge 1981. (*Cambridge Studies in Social Anthropology.* 32.)
40.13 Gibb, Hamilton Alexander Roskeen; Bowen, Harold: *Islamic society and the West. A study of the impact of Western civilization on Moslem culture in the Near East.* Vol. 1: *Islamic society in the eighteenth century.* Part 1.2. Oxford 1950-57; repr. 1969.
40.14 Guichard, Pierre: *Structures sociales 'orientales' et 'occidentales' dans l'Espagne musulmane.* Paris, La Haye 1977. (*École des Hautes études en sciences sociales. Centre de recherches historiques. Civilizations et sociétés.* 60.) – Cf. [54.06].
40.15 Hershlag, Zvi Yehuda: *Introduction to the modern economic history of the Middle East.* Leiden 1964.
40.16 *Individualism and Conformity in Classical Islam.* Ed. by A. Banani and S. Vryonis. Wiesbaden 1977 (*Fifth Giorgio Levi Della Vida Biennial Conference, 1975.*)
40.17 *The Islamic Middle East, 700-1900; studies in economic and social history.* Ed. by A. L. Udovitch. Princeton, NJ 1981.
40.18 Issawi, Charles [ed.]: *The economic history of the Middle East, 1800-1914. A book of readings.* Chicago, London 1966.
40.19 Lewis, Bernard: Sources for the economic history of the Middle East. In: *Studies in the economic history of the Middle East.* 1970 [40.26], pp.78-92 = *Wirtschaftsgeschichte des Vorderen Orients in islamischer Zeit.* 1. 1977 [40.27], pp.1-17.

40.20 Mez, Adam: *The renaissance of Islam [Die Renaissance des Islâms. 1922]*. Transl. by Salahuddin Khuda Bakhsh and D[avid] S[amuel] Margoliouth. London 1937; repr. 1987.

40.21 *The Middle Eastern economy. Studies in economics and economic history.* Ed. by Elie Kedourie. London 1977.

40.22 Owen, Roger: *The Middle East in the World Economy, 1800-1914.* London 1981.

40.23 Pipes, Daniel: *Slave soldiers and Islam. The genesis of a military system [A.D. 600-900].* New Haven, London 1981. – See also [33.59a].

40.24 Rodinson, Maxime: *Islam and capitalism (Islam et capitalisme. 1966).* London 1974.

40.25 Sellheim, Rudolf: Gelehrte und Gelehrsamkeit im Reiche der Chalifen. In: *Festgabe für Paul Kirn zum 70. Geburtstage.* Berlin 1962, pp.54-79.

40.26 *Studies in the economic history of the Middle East from the rise of Islam to the present day.* Ed. by M[ichael] A[llan] Cook. London [etc.] 1970.

40.26a Urvoy, Dominique: *Le monde des ulémas andalous du V/XIe au VII/XIIIe siècle; étude sociologique.* Genève 1978. (École pratique des Hautes études. Centre de recherches d'histoire et de philologie. Section 4. *Hautes études islamiques et orientales d'histoire comparée.* 8.)

—— Watt, William Montgomery: *Islam and the integration of society.* 1961 [30.16].

40.27 *Wirtschaftsgeschichte des Vorderen Orients in islamischer Zeit.* Teil 1. Mit Beiträgen von B. Lewis [*et al.*]. Leiden, Köln 1977. (*Handbuch der Orientalistik.* Abt. 1. Bd. 6: *Geschichte der islamischen Länder. Abschnitt 6.*)

B. Lewis: Sources. – M. Rodinson: Les conditions religieuses islamiques de la vie économique. – G. Baer: The organization of labour. – H. Müller: Sklaven. – A. S. Ehrenkreutz: Money. – E. Ashtor: The development of prices. – B. Spuler: Die wirtschaftliche Entwicklung des iranischen Raumes und Mittelasiens. – A. K. S. Lambton: Aspects of agricultural organisation and agrarian history in Persia [et al.].

Bedouins and sedentary peoples

41.01 Bräunlich, Erich: Beiträge zur Gesellschaftsordnung der arabischen Beduinenstämme. In: *Islamica.* Leipzig. 6. 1933, pp.68-111, 182-229.

41.02 Bulliet, Richard W.: *The camel and the wheel.* Cambridge, Mass. 1975.

41.03 Caskel, Werner: *Die Bedeutung der Beduinen in der Geschichte der Araber.* Köln and Opladen 1953. (*Arbeitsgemeinschaft für Forschung des Landes Nordrhein-Westfalen. Geisteswissenschaften.* H. 8.)

41.04 Carleton S. Coon, H[ermann] von Wissmann, F. Kussmaul, W[illiam] M[ontgomery] Watt: Badw. In: *EI*². 1, s. v. (1958).

41.05 Doughty, Charles M.: *Travels in Arabia Deserta.* Cambridge 1888. – With an introduction by T. E. Lawrence. 3rd ed. London, New York 1922.

41.06 Oppenheim, Max Freiherr von: *Die Beduinen.* Bd. 1-4. (1.2: Unter Mitbearbeitung von Ernst Bräunlich und Werner Caskel. 3.4: Bearb. und hrsg. von Werner Caskel.) Leipzig (3. 4.: Wiesbaden) 1939-68.

41.07 Ritter, Hellmut: Irrational solidarity groups. A socio-psychological study in connection with Ibn Khaldûn. In: *Oriens*. Leiden. 1. 1948, pp.1-44.
On Ibn Khaldūn, cf. also Chapter III [33.77-80].
41.08 Baer, Gabriel: *Fellah and townsman in the Middle East; studies in social history*. London 1981.
41.09 Cahen, Claude: Nomades et sédentaires dans le monde musulman du milieu du Moyen Age. In: *Islamic civilization, A.D. 950-1150*. Oxford 1973, pp.93-104.
41.10 Garcin, Jean-Claude: Note sur les rapports entre bédouins et fellahs à l'époque mamluke. In: *Annales islamologiques*. Le Caire. 14. 1978, pp.147-63.
41.11 Hütteroth, Wolf-Dieter: *Palästina und Transjordanien im 16. Jahrhundert. Wirtschaftsstruktur ländlicher Siedlungen nach osmanischen Steuerregistern*. Wiesbaden 1978. (*Tübinger Atlas des Vorderen Orients. Beihefte*. Nr. 33.)
41.12 Lambton, Ann Katherine Swynford: *Landlord and peasant in Persia*. London 1953.
41.13 Poliak, Abraham Nahum: Les révoltes populaires en Égypte à l'époque des mamelouks. In: *Revue des études islamiques*. Paris. 8. 1934, pp.251-73.
41.14 Sivers, Peter von: Military merchants and nomads: the social evolution of the Syrian cities and countryside during the classical period. In: *Der Islam*. Berlin. 56. 1979, pp.206-44.
41.15 Watson, Andrew M.: *Agricultural innovation in the early Islamic world: the diffusion of crops and farming techniques, 700-1100*. Cambridge 1983.
41.16 Weulersse, Jacques: *Paysans de Syrie et du Proche-Orient*. 2ème éd. Paris 1946.

Muslims and non-Muslims

42.01 Bulliet, Richard W.: *Conversion to Islam in the medieval period. An essay in quantitative history*. Cambridge, Mass. 1979.
42.02 Fattal, Antoine: *Le statut légal des non-musulmans en pays d'Islam*. Beirut 1958 (*Institut de Lettres orientales de Beyrouth. Recherches*. 10.)
42.03 Goitein, Shlomo Dov: *Jews and Arabs: their contacts through the ages*. New York 1964.
42.04 —: *A Mediterranean society. The Jewish community of the Arab world as portrayed in the documents of the Cairo Geniza*. Vol. 1-4. Berkeley 1967- .
1: Economic foundations. 1967.
2: The community. 1971.
3: The family. 1978.
4: Daily life. 1983.
5: The individual. 198 .
42.05 Hasluck, Frederick William: *Christianity and Islam under the Sultans*. 1.2. Oxford 1929.
42.06 Lewis, Bernard: *The Jews of Islam*. London 1985.
42.07 Motzki, Harald: *Ḏimma und Égalité. Die nichtmuslimischen Minderheiten Ägyptens in der zweiten Hälfte des 18. Jahrhunderts und die Expedition Bonapartes (1798-1801)*. Bonn 1979. (*Studien*

zum Minderheitenproblem im Islam. 5 = *Bonner Orientalistische Studien.* Bd. 27, 5.)
42.08 Spuler, Bertold: L'Islam et les minorités. In: *Die islamische Welt zwischen Mittelalter und Neuzeit. Festschrift für Hans Robert Roemer zum 65. Geburtstag.* Beirut, Wiesbaden 1979 (*Beiruter Texte und Studien.* 22), pp.609-19.
42.09 Tritton, Arthur Stanley: *The Caliphs and their non-Muslim subjects: a critical study of the covenant of 'Umar.* London 1930; ²1970.
42.10 Wirth, Eugen: Zur Sozialgeographie der Religionsgemeinschaften im Orient. In: *Erdkunde.* Bonn. 19. 1965, pp.265-84.

Government economy, taxation and feudalism
—— Ben Sheneb, A.: *Taxation in Islam.* 1965-69 [33.81].
43.01 Cahen, Claude: *Makhzūmiyyāt. Études sur l'histoire économique et financière de l'Égypte médiévale.* Leiden 1977.
Based on the Arabic manual of al-Makhzūmī (12 cent.) on financial administration.
43.01a Dennett, Daniel C.: *Conversion and the poll-tax in early Islam.* Cambridge, Mass. 1950 (*Harvard Historical Monographs.* 22.)
43.02 Gibb, Hamilton Alexander Roskeen: The Fiscal Rescript of 'Umar II. In: *Arabica.* Leiden. 2. 1955, pp.1-16.
43.03 Kremer, Alfred von: Über das Einnahmebudget des Abbasiden-Reiches vom Jahre 306 H. (918-919). In: *Denkschriften der Kais. Akademie der Wissenschaften.* Phil.-hist. Cl. Wien. Bd. 36. 1888, pp.283-362.
43.04 Løkkegaard, Frede: *Islamic taxation in the classic period. With special reference to circumstances in Iraq.* Copenhagen 1950; repr. 1977.
—— Puin, Gerd-Rüdiger: *Der Dīwān von 'Umar b. al-Ḫaṭṭāb.* 1970 [33.83].
43.05 Schmucker, Werner: *Untersuchungen zu einigen wichtigen bodenrechtlichen Konsequenzen der islamischen Eroberungsbewegung.* Bonn 1972. (*Bonner Orientalistische Studien.* N. S. Bd. 24.)

43.06 Cahen, Claude: L'évolution de l'iqta' du IXᵉ au XIIIᵉ siècle. Contribution à une histoire comparée des sociétés médiévales. In: *Annales. Économies-sociétés-civilizations.* Paris. 8. 1953, pp.25-52.
—— Halm, Heinz: *Ägypten nach den mamlukischen Lehensregistern.* 1979 [66.25].
43.07 Lambton, Ann Katherine Swynford: Reflections on the iqṭā'. In: *Arabic and Islamic Studies in honour of Hamilton A. R. Gibb.* Leiden 1965, pp.358-76.
43.08 Poliak, Abraham Nahum: *Feudalism in Egypt, Syria, Palestine and the Lebanon (1250-1900).* London 1939; repr. 1977.
43.09 Rabie, Hassanein: *The financial system of Egypt A.H. 564-741 / A.D. 1169-1341.* London 1972.
43.10 Beldiceanu, Nicoară: *Le timar dans l'État ottoman (début XIVᵉ-début XVIᵉ siècle).* Wiesbaden 1980.

Money, prices and salaries
43.11 Ashtor, Eliyahu: *Histoire des prix et des salaires dans l'Orient médiéval.* Paris 1969. (*Monnaie, Prix, Conjoncture.* 8.)

43.12 —: *Les métaux précieux et la balance des payements du Proche Orient à la basse époque.* Paris 1971. (*Monnaie, Prix, Conjoncture.* 10.)

43.13 Cahen, Claude: Contribution à l'étude de la circulation monétaire en Orient au milieu du moyen âge. In: *Annales islamologiques.* Le Caire. 15. 1979, pp.37-46.

43.14 Ehrenkreutz, Andrew S.: Monetary aspects of medieval history. In: *Studies in the Economic History of the Middle East.* 1970 [40.26], pp.37-50.

43.15 —: Money. In: *Wirtschaftsgeschichte.* 1977 [40.27], pp.84-97.

43.16 Hennequin, Gilles: Nouveaux aperçus sur l'histoire monétaire de l'Égypte à la fin du moyen-âge. In: *Annales islamologiques.* Le Caire. 13. 1977, pp.179-215.

43.17 Lombard, Maurice: *Études d'économie médiévale.* II: *Les métaux dans l'Ancien Monde du Ve au XIe siècle.* Paris, La Haye 1974.

The Islamic city

44.01 Beldiceanu, Nicoară: *Recherche sur la ville ottomane au XVe siècle. Étude et actes.* Paris 1973. (*Bibliothèque archéologique et historique de l'Institut français d'archéologie d'Istanbul.* 25.)

44.02 Bulliet, Richard W.: *The patricians of Nishapur. A study in medieval Islamic history.* Cambridge, Mass. 1972. (*Harvard Middle Eastern Studies.* 16.)

44.03 *L'espace social de la ville arabe.* Par Dominique Chevallier [et al.]. (Actes du colloque tenu les 24, 25 et 26 novembre 1977.) Paris 1979. (*Publications du Département d'Islamologie de l'Université de Paris-Sorbonne.* 7.)

44.04 Gaube, Heinz: *Iranian cities.* New York 1979. (*Hagop Kevorkian Series on Near Eastern Art and Civilisation.*)
Archaeology and historical topography, especially of Herat, Isfahan and Bam.

44.05 Grotzfeld, Heinz: *Das Bad im arabisch-islamischen Mittelalter. Kulturgeschichtliche Studie.* Wiesbaden 1970.

44.06 Grunebaum, Gustav Edmund von: Die islamische Stadt. In: *Saeculum.* Freiburg and München. 6. 1955, pp.138-53.

44.07 Havemann, Axel: *Ri'āsa und qaḍā'. Institutionen als Ausdruck wechselnder Kräfteverhältnisse in syrischen Städten vom 10. bis zum 12. Jahrhundert.* Freiburg 1975. (*Islamkundliche Untersuchungen.* 34.)

44.08 Hitti, Philip K.: *Capital cities of Arab Islam.* Minneapolis 1973.

44.09 *The Islamic city. A colloquium.* Ed. by Albert H[abib] Hourani and S[amuel] M[iklos] Stern. Oxford [etc.] 1970. (*Papers in Islamic History.* 1.)

44.10 *The Islamic City. Selected papers from the colloquium held at the Middle East Centre, Cambridge, 1976.* Ed. by R. B. Serjeant. Paris 1980.

44.11 Lapidus, Ira Marvin: *Muslim cities in the later Middle Ages.* Cambridge, Mass. 1967. (*Harvard Middle Eastern Studies.* 1.)
Damascus and Aleppo under the Mamluks.

44.12 *Middle Eastern cities. A symposium on ancient, Islamic, and contemporary Middle Eastern urbanism,* ed. by Ira M[arvin] Lapidus. Berkeley and Los Angeles 1969.

44.13 Petry, Carl Forbes: *The civilian élite of Cairo in the later Middle Ages.* Princeton, NJ. 1981.
44.14 Reitemeyer, Else: *Die Städtegründungen der Araber im Islam nach den arabischen Historikern und Geographen.* Leipzig 1912.
44.15 Wirth, Eugen: Die orientalische Stadt. Ein Überblick aufgrund jüngerer Forschungen zur materiellen Kultur. In: *Saeculum.* München and Freiburg. 26. 1975, pp.45-94.
44.16 Ziadeh, Nicola A.: *Urban life in Syria under the early Mamluks.* Beirut 1953. (*American University of Beirut. Publications of the Faculty of Arts and Sciences. Oriental Series.* 24.)
For the history of individual cities: Aleppo [52.11, 52.13], Baghdad [53.06-07], Damascus [52.09-10, 52.12, 52.14], Edirne [57.08], Fez [54.24-26], Herat [56.06a], Isfahan [56.14], [44.27], Istanbul [57.09], Cairo [44.13], [55.04-05], Marrakesh [54.23], Mecca [51.08], Qūṣ [55.06], Rabat [54.22], Samarra [53.05], Ṣanʻāʼ [51.07], Shiraz [56.13], Tehran [56.12].

Unions and guilds

44.17 Cahen, Claude: Zur Geschichte der städtischen Gesellschaft im islamischen Orient des Mittelalters. In: *Saeculum.* Freiburg and München. 9. 1958, pp.59-76.
44.18 —: Mouvements populaires et autonomisme urbain dans l'Asie musulmane au moyen âge. In: *Arabica.* Leiden. 5. 1958, pp.225-50; 6. 1959, pp.25-56, 233-65.
44.19 Taeschner, Franz: Das Futuwwa-Rittertum des islamischen Mittelalters. In: *Beiträge zur Arabistik, Semitistik und Islamwissenschaft.* Hrsg. v. R. Hartmann u. H. Scheel. Leipzig 1944, pp.340-85.
44.20 —: *Zünfte und Bruderschaften im Islam. Texte zur Geschichte der Futuwwa.* Zürich and München 1979. (*Die Bibliothek des Morgenlandes.*)

44.21 Baer, Gabriel: *Egyptian guilds in modern times.* Jerusalem 1964.
44.22 —: Guilds in Middle Eastern history. In: *Studies in the Economic history of the Middle East.* 1970 [40.26], pp.11-30.
44.23 —: The organization of labour. In: *Wirtschaftsgeschichte des Vorderen Orients in islamischer Zeit.* 1977 [40.27], pp.31-52.
44.24 Cahen, Claude: Y a-t-il eu des corporations professionelles dans le monde musulman classique? In: *The Islamic City.* 1970 [44.09], pp.51-63.
44.25 Elisséeff, Nikita: Corporations de Damas sous Nur ad-Din. Matériaux pour une topographie économique de Damas au 12e siècle. In: *Arabica.* Leiden. 3. 1956, pp.61-79.
44.26 Stern, Samuel Miklos: The constitution of the Islamic city. In: *The Islamic city.* 1970 [44.09], pp.25-50.

Markets and trade

44.27 Gaube, Heinz; Wirth, Eugen: *Der Bazar von Isfahan.* Wiesbaden 1978. (*Tübinger Atlas des Vorderen Orients.* Beihefte. Nr. 22.)
44.28 Al-Genabi, Hashim K. N.: *Der Suq (Bazar) von Bagdad. Eine wirtschafts- und sozialgeographische Untersuchung.* Erlangen 1976. (*Mitteilungen d. Fränkischen Geographischen Gesellschaft.* Bd. 21/22. 1974-5, pp.143-295 = *Erlanger Geographische Arbeiten.* H. 36.)

44.29 Raymond, André: *Artisans et commerçants au Caire au XVIIe siècle.* T. 1. 2. Damascus 1973-4.
44.30 Wirth, Eugen: Zum Problem des Bazars. In: *Der Islam.* Berlin. 51. 1974, pp.203-60; 52. 1975, pp.6-46.

44.31. 'Abd ar-Rāziq, Aḥmad: La ḥisba et le muḥtasib en Égypte au temps des Mamlūks. In: *Annales islamologiques.* Le Caire. 13. 1977, pp.115-78.
44.32 Klingmüller, Ernst: Agoranomos und Muhtasib. Zum Funktionswandel eines Amtes in islamischer Zeit. In: *Festschrift für E. Seidl zum 70. Geburtstag.* Köln 1975, pp.88-98.

44.33 Pirenne, Henri: *Mohammed and Charlemagne* (*Mahomet et Charlemagne.* 1937). London 1939.

More recent work on Pirenne's thesis:
44.34 Hübinger, Paul Egon [ed.]: *Bedeutung und Rolle des Islam beim Übergang vom Altertum zum Mittelalter.* Darmstadt 1968. (*Wege der Forschung.* 202.)
44.35 Ashtor, Eliyahu: Quelques observations d'un orientaliste sur la thèse de Pirenne. In: *Journal of the Economic and Social History of the Orient.* Leiden. 13. 1970, pp.166-94.
44.36 Ehrenkreutz, Andrew S.: Another orientalist's remarks concerning the Pirenne thesis. In: *Journal of the Economic and Social History of the Orient.* Leiden. 15. 1972, pp.94-104.

44.37 Cahen, Claude: Quelques mots sur le déclin commercial du monde musulman à la fin du moyen âge. In: *Studies in the Economic History of the Middle East.* 1970 [40.27], pp.31-36.
44.38 Goitein, Shlomo Dov: *Letters of medieval Jewish traders.* Transl. from the Arabic with introd. and notes. Princeton, NJ 1973.
—— —: *A mediterranean society.* 1967-78 [42.04].
44.39 Hourani, George Fadlu: *Arab seafaring in the Indian Ocean in ancient and early medieval times.* Princeton, NJ 1951.
44.40 Labib, Subhi Y.: *Handelsgeschichte Ägyptens im Spätmittelalter (1171-1517).* Wiesbaden 1965. (*Vierteljahresschrift für Sozial- und Wirtschaftsgeschichte.* Beihefte. Nr. 46.)
44.41 Lambton, Ann Katherine Swynford: The merchant in medieval Islam. In: *A locust's leg. Studies in honour of S. H. Taqizadeh.* London 1962, pp.121-30.
44.42 Rodinson, Maxime: Le marchand musulman. In: *Islam and the trade of Asia.* A colloquium, ed. by D. S. Richards. Oxford 1970, pp.21-36. (*Papers on Islamic history.* 2.)
44.43 Udovitch, Avrom L.: Formalism and information in the social and economic institutions of the medieval Islamic world. In: *Individualism and conformity in classical Islam. (Fifth Giorgio Levi Della Vida Biennial Conference, 1975.)* Wiesbaden 1977, pp.61-81.
44.44 —: *Partnership and profit in medieval Islam.* Princeton 1970.
44.45 Wirth, Eugen: *Der Orientteppich und Europa. Beitrag zu den vielfältigen Aspekten west-östlicher Kulturkontakte und Wirtschaftsbeziehungen.* Erlangen 1976. (*Erlanger geographische Arbeiten.* 37.)

V. Regions of Islamic History

Geography

50.01 Fisher, William Bayne: *The Middle East. A physical, social and regional geography.* 7th ed. London 1978.

50.02 Mensching, Horst; Wirth, Eugen: *Nordafrika und Vorderasien.* Frankfurt a.M. 1973. (*Fischer Länderkunden.* 4.)

50.03 Weekes, Richard V. [ed.]: *Muslim peoples: a world ethnographic survey.* Westport, Va., and London 1978; 2nd ed., rev., 1985.

On the cultural geography of the Islamic world, cf. Coon [40.02], Miquel [15.71], de Planhol [40.03].

Historical cartography

50.04 *Aṭlas-i tārīkhī-i Īrān. Historical atlas of Iran.* [Ed.:] Sayyid Ḥusayn Naṣr, Aḥmad Mustawfī, 'Abbās Zaryāb. Tehran 1350 H. Sh. / 1961.

50.05 Cornu, Georgette: *Atlas du monde arabo-islamique à l'époque classique IXe-Xe siècles.* [With] Répertoire des toponymes. Leiden 1985.

50.06 Hazard, Harry W.: *Atlas of Islamic history.* Compiled by Harry W. Hazard. Maps executed by H. Lester Cooke and J. McA. Smiley. 2nd ed., rev. and corr. Princeton 1952 (*Princeton Oriental Studies.* Vol. 12.)

50.07 *An historical atlas of Islam.* Ed. by William C. Brice under the patronage of the Encyclopaedia of Islam. Leiden 1981.

—— *A history of the Crusades.* Ed.: Kenneth M. Setton. Vol. 1.2: ^{2}1969; 3: 1975 [65.20].

Contains a number of good historical maps not only of the Crusades themselves but also of the general development of the Islamic lands in the east and west from the twelfth to the fifteenth century.

50.08 *The Times Atlas of World History.* Ed. by Geoffrey Barraclough. London 1978.

Contains clear presentations of different periods and regions of the Islamic world from the expansion of Islam until the present day.

50.09 *Tübinger Atlas des Vorderen Orients.* Hrsg. vom Sonderforschungsbereich 19 'Tübinger Atlas des Vorderen Orients' der Universität Tübingen. 1- . Wiesbaden 1977- .

Teil A: Geographie. Teil B: Geschichte.

Individual maps (format 72 × 50 cm) show developments in political, social, economic and cultural history. Each map is the result of extensive research which is documented in supplementary monographs ('Beihefte').

Historical topography and geography, regional and urban history according to individual countries:

1. The Arabian peninsula

51.01 *Gazetteer of Arabia. A geographical and tribal history of the Arabian Peninsula. (Based on the 1917 British Gazetteer of Arabia and other sources.)* Ed. by Sheila A. Scoville. Vol. 1-4. Graz 1979.

51.02 *Gazetteer of the Persian Gulf, Oman and Central Arabia.* Ed. by J. G. Lorimer, Vol. 1.2 [in 6]. Calcutta 1908-15. Repr. Westmead 1970.

51.03 Kiernan, Reginald Hugh: *The unveiling of Arabia. The story of Arabian travel and discovery.* London 1937.

51.04 Musil, Alois: *The Northern Ḥeǧāz. A topographical itinerary.* New York 1926. (*American Geographical Society. Oriental Explorations and Studies.* No. 1.)

51.05 —: *Arabia Deserta. A topographical itinerary.* New York 1927. (*American Geographical Society. Oriental Explorations and Studies.* No. 2.)

51.06 —: *Northern Neǧd. A topographical itinerary.* New York 1928. (*American Geographical Society. Oriental Explorations and Studies.* No. 5.)

51.07 Serjeant, Robert Bertram; Lewcock, Ronald [ed.]: *Ṣanʿāʾ, an Arabic Islamic city.* London 1983.

51.08 Snouck Hurgronje, Christian: *Mekka.* 1: *Die Stadt und ihre Herren.* 2: *Aus dem heutigen Leben.* Den Haag 1888-9.

2. Syria, Palestine and Lebanon

Syria

52.01 Charles, Henri: *Tribus moutonnières du Moyen-Euphrate.* Damas n.d. [1939]. (*Institut Français de Damas. Documents d'études orientales.* 8.)

52.02 Musil, Alois: *The Middle Euphrates. A topographical itinerary.* New York 1927. (*American Geographical Society. Oriental Explorations and Studies.* No. 3.)

52.03 —: *Palmyrena. A topographical itinerary.* New York 1928. (*American Geographical Society. Oriental Explorations and Studies.* No. 4.)

52.04 Weulersse, Jacques: *Le pays des Alaouites.* 1.2. Tours 1940.

52.05 Wirth, Eugen: *Syrien. Eine geographische Landeskunde.* Darmstadt 1971. (*Wissenschaftliche Länderkunden.* Bd. 4/5.)

—— Cahen, Claude: *La Syrie du Nord à l'époque des Croisades.* 1940 [65.19].

52.06 Dussaud, René: *Topographie historique de la Syrie antique et médiévale.* Paris 1927. (*Institut français d'archéologie de Beyrouth. Bibliothèque archéologique et historique.* 4.)

52.07 Dussaud, René; Deschamps, P.; Seyrig, Henri: *La Syrie antique et médiévale illustrée.* Paris 1931. (*Institut français d'archéologie de Beyrouth. Bibliothèque archéologique et historique.* 17.)

—— Gaudefroy-Demombynes, M.: *La Syrie à l'époque des Mamelouks.* 1923 [66.24].

52.08 Hitti, Philip Khûri: *History of Syria, including Lebanon and Palestine.* London 1951; ^{2}1957.

52.09 Dettmann, Klaus: *Damaskus. Eine orientalische Stadt zwischen Tradition und Moderne.* Erlangen 1969. (*Mitteilungen der Fränkischen Geographischen Gesellschaft.* 15-16. 1968-9, pp. 183-311 = *Erlanger Geographische Arbeiten.* Bd. 26.)

52.10 Elisséeff, Nikita: Dimashḳ. In: EI^2. 2 s. n. (1962).

52.11 Gaube, Heinz; Wirth, Eugen: *Aleppo. Historische und geographische Beiträge zur baulichen Gestaltung, zur sozialen Organisation und zur wirtschaftlichen Dynamik einer vorderasiatischen Fernhandelsmetropole.* [1:] Textband. [2:] Karten. Wiesbaden 1984. (*Tübinger Atlas des Vorderen Orients.* Beihefte. Reihe B. Nr. 58.)

52.12 Sauvaget, Jean: Esquisse d'une histoire de la ville de Damas. In: *Revue des études islamiques.* Paris. 8. 1934, pp.421-80.

52.13 —: *Alep. Essai sur le développement d'une grande ville syrienne des origines au milieu du XIXe siècle.* [1:] *Texte.* [2:] *Tables.* Paris 1941. (*Institut français d'archéologie de Beyrouth. Bibliothèque archéologique et historique.* 36.)

52.14 Ziadeh, Nicola A.: *Damascus under the Mamluks.* Norman, Oklahoma, 1964. (*The Centers of Civilization.*)
Cf. also Lapidus [44.11], Ziadeh [44.16].

Palestine

52.15 Hütteroth, Wolf-Dieter; Abdulfattah, Kamal: *Historical geography of Palestine, Transjordan and Southern Syria in the late sixteenth century.* Erlangen 1977. (*Erlanger Geographische Arbeiten.* Sonderband 5.)

52.16 Le Strange, Guy: *Palestine under the Moslems. A description of Syria and the Holy Land from A.D. 650 to 1500. Translated from the works of the mediaeval Arab geographers.* London 1890. Repr. Beirut 1965.

52.17 Marmardji, A.-Sebastianus: *Textes géographiques arabes sur la Palestine, recueillis, mis en ordre alphabétique et traduits en français.* Paris 1951. (*Études bibliques.*)

Lebanon

52.18 Vaumas, Étienne de: *Le Liban (Montagne libanaise, Bekaa, Anti-Liban, Hermon, Haute Galilée libanaise). Etude de géographie physique.* 1-3. Paris 1954.

52.19 Wild, Stefan: *Libanesische Ortsnamen. Typologie und Deutung.* Beirut, Wiesbaden 1973. (*Beiruter Texte und Studien.* Bd. 9.)

52.20 Hitti, Philip Khûri: *Lebanon in history.* London 1957.

3. Iraq

53.01 Thesiger, Wilfred: *The Marsh Arabs.* London 1964.

53.02 Wirth, Eugen: *Agrargeographie des Irak.* Hamburg 1962. (*Hamburger Geographische Studien.* 13.)

53.03 Al-Feel, Muhammad Rashid: *The historical geography of Iraq between the Mongolian and the Ottoman conquests, 1258-1534.* 1: Nejef 1965. 2: Baghdad 1967.

53.04 Le Strange, Guy: *The lands of the Eastern Caliphate. Mesopotamia, Persia and Central Asia from the Moslem conquest to the time of Timur.* Cambridge 1905. Repr. London 1966.

53.05 Herzfeld, Ernst: *Geschichte der Stadt Samarra.* Hamburg 1948. (*Forschungen zur islamischen Kunst.* Hrsg. v. Friedrich Sarre. 2: *Die Ausgrabungen von Samarra.* Bd. 6.)

53.06 Lassner, Jacob: *The topography of Baghdad in the early Middle Ages.* Detroit 1970.

53.07 Le Strange, Guy: *Baghdad during the Abbasid Caliphate from contemporary Arabic and Persian sources.* Oxford 1900. Repr. London 1972.

4. The West

54.01 Le Tourneau, Roger: Der Islam im Westen: Spanien und Nordafrika. In: *Historia Mundi.* Bd. 6. Bern 1958, pp.511-35.

54.02 —: [*et al.*]: Africa and the Muslim West. In: *The Cambridge History of Islam.* 1970 [14.03]. 2, pp.209-439.

(a) Spain

(On early Islamic Spain see also [64.31-33].)

54.03 Chejne, Anwar G.: *Muslim Spain. Its history and culture.* Minneapolis 1974.

54.04 Gonzáles Palencia, Angel: *Los Mozárabes de Toledo en los siglos XII y XIII.* Vol. 1-3 [with] volumen preliminar. Madrid 1926-30.
Vol. prelimin., pp.51-115: *Topografía de Toledo.*

—— Guichard, Pierre: *Structures sociales 'orientales' et 'occidentales' dans l'Espagne musulmane.* 1977 [40.14].

54.05 Hoenerbach, Wilhelm: *Islamische Geschichte Spaniens. Übersetzung der A'māl al-a'lām und ergänzender Texte.* Zürich and Stuttgart 1970. (*Die Bibliothek des Morgenlandes.*)
Translation and presentation according to one of the greatest historians of Islamic Spain, Lisān al-Dīn Ibn al-Khaṭīb (1313-75).

54.06 Imamuddin, S. M.: *Muslim Spain, 711-1492 A.D. A sociological study.* Leiden 1965; ^{2}1981.

—— Urvoy, D.: *Le monde des ulémas andalous du V/XIe au VII/XIIIe siècle.* 1978 [40.26a].

54.07 Watt, William Montgomery; Cachia, Pierre: *A history of Islamic Spain.* Edinburgh 1977. (*Islamic Surveys.* 4.)

(b) Sicily

54.08 Ahmad, Aziz: *A history of Islamic Sicily.* Edinburgh 1975. (*Islamic Surveys.* 10.)

54.09 Amari, Michele: *Storia dei Musulmani di Sicilia.* Sec. ed., modificata e accresciuta dall'autore, pubblicata con note a cura di C. A. Nallino. 1-3. Catania 1933-39.

(c) North Africa

54.10 Barbour, Nevill: *A survey of North West Africa (the Maghrib).* 2nd ed. London 1962.

54.11 Despois, Jean: *L'Afrique du Nord.* Paris 1949; ^{3}1964. (*Pays d'Outre-mer.* Série 4: *Géographie.* 1: *L'Afrique blanche.*)

54.12 Despois, Jean; Raynal, René: *Géographie de l'Afrique du Nord-Ouest.* Paris 1967.

54.13 Abun-Nasr, Jamil M.: *A history of the Maghrib.* 2nd ed. Cambridge 1975.

54.14 Bel, Alfred: *La religion musulmane en Berbérie; esquisse d'histoire et de sociologie religieuses.* I: *Établissement et développements de l'Islam en Berbérie du VIIe au XXe siècle.* Paris 1938.

54.15 Bousquet, Georges-Henri: *Les Berbères. (Histoire et institutions.)* 2ème éd., revue. Paris 1961. (*Que sais-je?* No. 718.)

54.16 —: *L'Islam maghrébin.* 4éme éd. Alger 1955.

54.17 Forstner, Martin: *Das Wegenetz des Zentralen Maghreb in islamischer Zeit. Ein Vergleich mit dem antiken Wegenetz.* Wiesbaden 1979.

54.18 Julien, Charles-André: *Histoire de l'Afrique du Nord. Tunisie, Algérie, Maroc.* 1.2. 2ème éd. Paris 1952; réimpr. 1961, 1978.
1: *Des origines à la conquête arabe (647).* Revue et mise à jour par Christian Courtois.
2: *De la conquête arabe à 1830.* Revue et mise à jour par Roger Le Tourneau.

54.19 Marçais, Georges: *La Berbérie musulmane et l'Orient au moyen-âge.* Paris 1946.
History of Islamic North Africa until the Ḥafṣid period. See also [65.50].

54.20 Sivers, Peter von: Nordafrika in der Neuzeit [1300-1985]. In: *Geschichte der arabischen Welt.* 1987 [14.05a], pp.502-90.

54.21 Terrasse, Henri: *Histoire du Maroc des origines à l'établissement du Protectorat français.* T. 1-2. Casablanca 1949-50.

54.22 Caille, Jacques: *La ville de Rabat jusqu'au Protectorat français. Histoire et archéologie.* T. 1-3. Paris 1949. (*Publications de l'Institut des Hautes-études marocaines.* 44.)

54.23 Deverdun, Gaston: *Marrakech des origines à 1912.* T. 1.2. Rabat 1959-66.

54.24 Le Tourneau, Roger: *Fès avant le Protectorat. Étude économique et sociale d'une ville de l'occident musulman.* Casablanca 1949. (*Publications de l'Institut des Hautes-études marocaines.* T.45.)

54.25 —: *Fez in the age of the Marinides.* Transl. by B. A. Clement. Norman, Oklahoma 1961.

54.26 —: *Les villes musulmanes de l'Afrique du Nord.* Alger 1957. (*Bibliothèque de l'Institut d'Études supérieures islamiques d'Alger.* 9.)

5. Egypt

55.01 Becker, Carl Heinrich: *Beiträge zur Geschichte Ägyptens unter dem Islam.* Heft 1.2. Straßburg 1902-3, repr. 1977.

55.02 Müller, Caspar Detlef G.: *Grundzüge des christlich-islamischen Ägypten von der Ptolemäerzeit bis zur Gegenwart.* Darmstadt 1969. (*Grundzüge.* Bd. 11.)

55.03 Wiet, Gaston: *L'Égypte arabe de la conquête arabe à la conquête ottomane, 642-1517 de l'ère chrétienne* (=G. Hanotaux: *Histoire de la nation égyptienne.* Paris 1931-40. 4.) Paris 1938.

55.04 Abu-Lughod, Janet L.: *Cairo. 1001 years of the City Victorious.* Princeton, NJ, 1971. (*Princeton Studies in the Near East.*)

—— Petry, C. F.: *The civilian elite of Cairo in the later Middle Ages.* 1981 [44.13].

55.05 Staffa, Susan Jane: *Conquest and fusion. The social evolution of Cairo, A.D. 462-1850.* Leiden 1977.

55.06 Garcin, Jean-Claude: *Un centre musulman de la Haute-Égypte médiévale, Qûṣ.* Le Caire 1974. (Institut français d'Archéologie orientale. *Textes arabes et études islamiques.* 6.)

6. *Iran and Central Asia*

—— *Bibliographical guide to Iran.* 1983 [11.10].

56.01 *Historical gazetteer of Iran.* Ed. by L. W. Adamec. Vol. 1-4. Graz 1976- .
1: *Tehran and Northwestern Iran.* 1976.
2: *Meshed and Northeastern Iran.*
3: *Shiraz and Southwestern Iran.*
4: *Bandar Abbas and Southeastern Iran.*
Based on archival material compiled by the General Staff of British India.

56.02 *Historical and political gazetteer of Afghanistan.* Ed. by L. W. Adamec. Vol. 1-6. Graz 1972-85.
Follows the official gazetteer of 1914.

56.03 Bobek, Hans: *Iran. Probleme eines unterentwickelten Landes alter Kultur.* Frankfurt, Berlin, Bonn 1962; ²1964. (*Themen zur Geographie und Gemeinschaftskunde.*)

56.04 Ehlers, Eckart: *Iran. Grundzüge der geographischen Landskunde.* Darmstadt 1980. (*Wissenschaftliche Länderkunden.* Bd. 18.)

56.05 Barthold, W. [Vasilij Vladimirovič Bartol'd]: *An historical geography of Iran* [*Istoriko-geografičeskij obzor Irana.* 1903]. Transl. by S. Soucek. Princeton, NJ 1984.

56.06 Gaube, Heinz: *Die südpersische Provinz Arrağān / Kūh-Gīlūyeh von der arabischen Eroberung bis zur Safawidenzeit. Analyse und Auswertung literarischer und archäologischer Quellen zur historischen Topographie.* Wien 1973. (*Österreichische Akademie der Wissenschaften. Denkschriften.* Bd. 107.)

56.06a —: Innenstadt – Aussenstadt: Kontinuität und Wandel im Grundriss von Herat (Afghanistan) zwischen dem x. und dem xv. Jahrhundert. In: *Beiträge zur Geographie orientalischer Städte und Märkte.* Hrsg. v. G. Schweizer. Wiesbaden 1977 (*Tübinger Atlas des Vorderen Orients.* Reihe B. Beihefte. Nr. 24), pp. 213-40.

56.07 Krawulsky, Dorothea: *Īrān – das Reich der Īlḫāne. Eine topographisch-historische Studie.* Wiesbaden 1978. (*Tübinger Atlas des Vorderen Orients.* Beihefte. Reihe B. Nr. 17.)

—— Le Strange, Guy: *The lands of the Eastern Caliphate.* 1905 [53.04].

56.08 Schwarz, Paul: *Iran im Mittelalter nach den arabischen Geographen.* Bd. 1-9. Leipzig 1896-1936.

56.09 *The Cambridge History of Iran.* Vol. 1- . Cambridge [etc.] 1968-
1: *The land of Iran.* Ed. by W. B. Fisher. 1968.
3, 1.2: *The Seleucid, Parthian and Sasanian periods.* Ed. by Ehsan Yarshater. 1983.
4: *The period from the Arab invasion to the Saljuqs.* Ed. by R. N. Frye. 1975.
5: *The Saljuq and Mongol periods.* Ed. by J. A. Boyle. 1968.
6: *The Timurid and Safavid periods.* Ed. by Peter Jackson and Laurence Lockhart. 1986.

56.10 Sykes, Percy: *A history of Persia.* Vol. 1.2. London 1915; ³1958.

56.11 Wilber, Donald N.: *Iran: past and present.* 8th ed. Princeton, NJ 1976.

56.12 Ahrens, Peter Georg: *Die Entwicklung der Stadt Teheran.* Opladen 1966.
56.13 Clarke, John Innes: *The Iranian city of Shiraz.* Durham 1963.
56.14 Quiring-Zoche, Rosemarie: *Isfahan im 15. und 16. Jahrhundert. Ein Beitrag zur persischen Stadtgeschichte.* Freiburg 1980. (*Islamkundliche Untersuchungen.* Bd. 54.)
See also H. Gaube, E. Wirth: *Der Bazar von Isfahan.* 1978 [44.27].

Central Asia

56.15 Barthold, W. [Vasilij Vladimirovič Bartol'd]: *Turkestan down to the Mongol invasion.* Third ed. with an additional chapter, ed. with further addenda and corrigenda by C. E. Bosworth. London 1968; 4th ed. (repr.) 1977. (*E. J. W. Gibb Memorial Series.* N. S. 5.)
56.16 Gabain, Annemarie von: *Einführung in die Zentralasienkunde.* Darmstadt 1979.
56.17 *Geschichte Mittelasiens.* Mit Beiträgen von K. Jettmar, H. W. Haussig, B. Spuler, L. Petech. Leiden and Köln 1966. (*Handbuch der Orientalistik.* Abt. 1. Bd. 5: *Altaistik.* Abschnitt 5.)
Pp. 123-310: Spuler, Bertold: *Geschichte Mittelasiens seit dem Auftreten der Türken.*
56.18 Hambly, Gavin [ed.]: *Central Asia.* London 1969.

7. *Anatolia and the Balkans*

57.01 Hütteroth, Wolf-Diether: *Türkei.* Darmstadt 1981. (*Wissenschaftliche Länderkunden.* Bd. 21.)

57.02 Babinger, Franz: Der Islam in Südosteuropa. In: *Völker und Kulturen Südost-Europas. Kulturhistorische Beiträge.* München 1959, pp.211-17.
57.03 Birken, Andreas: *Die Provinzen des Osmanischen Reiches.* Wiesbaden 1976. (*Tübinger Atlas des Vorderen Orients.* Reihe B. Beihefte. Nr. 13.)
57.04 Flemming, Barbara: *Landschaftsgeschichte von Pamphylien, Pisidien und Lykien im Spätmittelalter.* Wiesbaden 1964. (*Abhandlungen für die Kunde des Morgenlandes.* 35, 1.)
57.05 Hütteroth, Wolf-Dieter: *Ländliche Siedlungen im südlichen Inneranatolien in den letzten vierhundert Jahren.* Göttingen 1968. (*Göttinger Geographische Abhandlungen.* 46.)
57.06 Pitcher, Donald Edgar: *An historical geography of the Ottoman Empire from the earliest times to the end of the sixteenth century.* Leiden 1972.
57.07 Taeschner, Franz: *Das anatolische Wegenetz.* 1.2. Leipzig 1924-26. (*Türkische Bibliothek.* 22.23.)

57.08 Kreiser, Klaus: *Edirne im 17. Jahrhundert nach Evliyā Çelebī. Ein Beitrag zur Kenntnis der osmanischen Stadt.* Freiburg 1975. (*Islamkundliche Untersuchungen.* Bd. 33.)
57.09 Mantran, Robert: *Istanbul dans le seconde moitié du XVIIe siècle.* Paris 1962. (*Bibliothèque archéologique et historique de l'Institut français d'archéologie d'Istanbul.*)

8. The further Islamic lands

58.01 Arnold, Thomas Walker: *The preaching of Islam.* 2nd ed. London 1913.

India

58.02 Ahmad, Aziz: Indien. In: *Der Islam.* 11. 1971 [14.10], pp.226-87.

58.03 —: *An intellectual history of Islam in India.* Edinburgh 1969. (*Islamic Surveys.* 7.)

58.04 —: *Studies in Islamic culture in the Indian environment.* Oxford 1964.

58.05 *The Cambridge History of India.* Cambridge 1922ff.
3: *Turks and Afghans.* 1928.
4: *The Mughul period.* 1937.

58.06 Elliot, Henry M.; Dowson, John: *The history of India as told by its own historians. The Muhammadan period.* Ed. from the posthumous papers of the late Sir H. M. Elliot by John Dowson. Vols. 1-8. London 1867-77. Repr. Calcutta 1953; New York 1966.
Arabic and Persian historians in English translation.

58.07 Habib, Muhammad: *Politics and society during the early medieval period.* Collected works, ed. by K. A. Nizami. New Delhi 1974.

58.08 Ikram, Sheikh Mohamad: *Muslim rule in India and Pakistan.* Lahore 1966.

58.09 Lane-Poole, Stanley: *Medieval India under Mohammedan rule, 712-1764.* New York [etc.] 1903. (*The Story of the Nations.*)

58.10 Qureshi, Ishtiaq Husain: *The Muslim community of the Indo-Pakistan subcontinent, 610-1947; a brief historical analysis.* 's Gravenhage 1962; 2nd ed. Karachi 1977.

58.11 Schimmel, Annemarie: *Islam in the Indian Subcontinent.* Leiden 1980. (*Handbuch der Orientalistik.* Abt. 2. Bd. 4. Abschn. 3.)

58.12 —: *Der Islam im indischen Subkontinent.* Darmstadt 1983. (*Grundzüge.* Bd. 48.)

58.13 Sherwani, Haroon Khan; Joshi, P. M. [ed.]: *History of medieval Deccan, 1295-1724.* Vol. 1.2. Hyderabad 1973-4.

East and south-east Asia

58.14 Ferrand, Gabriel: *Relations de voyages et textes géographiques arabes, persans et turks relatifs à l'Extrême-Orient du VIIIe au XVIIIe siècle.* 1.2. Paris 1913-14.

58.15 Hartmann, Martin: *Zur Geschichte des Islam in China.* Leipzig 1921.

58.16 Hourani, George: *Arab seafaring.* Princeton 1951. (*Princeton Oriental Studies.* 13.)

58.17 Graaf, H. J. de [*et al.*]: South-East Asian Islam. In: *The Cambridge History of Islam.* 2. 1970 [14.03], pp.121-207.

58.17a Kähler, Hans: A short history of Indonesia. In: *The Muslim World.* 4, 1. 1981 [14.06], pp.236-337.

58.18 Sarkisyanz, Emanuel: China und Südostasien. In: *Der Islam.* 11. 1971 [14.10], pp.288-324.

58.19 Schwerin, Kerrin Gräfin: Der Islam in Südasien. Ein Literaturbericht. In: *Zeitschrift der Deutschen Morgenländischen Gesellschaft.* Wiesbaden. 128,2. 1978, pp.*35-*41.

58.20 Snouck Hurgronje, Christiaan: *Verspreide Geschriften.* Bonn,

Leipzig, Leiden 1923-27.
On South-East Asia, see esp. Vol. 4.
58.21 —: *The Achehnese* [De Atjèhers. 1893-94, Engl.] 1.2. Leiden 1906.
58.22 Tibbetts, Gerald Randall: *A study of the Arabic texts containing material on South-East Asia.* Leiden 1979. (*Oriental Translation Fund.* N. S. Vol. 44.)

Africa

58.23 O'Brian, Donald B. Cruise: *The Mourides of Senegal. The political and economical organisation of an Islamic brotherhood.* Oxford 1971.
58.24 Holt, Peter Malcolm; Daly, M. W.: *The history of the Sudan from the coming of Islam to the present day.* 3rd ed. London 1979.
58.25 Hopkins, John F. P.; Levtzion, Nehemia: *Corpus of early Arabic sources for West African history.* Cambridge 1981. (Union açadémique internationale. *Fontes Historiae Africanae. Series Arabica.* 4.)
58.26 *Studies in West African history.* Ed. with an introduction by John Ralph Willis. Vol. 1: *The cultivators of Islam.* London 1979.
58.27 Trimingham, John Spencer: *The influence of Islam upon Africa.* London, Harlow, Beirut 1968. (*Arab Background Series.*)
58.28 —: *Islam in the Sudan.* London 1949; ^{2}1965. – *Islam in Ethiopia.* 1952; ^{2}1965. – *Islam in West Africa.* 1959. – *A history of Islam in West Africa.* 1962. – *Islam in East Africa.* 1962.

VI. Periods of Islamic History

Periodisation. Reference works on genealogy and chronology

60.01 Paret, Rudi: Entwicklungsphasen und Metamorphosen in der Geschichte des Islam. In: *Arabic and Islamic studies in honor of H. A. R. Gibb.* Leiden 1965, pp.525-37.
60.02 Goitein, Shlomo Dov: A plea for the periodization of Islamic history. In: *Journal of the American Oriental Society.* New Haven. 88. 1968, pp.224-8.

60.03 Bacharach, Jere L.: *A Middle East Studies Handbook.* Rev. ed. (^{1}1974). Seattle and London 1984; repr. 1986.
Tables of dynasties and rulers (according to Bosworth), genealogies (according to Zambaur), 39 historical maps, comparative table of Islamic and Christian calendars, chronological tables and tables of linguistic families.
60.04 Bosworth, Clifford Edmund: *The Islamic dynasties. A chronological handbook.* Edinburgh 1967; rev. ed. 1980.
Tables of rulers and concise historical sketches of the most important Islamic dynasties. Within its limits the best and most reliable reference work.
60.05 Caskel, Werner: *Ǧamharat an-nasab. Das genealogische Werk des Hišām ibn Muḥammad al-Kalbī.* Bd. 1: *Einleitung. Tafeln* von Gert Strenziok. Bd. 2: *Erläuterungen zu den Tafeln. Register.* Leiden 1966.
60.06 Gomaa, Ibrahim: *A historical chart of the Muslim world.* Leiden 1972. (*Handbuch der Orientalistik.* Abt. 1. Erg.-Bd. VII.)
Linear, synoptic presentation of the dynastic history of the Islamic world on a map 105 × 65 cm.

60.07 Zambaur, Édouard de: *Manuel de généalogie et de chronologie pour l'histoire de l'Islam.* Hannover 1927.
Although it has been superseded in details, it is still the most comprehensive reference work for more obscure dynasties and minor office-holders. As far as they are known, dates are given with the month and day but only according to the Muslim calendar.

On the Islamic calendar, cf. also [73.01-3].

Islamic historians in translation
(see also [15.66-68], [58.06], [65.17], [65.18], [66.14], [67.02])

60.08 al-Ṭabarī, Muḥammad ibn Jarīr (d.923): *Geschichte der Araber und Perser zur Zeit der Sasaniden. Aus der arabischen Chronik des Tabari* [*Akhbār al-rusul wal-mulūk*, partial transl.] übersetzt und mit ausführlichen Erläuterungen und Ergänzungen versehen von Theodor Nöldeke. Leyden 1879.

60.09 al-Balādhurī, Aḥmad ibn Yaḥyā (d.892): *The origins of the Islamic state*, being a transl. of the *Kitâb Futûḥ al-buldân* of . . . al-Balâdhurî [1:] by Philip Khûri Hitti, [2:] by F. C. Murgotten. New York 1916-24. (*Columbia University Studies.* 68) Repr. [only part 1] Beirut 1966.

60.10 Ibn ʿAbdalḥakam, ʿAbdalraḥmān ibn ʿAbdallāh (d.871): *Conquête de l'Afrique du Nord et de l'Espagne* [*Futūḥ Miṣr wal-Maghrib*, partial ed. and transl.]. Texte arabe et traduction française par A. Gateau. Alger 1942; ²1947.

60.11 al-Ṭabarī, Muḥammad ibn Jarīr (d.923): *The reign of al-Muʿtaṣim (833-42)* [*Akhbār al-rusul wa'l-mulūk*, partial transl.]. Transl. and annotated by Elma Marin. New Haven, Conn. 1951.

60.11a —: *The History of al-Ṭabarī.* Ed. by Ehsan Yarshater [et al.]. Albany, NY 1987ff.
A complete translation of the Annals of al-Ṭabarī, the most important source for Islamic history until AD 915, prepared by a number of scholars. See also [60.08].

60.12 al-Masʿūdī, ʿAlī ibn al-Ḥusayn (d.957): *Les Prairies d'or* [*Murūj al-dhahab wa-maʿādin al-jawhar*]. Texte et traduction par [Adrien] Barbier de Meynard et [Abel] Pavet de Courteille. Paris 1861-77. – Trad. française, revue et corrigée par Charles Pellat. 1- . Paris 1962-

60.13 Miskawayh, Aḥmad ibn Muḥammad (d.1030): *The Eclipse of the Abbasid Caliphate.* Original chronicles of the fourth Islamic century. [1.2, 4.5:] The concluding portion of the *Experiences of the Nations* [*Tajārib al-umam*] by Miskawaih. [3.6]: Continuation . . . by Abū Shujāʿ Rudhrāwarī and Hilāl b. al-Muḥassin (aṣ-Ṣābi'). [1-3:] Arabic texts ed. by H. F. Amedroz, [4-6:] transl. from the Arabic, [7:] preface and index by D. S. Margoliouth. Oxford 1920-1.

60.14 Ibn al-Qalānisī, Ḥamza ibn Asad (d.555-1160): *The Damascus Chronicle of the Crusades* [*Dhayl Tārīkh Dimashq*]. Transl. by H. A. R. Gibb. London 1932.

60.15 Usāma ibn Munqidh (d.1188): *An Arab-Syrian gentleman and warrior in the period of the Crusades. Memoirs of Usāmah ibn Munqidh (Kitāb al-Iʿtibār).* Transl. by Philip K. Hitti. New York 1929. – Repr.: *Memoirs of an Arab-Syrian gentleman or An Arab knight in the Crusades.* Beirut 1964.

60.16 ʿImādaldīn al-Iṣfahānī, Muḥammad ibn Muḥammad (d.1201): *Conquête de la Syrie et de la Palestine par Saladin (al-Fatḥ al-qussî fî*

l-fatḥ al-qudsî). Trad. française par Henri Massé. Paris 1972.
Events of AD 1187-1193, ending with the death of Saladin.

60.17 Ibn Jubayr, Muḥammad ibn Aḥmad (d.1217): *The travels* [*Riḥla*] *of Ibn Jubair,* transl. from the original Arabic by R. J. C. Broadhurst. London 1952.
Account by an Andalusian traveller of his voyage to the Near East, AD 1183-5.

60.18 Ibn al-Ṭiqṭaqā, Muḥammad ibn ʿAlī: *Al Fakhri* [*al-Fakhrī,* written in AD 1302]. *On the system of government and the Muslim dynasties,* composed by Muhammad son of ʿAlī son of Tabataba . . ., transl. by C. E. J. Whitting. London 1947.

60.19 al-Dhahabī, Muḥammad ibn ʿUthmān Shamsaldīn (d.1348): *K. Duwal al-Islam. Les dynasties de l'Islam.* Traduction annotée des années 447 / 1055-1056 à 656 / 1258. Introduction, lexique et index par A. Nègre. Damas 1979.

60.20 Ibn Bībī, al-Ḥusayn ibn Muḥammad (d. after 1285): *Die Seltschukengeschichte des Ibn Bībī* [*al-Awāmir al-ʿalāʾiyya fī l-umūr al-ʿAlāʾiyya*]. Übersetzt von Herbert W. Duda. Kopenhagen 1959.
History of the Seljuqs of Anatolia, 1192-1280.

60.21 al-Juwaynī, ʿAlāʾaldīn ʿAṭāʾmalik ibn Muḥammad (d.1283): *The History of the World-Conqueror* [*Tārīkh-i Jahāngushā*]. Transl. by John Andrew Boyle. Vol. 1.2. Manchester 1958.
An account of the conquests of Chingiz-Khān (1206-27).

60.22 Rashīdaldīn Faḍlallāh (d.1318): *The successors of Genghis Khan* [*Jāmiʿ al-tawārīkh,* partial transl.]. Transl. from the Persian of Rashīd al-Dīn by John Andrew Boyle. New York 1971.
Extending to the reign of Öljeytü (1294-1307).

60.23 Abū l-Fidāʾ Ismāʿīl ibn ʿAlī: *The memoirs of a Syrian prince: Abū'l-Fidāʾ, Sultan of Ḥamāh (672-732 / 1273-1331)* [*al-Mukhtaṣar fī akhbār al-bashar*]. Transl. with an introduction by P[eter] M[alcolm] Holt. Wiesbaden 1983. (*Freiburger Islamstudien.* 9.)

60.24 Ibn Baṭṭūṭa, Muḥammad ibn ʿAlī (d.1368 or 1377): *The travels of Ibn Baṭṭūṭa, A.D. 1325-1354* [*Tuḥfat al-nuẓẓār fī gharāʾib al-amṣār wa-ʿajāʾib al-asfār*]. Transl. with revisions and notes . . . by H. A. R. Gibb. 1-3 [all published]. Cambridge 1958-71.
An account of travels extending from Morocco beyond the Near and Middle East to East and South-East Asia. The fourth part is available in the edition and French translation of C. Defrémery and B. R. Sanguinetti: *Voyage d'Ibn Batoutah.* Paris 1853-8.

60.25 al-Maqrīzī, Aḥmad ibn ʿAlī (d.1442): *Histoire des sultans mamlouks de l'Égypte, écrite an arabe par Taki-eddin-Ahmed-Makrizi* [*Kitāb al-Sulūk li-maʿrifat al-mulūk*], traduite en français et accompagnée de notes philologiques, historiques et géographiques par É[tienne] Quatremère. Vol. 1.2. Paris 1837-44.

60.26 al-Ẓāhirī, Khalīl ibn Shāhīn (d.1468): *La Zubda kachf al-mamālik* [*Zubdat kashf al-mamālik*]. Trad. française par Jean-Michel Venture de Paradis avec une notice sur le traducteur. [Ed.:] Jean Gaulmier. Beyrouth 1950.
A description of Egypt and Syria under the Mamlūks in the fifteenth century.

60.27 Ibn Taghrībirdī, Abū l-Maḥāsin Yūsuf (d.1470): *History of Egypt, 1382-1469 A.D.* [*al-Nujūm al-ẓāhira fī mulūk Miṣr wal-Qāhira*].

Transl. from the Arabic annals of Abu l-Maḥâsin ibn Taghrî Birdî by William Popper. Part 1-7 [with] Indices. Berkeley, Los Angeles 1954-63.

—— al-Qalqashandī, Aḥmad ibn ʿAlī (d.1418): *Ṣubḥ al-aʿshā fī ṣināʿat al-inshāʾ* [excerpts] in: Gaudefroy-Demombynes, M.: *La Syrie à l'époque des Mamelouks.* 1923 [66.24].

60.28 Ibn ʿArabshāh, Aḥmad ibn Muḥammad (d.1450): *Tamerlane, or Timur the Great Amir* [*ʿAjāʾib al-maqdūr fī nawāʾib Tīmūr*]. Transl. by J. H. Sanders from the Arabic life by Ahmed ibn Arabshah. London 1936.

60.29 Ḥasan-i Fasāʾī: *History of Persia under Qājār rule.* Transl. from the Persian of Ḥasan-e Fasāʾī's *Fārsnāma-ye Nāṣerī* by Heribert Busse. New York, London 1972.

Historians of Spain and the Maghrib

60.30 Ibn ʿIdhārī al-Marrākushī, Aḥmad ibn Muḥammad (fl.1312-13): *Histoire de l'Afrique du Nord et de l'Espagne* [*Kitāb al-Bayān al-mughrib fī akhbār mulūk al-Andalus wal-Maghrib*]. Trad. française par Éd. Fagnan. 1.2. Alger 1901-4.
Annals of the Muslim West to AD 997.

60.31 Ibn Ḥayyān, Ḥayyān ibn Khalaf (d.1076): *Cronica del Califa ʿAbdarraḥmān III an-Nāṣir entre los años 912 y 942 (al-Muqtabis. V).* Traducción, notas e indices por Jesús Viguera y Federico Corriente. Zaragoza 1981.

60.32 ʿAbdalwāḥid ibn ʿAlī al-Marrākushī: *Histoire des Almohades* [*Kitāb al-Muʿjib fī talkhīṣ akhbār al-Maghrib,* written AD 1224]. Trad. française par Éd. Fagnan. Alger 1893.

60.33 Ibn al-Khaṭīb, Lisānaldīn Muḥammad ibn ʿAbdallāh (d.1375): *Kitāb Aʿmāl al-aʿlām.* Parte 3ª: *Historia medieval islámica de Norte de Africa y Sicilia.* Traducción, notes e indices por Rafaela Castrillo. Madrid 1983.

—— *Aʿmāl al-aʿlām* [excerpts] *v.* Hoenerbach, W.: Islamische Geschichte Spaniens. 1970 [54.05].

60.34 Ibn Khaldūn, ʿAbdalraḥmān ibn Muḥammad (d.1406): *Histoire des Berbères et des dynasties musulmanes de l'Afrique septentrionale* [*Kitāb al-ʿIbar wa-dīwān al-mubtadaʾ wal-khabar,* partial transl.]. Trad. française par [MacGuckin] de Slane. 1-4. Paris 1852-6. – Nouvelle éd. par Paul Casanova, [4:] Henri Pérès. Paris 1925-56 (1-3: [2]1968-9).
For Ibn Khaldūn's *Introduction, v.* [33.77].

60.35 al-Maqqarī, Aḥmad ibn Muḥammad (d.1632): *The history of the Mahommedan dynasties in Spain, extracted from the Nafhu-t-tíb* . . . [*Nafḥ al-ṭīb min ghuṣn al-Andaluṣ al-raṭīb*]. Transl. . . . by Pascual de Gayangos. Vol. 1.2. London 1840-3; repr. New York 1964.

Literature on the history of individual periods

Not all periods, regions and personalities have yet been adequately studied and treated in monographs. For many subjects therefore only the general and collaborative works mentioned for Chapter I (General surveys) and Chapter V (Regions) can be cited.

1. Arabia and the Arabs before Islam

61.01 Altheim, Franz; Stiehl, Ruth [ed.]: *Die Araber in der Alten Welt.* Bd. 1-5. Berlin 1964-68.

61.02 Caskel, Werner: Der arabische Stamm vor dem Islam und seine gesellschaftliche und juristische Organisation. In: Accademia Nazionale dei Lincei. *Atti del Convegno internazionale sul tema: Dalla tribù allo stato, 1961.* Roma 1962, pp.139-49.

61.03 Crone, Patricia: *Meccan trade and the rise of Islam.* Cambridge 1987.

61.04 Dietrich, Albert: Geschichte Arabiens vor dem Islam. In: *Handbuch der Orientalistik.* Abt. 1. Bd. 2: *Keilschriftforschung und alte Geschichte Vorderasiens.* Abschnitt 4: *Orientalische Geschichte von Kyros bis Mohammed.* Lfg. 2. Leiden and Köln 1966, pp.291-336.

61.05 Grohmann, Adolf: *Arabien.* München 1963. (*Handbuch der Altertumswissenschaft.* Abt. 3, T. 1, Bd. 3: *Kulturgeschichte des Alten Orients.* Abschnitt 3,4.)

61.06 Grohmann, Adolf; Caskel, Werner; Spuler, Bertold; Wiet, Gaston; Marçais, Georges: al-ʿArab. In: *EI*² 1, s. n. (1957).

61.07 Grunebaum, Gustav Edmund von: The nature of Arab unity before Islam. In: *Arabica.* Leiden. 10. 1963, pp.5-23.

61.08 Kister, Meir Jacob: *Studies in Jāhiliyya and early Islam.* London 1980. (*Collected Studies Series.* 123.)

61.09 Lammens, Henri: *L'Arabie occidentale avant l'Hégire.* Beyrouth 1928.

61.10 —: *Le berceau de l'Islam. L'Arabie occidentale avant l'Hégire.* Vol. 1: *Le climat – les bédouins.* Romae 1914. (*Scripta Pontificii Instituti Biblici.*)

—— Meyer, E.: *Der historische Gehalt der Aiyām al-ʿArab.* 1970 [15.59].

61.11 Rentz, G.: Djazīrat al-ʿArab. VII: History. In: *EI*² 1, s. n. (1957).

61.12 Brünnow, Rudolf E.; Domaszewski, A. von: *Die Provincia Arabia auf Grund zweier in den Jahren 1897 bis 1898 unternommener Reisen und der Berichte früherer Reisender.* Bd. 1-3. Strassburg 1904-9.

61.13 Christensen, Arthur: *L'Iran sous les Sassanides.* 2ème éd. Copenhague, Paris 1944. (*Annales du Musée Guimet. Bibliothèque d'études.* 48.)

61.14 Dussaud, René: *La pénétration des Arabes en Syrie avant l'Islam.* Paris 1955. (*Bibliothèque archéologique et historique de l'Institut français d'archéologie de Beyrouth.* 5.)

61.15 Maier, Franz Georg: *Die Verwandlung der Mittelmeerwelt.* Frankfurt, Hamburg 1968. (*Fischer Weltgeschichte.* Bd. 9.)
The Mediterranean area from the third until the beginning of the eighth century: collapse and Christianisation of the Imperium Romanum, the rise of the Byzantine empire, the emergence of Islam.

61.16 Moubarac, Youakim: Les études d'épigraphie sud-sémitiques et la naissance de l'Islam. Eléments de bibliographie et lignes de recherches. In: *Revue des études islamiques.* Paris 23. 1955, pp.121-76; 25. 1957, pp.13-68.

61.17 Nöldeke, Theodor: *Die ghassânischen Fürsten aus dem Hause Gafna's.* Berlin 1887. (*Abhandlungen d. Kgl. Preußischen Akademie d. Wissenschaften.*)

61.18 Rothstein, Gustav: *Die Dynastie der Lahmiden in al-Ḥîra. Ein*

Versuch zur arabisch-persischen Geschichte zur Zeit der Sasaniden. Berlin 1899.
61.19 Wissmann, Hermann von: *Über die frühe Geschichte Arabiens und das Entstehen des Sabäerreiches. Die Geschichte von Saba'.* 1. Wien 1975. (Österr. Akad. d. Wissenschaften. Phil.-hist. Kl. *Sitzungsberichte.* Bd. 301. Abh. 5 = *Sammlung Eduard Glaser.* 13.)

61.20 Bravmann, Meir Max: *The spiritual background of early Islam.* Leiden 1972.
61.21 Fahd, Toufic: *Le panthéon de l'Arabie centrale à la veille de l'Hégire.* Paris 1968. (Institut français d'archéologie de Beyrouth. *Bibliothèque archéologique et historique.* 88.)
61.22 Lammens, Henri: La Mecque à la veille de l'Hégire. In: *Mélanges de l'Université Saint-Joseph.* Beirut. 9. 1924, pp.99-439.
61.23 Snouck Hurgronje, Christiaan: *Het Mekkaansche Feest.* Leiden 1880 = *Verspreide Geschriften.* 1. Bonn and Leipzig 1923, pp.1-124.
61.24 Trimingham, J. Spencer: *Christianity among the Arabs in pre-Islamic times.* London, Beirut 1979 (*Arab Background Series.*)
61.25 Wolf, Eric R.: The social organization of Mecca and the origins of Islam. In: *Southwestern Journal of Anthropology.* Albuquerque 7. 1951, pp.329-56.

2. *Muḥammad (c.610-632)*

Cf. Chapter III above [31.01-35].

3. *The caliphate until the end of the Umayyad period (632-750)*

63.01 Caetani, Leone: *Annali dell'Islam.* Vol. 1-10. Milano 1905-18, (9.10:) Roma 1926. Repr. Hildesheim 1971-3.
Detailed synopsis of primary accounts in chronological order for the events of the years 1-40 AH/622-61 AD.
63.02 —: *Chronographia Islamica ossia riassunto chronologico della storia di tutti i popoli musulmani.* Vol. 1-5. Paris 1913-23.
Concise chronological survey of events until the end of the Umayyad caliphate.
—— Donner, F. M.: The formation of the Islamic state. 1986 [33.59c].
63.03 Shaban, Muhammad Abdalhayy: *Islamic history. A new interpretation.* [*1*:] *A.D. 600-750 (A.H. 132).* Cambridge 1971.
See also [64.01].
63.04 Veccia Vaglieri, Laura: The Patriarchal and Umayyad caliphates. In: *The Cambridge History of Islam.* 1970 [14.03], pp.57-103.
63.05 Wellhausen, Julius: *Das arabische Reich und sein Sturz.* Berlin 1902.
English transl.: *The Arab Kingdom and its fall.* Transl. by Margaret Graham Weir. Calcutta 1927; repr. Beirut 1963.

The Islamic conquests

63.06 Becker, Carl Heinrich: Die Ausbreitung der Araber im Mittelmeergebiet. (1912.) In: Becker: *Islamstudien.* 1924 [14.17]. 1, pp.66-145.
63.07 Butler, Alfred J.: *The Arab conquest of Egypt and the last thirty years of the Roman dominion.* (First publ. 1902.) Second ed. by P. M. Fraser with a critical bibliography and additional documentation. [Also contains:] Butler: *The treaty of Miṣr in Ṭabarī.* (1913.) *Babylon of*

Egypt. A study in the history of Old Cairo. (1914.) Oxford 1978.
63.08 Donner, Fred McGraw: *The early Islamic conquests.* Princeton, NJ, 1981. (*Princeton Studies on the Near East.*)
63.09 Gibb, Hamilton Alexander Roskeen: *The Arab conquests in Central Asia.* London 1923. (*James G. Forloy Fund.* 3.)
63.10 Hill, Donald Routledge: *The termination of hostilities in the early Arab Conquests, A.D. 634-656.* London 1971.
63.11 Mantran, Robert: *L'expansion musulmane (VIIe-XIe siècles).* Paris 1969; ²1979. (*Nouvelle Clio.* 20.)
63.11a Morony, M. G.: *Iraq after the Muslim Conquest.* Princeton, NJ, 1984.

63.12 Eickhoff, Ekkehard: *Seekrieg und Seepolitik zwischen Islam und Abendland. Das Mittelmeer unter byzantinischer und arabischer Hegemonie (650-1040).* Berlin 1966.
63.13 Hoenerbach, Wilhelm: *Araber und Mittelmeer. Anfänge und Probleme arabischer Seegeschichte.* Kiel 1967.
63.14 Vasiliev, Aleksandr Aleksandrovič: *Byzance et les Arabes.* Éd. Française préparée par Henri Grégoire et Marius Canard. 1-3. Bruxelles 1935-68.
3: Ernst Honigmann: *Die Ostgrenze des byzantinischen Reiches von 363 bis 1071.* 1935.

On administration and taxation law, cf. Dennett [43.01a], Gibb [43.02], Løkkegaard [43.04], Puin [33.83], Schmucker [43.05], Tritton [42.09].

(a) The period of the 'orthodox' caliphs (al-Rāshidūn, 632-61)

63.15 Hinds, Martin: The murder of the Caliph ʿUthmân. In: *International Journal of Middle East Studies.* Cambridge. 3. 1972, pp.450-69.
63.16 —: The Siffin arbitration agreement. In: *Journal of Semitic Studies.* Manchester. 17. 1972, pp.93-129.
63.17 Veccia Vaglieri, Laura: ʿAlī b. Abī Ṭālib. In: *EI²*. 1, s. n. (1956).
63.18 —: Il conflitto ʿAlī-Muʿāwiya e la secessione khārigita riesaminati alla luce di fonti ibāḍite. In: *Annali dell'Istituto Universitario Orientale di Napoli.* N. S. 4. 1952, pp.1-94; 5. 1953, pp.1-98.
63.19 Wellhausen, Julius: Prolegomena zur ältesten Geschichte des Islams. In: Wellhausen: *Skizzen und Vorarbeiten.* H. 6. Berlin 1899, pp.1-110.
—— *Die religiös-politischen Oppositionsparteien im alten Islam.* 1901 [32.10].

(b) The caliphate of the Umayyads (661-750)

Until the second civil war:

63.20 Lammens, Henri: Le califat de Yazîd Ier. In: *Mélanges de la Faculté Orientale, Université Saint-Joseph.* Beyrouth. 4. 1910, pp.233-312; 5. 1911-12, pp.79-267, 589-724; 6. 1913, pp.401-92; 7. 1914-21, pp.211-44.
63.21 —: Études sur le règne du calife omaiyade Moʿâwia Ier. In: *Mélanges de la Faculté Orientale, Université Saint-Joseph.* Beyrouth. 1. 1906, pp.1-108; 2. 1907, pp.1-172; 3. 1908, pp.145-312. [Also separately:] Paris 1908.
63.22 —: Moʿāwia II ou le dernier des Sofiānides. In: *Rivista degli Studi*

Orientali. Roma. 7. 1915, pp.1-49 = Lammens: *Études sur le siècle des Omayyades.* Beyrouth 1930, pp.163-210.
63.23 —: Ziād ibn Abīhi, vice-roi de l'Iraq, lieutenant de Mo'āwia Ier. In: *Rivista degli Studi Orientali.* Roma. 4. 1911-12, pp.1-45, 199-250, 653-92 = Lammens: *Études* [63.22], pp.27-161.
63.24 Rotter, Gernot: *Die Umayyaden und der zweite Bürgerkrieg (680-692).* Wiesbaden 1983. (*Abhandlungen für die Kunde des Morgenlandes.* 45, 3.)
63.25 Sellheim, Rudolf: *Der zweite Bürgerkrieg im Islam (680-692). Das Ende der mekkanisch-medinensischen Vorherrschaft.* Wiesbaden 1970. (*Sitzungsberichte der Wissenschaftl. Gesellschaft an der J.-W.-Goethe-Universität Frankfurt/Main.* Bd. 8. Jhg. 1969. Nr. 4.)

The Marwānids

63.26 Barthold, W. W. [Vasilij V. Bartol'd]: Caliph 'Umar II and the conflicting reports on his personality (1922) [transl. from the Russian]. In: *The Islamic Quarterly.* London. 15. 1971, pp.69-95.
63.27 Bosworth, Clifford Edmund: Rajā' ibn Ḥaywa al-Kindī and the Umayyad caliphs. In: *The Islamic Quarterly.* London. 16. 1972, pp.36-80.
63.28 Caskel, Werner: *Der Felsendom und die Wallfahrt nach Jerusalem.* Köln, Opladen 1963. (*Arbeitsgemeinschaft für Forschung des Landes Nordrhein-Westfalen. Geisteswissenschaften.* 114.)
On the Dome of the Rock also:
63.29 Grabar, Oleg: The Umayyad Dome of the Rock. In: *Ars Orientalis.* Washington. 3. 1959, pp.33-62.
63.30 Dennett, David Clement: *Marwan ibn Muhammed: the passing of the Umayyad Caliphate.* Cambridge, Mass. 1939.
63.31 Gabrieli, Francesco: *Il califfato di Hishâm. Studi di storia omayyade.* Alexandrie 1935. (*Mémoires de la Société royale d'archéologie d'Alexandrie.* 7,1.)
63.32 —: Al-Walīd ibn Yazīd. Il califfo e il poeta. In: *Rivista degli Studi Orientali.* Roma. 15. 1935, pp.1-64.
—— Gaube, H.: *Die syrischen Wüstenschlösser.* 1979 [15.36].
63.33 Gibb, Hamilton Alexander Roskeen: The Fiscal Rescript of 'Umar II. In: *Arabica.* Leiden. 2. 1955, pp.1-16.
63.34 Lammens, Henri: L'avènement des Marwānides et le califat de Marwān Ier. In: *Mélanges de l'Université Saint-Joseph.* Beyrouth. 12. 1927, pp.43-147.
63.35 Périer, Jean: *Vie d'al-Ḥadjdjâdj ibn Yousof (41-95 de l'Hégire = 661-714 de J.-C.) d'après les sources arabes.* Paris 1904. (*Bibliothèque de l'École des Hautes Études. Sciences historiques et philologiques.* Fasc. 151.)
Cf.also
63.36 Dietrich, Albert: al-Ḥadjdjādj b. Yūsuf. In: *EI*². 3, s. n. (1965).
63.37 Sayed, Redwan: *Die Revolte des Ibn als-Aš'aṯ und die Koranleser. Ein Beitrag zur Religionsgeschichte der frühen Umayyadenzeit.* Freiburg i. Br. 1977. (*Islamkundliche Untersuchungen.* 45.)

4. The caliphate of the 'Abbāsids and its successor states from 749 until the middle of the eleventh century

64.01 Shaban, Muhammad Abdalhayy: *Islamic history. A new interpreta-*

tion. 2: *A.D. 750-1055 (A.H. 132-448).* Cambridge 1976.
See also above [63.03].
64.02 Sourdel, Dominique: The 'Abbāsid Caliphate. In: *The Cambridge History of Islam.* 1970 [14.03]. 1, pp.104-39.
64.03 —: *Le vizirat abbaside, 749-936.* 1.2. Damas 1959-60.
—— Vasiliev, A. A. [*et al.*]: *Byzance et les Arabes.* 1935-68 [63.14].

The 'Abbāsid revolution

64.04 Cahen, Claude: Points de vue sur la 'révolution 'abbâside'. In: *Revue historique.* Paris. Ann. 87, t. 230, 1963, pp.295-338.
64.05 Moscati, Sabatino: Studi su Abū Muslim. 1-3. In: Accademia Nazionale dei Lincei. *Rendiconti cl. sc. mor.* Roma. Ser. 8, v. 4. 1949-50, pp.323-35, 474-95; 5. 1950-51, pp.89-105.
64.06 Nagel, Tilman: *Untersuchungen zur Entstehung des abbasidischen Kalifates.* Bonn 1972. (*Bonner Orientalistische Studien.* N. S. 22.)
64.07 Shaban, Muhammad Abdalhayy: *The 'Abbāsid revolution.* Cambridge 1970.
64.07a Sharon, Moshe: *Black banners from the East: the establishment of the 'Abbāsid state – incubation of a revolt.* Jerusalem; Leiden 1983. (*The Max Schloessinger Memorial Series.* Monograph 2.)
64.08 Vloten, Gerlof van: *De opkomst der Abbasiden in Chorasan.* Leiden 1890.

(a) The first century of the 'Abbāsids (749-847)

64.09 Daniel, Elton Lee: *The political and social history of Khurasan under Abbasid rule, 747-820.* Minneapolis, Chicago 1979.
64.10 Dietrich, Albert: Das politische Testament des zweiten 'Abbāsidenkalifen al-Manṣūr. In: *Der Islam.* Berlin. 30. 1952, pp.133-65.
64.11 Gabrieli, Francesco: *al-Ma'mūn e gli 'Alidi.* Leipzig 1929. (*Morgenländische Texte und Forschungen.* Bd. 2. H. 1.)
64.12 —: La successione di Hārūn ar-Rashīd e la guerra fra al-Amīn e al-Ma'mūn. (Studio storico su un periodo del califfato 'abbāside.) In: *Rivista degli Studi Orientali.* Roma. 11. 1926-28, pp.341-97.
—— Goitein, S. D.: *A turning-point in the history of the Muslim state.* 1949 [33.66].
64.13 Kennedy, Hugh: *The early Abbasid Caliphate: a political history.* London 1981.
64.14 Lassner, Jacob: *The shaping of 'Abbāsid rule.* Princeton, NJ, 1979. (*Princeton Studies on the Near East.*)
Part 1: *The political setting.* Part 2: *The physical setting.*
—— *The topography of Baghdad.* 1970 [53.06].
64.15 On the foundation and layout of Baghdad, cf. Duri, Abdal-Aziz: Baghdad. In: *EI*². 1, s. n. (1958-59), and the special volume of the journal *Arabica* (t. 9, fasc. 3): *Baġdād. Volume spécial du mille deux centième anniversaire de sa fondation.* Leiden 1962.
64.17 Moscati, Sabatino: Le califat d'al-Hādī. In: *Studia Orientalia.* Helsinki. 13,4. 1946, pp.1-28.
64.18 —: Studi storici sul califfato di al-Mahdī. In: *Orientalia.* Roma. N. S. 14. 1945, pp.300-54; 15. 1946, pp.155-79.
—— Patton, W. M.: *Aḥmed ibn Ḥanbal and the Miḥna.* 1897 [32.38].
64.19 Sourdel, Dominique: La politique religieuse du calife 'abbâside

al-Ma'mûn. In: *Revue des études islamiques.* Paris. 30. 1962, pp.27-48.
Watt, W. M.: *The formative period of Islamic thought.* 1973 [30.15].

(b) The decline of the caliphate (ninth-tenth centuries)

64.20 Bowen, Harold: *The life and time of 'Alí ibn 'Ísà 'the good vizier'.* Cambridge 1928.
64.21 Busse, Heribert: *Chalif und Großkönig. Die Buyiden im Iraq (945-1055).* Beirut, Wiesbaden 1969 (*Beiruter Texte und Studien.* 6.)
64.22 Forstner, Martin: *Das Kalifat des Abbasiden al-Musta'īn (248/862-252/866).* Mainz 1968.
64.23 —: *Al-Mu'tazz billāh (252/866-255/869). Die Krise des abbasidischen Kalifats im 3./9. Jahrhundert. Beitrag zur politischen Geschichte der sog. Periode der Anarchie von Samarra.* Germersheim 1976.
—— Gibb, H. A. R.: Government and Islam under the early 'Abbāsids. The political collapse of Islam. 1961 [33.62].
64.24 Glagow, Rainer: *Das Kalifat des al-Mu'taḍid Billāh (892-902).* Phil. Diss. Bonn 1968.
64.25 Halm, Heinz: *Die Traditionen über den Aufstand 'Alī ibn Muḥammads, des 'Herrn der Zanǧ'. Eine quellenkritische Untersuchung.* Phil. Diss. Bonn 1967.
64.26 Hellige, Walther: *Die Regentschaft al-Muwaffaqs. Ein Wendepunkt in der 'Abbâsidengeschichte.* Berlin 1936.
—— Herzfeld, Ernst: *Geschichte der Stadt Samarra.* 1948 [53.05].
64.27 Laoust, Henri: Les agitations religieuses à Baghdād aux IVe et Ve siècles de l'Hégire. In: *Islamic civilization, A.D. 950-1150.* Oxford 1973, pp.169-85.
64.28 Mottahedeh, Roy P.: *Loyalty and leadership in an early Islamic society.* Princeton, NJ, 1980.
64.29 Popovic, Alexandre: *La révolte des esclaves en Iraq au IIIe/IXe siècle.* Paris 1976. (*Bibliothèque des études islamiques.* T. 6.)
64.30 Töllner, Helmut: *Die türkischen Garden am Kalifenhof von Samarra. Ihre Entstehung und Machtergreifung bis zum Kalifat Al-Mu'taḍids.* Walldorf 1971. (*Beiträge zur Sprach- und Kulturgeschichte des Orients.* 21.)

(c) The rise of local autonomous states and the successor states of the caliphal empire (mid ninth-mid eleventh centuries)

The West

Spain under the Umayyads:

64.31 Dozy, Reinhart Pieter Anne: *Histoire des Musulmans d'Espagne jusqu'à la conquête de l'Andalousie par les Almoravides (711-1110).* Leiden 1861. – Nouvelle éd., revue et mis à jour par É. Lévi-Provençal. 1-3. Leiden 1932.
—— Hoenerbach, W.: *Islamische Geschichte Spaniens.* 1970 [54.05]. T. 1: *Von der Eroberung bis zum Sturz des Kalifates (711-1031).*
64.32 Lévi-Provençal, Évariste: *La civilisation arabe en Espagne. Vue générale.* Paris 1961; repr. 1967. (*Islam d'hier et d'aujourd'hui.* 1.)
64.33 —: *Histoire de l'Espagne musulmane.* T. 1-3. Paris [etc.] ²1950, 1953.

1: *La conquête et l'émirat hispano-umaiyade (710-912).* ²1950.
2: *Le califat umaiyade de Cordoue (912-1031).* ²1950.
3: *Le siècle du califat de Cordoue.* 1953.
64.34 —: *Islam d'Occident.* Paris 1948. (*Islam d'hier et d'aujourd'hui.* 7.)

North Africa:
64.35 Idris, Hady Roger: *La Berbérie orientale sous les Zīrīdes, Xe-XIIe siècles.* T. 1.2. Paris 1962. (*Faculté des Lettres et sciences humaines d'Alger. Publications de l'Institut d'études orientales.* 22.)
64.36 Talbi, Mohamed: *L'émirat aghlabide, 184-296/800-909. Histoire politique.* Paris 1966. (*Publications de la Faculté des Lettres, Tunis.*)

Egypt before the Fāṭimids:
64.37 Hassan, Zaky Mohamed: *Les Tulunides. Etudes de l'Egypte à la fin du IXe siècle, 868-905.* Paris 1933.

The Fāṭimids in North Africa and in Egypt
(cf. also Section 3 [32.17-23] on the Ismāʿīliyya and the origins of the Fāṭimid movement):
64.38 O'Leary, de Lacy E.: *A short history of the Fatimid Khalifate.* London 1923.
64.39 Wüstenfeld, Ferdinand: *Geschichte der Fatimiden-Chalifen. Nach arabischen Quellen.* Göttingen 1881. (*Abhandlungen der Kgl. Gesellschaft der Wissenschaften.* 26. 27.)
64.40 Ess, Josef van: *Chiliastische Erwartung und die Versuchung der Gottheit. Der Kalif al-Ḥākim (386-411 H.).* Heidelberg 1977. (*Abh. d. Heidelberger Akad. d. Wiss. Phil.-hist. Kl.* Jhg. 1977. Abh. 2.)
64.41 Stern, Samuel Miklos: The succession to the Fatimid Imam al-Āmir, the claims of the later Fatimids to the Imamate, and the rise of Ṭayyibī Ismailism. In: *Oriens.* Leiden. 4. 1951, pp.193-255 = Stern: *History and culture of the medieval Muslim world.* London 1987, no. xi.

The East
64.42 Bosworth, Clifford Edmund: *The Ghaznavids. Their empire in Afghanistan and Eastern Iran, 944-1040.* Edinburgh 1963.
See also [65.02].
64.43 —: *The medieval history of Iran, Afghanistan and Central Asia.* London 1977.
Collected articles 1960-76.
64.44 —: *Sīstān under the Arabs from the Islamic conquest to the rise of the Ṣaffārids (30-250/651-864).* Rome 1968. (Istituto Italiano per il Medio ed Estremo Oriente. *Reports and Memoirs.* 11.)
64.45 *The Cambridge History of Iran.* Vol. 4: *The period from the Arab invasion to the Saljuqs.* Ed. by R. N. Frye. Cambridge 1975.
90-135 C. E. Bosworth: *The Ṭāhirids and the Ṣaffārids.*
136-61 R. N. Frye: *The Sāmānids.*
162-97 C. E. Bosworth: *The early Ghaznavids.*
198-249 W. Madelung: *The minor dynasties of Northern Iran.*
250-304 H. Busse: *Iran under the Būyids.*
64.46 Canard, Marius: *Histoire de la dynastie des H'amdanides de Jazîra et de Syrie.* 1. Alger 1951.

64.47 Frye, Richard Nelson: *The Golden Age of Persia: the Arabs in the East.* London 1975; repr. 1977.
64.48 Minorsky, Vladimir: *La domination des Dailamites.* Paris 1932. (*Publications de la Société des études iraniennes et de l'art persan.* 3.)
64.49 —: *Studies in Caucasian history.* London 1953.
64.50 Nöldeke, Theodor: Yakúb the coppersmith and his dynasty. In: Nöldeke: *Sketches from Eastern history.* London and Edinburgh 1892, pp.176-206.
64.51 Spuler, Bertold: *Iran in früh-islamischer Zeit. Politik, Kultur, Verwaltung und öffentliches Leben zwischen der arabischen und der seldschukischen Eroberung, 633-1055.* Wiesbaden 1952. (Akademie der Wissenschaften und der Literatur. *Veröffentlichungen der Orientalischen Kommission.* 2.)

5. The Seljuq period (mid eleventh-mid thirteenth centuries)

65.01 Barthold, W. [Vasilij Vladimorovič Bartol'd]: *Zwölf Vorlesungen über die Geschichte der Türken Mittelasiens.* Berlin 1935. (*Die Welt des Islam.* Beiheft zu Bd. 14-17.)
—— —: *Turkestan down to the Mongol invasion.* 1968 [56.15].
65.02 Bosworth, Clifford Edmund: *The later Ghaznavids. Splendour and decay.* Edinburgh 1977. (*Persian Studies Series.*)
65.03 Cahen, Claude: The historiography of the Seljuqid period. In: *Historians of the Middle East.* 1962 [15.53]. pp.59-78.
65.04 —: *Turcobyzantina et Oriens Christianus.* London 1974. (*Collected Studies.* 34.)
65.05 *The Cambridge History of Iran.* Vol. 5: *The Saljuq and Mongol periods.* Ed. by J. A. Boyle. Cambridge 1968.
65.06 Holt, Peter Malcolm: *The age of the Crusades: the Near East from the eleventh century to 1517.* London 1986.
65.06a *Islamic civilization, A.D. 950-1150.* Ed.: D. S. Richards. Oxford 1973. (*Papers on Islamic History.* 3.)
Pp. 1-16: C. E. Bosworth: Barbarian invasions. The coming of the Turks into the Islamic world.

On the sultanate of Delhi, see below [66.15-16].

(a) The Seljuqs (Iran, Iraq, Anatolia)

65.07 Cahen, Claude: The Turkish invasion: the Selchükids. In: *A History of the Crusades* [65.20]. 1, pp.135-76.
65.08 Klausner, Carla L.: *The Seljuk vizierate. A study of civil administration, 1055-1194.* Cambridge 1973.
65.09 Lambton, Ann Katherine Swynford: The internal structure of the Saljuq empire. In: *The Cambridge History of Iran.* 5. 1968 [65.05], pp.203-82.

The Seljuqs of Rūm and other Turkish principalities of Asia Minor:

65.10 Cahen, Claude: La campagne de Mantzikert d'après les sources musulmanes. In: *Byzantion.* Bruxelles. 9. 1934, pp.613-42.
65.11 —: *Pre-Ottoman Turkey. A general survey of the material and spiritual culture and history, c. 1071-1330.* Transl. from the French by J. Jones-Williams. London, New York 1968.
65.12 —: The Turks in Iran and Anatolia before the Mongol invasion. In: *A history of the Crusades* [65.20]. 2, pp.661-92.

65.13 Rice, Tamara Talbot: *The Seljuks in Asia Minor.* London 1961.

(b) Syria and Egypt under Atabegs and Ayyūbids; the Islamic confrontation with the Crusaders. The final phase of the 'Abbāsid caliphate (12th–mid-13th centuries)

The Crusades

65.14 Atiya, Aziz Suryal: *The Crusade: historiography and bibliography.* Bloomington 1962.

65.15 Mayer, Hans Eberhard: *Bibliographie zur Geschichte der Kreuzzüge.* Hannover 1960.

65.16 —: Literaturbericht über die Geschichte der Kreuzzüge. Veröffentlichungen 1958-1967. In: *Historische Zeitschrift.* Sonderheft 3. München 1969, pp.641-731.

Sources:

65.17 *Recueil des historiens des Croisades.* Publié par les soins de l'Académie des Inscriptions et des Belles-Lettres. Paris 1844-1906. [2:] *Historiens orientaux.* T. 1-5. 1872-1906.
Extracts from Arabic historians with text and French translation. The sole major collection of sources accessible to non-Arabists, obsolete in selection and translation.

65.18 Gabrieli, Francesco: *Arab Historians of the Crusades.* Selected and translated from the Arabic sources. Translated from the Italian by E. J. Costello. London 1978.
Well translated and informative anthology of (mainly contemporary) Arab historians.

65.19 Cahen, Claude: *La Syrie du Nord au temps des Croisades et la principauté franque d'Antioche.* Paris 1940. (Institut français de Damas. *Bibliothèque orientale.* T. 1.)
The introduction ('Les sources', pp.33-93) comprises the most detailed and still the most comprehensive survey of the sources and their relationship with each other. Updated summary in *EI*². 2, s. v. Crusades / Croisades (1960-61).

General surveys:

65.20 *A history of the Crusades.* General ed.: Kenneth M. Setton. Philadelphia 1955-62; Madison, Wisc. 1969-85.
1: *The first hundred years.* 1955; ²1969.
2: *The latter Crusades, 1189-1311.* 1962; ²1969.
3: *The fourteenth and fifteenth centuries.* 1975.
4: *The art and architecture of the Crusader states.* 1977.
5: *The impact of the Crusades on the Near East.* 1985.

65.21 Mayer, Hans Eberhard: *Geschichte der Kreuzzüge.* Stuttgart 1965; ⁴1976. (*Urban Taschenbücher.* 86.)

65.22 Runciman, Steven: *A History of the Crusades.* Vols 1-3. Cambridge 1951-5.

Individual themes:

65.23 Atiya, Aziz Suryal: *The Crusade in the later Middle Ages.* London 1938; 2nd ed. New York 1970.

65.24 —: *Crusade, commerce and culture.* Bloomington 1962.

—— Cahen, C.: *Turcobyzantina.* 1974 [65.04].

65.25 Cahen, Claude: *Orient et Occident au temps des Croisades.* Paris 1983.

65.26 Noth, Albrecht: *Heiliger Krieg und heiliger Kampf in Islam und Christentum. Beiträge zur Vorgeschichte und Geschichte der Kreuzzüge.* Bonn 1966. (*Bonner Historische Forschungen.* 28.)

65.27 Prawer, Joshua: *The Latin Kingdom of Jerusalem. European colonialism in the Middle Ages.* London 1972.

The Zengids

65.28 Élisséeff, Nikita: *Nūr ad-Dīn. Un grand prince musulman de Syrie au temps des Croisades (511-569 H./1118-1174).* T. 1-3. Damas 1967.

65.29 Gibb, Hamilton Alexander Roskeen: Zengi and the fall of Edessa. In: *A history of the Crusades* [65.20]. 1, pp.449-62. – The career of Nūr-ad-Dīn. Ibid. 1, pp.513-27. – The Aiyūbids. Ibid. 2, pp.693-714.

Saladin and the Third Crusade

65.30 Baldwin, Marshall Whithed: *Raymond III of Tripolis and the fall of Jerusalem (1140-1187).* Princeton, NJ, 1936.

65.31 Ehrenkreutz, Andrew Stefan: *Saladin.* Albany, NY, 1972.

65.32 Gibb, Hamilton Alexander Roskeen: *The life of Saladin from the works of 'Imād ad-Dīn and Bahā' ad-Dīn.* Oxford 1973.

65.33 Lyons, Malcolm Cameron; Jackson, David Edward Pritchett: *Saladin. The politics of the Holy War.* Cambridge 1982. (*Cambridge University Oriental Publications.*)

65.34 Möhring, Hannes: *Saladin und der Dritte Kreuzzug. Aiyubidische Strategie und Diplomatie im Vergleich vornehmlich der arabischen mit den lateinischen Quellen.* Wiesbaden 1980. (*Frankfurter Historische Abhandlungen.* Bd. 21.)

The Ayyūbids after Saladin

65.35 Dahlmanns, Franz-Josef: *Al-Malik al-'Ādil. Ägypten und der Vordere Orient in den Jahren 589/1193 bis 615/1218. Ein Beitrag zur ayyubidischen Geschichte.* Diss. Gießen 1975.

65.36 Gibb, Hamilton Alexander Roskeen: The Aiyūbids. In: *A history of the Crusades* [65.20]. 2. 1962, pp.693-714.

65.37 Gottschalk, Hans L.: *Al-Malik al-Kāmil von Egypten und seine Zeit. Eine Studie zur Geschichte Vorderasiens und Egyptens in der ersten Hälfte des 7./13. Jahrhunderts.* Wiesbaden 1958.

65.38 Humphreys, R. Stephen: *From Saladin to the Mongols. The Ayyubids of Damascus, 1193-1260.* Albany, NY, 1977.

65.39 Smith, G. R.: The Ayyūbids and Rasūlids – the transfer of power in 7th/13th century Yemen. In: *Islamic Culture.* Hyderabad. 43. 1969, pp.175-88.

The final phase of the 'Abbāsid caliphate

65.40 Hartmann, Angelika: *An-Nāṣir li-Dīn Allāh (1180-1225). Politik, Religion, Kultur in der späten 'Abbāsidenzeit.* Berlin [etc.] 1975. (*Studien zur Sprache, Geschichte und Kultur des islamischen Orients. Beihefte zur Zeitschrift 'Der Islam'.* N. F. Bd. 8.)

On the assassins, cf. Hodgson [32.24-25] and Lewis [32.26].

(c) Small states, Almoravids and Almohads in North Africa and Spain
65.41 Bosch Vilá, Jacinto: *Los Almorávides.* Tetuán 1956.
65.42 Golvin, Lucien: *Le Maghrib central à l'époque des Zirides. Recherches d'archéologie et d'histoire.* Paris 1957.
Esp. on the dynasty of the Ḥammādids (1015-1152).
65.43 Handler, Andrew: *The Zirids of Granada.* Coral Gables 1974.
65.44 Hazard, Harry W.: Moslem North Africa, 1049-1394. In: *A history of the Crusades* [65.20]. 3. 1975, pp.457-85.
—— Hoenerbach, W.: *Islamische Geschichte Spaniens.* 1970 [54.05].
T. 2.: *Die Kleinstaaten* (1031-1248).
65.45 Hopkins, John Francis Price: *Medieval Muslim Government in Barbary until the sixth century of the Hijra.* London 1958.
History, institutions and government organisation in the Maghrib until the Almohad period.
65.46 Huici Miranda, Ambrosio: *Historia politica del imperio almohade.* 1.2. Tetuán 1956-57.
65.47 Idris, Hady Roger: De la réalité de la catastrophe hilalienne. In: *Annales. Économies – sociétés – civilizations.* Paris. 23. 1968, pp.390-96.
—— *La Berbérie orientale sous les Zīrīdes, Xe-XIIe siècles.* 1962 [64.35].
65.48 —: Le Maghrib des Almoravides à la domination turque. In: *Regierung und Verwaltung des Vorderen Orients in islamischer Zeit.* T. 1. Leiden, Köln 1979 (*Handbuch der Orientalistik.* Abt. 1. Bd. 6. Abschn. 5), pp.1-16.

65.49 Le Tourneau, Roger: *The Almohad movement in North Africa in the twelfth and thirteenth centuries.* Princeton, NJ 1969.
65.50 Marçais, Georges: *Les Arabes en Berbérie du XIe au XIVe siècle.* Constantine, Paris 1913.
Crucial work on the invasion of the Hilāl Arabs and the subsequent history of the Arab tribes in the Maghrib. See also [54.19].

6. The Mongol period. From the conquest of Baghdad by the Mongols until the establishment of the Ottoman empire in the Near East (1258-1517)
—— Spuler, Bertold: *The Mongol period.* 1960 [14.05].

(a) The Mongol invasion and the Mongol period in the Islamic east (thirteenth-fifteenth centuries)
66.01 Alexandrescu-Dersca, Maria-Matilda: *La campagne de Timur en Anatolie (1402).* (1942.) Revised ed. London 1977.
The campaign of Tīmūr against Bāyezīd and the battle of Ankara 1402.
66.02 Barthold, V. V. [Vasilij Vladimirovič Bartol'd]: *Four studies in the history of Central Asia.* Leiden 1956-62.
Vol. 2: *Ulugh Beg* [*Ulugbek i ego vremja.* 1918].
Vol. 3, pp.1-72: *Mīr 'Alī Shīr* [*Mir Ali-Šir i političeskoja žizn'.* 1928].
66.03 Boyle, John Andrew: Dynastic and political history of the Īl-Khāns. In: *The Cambridge History of Iran.* Vol. 5. Cambridge 1968, pp.303-422.
66.04 —: *The Mongol World Empire, 1206-1370.* Preface by Owen

Lattimore. London 1977. (*Collected Studies.* 58.)
Collected studies 1952-75.

66.05 Cahen, Claude: The Mongols and the Near East. In: *A history of the Crusades* [65.20]. 2. ^{2}1969, pp.715-32.

66.06 Howorth, Sir Henry: *History of the Mongols.* 1-3. London 1876-88. Supplementary vol. with indices to the whole work. 1927. Repr. 1965.

66.07 Ohsson, Mouradja d': *Histoire des Mongols depuis Tchinguiz-Khan jusqu'à Timour Bey.* 1-4. Amsterdam 1824; ^{2}1834; ^{3}1852.

66.08 Roemer, Hans Robert: Veröffentlichungen zur Geschichte Timurs und seiner Nachfolger. In: *Central Asiatic Journal.* The Hague, Wiesbaden. 2. 1956, pp.219-32.

66.09 —: The Jalayirids, Muzaffarids and Sarbadārs (pp.1-41); Tīmūr in Iran (pp.41-97); The successors of Tīmūr (pp.98-146); The Türkmen dynasties (pp.147-88). In: *The Cambridge History of Iran* [56.09]. Vol. 6: The Timurid and Safavid periods. 1986, pp.1-188.

66.10 Saunders, John Joseph: *The history of the Mongol conquests.* London 1971.

66.11 Smith, John Masson: *The history of the Sarbadār dynasty, 1336-1381 A.D., and its sources.* The Hague, Paris 1970. (*Publications in Near and Middle East Studies, Columbia University.* Series A. 11.)

66.12 Spuler, Bertold: *Die Mongolen in Iran. Politik, Verwaltung und Kultur der Ilchanzeit 1220-1350.* 4. Aufl. Leiden 1985.

66.13 —: *Die Goldene Horde. Die Mongolen in Rußland 1223-1502.* 2. Aufl. Wiesbaden 1965.

66.14 —: *History of the Mongols, based on Eastern and Western accounts of the thirteenth and fourteenth Centuries.* Transl. by Helga and Stuart Drummond. London 1972.
Selections from the sources in translation with introduction and comments.

India: the Sultanate of Delhi
(see also [58.05-13])

66.15 *The Cambridge History of India.* Vol. 3: *Turks and Afghans.* Ed. by Sir Wolseley Haig. Cambridge 1928.

66.16 *A comprehensive history of India.* Vol. 5: *The Delhi Sultanate, A.D. 1206-1526.* Ed. by Mohammed Habib and Khaliq Ahmed Nizami. Delhi 1970.

Turcomans in Iran and Anatolia

66.17 Woods, John E.: *The Aqquyunlu. Clan, confederation, empire. A study in 15th/9th century Turko-Iranian politics.* Minneapolis, Chicago 1976.

66.18 Wittek, Paul: *Das Fürstentum Mentesche. Studie zur Geschichte Westkleinasiens im 13.-15. Jahrhundert.* Istanbul 1934. (*Istanbuler Mitteirlungen.* H. 2.)

On the origin and rise of the Ottomans, see below [67.03-05].

(b) The Mamlūks in Egypt and Syria (1250-1517)

66.19 Ayalon, David: Aspects of the Mamlūk phenomenon. In: *Der Islam.* Berlin. 53. 1976, pp.196-225; 54. 1977, pp.1-33.

66.20 —: *L'esclavage du Mamelouk.* Jerusalem 1951. (The Israel Oriental Society. *Oriental Notes and Studies.*)

66.21 —: *Gunpowder and fire-arms in the Mamluk kingdom. A challenge to medieval society.* London 1956; 2nd ed. 1978.

66.22 —: *The Mamlūk military society.* London 1979. (*Collected Studies Series.* 104.)

66.23 —: *Studies on the Mamlūks of Egypt (1250-1517).* London 1977. (*Collected Studies.* 62.)

66.24 Gaudefroy-Demombynes, Maurice: *La Syrie à l'époque des Mamelouks d'après les auteurs arabes. Description géographique, économique et administrative.* Paris 1923. (*Bibliothèque archéologique et historique de l'Institut français d'archéologie de Beyrouth.* 3.)

66.25 Halm, Heinz: *Ägypten nach den mamlukischen Lehensregistern.* 1.2. Wiesbaden 1979-82. (*Tübinger Atlas des Vorderen Orients. Beihefte.* Reihe A. Nr. 38.)
1: *Oberägypten und das Fayyūm.* 1979. 2: *Das Delta.* 1982.

66.26 Hartmann, Richard: *Zur Vorgeschichte des 'abbāsidischen Schein-Chalifats von Cairo.* Berlin 1950.

66.27 Holt, Peter Malcolm: The structure of government in the Mamluk sultanate. In: *The Eastern Mediterranean lands in the period of the Crusades.* Ed. by P. M. Holt. Warminster 1977, pp.44-61.

—— Rabie, H.: *The financial system of Egypt.* 1972 [43.09].

66.28 Irwin, Robert: *The Middle East in the Middle Ages: the early Mamlūk sultanate, 1250-1382.* Carbondale, Ill., 1986.

66.29 Ziada, Mustafa M.: The Mamluk Sultans to 1293. In: *A history of the Crusades* [65.20]. 2. [2]1969, pp.735-58.

—— Ziadeh, N. A.: *Damascus under the Mamluks.* 1964 [52.14].

—— —: *Urban life in Syria under the early Mamluks.* 1953 [44.16].
See also Lapidus [44.11].

(c) The West under the last Berber dynasties (mid-thirteenth–mid-sixteenth centuries)

66.30 Arié, Rachel: *L'Espagne musulmane au temps des Naṣrides (1232-1492).* Paris 1973.

66.31 Cour, Auguste: *La dynastie marocaine des Beni Waṭṭâs, 1420-1554.* Constantine 1920.

66.32 Brunschvig, Robert: *La Berbérie orientale sous les Hafsides.* 1.2. Paris 1940-47.

—— Le Tourneau, Roger: *Fez in the age of the Marinides.* 1961 [54.25].

7. *The Ottoman period (sixteenth-eighteenth centuries)*

(a) The Ottoman Empire

—— Kornrumpf, H. J.: *Osmanische Bibliographie.* 1973 [11.14].

Sources:

—— Babinger, Franz: *GOW* [13.17].

—— Deny, Jean: *Sommaire des archives turques du Caire.* 1930 [15.19].
Containing an introduction to Ottoman administration in Egypt.

67.01 Moravcsik, Gyula: *Byzantinoturcica.* 1.2. Berlin [2]1958.
On the Greek sources.

Collection of sources in translation:

67.02 *Osmanische Geschichtsschreiber.* Hrsg.: Richard F. Kreutel. Bd. 1-10. Graz [etc.] 1955-81. Neue Folge. Bd. 1ff. Graz 1982ff.

Beginnings and rise to power of the Ottomans:

67.03 Köprülü, Mehmed Fuad: *Les origines de l'Empire ottoman.* Paris 1935. (*Études orientales de l'Institut français d'archéologie de Stamboul.* 3.)

67.04 Werner, Ernst: *Die Geburt einer Großmacht – die Osmanen (1300-1481). Ein Beitrag zur Genesis des türkischen Feudalismus.* Berlin 1966; [3]1978. (*Forschungen zur Mittelalterlichen Geschichte.* Bd. 13.)

67.05 Wittek, Paul: *The rise of the Ottoman Empire.* London 1938; repr. 1965. (*Royal Asiatic Society Monographs.* Vol. 23.)

General surveys:

67.06 Hammer-Purgstall, Joseph von: *Geschichte des osmanischen Reiches; großenteils aus bisher unbenützten Handschriften und Archiven.* 1-10. Budapest 1827-35. – 2. Aufl. 1-4. Pesth 1834-36.

67.07 Inalcik, Halil: *The Ottoman Empire. The Classical Age, 1300-1600.* Transl. by Norman Itzkowitz and Colin Lumber. London 1973.

67.08 —: *The Ottoman Empire: conquest, organization and economy.* London. 1978. (*Collected Studies.* 87.)

67.09 Jorga, Nicolae: *Geschichte des Osmanischen Reiches, nach den Quellen dargestellt.* Bd. 1-5. Gotha 1908-13. (*Allgemeine Staatengeschichte.* Abt. 1. Bd. 37-41.)

67.10 Shaw, Stanford Jay; Shaw, Ezel Kural: *History of the Ottoman Empire and modern Turkey.* Vol. 1.2. Cambridge [etc.] 1976-77.
1: *Empire of the Gazis: The rise and decline of the Ottoman Empire, 1280-1808.* Stanford J. Shaw.
2: *Reform, revolution and republic: The rise of modern Turkey, 1808-1975.* Stanford J. Shaw, Ezel Kural Shaw.

67.11 —: Das osmanische Reich und die moderne Türkei. In: *Der Islam II.* 1971 [14.10], pp.24-159.

67.12 Uzunçarşılı, Ismail Hakkı; (5-8:) Karal, Enver Ziya: *Osmanlı tarihi.* Cilt 1-8. Ankara 1947-62 (1.2: [2]1961-64). (*Türk Tarih Kurumu yayınları.* Seri XIII. 16.)

Individual themes:

67.13 Alderson, Anthony Dolphin: *The structure of the Ottoman dynasty.* Oxford 1956.
With genealogical tables.

67.14 Babinger, Franz: *Mehmed der Eroberer und seine Zeit. Weltenstürmer einer Zeitenwende.* München [2]1959.

67.15 *The fall of Constantinople. A symposium held at the School of Oriental and African Studies, 29 May 1953.* [Contributions from:] S. Runciman, B. Lewis, R. R. Betts, N. Rubinstein, P. Wittek. London 1955.

—— Gibb, H. A. R.; Bowen, H.: *Islamic society and the west.* 1950-57 [40.13].
Cf. also the critique of N. Itzkowitz: Eighteenth century Ottoman realities. In: *Studia Islamica.* Paris. 16. 1962, pp.73-94.

67.16 Itzkowitz, Norman: *Ottoman Empire and Islamic tradition.* New York 1972; 2nd ed. Chicago, London 1980.

67.17 Lewis, Bernard: *Istanbul and the civilization of the Ottoman Empire.* Norman, Oklahoma 1963.

—— Pitcher, D. E.: *A historical geography of the Ottoman Empire.* 1972 [57.06].

67.18 Röhrborn, Klaus: *Untersuchungen zur osmanischen Verwaltungsgeschichte.* Berlin 1972. (*Studien zur Sprache, Geschichte und Kultur des islamischen Orients.* N. F. Bd. 5.)

Balkans:

67.19 Babinger, Franz: Die Osmanen auf dem Balkan. In: *Völker und Kulturen Südost-Europas. Kulturhistorische Beiträge.* München 1959, pp.199-210.

67.20 Beldiceanu, Nicoară: *Le monde ottoman des Balkans (1402-1566). Institutions, société, économie.* London 1976. (*Collected Studies.* 53.)

67.21 Sugar, Peter F.: *Southeastern Europe under Ottoman rule, 1354-1804.* Seattle, London 1977. (*A History of East Central Europe.* Vol. 5.)

67.22 Vaughan, Dorothy M.: *Europe and the Turk. A pattern of alliance, 1350-1700.* Liverpool 1954.

67.23 Zernack, Klaus: *Osteuropa. Eine Einführung in seine Geschichte.* München 1977. (*Beck'sche Elementarbücher.*)

67.24 Zinkeisen, Johann Wilhelm: *Geschichte des Osmanischen Reiches in Europa.* Th. 1-7. Hamburg, Gotha 1840-63.

Arab Near East:

67.25 Barbir, Karl K.: *Ottoman rule in Damascus, 1708-1758.* Princeton, NJ 1980. (*Princeton Studies on the Near East.*)

67.26 Cohen, Amnon: *Palestine in the 18th century. Patterns of government and administration.* Jerusalem 1973.

67.27 Holt, Peter Malcolm: *Egypt and the Fertile Crescent, 1516-1922. A political history.* Ithaca, NY, 1966; ^{2}1967.

67.28 Ma'oz, Moshe: *Ottoman reform in Syria and Palestine, 1840-1861. The impact of the Tanzimat on politics and society.* Oxford 1968.

67.29 Ma'oz, Moshe [ed.]: *Studies on Palestine during the Ottoman Period.* Jerusalem 1975.

(b) North Africa

67.30 Lévi-Provençal, Évariste: *Les historiens des Chorfa. Essai sur la littérature historique et biographique au Maroc du XVIe au XXe siècle.* Paris 1922.

67.31 Le Tourneau, Roger: *Les débuts de la dynastie sa'dienne.* Alger 1954.

(c) Iran since the Ṣafavid period

67.32 *The Cambridge History of Iran.* Vol. 6: *The Timurid and Safavid periods.* Ed. by Peter Jackson and Laurence Lockhart. Cambridge 1986.

H. R. Roemer: The Safavid period (pp.189-350). R. M. Savory: The Safavid administrative system (pp.351-72), and further contributions on literature, art, science and philosophy under the Safavids.

67.33 Hinz, Walter: *Irans Aufstieg zum Nationalstaat im fünfzehnten Jahrhundert.* Berlin 1936.

67.34 Lockhart, Laurence: *The fall of the Ṣafavī dynasty and the Afghan occupation of Persia.* Cambridge 1958.

67.35 —: *Nadir Shah. A critical study based mainly upon contemporary sources.* London 1938.
67.36 Luft, Paul: *Iran unter Schah ʿAbbās II (1642-1666).* Diss. Göttingen 1969.
67.37 Mazzaoui, Michel M.: *The origins of the Ṣafawids: Šīʿism, Ṣūfism and the Ġulāt.* Wiesbaden 1972. (*Freiburger Islamstudien.* 3.)
67.38 Perry, John R.: *Karim Khan Zand; a history of Iran, 1747-1779.* Chicago, London 1979. (*Publications of the Center for Middle Eastern Studies.* No. 12.)
67.39 *Qajar Iran. Political, social and cultural change, 1800-1925.* (Studies presented to Professor Laurence P. Elwell-Sutton.) Ed. by Edmund Bosworth and Carole Hillenbrand. Edinburgh 1983.
67.40 Röhrborn, Klaus: Regierung und Verwaltung Irans unter den Safawiden. In: *Regierung und Verwaltung des Vorderen Orients in islamischer Zeit.* T. 1. Leiden, Köln 1979 (*Handbuch der Orientalistik.* Abt. 1. Bd. 6: *Geschichte der islamischen Länder.* Abschnitt 5), pp. 17-50.
67.41 Roemer, Hans Robert: *Der Niedergang Irans nach dem Tode Ismāʿīls des Grausamen, 1577-1581.* Würzburg 1939.
67.42 Savory, Roger: *Iran under the Safavids.* Cambridge 1980.

(d) India under the Mughal emperors (1526-1858)

Cf. also the general surveys of the Islamic history of India mentioned above [58.02-10].

67.43 *The Cambridge History of India.* Vol. 4: *The Mughul period.* Planned by Sir Wolseley Haig, ed. by Sir Richard Burn. Cambridge 1937.
67.44 Sarkar, Sir Jadunath: *History of Aurangzib, mainly based on Persian sources.* Vol. 1-5. Delhi [etc.] 1912-24; ²1925-52; repr. 1972-4.
67.45 —: *Mughal administration.* Calcutta 1963.
67.46 —: *Fall of the Mughal empire.* Vol. 1-4. Calcutta 1932-50; 1-3: ²1949-52.

8. The emergence of nation states. Westernisation and reform (since the beginning of the nineteenth century)

See also [20.15-16], [33.84-97].

68.01 Antonius, George: *The Arab awakening. The story of the Arab national movement.* 2nd ed. London 1945. Repr. New York 1965.
68.02 Grunebaum, Gustav Edmund von: *Modern Islam: the search for cultural identity.* Berkeley, Los Angeles 1962.
68.03 Hanna, Sami A.; Gardner, George H.: *Arab socialism; a documentary survey.* Leiden 1969.
68.04 Hartmann, Richard: *Islam und Nationalismus.* Berlin 1948. (*Abhandlungen der Deutschen Akademie der Wissenschaften zu Berlin. Jahrgang 1945/46. Phil.-hist. Kl.* Nr. 5.)
68.05 Hourani, Albert Habib: *Arabic thought in the liberal age, 1798-1939.* London [etc.] 1962; ²1970; new ed., Cambridge 1983.
68.06 —: *The emergence of the modern Middle East.* London 1980.
68.07 Hurewitz, J. C.: *The Middle East and North Africa in world politics. A documentary record.* 2nd ed. Vols 1-3. New Haven, London 1975-85.
1: *European expansion, 1535-1914.* 1975.
2: *British-French supremacy, 1914-1945.* 1979.

3: *British-French withdrawal and Soviet-American rivalry, 1945-75.*
68.08 Hussain, Asaf: *Islamic movements. An annotated bibliography of political Islam in Egypt, Pakistan and Iran.* London 1982.
68.09 *Der Islam in der Gegenwart.* Hrsg. von Weiner Ende und Udo Steinbach, unter red. Mitarbeit von Michael Ursinus. München 1984.
Individual contributions on the political rôle of Islam in different regions, reform movements, culture, literature, and the arts.
68.10 Keddie, Nikki R.: *Sayyid Jamāl ad-Dīn 'al-Afghānī': a political biography.* Berkeley, Los Angeles, London 1972.
68.11 Kedourie, Elie: *Afghani and Abduh: an essay on religious unbelief and political activism in modern Islam.* London 1966.
68.12 —: *England and the Middle East. The destruction of the Ottoman Empire, 1914-1921.* London 1956.
68.13 *Politisches Lexikon Nahost.* Hrsg. v. Udo Steinbach, Rolf Hofmeier und Mathias Schönborn. München 1979. (*Beck'sche Schwarze Reihe.* Bd. 199.)
68.14 Rodinson, Maxime: *Marxisme et monde musulman.* Paris 1972.
68.15 Steppat, Fritz: Die arabische Welt in der Epoche des Nationalismus. In: Taeschner, F.: *Geschichte der arabischen Welt.* 1964 [14.15], pp.178-236.

Arabia
68.16 Ende, Werner: Religion, Politik und Literatur in Saudi-Arabien: der geistesgeschichtliche Hintergrund der heutigen religiösen und kulturpolitischen Situation. In: *Orient.* Opladen. 22. 1981, pp.377-90; 23. 1982, pp.21-35; 378-93; 524-39.
68.16a Helms, Christine Moss: *The cohesion of Saudi Arabia; evolution of political identity.* London 1981.
68.16b al-Rashid, Ibrahim: *Documents on the history of Saudi Arabia.* Vol. 1-3. Salisbury, North Carolina 1976.
68.16c Habib, John S.: *Ibn Sa'ud's warriors of Islam. The Ikhwan of Najd and their rôle in the creation of the Sa'udi Kingdom, 1910-1930.* Leiden 1978. (*Social, Economic and Political Studies of the Middle East.* 27.)
68.17 Hartmann, Richard: Die Wahhābiten. In: *Zeitschrift der Deutschen Morgenländischen Gesellschaft.* 78. 1924, pp.76-213.
See also H. Laoust: *Essai sur ... b. Taimīya.* 1939 [33.19a], pp.506-40; G. Rentz: *The Wahhābīs.* 1969 [33.24].
68.18 Philby, Harry St John Bridger: *Sa'udi Arabia.* London 1955; repr. Beirut 1968; New York 1972.
68.19 Winder, Richard Bayly: *Saudi Arabia in the 19th century.* New York 1966.

Egypt
68.20 Ahmed, Jamal Mohamed: *The intellectual origins of Egyptian nationalism.* Oxford 1960. Repr. London 1968. (*Middle East Monographs.* 3.)
68.21 Berque, Jacques: *L'Égypte: impérialisme et révolution.* Paris 1967.
68.22 Dodwell, Henry Herbert: *The founder of modern Egypt. A study of Muhammad Ali.* Cambridge 1931; repr. 1967.
68.23 Holt, Peter M. [ed.]: *Political and social change in modern Egypt.*

Historical studies from the Ottoman conquest to the United Arab Republic. London 1968.
68.24 Marsot, Afaf Lutfi al-Sayyid: *Egypt in the reign of Muhammad Ali.* Cambridge 1983.
68.25 Mitchell, Richard P.: *The society of the Muslim Brothers.* London [etc.] 1969. (*Middle Eastern Monographs.* 9.)

68.26 Schölch, Alexander: *'Ägypten den Ägyptern!' Die politische und gesellschaftliche Krise der Jahre 1878-1882 in Ägypten.* Vorwort von Albert Hourani. Zürich, Freiburg 1972. (*Beiträge zur Kolonial- und Überseegeschichte.* 9.)
68.27 —: Die europäische Expansion und die Transformation Ägyptens 1760-1922. In: *Traditionelle Gesellschaften und europäischer Kolonialismus.* Hrsg. v. J.-H. Grevemeyer. Frankfurt a.M. 1981, pp.131-57.
68.28 Vatikiotis, Panayiotis J.: *The modern history of Egypt.* New York 1969; repr. London 1976. 2nd ed. as: *The history of Egypt.* London 1980.

India and Pakistan

68.29 Ahmad, Aziz: *Islamic modernism in India and Pakistan, 1857-1964.* London [etc.] 1967.
68.30 Ahmad, Aziz; Grunebaum, Gustav Edmund von: *Muslim self-statement in India and Pakistan, 1857-1968.* Wiesbaden 1970.
Selected documents in English translation.
68.31 Gupta, Narayani: *Delhi between two empires, 1803-1931.* New Delhi [etc.] 1980.
From the time of the British conquest to the foundation of New Delhi.
68.32 Hamid, Abdul: *Muslim separatism in India. A brief survey, 1858-1947.* Lahore 1967; repr. with corrections 1971.
68.33 Ikram, S. M.: *Modern Muslim India and the birth of Pakistan, 1858-1951.* 2nd ed. Lahore 1965.
— Smith, W. C.: *Islam in modern history.* 1977 [33.93].

Iran

68.34 Algar, Hamid: *Religion and State in Iran, 1758-1906. The role of the Ulama in the Qajar period.* Berkeley, Los Angeles 1969.
68.35 —: The oppositional rôle of the ulama in twentieth century Iran. In: *Scholars, Saints and Sufis.* 1972 [32.07], pp.231-55.
68.36 Avery, Peter W.: *Modern Iran.* 2nd ed. London 1967.
— Bosworth, C. E.; Hillenbrand, C.: *Qajar Iran.* 1934 [67.39].
68.37 Browne, Edward Granville: *The Persian revolution, 1905-1909.* Cambridge 1910.
68.38 Fischer, Michael M. J.: *Iran: from religious dispute to revolution.* Cambridge, Mass. 1980.
68.39 Keddie, Nikki R.: *Religion and rebellion in Iran: the tobacco protest of 1891-1892.* London 1966.
Cf. also Lambton, A. K. S.: The tobacco régie: prelude to revolution. In: *Studia Islamica.* Paris. 22. 1965, pp.119-57; 23. 1965, pp.71-90.
68.40 Keddie, Nikki R.: The roots of the ulama's power in modern Iran. In: *Scholars, Saints and Sufis.* 1972 [32.07], pp.211-29.

Iraq

68.41 Longrigg, Stephen H.: *Four centuries of modern Iraq*. Oxford 1925. Repr. Beirut 1968; Farnborough 1969.

68.42 —: *Iraq, 1900 to 1950. A political, social and economic history.* London 1953; repr. 1968.

Jordan

68.43 Goichon, Amélie-Marie: *Jordanie réelle.* 1.2. Paris 1967-72.

North Africa

68.44 Ageron, Charles Robert: *Les Algériens musulmans et la France, 1871-1919.* T. 1.2. Paris 1968. (Université de Paris. Faculté des Lettres et sciences humaines. *Recherches.* 44.45.)

68.45 Brown, Leon Carl: *The Tunisia of Ahmad Bey, 1837-1855.* Princeton, NJ 1974. (*Princeton Studies on the Near East.*)

68.46 Julien, Charles-André: *L'Afrique du Nord en marche. Nationalismes musulmans et souveraineté française.* Paris 1952.

68.47 —: *Histoire de l'Algérie contemporaine.* T. 1: *La Conquête et les débuts de la colonisation (1827-1871).* Paris 1964; ²1979.

68.48 Krieken, G. S. van: *Khayr al-Dīn et la Tunisie (1850-1881).* Leiden 1976.

68.49 Le Tourneau, Roger: *Évolution politique de l'Afrique du Nord musulmane, 1920-1961.* Paris 1962.

Palestine

Cf. also [67.28], [67.29].

68.50 *The Arab-Israeli conflict.* Vol. 1-3. Ed. by John Norton Moore. Princeton, NJ, 1974.
1. 2: *Readings.* 3: *Documents.*

68.51 Khalidi, Walid; Khadduri, Jill: *Palestine and the Arab-Israeli conflict. An annotated bibliography.* Beirut 1974.

Sudan

68.51 Holt, Peter Malcolm: *The Mahdist state in the Sudan, 1881-1898.* Oxford 1958; ²1970.

68.52 —: *A modern history of the Sudan.* London 1961. – 3rd ed.: *The history of the Sudan from the coming of Islam to the present day.* [Co-author:] M. W. Daly. London 1979.

Syria and Lebanon

Cf. also [67.27], [67.28].

68.53 Harik, Ilya F.: *Politics and change in a traditional society: Lebanon 1711-1845.* New Jersey 1968.

68.54 Hourani, Albert H.: *Syria and Lebanon. A political essay.* London [etc.] 1946; ³1954. (*Royal Institute of International Affairs.*)

68.55 Longrigg, Stephen H.: *Syria and Lebanon under French mandate.* London [etc.] 1958; repr. 1968.

68.56 Reissner, Johannes: *Ideologie und Politik der Muslimbrüder Syriens. Von den Wahlen 1947 bis zum Verbot unter Adīb aš-Šīšaklī 1952.* Freiburg 1980. (*Islamkundliche Untersuchungen.* Bd. 55.)

68.57 Salibi, Kamal Suleiman: *The modern history of Lebanon.* London 1965.

68.58 Tibawi, Abdul Latif: *A modern history of Syria, including Lebanon and Palestine.* London 1959; ²1969.
68.59 Ziadeh, Nicola A.: *Syria and Lebanon.* London 1957.

Turkey

68.60 Berkes, Niyazi: *The development of secularism in Turkey.* Montreal 1964.
68.61 Davison, Roderic H.: *Reform in the Ottoman Empire, 1856-1876.* Princeton, NJ, 1963.
68.62 Duda, Herbert W.: *Vom Kalifat zur Republik.* Wien 1948.
68.63 Lewis, Bernard: *The emergence of modern Turkey.* London 1961; ²1968.
Ma'oz, Moshe: *Ottoman reform in Syria and Palestine, 1840-1861.* 1968 [67.28].
68.64 Mardin, Şerif: *The genesis of Young Ottoman thought. A study in the modernization of Turkish political ideas.* Princeton, NJ, 1962. (*Princeton Oriental Studies.* Vol. 21.)

VII. Appendix

1. Language and script

71.01 *Semitistik.* Mit Beiträgen von Anton Baumstark [*et al.*]. Leiden, Köln 1953-4. (*Handbuch der Orientalistik.* Abt. 1. Bd. 3.)
Containing, pp.207-45: C. Brockelmann: Das Arabische und seine Mundarten; pp.253-314: id.: Geschichte der arab. Literatur; pp.245-52: B. Spuler: Die Ausbreitung der arab. Sprache.
71.02 Fleisch, Henri: *Traité de philologie arabe.* Vol. 1.2. Beyrouth 1961, 1979. (*Recherches publiées sous la dir. de l'Institut d'études orientales.* 16.)
71.03 Fück, Johann: *'Arabīya. Recherches sur l'histoire de la langue et du style arabe.* Trad. par C. Denizeau avec une préface del'auteur et une introduction par J. Cantineau. Paris 1955.
71.04 *Grundriss der Arabischen Philologie.* Hrsg. v. Wolfdietrich Fischer und Helmut Gätje. T. 1.2. Wiesbaden 1982-87.
1: *Sprachwissenschaft.* [Arabic linguistics, palaeography and codicology.] 1982.
2: *Literaturwissenschaft. 1987.*
71.05 *Handbuch der arabischen Dialekte.* Bearb. u. hrsg. v. Wolfdietrich Fischer und Otto Jastrow. Wiesbaden 1980. (*Porta Linguarum Orientalium.* N. S. Bd. 16.)
71.06 Wild, Stefan: Sprachpolitik und Nationalismus. Arabisch und Ivrit. Leiden 1975. (*Oosters Genootschap in Nederland.* 6 = pp.137-64.)
71.07 *Iranistik.* Abschnitt 1: *Linguistik.* Leiden, Köln 1958 (*Handbuch der Orientalistik.* Abt. 1. Bd. 4.)
71.08 Lazard, Gilbert: The rise of the New Persian language. In: *The Cambridge History of Iran.* Vol. 4. 1975 [64.45], pp.595-632.
71.09 *Philologiae Turcicae Fundamenta.* [Ed.:] Jean Deny [*et al.*]. T. 1.2. Wiesbaden 1959-64.
71.10 *Turkologie.* Mit Beiträgen von Annemarie von Gabain [*et al.*]. Leiden, Köln 1963. (*Handbuch der Orientalistik.* Abt. 1. Bd. 5: *Altaistik.* Abschn. 1.)

2. Names and titles

72.01 Ism. In: *EI²*. 3. s.v.
72.02 Caetani, Leone; Gabrieli, Giuseppe: *Onomasticon arabicum ossia repertorio alfabetico dei nome di persona e di luogo contenuti nelle principali opere storiche, biografiche e geografiche, stampate e manoscritte, relative all'Islam. I: Fonti, introduzione.* Roma 1915 [all published], pp.49-314.
Contains introduction to Arabic names and their constituent parts.
72.03 al-Bāshā, Ḥasan: *al-Alqāb al-islāmiyya fi'l-tārīkh wa'l-wathā'iq wa'l-āthār.* Cairo 1957, ²1978.
72.04 Berchem, M. van: *Opera minora* [15.09b]. 1, pp.539-560; 2, pp.787-877.
72.05 Bosworth, C. E.: The titulature of the early Ghaznavids. In: *Oriens.* Leiden. 15. 1962, pp.210-33.
72.06 Busse, H.: *Chalif und Großkönig* [64.21], pp.159-84.
72.07 Dietrich, A.: Zu den mit ad-dīn zusammengesetzten islamischen Personennamen. In: *Zeitschrift der Deutschen Morgenländischen Gesellschaft.* Wiesbaden. 110. 1960, pp.43-54.
72.08 Élisséeff, N.: La titulature de Nūr ad-Dīn d'après ses inscriptions. In: *Bulletin d'études orientales.* Damas. 14. 1952-54, pp.155-96.
72.09 Goldziher, I.: *Gesammelte Schriften* [30.04], pp.133-40, 144-54, 195-203.
72.10 Kramers, J. H.: Les noms musulmans composés avec Dīn. In: *Acta Orientalia.* Lund, Copenhagen. 5. 1927, pp.53-67.
72.11 Richter-Bernburg, L.: Amīr-Malik-Shāhānshāh; 'Aḍud ad-Dawla's titulature re-examined. In: *Iran.* London. 18. 1980, pp.83-102.
72.12 Sauvaget, J.: Noms et surnoms des Mamlouks. In: *Journal Asiatique.* Paris. 238. 1950, pp.31-58.
72.13 Schimmel, Annemarie: *Islamic Names.* Edinburgh 1988. (Islamic Surveys, 12.)
72.14 Spitaler, A.: Beiträge zur Kenntnis der Kunya-Namengebung. In: *Festschrift für Werner Caskel.* Leiden 1968, pp.336-50.
72.15 Spuler, B.: *Iran in frühislamischer Zeit* [64.51], pp.356-60.

3. Islamic chronology

73.01 Grohmann, Adolf: Arabische Chronologie. Mit Beiträgen von Joachim Mayr und Walter C. Till. In: *Handbuch der Orientalistik.* Abt. 1. Erg.-Bd. 2, Halbband 1. Leiden, Köln 1966, pp.1-48.
73.02 Taqizadeh, Sayyid Hasan: Various eras and calendars used in the countries of Islam. In: *Bulletin of the School of Oriental and African Studies.* London. 9. 1937-39, pp.903-22; 10. 1940-42, pp.107-32.
73.03 Wüstenfeld, Ferdinand: *Wüstenfeld-Mahler'sche Vergleichungs-Tabellen zur muslimischen und iranischen Zeitrechnung.* Unter Mitarbeit von Joachim Mayr bearb. v. B. Spuler. Wiesbaden 1961.

INDEX

al-ʿAbbās, 39, 42
ʿAbbāsids, 3, 48, 62-4, 82, 83-4, 91, 95, 105, 121-3
  and the West, 106
  capital, 88
  concept of heredity, 38
  conflict about legitimacy, 69
  rise to power, 39-42
  titles, 154-6
  use of names, 154
ʿAbd al-Malik, 39, 59, 83, 103, 105, 120
  reforms, 161
ʿAbd al-Qādir al-Jīlanī, 57
ʿAbd al-Raḥmān I, 106
ʿAbd al-Raḥmān ibn Rustam, 106
ʿAbd al-Raḥmān II al-Nāṣir, 106
ʿAbdallāh ibn al-Zubayr, 38, 61, 102, 103, 120
ʿAbdalwādids, 108-9
Abū Bakr, 35, 101, 118
Abu'l-Fidā', 9, 11
Abū Ḥanīfa, 59, 65
Abū Hāshim, 39
Abu'l-Hudhayl, 48
Abū Yazīd al-Bisṭāmī, 54-5
Abū Yūsuf Yaʿqūb, 65
administration, 63, 64, 102
  and calendar, 162
ʿAḍud al-Dawla, 70, 110
Africa, 114
  North, 106, 107-9, 128, 131
Aghlabids, 44, 106
agriculture, 83, 91-2
Ahlwardt, Wilhelm, 16
Aḥmad ibn Ḥanbal, 50, 67, 95
Aḥmad ibn Ṭulūn, 109
ʿĀ'isha, 36
Āl Saʿūd, 74, 79, 102
Alamūt, 44
Aleppo, 89, 104
Algeria, 106, 108
ʿAlī, 36-7, 46, 61, 105, 120
ʿAli, Muḥammad Kurd, 20
ʿAlī al-Riḍā, 49
ʿAlids, 42
Allāh
  concept of, 28
  origin of name, 26
Almohads, 107, 108, 128, 131
Almoravids, 79, 107, 108, 114, 128
almsgiving, 33
Alp Arslan, 111
alphabets, 146, 147
Amari, Michele, 14
Anatolia, 112-13
Andalusia, *see* Spain
anti-caliphate, 44, 102, 127
Aq-Qoyunlu, 112
Arabia, 76-8, 81, 102, 117
Arabic (language), 138-42
  and Persian, 143-4
  dialects, 82, 90, 141, 142
  grammars of, 8
  script, 146-9
  see also names
Arabic studies (in the West), 8-18
Arabisation, 101-3, 104, 106, 110, 113
  and language, 139, 146, 147
Aramaic, 90, 139, 140, 146, 147, 161
  script, 146-7
Arkoun, M., 27
armies, 63, 84; *see also* military
asceticism, 53, 54, 55
al-Ashʿarī, 50
  creed, 51-3
Ashʿariyya, 51-3, 67
assassins, 44
ʿAṭṭār, 58
authenticity of ḥadīth, 60, 62, 66